The Revolutionary World Of a Free Black Man

Jacob Francis

1754-1836

Other Books by William L. (Larry) Kidder

The Pleasant Valley School Story: A Story of Education and Community in Rural New Jersey (2012)
(Winner of the 2013 Scholarship and Artistry Award presented by the Country School Association of America)

A People Harassed and Exhausted: The Story of a New Jersey Militia Regiment in the American Revolution (2013)

Farming Pleasant Valley: 250 Years of Life in Rural Hopewell Township, New Jersey (2014)

Crossroads of the Revolution: Trenton, 1774-1783 (2017)

Ten Crucial Days: Washington's Vision for Victory Unfolds (2019)

Revolutionary Princeton 1774-1783: The Biography of an American Town During a Civil War (2020)

Books edited by William L. Kidder

Meet Your Revolutionary Neighbors (2015)

Book chapters by William L. Kidder

"A Disproportionate Burden on the Willing," in James J. Gigantino II, ed., *The American Revolution in New Jersey: Where the Battlefront Meets the Home Front* (2015)

"The Times That Try Men's Souls: The Crossing and the Ten Crucial Days," in Edward G. Lengel, Ed., *The 10 Key Campaigns of the American Revolution* (2020)

The Revolutionary World Of a Free Black Man

Jacob Francis, 1754-1836

by

William L. Kidder

The Revolutionary World of a Free Black Man:
Jacob Francis, 1754-1836

ISBN: 978-0-578-34185-9

Dedication

to Hannah, Karla, and Reed

Author's Note

In thinking about doing this book, at my current advanced stage of life, I had to choose between learning about Jacob Francis just to satisfy my curiosity or to write a book to introduce Jacob to a broad audience.

My final decision to research and write this book came first from my deep interest in the life of Jacob Francis. That interest grew deeper due to the inspiration of two sets of my friends. Sharon Elaine Buck and Beverly Mills have done incredible work to bring out and make known the lives of Black people who have lived in the Sourland Mountain region of New Jersey. Their wonderful book, *If These Stones Could Talk* immediately came to mind when I discovered the tombstones for Jacob and Mary Francis. I wanted to help make those stones "talk." At that time, I was also working with Jason Huza and John Allen Watts as they wrote a stage musical based on *The Crossing and the Ten Crucial Days*. In their work, they highlighted "ordinary" people who experienced and contributed to those historic, not just the usual already famous people. They enthusiastically welcomed my suggestion to include Jacob Francis as a character in the production. One song in particular contributed to my determination to tell his story more fully. He seemed to epitomize the theme and words of the song.

These are the days – these are the moments
These are the Times that will try a man's soul
These are the stakes – these are the torments
Hope and despair vie for who gets control
These are the means, we are the people
Who haven't forgotten why our fathers came
One congregation, a righteous upheaval
We'll be remembered, We'll be remembered
We'll be remembered, We'll be remembered
We'll be remembered – though not by our name

I wanted to help people remember the name Jacob Francis and the life story associated with it that helps us to better understand what it means to be a human being in a continuously revolutionary world.

I never write in order to prove something, but rather to explore and uncover a human story. Nor, did I write this story to justify anything or create feelings of guilt for past events and attitudes, but rather to shed light on the longstanding revolution in expanding human rights that continues to this day. The only guilt people today should feel is for actions they make that perpetuate the problems of the past rather than continue to move forward the revolution towards equality for all.

Terminology Note

As a White man writing about the life of a Black man and his family, my ability and motives for writing his story might be suspect by some, and how I tell the story might bring criticism. I am well aware that because I am White and living in a society with a long history of systemic racism, I cannot be immune from inadvertently using language or explaining situations in ways that may have racist implications to some people. Should that happen, I apologize and can confidently say that my family raised me to respect all human beings equally, regardless of their skin color, country of origin, native language, religion, or any other differences. No member of my extended family ever suggested that being White made me better than other people. However, from a young age, I have been well aware that the society in which I live has many systemic racist elements that put me in a position of White privilege.

Choice of words can be very tricky because the English language develops nuances of meaning that may strike individuals differently. With this in mind, I have chosen to avoid the words slave and slavery, except in direct quotations, and generally use the words **enslaved** and **enslavement**. Slave is a dehumanizing term reducing a human to being bound property. Enslavement is a process inflicted on humans by other humans for the enhancement of the enslaver.

While the writer believes in the absolute equality of all human beings and that skin color or tone is no indication of the quality of an individual, the terms **White** and **Black** have developed different meanings to different people through historical processes relative to this story. The terms "black" and "white" are charged with nuances of meaning in our world today. It is usually considered proper today to capitalize Black when referring to people of color but not necessarily when referring to White people. Some people believe the terms should not be capitalized while others do. This author has chosen to capitalize White because not to do so could be taken to mean white is the "normal" when referring to human beings. The augthor uses the term White to denote eighteenth and nineteenth century humans with privileges and liberties not yet given to Black humans. Capitalizing White should not be taken as belief in White Supremacy as the norm. The author fully accepts, and respects, that others may disagree with this style decision.

Terms to describe the various groups involved in the American Revolution can also be tricky. The author has chosen to use the term **Whig** to denote people who supported the protests against the acts of Parliament before formal war broke out. As hostilities approached and war broke out, the term **Patriot** denotes those people who supported the new government that was first an extralegal entity and then became official after the Declaration of Independence. The term **Tory** denotes people who opposed the protests against the act of Parliament before the war broke out, while the term **Loyalist** denotes those people who continued to support the British government after the Declaration of Independence.

Systemic racism can be a charged phrase. This author uses the term to indicate inequalities brought about through legislation or practices in economic or social organizations, not to describe the beliefs and actions of a group of people. The "system" is not necessarily indicative of the feelings or actions of individual human beings. Not all people are "racist" in a grouping that inflicts systemic racism. For example, while Jacob Francis experienced living under "systemic racism" he encountered people holding differing, and often evolving, feelings about Black people. He lived through a time when negative racist attitudes were changing, although the progress was very slow, and they have not yet been erased in our time.

Throughout the text I use the given name **Jacob** and seldom refer to the subject of this book by his surname Francis although most men are identified by surname or both given name and surname. This should not be construed as the author demeaning Jacob Francis in any way. I chose to do this because through much of his life he did not know or use the surname. Only his given name was consistent throughout his life. That is an important point for the reader to keep in mind.

Contents

Part III

Aftermath of War: Life as a Black Veteran Seeking Equality

Part IV

Continuing the Fight for Equal Rights for All

Maps

Illustrations

The Revolutionary World of a Free Black Man

THE REVOLUTIONARY WORLD OF A FREE BLACK MAN

"America was born in a revolution and will continue to be defined by that revolution as each generation renews the struggle to measure up to the ideals with which this country began – that all of us are created equal." Nathaniel Philbrick – *Travels with George*, 172

"Protests had sparked the American Revolution, and protests would continue to define the United States as each generation has struggled to live up to the ideals set forth in the Declaration of Independence." Nathaniel Philbrick – *Travels with George*, 203

Introduction

On a warm August 18, 1832, 78-year-old Jacob Francis walked up several blocks from his home on Main Street in Flemington, New Jersey, to the Hunterdon County Court House. The United States Congress had passed a law on June 7 authorizing government pensions for men who had served for at least two years in some form of Continental or State military service during the American Revolution. Veterans did not have to prove gallantry or any quality of service, just time in service. Like other local veterans, Jacob appeared before Judge Benjamin Egbert of the Court of Common Pleas for Hunterdon County and, under oath, dictated his statement of service while Judge Egbert recorded it. As Egbert wrote the introductory paragraph, he paused after writing Jacob's name and age and then inserted the words "a colored man" above them.

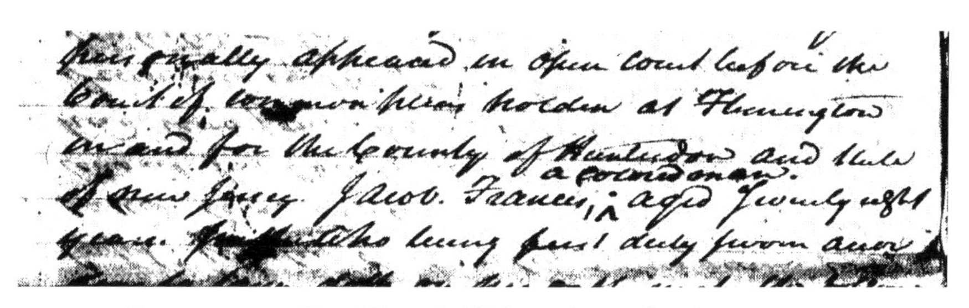
[illegible] appeared in Open Court before the
Court of Common Pleas holden at Flemington
in and for the County of Hunterdon and State
a colored man
of New Jersey Jacob Francis aged Seventy eight
years [illegible] who being first duly sworn [illegible]

From page one of Jacob Francis 1832 pension application statement

In accord with the systemic racism of his time, many documents noted Jacob's race. In this particular situation, the veracity of Jacob's statement would be suspect simply because he was "colored." While only required to prove two years of service, either at Judge Egbert's encouragement or simply because he wanted to, Jacob also outlined his life before enlisting in the Continental Army, and Egbert recorded it. The depth of Jacob's statement about his life and military service demonstrated that his mind and memory were excellent, even at his advanced age.

—

I came across Jacob's engrossing pension application statement while researching New Jersey's Hunterdon County militia and immediately realized he was a person with an interesting, enlightening, and important life story. The search to know more about Jacob and his family helped me to understand his world and the obstacles it presented for a free Black man living in America during the late eighteenth and early nineteenth centuries. Writing this book provided a way to historically remember the name and person of Jacob Francis, along with his wife, Mary, and their children. To reject writing it would contribute to our forgetting or dismissing them. It would also dismiss a chance to examine how the several revolutions that Jacob and Mary lived through were part of what we are still fighting for today.

Investigations of the Black experience in pre-1865, Thirteenth Amendment American history generally focus on slavery, and often overlook the stories of free Black people living between the worlds of privileged White people and enslaved Black people. Enslavement had been supported by the development of prejudicial racist lies about the very nature of Black people – enslaved or free. While not diminishing the importance of understanding slavery, this study seeks to widen our knowledge of the Black experience imposed by the White controlled political, economic, and social system.

It is important not to stereotype human experience but rather examine as many lives as possible to understand the diversity in that experience. Therefore, Jacob's story is not presented here as that of a "typical" free Black man, but rather as one example among thousands of stories of individual free Black people living at that time. Examining Jacob's life, we can see what challenges his revolutionary world presented to free Black people living in a society undergoing very slow changes in its attitudes toward Black enslavement and the qualities of Black people. It is not the author's purpose to promote Jacob as a hero or victim. Instead, this story about Jacob has helped the author enhance his understanding of humanity and its struggles, and he hopes it will do the same for readers.

While we should always bring attention to the lives of inspirational free Black leaders who escaped enslavement, such as Frederick Douglass and Harriet Tubman, we should also acknowledge the lives and contributions of "ordinary" people of color. They also helped build this nation and strove to create a political system based on the idea that "all men are created equal." Jacob and his family represent the many forgotten people of color whose contributions echo in our lives today.

While every work of history involves discoveries that only reveal possibilities for interpretation, this work is heavy with them. Except for Jacob's pension application papers, and the extensive writings of his youngest son, Abner, there are no extensive family writings to explain the events in their lives and their feelings about those experiences. This story, therefore, becomes an imperfect search for Jacob's personal feelings about the events he participated in and the reasoning behind his decisions. We get hints, but nothing definitive. It is possible to learn the "who," "what," and "where" for milestones in his life, but the "why" and "how" cannot always be definitively known. By necessity, this story must focus mainly on the nature of the revolutionary world Jacob and his family inhabited. While we know many of the things they did in that world, we do not know very much about how they felt about them. We can gather clues from later actions, possibly influenced by those events, but we cannot be entirely sure.

By examining Jacob in his revolutionary world, we better understand that all human lives are presented with choices and obstacles beyond their control. The lives of unheralded individuals are as essential to understand as are those of the famous. Life placed Jacob Francis in a very different situation than George Washington, but that does not mean his life is less important to understand. Although Washington left a vast amount of written material to study, historians still continually try to improve their understanding of him and must sometimes deal only with possibilities. Jacob presents a bigger problem by not leaving so many letters, diaries, memoirs, and other personal writings. However, in that way, he is more like the vast majority of humans who have lived vibrantly and contributed to the history that more famous figures symbolize. Like all human beings, fully understanding his life presents many obstacles.

—

Years passed while Jacob's story kept circulating in my mind, and I wrote several short pieces about him. I finally decided that a complete biographical sketch, placing him in the context of the world he lived in, was not only possible but important to tell. I never try to prove some preconceived idea, rather simply endeavor to uncover and tell a story. I came to understand Jacob as a tough survivor who overcame life's obstacles to live a highly respected life at a time when free Black men were "expected" by White racists to be indigent and possible threats to society. His is a unique story and reminds us that each person who lived in the past was important. History is ultimately very personal, and the "big picture" comprises millions of individual lives that interacted with each other.

Jacob lived in a revolutionary world throughout his life, not just during the years when Great Britain's thirteen North American colonies fought for independence. In addition to independence, a stated goal of the American Revolution was to guarantee certain "inalienable" rights of "life, liberty, and the pursuit of happiness" to "all men." However, the full understanding of those rights continues to evolve, as does the concept of "all men." Does "all men" mean White males owning property of a minimum value, or does it mean all human beings? From its beginnings, United States history has been the story of the expansion and contraction of the meanings of "all men" and "equal rights." This author hopes that Jacob Francis's story will play a role in helping the concepts of "all men" and "equal rights" continue to move forward.

Jacob's life is a series of interrelated stories. It begins with a story about a youngster who had to endure a life of indentured servitude to age twenty-one. That story has several twists and turns that bring Jacob face-to-face with the accelerating pace of the American Revolution. The second story looks at his life and service in the Continental Army during the early campaigns against the British around Boston and New York and culminating with the Battle of Trenton in December 1776. The third story looks at Jacob's efforts to establish a life in rural New Jersey while the war continued and he was torn between the work needed to establish a farm and service in the New Jersey militia as he continued fighting for the ideals of the Revolution. The fourth story concerns how he married and established a family while developing his farm near Flemington, New Jersey and then his move into the village of

Flemington. The fifth story looks at his senior years and effort to obtain a government pension for his military service. That story merges into the sixth story that looks at how his children, and especially one of them, was inspired to take on a significant role in the continuing work to guarantee the equal citizen and human rights promised in the Declaration of Independence and the United States Constitution.

While all these stories reveal information about life in general during the late eighteenth and early nineteenth centuries, they are especially helpful in understanding how the systemic racism of the time complicated and shaped this particular man's life and that of his family. Jacob lived his life surrounded by various, often interconnected revolutions, but the revolution for human rights and all men being created equal, that continues to this day, was at the base of his revolutionary world.

THE REVOLUTIONARY WORLD OF A FREE BLACK MAN

Part I

Prelude to War:

Growing to Manhood During a Developing Political Revolution

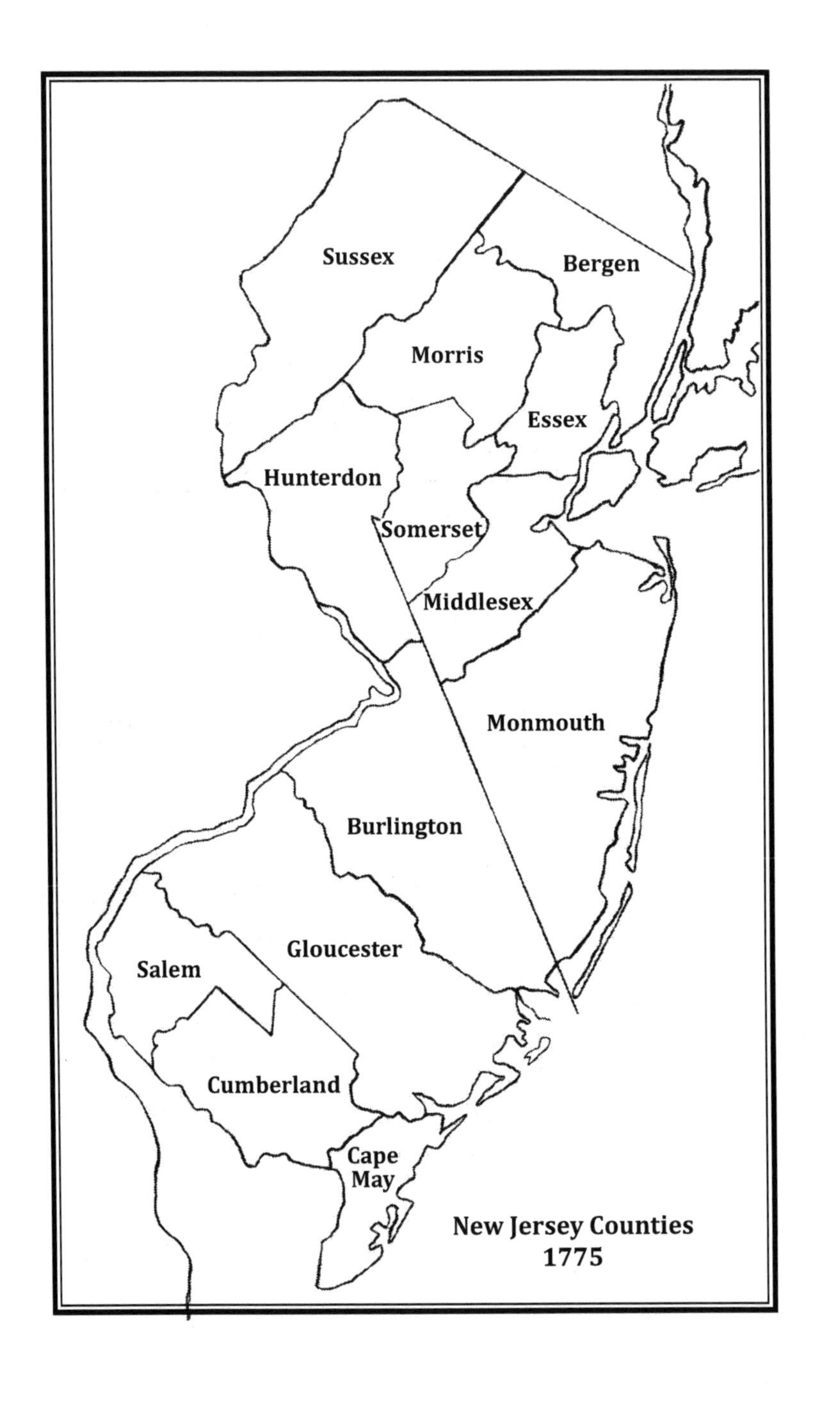
Sussex
Bergen
Morris
Essex
Hunterdon
Somerset
Middlesex
Monmouth
Burlington
Gloucester
Salem
Cumberland
Cape May
New Jersey Counties 1775

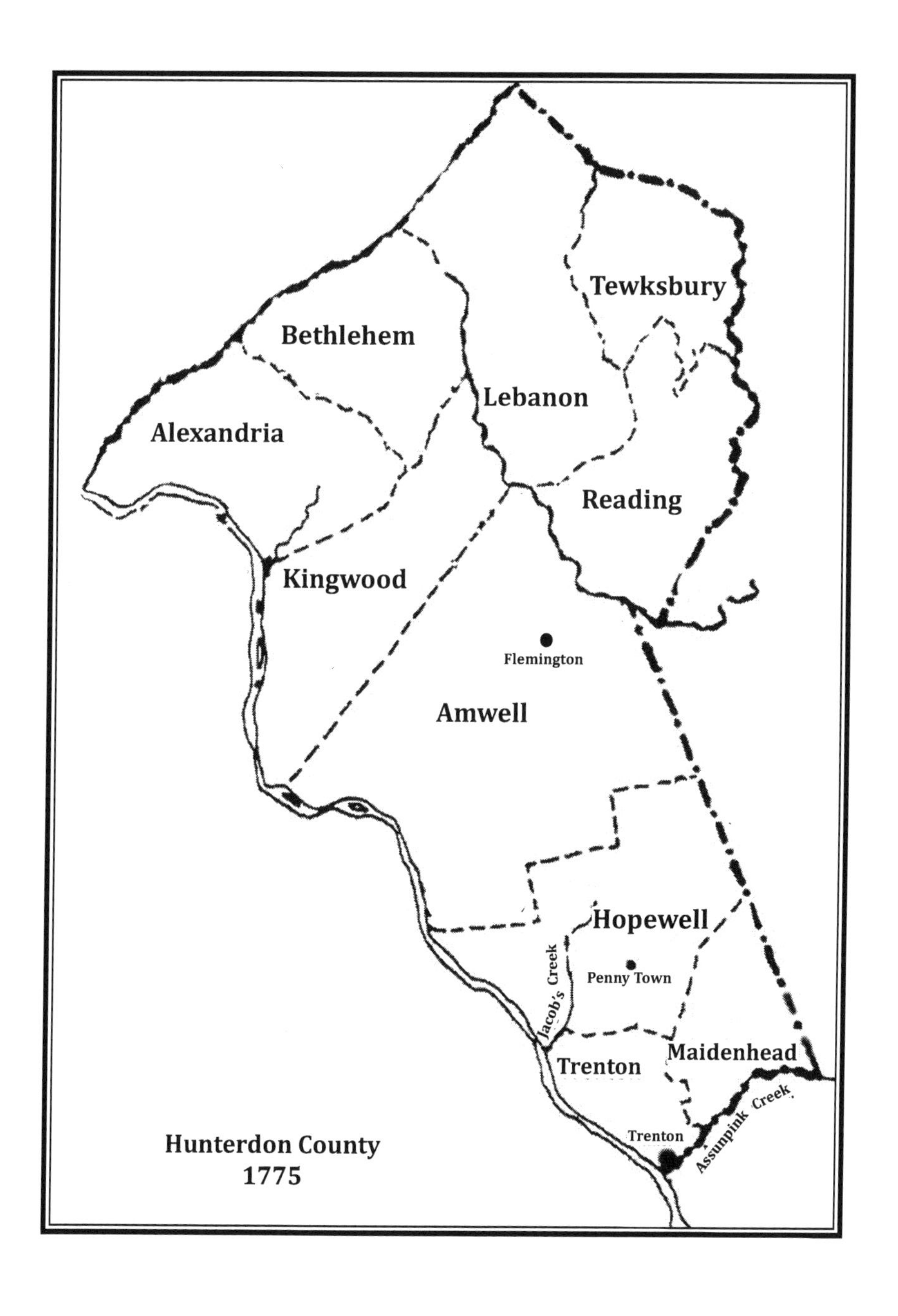
Tewksbury
Bethlehem
Lebanon
Alexandria
Reading
Kingwood
Flemington
Amwell
Hopewell
Jacob's Creek
Penny Town
Maidenhead
Trenton
Assunpink Creek
Trenton
Hunterdon County
1775

I was born in the township of Amwell in the County of Hunterdon, on ye 15 January 1754. I never had or saw any record of my age. I learned it from my mother & the persons with whom I serv'd my time til I was of age. – Jacob Francis

1

She Named Him Jacob

SHE WAS A FREE BLACK WOMAN LIVING IN AMWELL TOWNSHIP, HUNTERDON County, New Jersey, part of the small, free Black population struggling to secure successful lives in White-controlled Hunterdon County, where most resident Black people lived enslaved. We do not know if she had been formerly enslaved or had been free from birth. Her complete identity and life situation remain a mystery. However, we do know that she gave birth to a baby boy on January 15, 1754, and named him Jacob.[1]

The dispersed New Jersey Black population had a difficult time creating a close community. Despite this, according to historian Clement Price, in West Jersey, "The combination of a rural economy based upon free labor with an aggressive Quaker religious credo opposed to slavery fostered the development of free Black communities acutely aware of their human dignity."[2] Throughout their lives, Jacob and his family would strongly demonstrate that awareness of human dignity and fight for equality.

Hunterdon County was established in 1714 in the territory of the former proprietary colony of West Jersey that had united in 1702 with the proprietary colony of East Jersey to become the royal colony of New Jersey. Different settlement patterns had produced strongly persisting cultural and economic differences in the two "Jerseys." Residents in western New Jersey enslaved fewer Black people than their counterparts in the east, partially due to Quaker efforts to eliminate it among their members. The Quakers had initiated a late-seventeenth century revolution in human rights, related to their belief in the fundamental equality of all human beings in the eyes of God. However, that revolution was still developing, and some West Jersey Quakers still enslaved Black people in the eighteenth century. However, the density of enslaved people in Hunterdon County never approached that found in the northeastern counties of the colony.[3]

Observers have described the province of New Jersey as "a society with slaves rather than a slave society." Most Hunterdon County enslavers held only one or two persons in bondage either as domestics, farmhands, or craftsmen. Only a few businesses, such as an ironworks or a ferry, enslaved larger groups of people.[4] Eighteenth-century travelers commented that the colony's relatively few enslaved people were well-treated, perhaps because they tended to live with their enslavers as individuals or small families rather than in larger, separate groups.[5] Whatever the accuracy of this description, it did not alleviate the inhumane fact that all the enslaved people lacked the freedom to live their lives as they wished and were subject to whatever harsh conditions their enslaver for life inflicted on them. One of the revolutions Jacob would encounter in his world throughout his lifetime concerned the institution of enslavement and how it affected the enslaved as well as the free Black people like him.

Jacob never mentions his father or any siblings, so his mother was likely a single parent. He also never describes what type of home he and his mother occupied. We are left to wonder whether she owned a residence or boarded with a relative, a friend, or a farm family employing her as a house servant. Regardless, in addition to housework, she probably worked with poultry, dairy cattle, and other aspects of farm life like most women of her time.

Jacob's father is an even greater mystery. Was his biological father his mother's employer? Had her husband abandoned her? Did he live nearby, or was he a transient who had moved on? Was she a victim of rape? Did his father die before Jacob's birth, or shortly afterward, leaving Jacob with no memory of him? Was his father a Black man or a White man? According to historian Clement Price, colonial New Jersey records make frequent references to mixed-race individuals, identified as mulattos, among the Black population. While no records describe Jacob as mulatto, several of his children and grandchildren carry that label in some documents, so Jacob's father or maternal grandfather may have been White. Individuals with any degree of African ancestry were considered to be mulatto and suffered the same denial of liberties and privileges as those of pure African descent.[6]

—

Unlike Jacob's mother, most of the Black people living near her were enslaved. For their entire lifespan, enslaved people were the property of their enslavers. Children of enslaved women contributed to the wealth of their mother's enslaver. The enslaved person's work recouped their purchase price and then added to their enslaver's wealth throughout their entire life unless sold, freed, or unable to work due to injury, illness, or age. The enslaver could sell the person they "owned" when their labor was no longer needed, the worker violated trust, or the enslaver required money more than the labor. In the British colonies, Black people and sometimes Native Americans could be enslaved, while White people could not.

Early colonial laws supported enslavement. The 1713-14 colonial slave code specified punishments for enslaved persons who absented themselves or stole items from owners, had intercourse with White women, or committed other crimes. Racist beliefs supported and justified enslavement while also discouraging freeing enslaved persons. The code stated, "It is found by experience, that free Negroes are an idle, slothful people, and proved very often a charge to the place where they are."[7] However, the physical and psychologically debilitating effects resulting from long years of enslavement and the laws restricting opportunities for free Black people received no mention as factors contributing to these negative behaviors.

The law required enslavers to sign a "security" guaranteeing that they would financially support any person they manumitted, set free, who failed to become self-supporting and sought public assistance. However, the code handicapped freedmen by creating conditions conducive to failure, including disallowing them to own land, which deprived them of a source of revenue and a commodity required to be owned to qualify as a voter. Colonial New Jersey passed laws regulating the lives of enslaved persons similar to legislation enacted in southern colonies, where slaves comprised a more significant portion of the population. For example, in 1751, a law prohibited enslaved persons from meeting in large groups, being out and about at night, and hunting or carrying a gun on Sundays.[8]

The same year as Jacob's birth, John Woolman, a Quaker tailor and storekeeper from Mount Holly, Burlington County, New Jersey published a tract in Philadelphia entitled *Some Considerations on the Keeping of Negroes.* Woolman's publication spurred the Quaker movement toward abolition, which had begun as early as 1693. Although most White people believed that Black and White people had no common origin, he accepted and defended Black people's full humanity. However, like most of his contemporaries, Woolman believed that White people possessed positive attributes that Black people lacked. But, he paternalistically argued that White people should use their superior qualities for good. Additionally, unlike many other opponents of enslavement, Woolman believed that White beliefs and actions, combined with the stigma of enslavement, had created the *acquired*, not inborn, detrimental traits that White individuals attributed to both enslaved and free Black people.[9]

Few White people agreed with Woolman. Even a century after Jacob's birth, White pastor Reverend Samuel B. How in New Brunswick used the exact words often expressed by White people during New Jersey's colonial history to describe Black people. He argued that "Selfishness, absolute and lawless selfishness, is the master passion of their hearts, -- a selfishness which regards neither justice, nor humanity, nor decency, nor friendship; -- a selfishness which is universal, and which produces falsehood, theft, fraud, drunkenness, gluttony, and debauchery."[10] Since White people frequently demonstrated the same characteristics one wonders why he did not condemn similar shortcomings among the members of his White congregation and White enslavers in their actions toward each other.

Systemic racism has existed in New Jersey since its colonial beginning when it was the underpinning to justify enslavement. White New Jerseyans generally did not believe that Black people, enslaved or free, were equal to White people and deserved the same rights and respect. Free Black people could quickly find life unpleasant unless one "knew their place" and accepted a social and legal status below White people.[11] Today, legal, economic, and cultural relics remain from the racism employed to justify enslavement and continue to prevent Black citizens from thoroughly enjoying equal rights and opportunities with White citizens.

—

As young Jacob became more aware of a world wider than life with his mother, he had to begin dealing with being a Black person in a predominantly White peopled world. The fact that "Black" people varied in skin tone, presenting various shades of brown, complicated that world. He discovered early in life that White people, also displaying multiple skin tones, did not treat Black people the same way they did each other. Upon encountering Jacob or his mother for the first time, people tended to believe them to be enslaved just because they were "colored." Many White people were prone to negatively judge the never enslaved Jacob the same way they did formerly enslaved men. Enslaved Black people Jacob encountered recognized that he had a degree of freedom that they did not. Being neither enslaved nor White, Jacob must have found the world continuously confusing for a young boy to grow up in as he developed his self-identity.

Jacob spent the first years of his childhood in this racially divided world while developing a sense of who he was and how to navigate his world. He must have wondered why other children had fathers and siblings. For Jacob, family meant just himself and his mother. We don't know what skills she may have taught him which he could use to help her, but he must have appreciated his mother's guidance and protection during those early years. She must have been a remarkable woman who instilled in him the foundation for the high degree of strength, dignity, persistence, and fight for equality he demonstrated throughout his life.

—

Toward the end of his life's first decade, Jacob departed his mother's home and found himself in a new situation controlled by a White man and his family.

As I always understood I was bound by my mother, a colored woman, when I was young to one Henry Wambough, (or Wambock) in Amwell. He parted with me to one Michael Hart, he sold my time to one Minner Gulick (called Hulick) a farmer in Amwell. He sold my time when I was a little over 13 years of age to One Joseph Saxton. He went in the Spring of the year 1768 and took me with him as his servant to New York, from there to Long Island where we took shipping in May 1768 and went to the Island of St. John. We visited different parts of that Island and spent the summer there. Towards fall we came to the town of St. Peters where we took shipping and returned to Salem, Massachusetts where we arrived about the month of November 1768. – Jacob Francis

2

Indenture in New Jersey

SOMETIME IN THE EARLY 1760S, JACOB'S MOTHER INFORMED HIM THAT she had bound him out as an indentured servant to local German-born Amwell farmer Henry Wambaugh, then in his mid-forties. Wambaugh's family included his much younger wife, Ann (Snook), and young son, Peter, born in 1760. Jacob's mother may have lived nearby, or even with, the Wambaugh family.

Why Jacob's mother indentured him out is unknown. Whatever her circumstances, she does not appear in the Amwell town records as a pauper whose child was bound out, indentured, by the Overseer of the Poor.[1] She is one of those many people who seldom show up in official documents, so her story before the birth of Jacob and during his early life can only be the subject of speculation. Perhaps she lived and worked in the household of a farmer who did not want to help support her child, possibly the product of rape. Or, as a hired servant, she could not both care for Jacob and perform her work or afford to support him on her salary. Perhaps her employer had no work for her child, and Jacob needed more supervision than she could provide.

It is also possible that his mother believed Jacob would benefit from a father-like figure to help him mature as a man. She likely wanted Jacob to have an opportunity to learn skills, even if just farming ones, and perhaps reading and writing, which he could use to better himself in life. However, throughout his life, Jacob always signed with his mark rather than his name. In many areas teaching enslaved persons to read and write was banned. On some occasions, enslavers arranged for enslaved people to learn to read and work from written instructions. However, they considered it dangerous for enslaved men to know how to write because they could communicate with distant locations to organize rebellions and other unwanted activities. Jacob may have only learned to read if he received any education at all.[2]

Other than Henry Wambaugh owning Jacob's time until his twenty-first birthday, we don't know the details of the indenture agreement. We do not understand why Wambaugh wanted to take on a relatively young person, with limited skills. While Wambaugh's specific land holdings when he took on Jacob sometime in the early 1760s are unknown, he paid taxes in 1780 for a 106-acre farm, along with three horses, five cattle, and six pigs,[3] indicating he was roughly middle class.

Hunterdon County's many diversified farms produced plentiful food crops for sale in New York and Philadelphia and shipment to the West Indies. The many farm animals required daily care, and the variety of crops had overlapping growth, harvest, and processing cycles requiring farm work throughout the calendar year. To undertake this unending labor, farmers utilized combinations of family members, neighbors, hired help, apprentices, indentured servants, and enslaved persons. Each labor source presented advantages and disadvantages for the farm owner.[4]

Virtually all family members contributed labor on a family farm, but the family workforce kept changing in numbers, ages, and personal relationships. To supplement family labor, neighbors often combined efforts for short periods to help each other. But this labor source could also fluctuate in numbers and skill. Farmers could hire help when needed and then dismiss the worker when no longer required. However, hired labor could be expensive or not available in sufficient quantity when required. Wambaugh must have had some vision of how Jacob could fit into his workforce, beginning at a young age and gathering skills as he matured.

Indentured servitude was similar to an apprenticeship where a "master" would take on a person for a contracted number of years to learn and perform a particular set of skills. During those years, the "master" supported the student of his trade and benefited economically from the apprentice's improving skills. An apprenticeship prepared a person for a successful life if he learned his lessons well and employed them effectively.

As an indentured person, Jacob would essentially be like a person in an apprenticeship, except that learning a specific trade was not the agreement's primary purpose. Like an apprentice, Jacob's *time* would be "owned" until a specified date. Like apprentices, indentured servants were primarily White. The number of indentured servants began to increase in Hunterdon County about the middle of the eighteenth century.[5]

In an indenture agreement, both parties signed a contract specifying the length of time purchased, expectations for providing the necessities of life during the term of service, and any gifts to be given at the termination of service to assist the newly independent person in establishing a free life. Then the document was divided into two pieces with a jagged cut, and each party kept half of it. Because Jacob was a free Black child, his mother participated in wording the agreement. Although we do not know the precise physical nature or contents of the contract, we know it contained Jacob's given name, but not his family name, and his exact birthdate of January 15, 1754.

If Jacob or his "master" felt the other party violated the agreement during his indenture, especially the termination date, each party could produce half of the contract in court. When the jagged cut edges, with their indentations, fit together, the contract contents would be apparent to the judge.

Even though the law protected indentured free Black people better than enslaved Black people, free Black indenture would not provide Jacob with the same benefits available to White servants. White indentured servitude offered a way to establish a footing in society that, with effort, could lead to a successful and respected life, fully equal with other whites. However, the expectation for Jacob as an indentured Black servant was that he would remain a low-class unskilled laborer.

—

Jacob's indenture does prove that his mother was a free Black woman. To arrange for Jacob's indenture, his mother had to be free and not have a living husband. Had she been married, her husband would be the one to indenture Jacob out. If enslaved, Jacob would have been the property of her enslaver. The enslaver might hire him out to others periodically, but not usually as a formal indenture. If an enslaver did indenture out an enslaved person, when the indenture time expired that person would return to the enslaver for life or until sold.

During his defined indenture time, Jacob lived much like an enslaved person and came to understand the greater severity of enslavement for life. Both indentured and enslaved people had to live with "masters" possessing various temperaments and beliefs. While Jacob was not subject to being sold like an enslaved person, at any point, the owner of his indenture time could sell the remaining portion of it. This possibility resulted in unanticipated and uncontrolled changes to his life, just like the sale of an enslaved person. Selling a worker or a worker's time might occur because of dissatisfaction with work or attitude, the need for a worker had ceased, or the owner needed some cash.

Just how long Jacob worked for and lived with the Wambaugh family is not known. However, within a short time, Wambaugh decided to sell Jacob's remaining indenture time to another local farmer, Michael Hart. After another undetermined but probably short period, Hart sold Jacob's remaining time to Minne Gulick (apparently pronounced Hulick according to Jacob).

Born in 1731, Gulick was a young farmer in his mid-thirties. Minne and his wife, Elizabeth, had no children yet, so Jacob probably fit into their family setting almost like a son.[6] Although Jacob says that Minne Gulick lived in Amwell, by 1778, he had land in neighboring Hopewell Township, where he paid taxes for a 199-acre farm and six horses, nine cattle, and three pigs. In 1780, he paid taxes for ten horses, fifteen cattle, and ten pigs.[7]

Jacob does not indicate how long he spent living with and working for each of these three men, so we don't know if each term was for months or years. Neither did he comment on the nature of his life with them or the reasons each man transferred his contract to another man. Wambaugh and Gulick had very young or no children and may have required the labor of a person older than Jacob. Another contributing factor may have been Jacob's needs as a growing child. Recounting these three transactions later in life, Jacob consistently and pointedly stated that each man had owned his remaining indenture time, not his person. Jacob wanted it to be clear that he was not enslaved. However, these masters controlled his life much like an enslaver could while they owned his time.[8]

Although these three men lived near his birthplace, allowing Jacob to possibly keep in contact with his mother and others in the area of his early childhood, the indenture meant that Jacob experienced four different household environments during the first dozen years of his youth. Each relocation required adaptation to new conditions and developing relationships with the White males and their wives who controlled his indenture. Jacob seems to have adapted very well to these changing conditions and, as a result, may have developed better-than-average interpersonal and adaptive skills.

—

Sometime about 1767, Gulick sold thirteen-year-old Jacob's remaining indenture time to a fourth man, Joseph Saxton. Saxton was not a local farmer but a merchant who took Jacob to New York City in the spring of 1768 and then to Long Island, perhaps as his personal servant or valet. No longer living with a farm family, Jacob developed a new set of skills while adapting to Saxton's personality and expectations. Just who Saxton was and why he wanted to purchase the time of a young indentured servant possessing only farm skills is not known. However, this change began a new chapter in Jacob's life by removing the possibility of visiting his mother and maintaining ties to the community of his birth. In many ways, each sale of his time was similar to the sales of enslaved persons that broke up families, except that Jacob knew he could rejoin his mother upon reaching age twenty-one when his indenture expired. However, that would be almost a decade away.

—

Jacob's world changed even more dramatically in May 1768, when Saxton took fourteen-year-old Jacob with him by ship to St. John Island in the Caribbean and spent the summer there. As a free man, although indentured, Jacob needed to provide his surname for the ship's passenger manifest. Since neither Jacob nor Saxton knew it, Jacob adopted the name Gulick, much like enslaved people sometimes took the surname of their enslaver. Perhaps this was a tribute to Minne Gulick, or maybe it was just because Gulick had been the most recent, or perhaps the most prolonged, owner of Jacob's time before Saxton.

Traveling at sea presented Jacob with an entirely new experience that soon revealed to him a new world in the terrain, climate, and culture of the West Indies, far removed from the Hunterdon County farms. He saw the cleared and terraced St. John hills and the vast cotton and sugar cane plantations with their thin soil requiring applications of ashes and dung to maintain fertility. African enslavement and indentured servitude were the primary labor sources, and enslaved people made up most of the population.

Unlike the scattering of enslaved people who usually lived with their enslavers in Hunterdon County, Jacob saw the vast enslaved labor force mostly living and working at a distance from their enslavers on the sugar plantations. This observation must have shocked him and caused him to think even more negatively than he already did about the practice of enslavement. While on the island, he may well have feared being sold into enslavement, and the White people he encountered at first probably considered and treated him like an enslaved man.

As autumn approached, Jacob and Saxton traveled to a town on St. John where they took ship for Salem, Massachusetts.[9]

—

Jacob's frequently changing world was about to change again. He had lived his first fourteen years as a British colonial subject when the colonists began protesting British laws that they considered unfair to them. Just at the time of increasing agitation in New England, Jacob would find himself in that center of the brewing storm, while adapting to a way of life once again entirely new to him. Jacob's life as an indentured servant had introduced him to farming and a merchant's life in New York and the West Indies. Now, he headed for life in an important New England seaport. There, the next six years leading to his adulthood and freedom from indenture would coincide with the rising anger against the British Parliament and the outbreak of a war for independence, all amid cries protesting Great Britain's "enslavement" of its White colonists. Jacob's world was revolutionary both in terms of his situation and that of the world around him.

After the Treaty of Paris ended the French and Indian War in 1763, just about the time Jacob's indentured servitude had begun, British military policy took a new direction that inflamed its colonies. British leaders decided to keep troops in America and tax the colonists, the beneficiaries of their presence, to pay the cost. Establishing a permanent military force in the colonies would allow Britain to maintain a larger army than usual in peacetime. The regiments stationed in America would defend the territory won from the French in Canada and the Spanish in Florida, while protecting colonists living on the frontier from conflict with Native Americans.

However, Americans did not see these British soldiers as effective protectors when most troops occupied cities on the coast, such as Boston, to facilitate supplying them. This situation intensified the colonial fear of the soldiers becoming a standing army to control the colonists whenever they resisted British policies. That fear increased in Massachusetts when several British army regiments arrived at Boston in 1768 to deal with the protests against the Townshend Act taxes.[10]

Jacob heard the complaints as people discussed them and the protests they ignited around him. However, any complaints he heard from the mouths of White enslavers, arguing that Britain wanted to enslave them and deny them their rights, must have seemed highly hypocritical to him. During his time with Saxton, things were nearing a boiling point for merchants, ship owners, and captains. By sailing for Salem, Jacob headed into the heart of revolutionary activity that would one day result in the outbreak of a war for freedom and independence in which he became a participant.

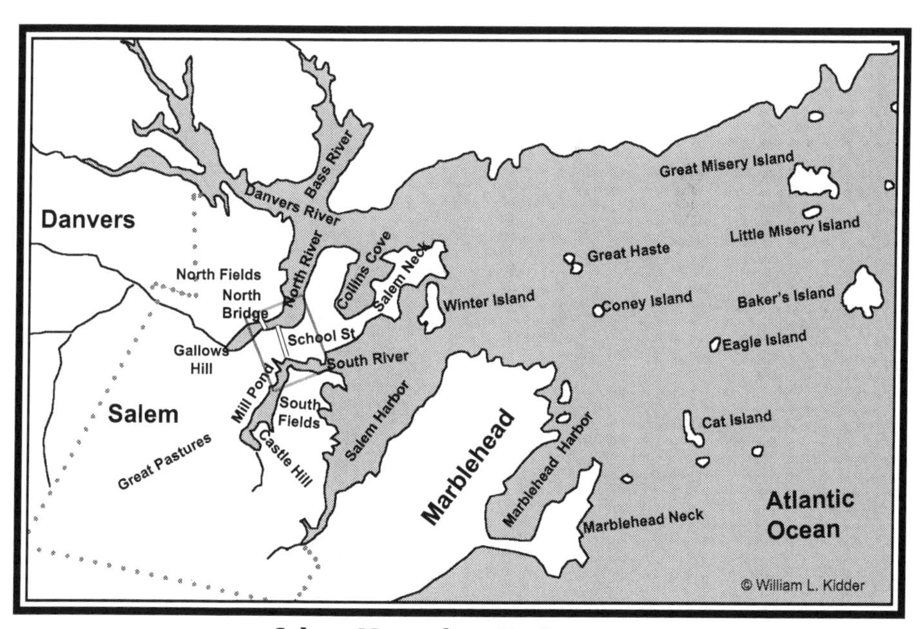

Salem, Massachusetts Area

Box indicates area included on the following map.

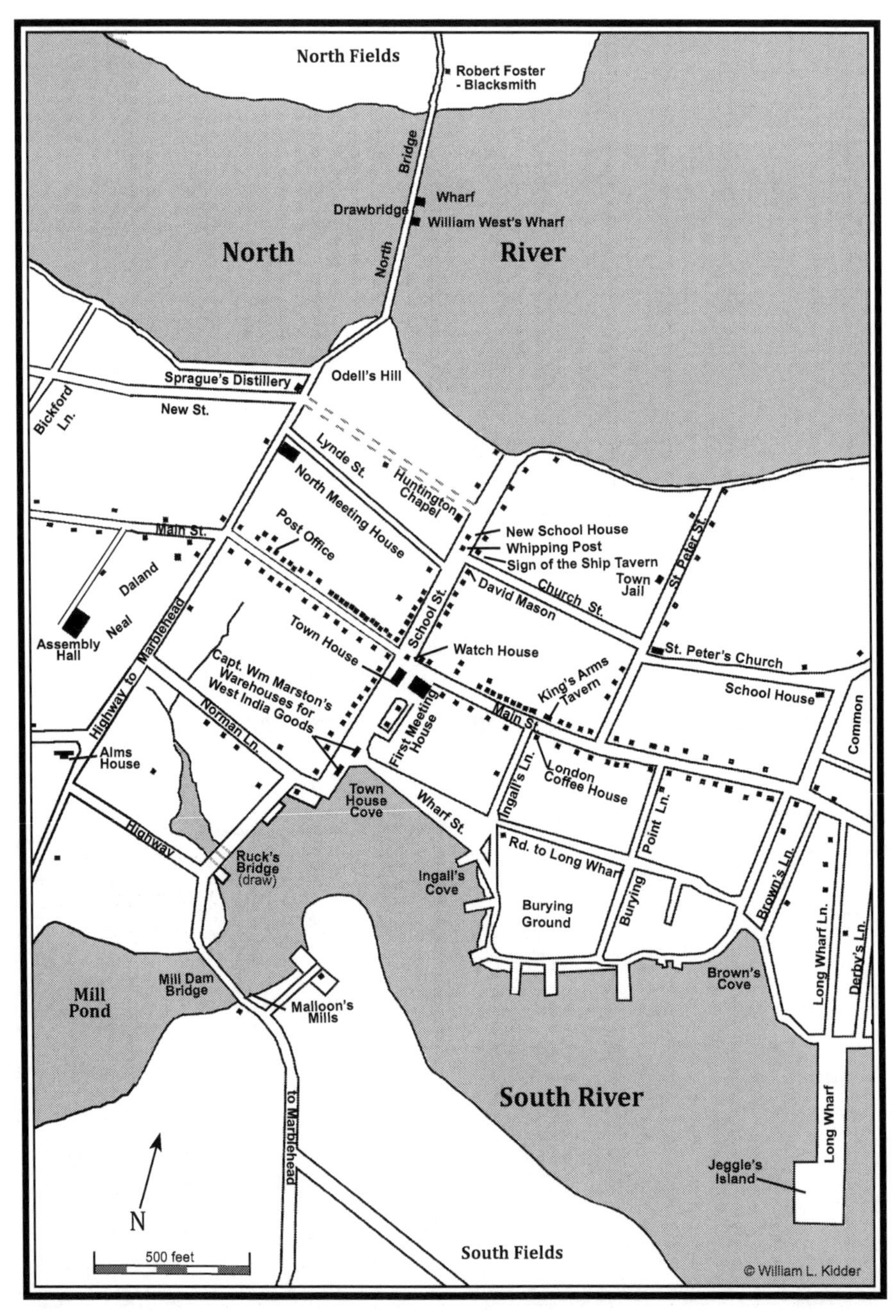

Salem as Jacob Francis Knew It - 1768-1775

In Salem Mr. Saxton sold my time to one Benjamin Dealon [Deland] with whom I was to serve 6 years & until I was 21 years of age. With him I lived and served in Salem until my time was out which was in January 1775. - Jacob Francis

3

Indenture in Salem, Massachusetts 1768-1774

AFTER A MONTH OR SO ROLLING ON THE OPEN OCEAN, THE SOUNDS AND SMELLS that had permeated fourteen-year-old Jacob's senses combined with new ones as the small sailing ship approached the Massachusetts seaport town of Salem. The distinctive aromas of salt air, ship's wood, rope, canvass, and tar, became mixed with the harbor smells. The constantly creaking wooden vessel, the seawater crashing against and rushing along the ship's hull as it plowed through the Atlantic swells, the wind pressing the sails and singing in the rigging, and the commotion of the crew and officers carrying out their duties, now combined with the harbor sounds. Wharves* jutted into the South River and just to their west, near Norman Lane and School Street, shipyards propagated the sounds of broad axes and caulking hammers as carpenters built more sloops, schooners, and brigs to serve the port's thriving commerce.[1]

After the ship tied up to a wharf, Jacob disembarked with Mr. Saxton. The ship's captain probably greeted its owner, who immediately initiated a discussion about various aspects of the voyage. Walking proved a little uneasy as his legs got used to the return to firm land. He entered a world crowded with warehouses, ship chandlers selling supplies and equipment for ships and boats, counting houses, cooperages, block makers, and other

*Piers

maritime trade shops. The streets running up into town from Wharf Street presented Jacob with a vibrant population immersed in the activities of maritime commerce. Among the primarily White people, Jacob also noticed Black laborers, seamen, and servants. Jacob heard ship captains and owners comparing the advantages and disadvantages of the rigging and sail combinations distinguishing their various vessels. He may well have spotted a ship captain recruiting White, Black, and American Indian men for his crew, a street merchant selling exotic items from afar, or a woman accompanied by her enslaved servant examining wares from the West India Goods Store. He saw customs officers bring their scales to ships to weigh items such as cotton bales, coffee bags, pepper bags, and wine casks lifted from the ships' holds by human or horse-powered windlasses.[2]

Jacob saw horse-drawn "trucks" carrying large loads of merchandise. Laws regulated those two-horse wagons to be no more than eighteen feet long, run on four-inch wide wheels, and limit their loads to one ton. The driver usually walked at the head of a horse. In Boston, and presumably Salem, truckers were generally hardy and athletic men wearing white frocks and black hats.[3]

Among all the commercial activity, Jacob may have overheard both positive and negative comments about the British troops that had arrived the previous month in nearby Boston, about sixteen miles south.

—

Although Jacob had experienced various environments during his first fourteen years, Salem presented much to absorb. As one of the leading towns in the Province of Massachusetts Bay, it ranked next to Boston in political and economic importance and was home to many of the colony's leaders in various aspects of life, including commerce, law, religion, public service, and the military.[4] Cod fishing was the principal business, and one contemporary visitor reported that the port employed fifty or sixty fishing schooners. Wooden racks for curing cod, known as flakes, had been erected alongside the North River stretching from the North Bridge to the east. Merchants sent dried cod to a wide variety of markets, and their ships brought back various trade goods. During Jacob's first year in Salem, more than 250 vessels cleared from the custom-house, carrying cargoes to ports in Virginia, Maryland, Philadelphia, North and South Carolina, Georgia, Nova Scotia, Newfoundland, and Quebec; the European ports of Lisbon, Cadiz, Bilbao, Gibraltar, Liverpool;

and to various ports in the West Indies, such as the island of St. John. Occasionally, a Salem-owned vessel participated in the African slave trade, although few enslaved people landed at Salem.[5]

Jacob saw other industries operating in Salem including distilleries, leather tanneries, and long rope walks. In one part of town, Jacob might find the air around him filled with spice aromas, while in another, he could not escape the foul odors emanating from tanneries, restricted to the eastern side of town between the Town Common and Collins Cove. Local merchants dealing with molasses operated distilleries that produced rum from sugar cane, including the crops Jacob had seen growing and cut by enslaved labor on St. John in the West Indies.

Many merchants and crafts people provided retail goods to the residents of Salem and surrounding towns. Stores carried a wide variety of items brought from faraway places, in addition to products made locally in Salem. In addition to the retail stores, public auctions, or vendues, often held at taverns, attracted potential buyers for a wide variety of products as well as curious onlookers. For example, on July 23, 1770, Robert Bell advertised that he would sell a variety of books for three evenings at the King's Arms Tavern, an old colonial building on the main street surrounded by extensive grounds.[6]

—

Jacob found the New England seacoast climate quite different from that of western New Jersey. Only about a month after he arrived in Salem, a late December storm hit the area, and "the tide arose to an unusual height, and overflowed many of the wharves, but did no great damage."[7] Jacob's first winter in Salem was quite cold, with the harbor freezing in February as far as Baker's, Great Misery, and Little Misery islands. Ferry routes froze so hard that men and horses safely walked them on the ice. Snow fell for twelve hours as late as May 11, 1769, but not long after, on June 27, the temperature at 3:00 pm registered 92½ degrees. Then, on September 8, a severe northeast storm associated with a hurricane uprooted trees.[8] Similar winter and summer temperature fluctuations and extremes characterized Jacob's years in Salem.

The severe weather often produced deadly and destructive lightning. During the morning of August 18, 1770, a whirlwind accompanied by thunder and lightning damaged several chimneys and trees. On October 20, a severe northeast gale collapsed fences and uprooted trees, while an excessively high tide damaged bridges and drove many vessels ashore.[9] In late May 1773, when lightning struck a tree in the lower part of the town, a nearby mare was killed, while her colt remained unharmed, and a set of hay scales was damaged. A month later, lightning struck in at least eight places, including a store on Derby's Wharf and a large elm tree up in town, and damaged the masts of a brig and schooner sitting in the harbor and a sloop tied up at one of the wharves. On July 10, lightning struck a tree on Gallows Hill, tearing it into a "thousand pieces," leaving the upper trunk looking like a broom.[10] Lightning struck and heavily damaged a house on August 22, 1774, but surprisingly no one was hurt.[11]

—

Despite the sometimes severe weather, the town impressed visitors as a place of "comparative ease and comfort, as the reward of thrift and industry," where people of varying economic status lived near each other. Most of Salem's inhabitants were neither wealthy nor destitute.[12] However, a small but showy aristocracy loyal to the King and thoroughly colonial in feeling and sentiment dominated town leadership at the time of Jacob's arrival. They dressed in costly imported velvets and splendid satins dyed in rich colors, such as purple and scarlet, and wore their hair in conspicuous eye-catching styles.

Merchant Samuel Archer had recently arrived from London and set up his shop where "Ladies' hair is dressed in different manners, viz. French curls, rough tupees, plain tops, and in many other forms, too tedious to mention. Gentlemen's hair is also dressed in the best manner and newest fashions from London. Wigs made, of all sorts. Towers and false curls and rolls for ladies." Women piled their hair often to ridiculous heights on crape cushions. Hoops were deemed indispensable. Most upper-class men appeared in public decked out in knee-breeches with silver buckles, while their powdered hair and wigs supported cocked hats. Jacob saw even young boys wearing wigs and cocked hats. Gentlemen usually wore cloaks, except in winter when they wore knee-length "round coats," stiffened with buckram. Visitors and newcomers could quickly recognize ordinary people belonging to a subordinate class by their homespun clothing.[13]

In sum, Salem was a lively and exciting place. Its fisheries were far more extensive than Boston's, while its nearly equal overseas trade brought vast sums of money to the town, making people feel they had a material culture rivaling Boston's. The common perception that more people moved from

Boston to Salem, rather than in the other direction, reflected that to reside in Salem was not considered a step down in society.[14]

During the six years Jacob spent in Salem, its very diverse population was about 5,000, growing toward 6,000. Girls and women outnumbered boys and men mainly because so many males engaged from a young age in the dangerous occupations associated with the sea. English Puritans had established Salem in the 1630s and had been joined by French Huguenots, Irish, Scots, Dutch, and Germans as the population became more diverse. Jacob encountered both enslaved and free Black people. Since Salem was a busy and growing seaport, he also met transient people of various European backgrounds such as Spanish and Portuguese sailors or possibly a French-speaking trader, among other nationalities.[15]

—

This varied population suffered many health concerns that equally affected everyone regardless of wealth or skin tone. During Jacob's teenage years between 1769 and 1773, diseases, old age, and accidents took between 100 and 115 lives each year, with chronic complaints, consumption [tuberculosis], and fevers taking the most lives. Then, in 1773, deaths virtually doubled to 208, with cholera morbus (15), drownings (10), fluxes [dysentery] (46), Thrush (10), and small pox (17) leading the increase. The drownings occurred when a custom house boat sank, and three men and seven women drowned. Six drowned bodies were found the next day, brought to Derby Wharf, and buried the following day with many people in attendance. Two more bodies were discovered later and buried.[16]

The outbreak of smallpox was a frequent topic of conversations that Jacob must have heard. The town even ordered the killing of cats and dogs lest they spread the disease, and people also debated the safety and effectiveness of inoculation.[17] In mid-October 1773, the number of cases declined, and the town selectmen saw no "danger to market people or others going through every part of the town."[18] However, the outbreak continued into 1774 amid public debate about the qualities of several doctors and their methods of inoculation.[19] By the end of March, the *Essex Gazette* announced that "Salem Hospital, being now clear of patients, is to be shut up, by order of the Town."[20] Jacob appears to have had a strong constitution and avoided severe illness throughout his life.

—

Salem was no exception to the frequent problem found in all the colonies of a high rate of alcohol consumption. Many people consumed alcoholic punch about 11:00 am as a regular practice. Jacob could not help encountering drunkenness, not only among the stereotyped sailors but among all classes. Salem's Deacon Timothy Pickering had written a piece in the *Boston Gazette* in 1766 that criticized people who drank excessively as well as those who sold liquor to known abusers rather than help them reform. During Jacob's first year in Salem, the town's selectmen warned all who sold alcohol to refrain from selling to "tipplers" or possibly lose their licenses.[21]

The public debates over alcohol persisted, and on July 14, 1773, a newspaper item noted fifteen retailers and innkeepers sold liquor in Salem. Although the town selectmen believed the merchants involved were all good men and fit to sell alcohol, they addressed the colony's Court of General Sessions, which dealt with liquor licenses, when it convened at Salem. After describing the problems associated with strong drink, they recommended to the Court that just eight such businesses, two for each of Salem's four wards, should be allowed to operate. This action would help reduce but not eliminate the problem, so other approaches would also be necessary.[22] There is no indication that Jacob ever had a problem with alcohol consumption, but its abuse was undoubtedly a part of his surroundings.

—

Soon after arriving in Salem, Jacob's indentured life took its fifth turn when Saxton sold his remaining six years to Benjamin Deland* about the time Jacob turned fifteen years old. Benjamin Deland descended from an immigrant French Huguenot family that had resided in Salem and neighboring Danvers for several generations. Deland married Hannah Cook of Salem on September 20, 1752, and was about 40 years old when he purchased Jacob's remaining indenture time.

Benjamin and Hannah had three boys and three girls, ranging from 15-year-old Joseph to ten-month-old John, when Jacob joined their household. Another four children had died young. During the six years Benjamin owned Jacob's time, Hannah gave birth to two more children; daughter Mary, baptized January 14, 1770, and son George, baptized on

---

**Often spelled Daland.*

September 22, 1771.[23] Because the Deland family had lived in the area for several generations, Benjamin also had extended family living nearby, including a cousin, Benjamin, of similar age, who lived in Danvers and had an adult son also named Benjamin.

Benjamin Deland had a reputation as a man of many virtues, "a worthy and respectable citizen," who maintained a "tender and affectionate" relationship with Hannah and "strove with the utmost solicitude to promote" the welfare of his children.[24] Hopefully, his relationship with Jacob was also benevolent. While not among the town's elite, on two occasions while Jacob lived with him, his fellow citizens elected Benjamin to town office at the annual town meeting; on March 11, 1771, to be one of the four wardens, and in March 1773, one of two collectors of taxes.[25]

Benjamin owned enough property in Salem to be described as "Yeoman" in several documents, including land deeds. However, documents more often characterized him as "truck man," indicating his occupation operating those regulated horse-drawn "trucks" for transporting items to and from the seaport that Jacob had seen upon his arrival in Salem. The house and "trucking stable" that Benjamin purchased in October 1754, the year of Jacob's birth, sat on the highway to Marblehead bordering land belonging to David Neal and near the highway's intersection with Main Street.[26]

Along with his house and business, Benjamin owned other properties in Salem and across the North River in the North Fields.[27] A December 1771 newspaper advertisement described one property on the western edge of Salem on Bickford's Lane which Deland offered for rent. It contained a house with two rooms on each floor, besides a kitchen and good cellar, and the yard had a well and a large garden spot. The property could be "let all together, to one or two families, or only one end, as may be most agreeable."[28]

An adjoining lot behind the Deland house contained a large Assembly Hall constructed in 1766 that accommodated significant social events and other activities, many of which the solemn clergy of Salem probably did not approve. On December 31, 1773, amid the heightened concern following the destruction of tea in Boston Harbor earlier that month, Benjamin purchased the Assembly Hall lot from Ebenezer Putnam.[29]

In the eighteenth century, virtually everyone was a farmer, even those living in towns and practicing other occupations. Benjamin Deland kept a cow for milk and some chickens for eggs, grew some vegetables, and had a few fruit trees. In December 1774, Benjamin reported the loss of a "dark-colour'd broad-cloath cloak" in the same newspaper advertisement in which he noted he would "give a good price for a new milch cow."[30]

Jacob's experience in farming made him helpful to the Delands, but Jacob never mentioned what duties he performed. His skills at some point may have benefitted the Deland trucking business, whose horse-drawn wagons moved merchandise to and from the Salem wharves and to and from Salem and nearby towns. Very likely, Jacob's duties varied over his six years with Deland as he matured from a fifteen-year-old boy to a twenty-year-old adult. Perhaps he cared for horses at some point, since he had farming experience, or even drove wagons to make pick-ups and deliveries, possibly wearing a white frock and black hat. Jacob could not write, so he could not help Deland with business matters requiring that skill.

—

Salem's religiously diverse population supported three Congregational denomination churches, a Society of Friends meetinghouse, and the Anglican St. Peter's Church. Many religious leaders in Salem denounced entertainment and "worldly pleasures," including the theatre, which a government act also prohibited. Dancing was considered to be abominable but was indulged in by the "ungodly" in spare moments. The clergy permitted participation in singing schools that featured psalm singing. Less religious folks indulged in hilarity and noisy enjoyments on Pope's Day, Election Day, and militia training days. The more serious-minded found satisfaction in the many religious meetings featuring extensive sermonizing. During Jacob's years in Salem, the political events and protest demonstrations leading up to the outbreak of war crowded out the pleasurable activities people customarily employed to relieve the drudgery of life.[31]

The Deland family, accompanied by Jacob, worshiped at the Second Church in Salem, called the Huntington Chapel. Rev. Nathaniel Whitaker became its pastor on July 28, 1769, and he gives us a glimpse of the Deland family on February 21, 1771, when he visited them as part of his survey of church families. Rev. Whitaker's congregation consisted of 660 adults. The families, some headed by women, contained a total of 841 children. Benjamin and Hannah had seven children and Deland also had four servants and other domestics, some enslaved and some indentured. The nine family members were baptized, while the four servants, including Jacob, were not.[32] Jacob probably heard Whitaker's preaching from the balcony of the meeting-house, where the church relegated Black people.

The outspoken Rev. Whitaker became involved in many controversies concerning resistance to British laws and published several pamphlets during the Revolution. While his thoughts on the troubles leading up to the Revolution were consistent with those of most of his congregants, he raised more divisive debates over how the church should function. He insisted that his currently Congregational style church should adopt the Presbyterian system of governance and that he, as the minister, have the final word on any issue.[33] By 1773, when Jacob was nineteen, Rev. Whitaker's congregation was dividing over allegiance to him. In February 1774, Benjamin Deland was one of at least thirty people who sold their pews in Rev. Whitaker's meeting-house, indicating they were leaving the church.[34]

Having owned the Assembly Hall for just eleven months, Benjamin sold it on November 25, 1774, to a group of former Second Church parishioners, including himself, who planned to convert the building to a church.[35] On November 30, Benjamin was one signer of a letter to Justice of the Peace, Peter Frye. The letter stated, "We the subscribers proprietors in common of a house & land in Salem bounded Westerly by a Lane leading from the Main Street to Neale land, southerly on Neale land, easterly on land of Benj Daland, and northerly on land of said Daland," and asking for a meeting on December 19 to choose church officers.[36] Local Congregational minister Dr. Thomas Barnard began preaching there by December 18.[37] The new church would become known as the South Meeting House.[38]

—

Jacob walked on Salem's unpaved streets lacking sidewalks that could become a morass during spring thaw season or heavy rains. People generally walked in the middle of the road. Jacob saw wealthy women going to market riding in sedan chairs carried by enslaved men. Well-to-do men traveled on horseback or in a two-wheeled curricle, or chaise. A curricle, drawn by two horses, accommodated just one or two people and had an open top. Travel in carriages was often tricky on the uneven dirt streets, especially in deep mud. There were no street lights and no watchmen patrolled until 1774, when, coinciding with the rise in protest activity and removal of the provincial government from Boston to Salem, citizens formed themselves into groups of ten that took turns patrolling. [39]

In 1773, the town paved one block of Main Street between School Street and the Highway to Marblehead, formerly a swamp, using cobblestones brought from the beach at Baker's Island. Since Salem paved no other roads until after the Revolution it became the best street in town. The corner at the end of the paved portion lay just across the highway from the Deland home, and Jacob must have walked it often when running errands for Benjamin to local merchants.[40]

The houses lining the streets in Salem, including the Deland's, were chiefly constructed of wood and generally stood two stories tall. Early settlers had built many homes in a style featuring gables, overhanging second stories, and diamond-shaped leaded glass in the windows. Jacob saw more elegant Georgian-style dwellings, some constructed of brick and some with gambrel roofs, gradually replace the two-and-a-half-story boxlike homes of early wealthy ship owners and merchants. Most buildings remained unpainted both outside and inside, and floors were usually just sanded and the walls left in plaster. The buildings stood comfortably spaced apart and had gardens in back on their lots. In 1766, when thirty-year-old John Adams visited the town he commented that several newly built houses were "the most elegant and grand I have seen in any of our maritime towns."[41]

Fire was always a danger. On August 23, 1774, at about 2:00 am, Jacob and other residents heard the cry of fire. Despite the townspeople turning out and working eight fire engines until 6:00 am to get the fire under control, it severely burned eight shops and a warehouse. However, they saved several buildings, including three distilleries and a large dwelling house. The intense fire melted the glass in the warehouse windows and consumed between 400 and 500 bushels of corn and twelve hundredweight of molasses and other items. Disasters often occurred in clusters, and about 11:00 am the same day, a seven-year-old child drowned, and a coastal vessel sank in the bay.[42]

Just over a month later, about 3:00 am on October 6, a fire broke out in Colonel Peter Frye's warehouse near Town House square, also destroying his store and dwelling house. The fire then spread along both sides of Queen Street, then around the corners to race up and down the western side of School Street. It consumed "Dr. Whitaker's Meeting House, Coats' house & shop, Northey's shops, Field's, Bartlet's, Cheever's, Appleton's, Britton's, Hathorn's & Ropes' dwelling houses & outhouses."

Burning shingles blew across the square and set the Town House on fire. With valuable assistance from Marblehead residents, they saved the Town House. However, it had been "ruined" with its front blistered and scorched, the windows cracked, and a front cornice mostly destroyed.[43] All these fires occurred near the Deland house, and twenty-year-old Jacob likely helped fight them.

—

Part of adapting to life in Salem involved Jacob developing a complete understanding of the restrictions imposed by White society on people of color. As a free Black indentured servant, Jacob associated with other free and enslaved Black people, primarily domestic servants, and heard when someone he knew was sold or ran away. Many families held no servants and those that did usually had just one or two. Benjamin Deland was among the few in his church congregation who had between four and seven, and he held both enslaved and indentured servants.[44]

In 1770, he owned "A likely, strong, healthy young Negro woman, being but about 20 years of age." She was the mother of "a hearty, strong boy, about three years and an half old." Deland advertised both mother and child for sale in December. We can only wonder how sixteen-year-old Jacob felt about this woman and her child, but he was undoubtedly offended by their sale, especially if it separated mother and child.[45] It is unclear why Deland was selling her or whether he had considered setting her free, as some New England people were doing. If not yet sold, she might have been one of the four servants counted in the household two months later in February 1771.

Even as a teenager, Jacob undoubtedly opposed enslavement and the endemic racial prejudice supporting it that was a ubiquitous part of his daily life. He had seen the stark differences between the conditions of enslaved people in New Jersey and on the plantations of the West Indies, and now he saw yet another version. New England had progressed further along the path to abolition than New Jersey, and Jacob arrived in Salem during a period of increasing discussions opposing slavery and the slave trade.

Deacon Timothy Pickering had been striving to end the importation of enslaved people as early as the 1750s.[46] Nineteen-year-old Jacob may have heard that the May 11, 1773 town meeting voted "that the Representatives of the Town be instructed to use their utmost endeavours to prevent the future importation of Negroes into this province; their slavery being repugnant to the natural Rights of Mankind, and highly prejudicial to the Province."[47] When the legislature assembled, a bill for that purpose passed both houses but then deferred until the following year. Governor Thomas Hutchinson refused to sanction it, judging that it required an act of Parliament. His successor, General Thomas Gage, took the same stance.[48]

Slavery had been introduced to Massachusetts Bay as early as 1633 and legalized in 1641. During Jacob's time in Salem, only between 120 and 190 of the 5,000 inhabitants were enslaved or free people of color. Members of Dr. Whitaker's congregation that the Deland's belonged to in early 1771 owned a total of 250 servants, so most of them may have been White or Black indentured servants.[49]

Some Salem people freed their slaves, but, as in New Jersey, enslavers had to provide bonds to the town selectmen guaranteeing that the released individuals would not become a financial burden on the town. For example, Blacksmith Jonathan Phelps placed a notice in the *Essex Gazette* on October 4, 1773 advertising to lease "A Blacksmith's Shop, with the tools and appurtenances, near the Long-Wharf, in Salem; which shop is well accustomed, and is in the best part of the Town for the business of a blacksmith. Also a Negro man, who is an excellent workman, will be let to hire with the said shop." That man was probably the "valuable negro slave" Phelps freed the following August. Along with a growing number of people in New England, Phelps recognized the conflict involved in demanding freedom from the acts of Parliament while enslaving people yourself.[50] Some New England enslaved persons tried suing for their liberty in court, as the law allowed, and while most failed, Jacob may have been aware of the enslaved man James who sued his master, Richard Lechmere, of Cambridge, for his liberty and won his case.[51]

Toward the end of May 1769, 15-year-old Jacob may have witnessed the "Slave Election Day" festivities, a traditional event he would observe each year he lived in Salem. This New England tradition began when Puritans traveled into town to elect their local leaders each spring and celebrated with rum, gingerbread, and thick election cakes filled with fruit. Lacking supervision, their bondsmen were given time off or came to town with their enslaver. It became customary to give the enslaved people a three-day vacation or holiday in late May when they celebrated and imitated the election of town and colony officials.

In pre-Revolution Salem, the bondsmen elected a king, rather than a governor, as in other colonies, because Massachusetts was a Royal colony where the King selected the governor. The event could get rowdy, and in 1768 Salem's leaders had agreed that "it was the mind of the town that means be used to prevent slaves especially on election days (so called) from wearing swords, beating drums and making use of [gun] powder." White onlookers failed to realize that the swaggering and other antics of their enslaved Black residents seen during these events were satires on White stiffness and pretentious attitudes. Other elements of the celebrations expressed pride in their African heritage. Whites regarded the observed behavior and clothing as "fantastic." However, being neither enslaved nor White, what Jacob thought about the festivities is difficult to speculate, although he probably was amused by the misunderstandings of the White people.

The celebration began with a parade led by the current elected "king." A gunshot started things off, and the "marchers made a happy racket with many African languages, more gunshots and music from tambourines, banjos, fiddles and drums. All the slaves wore their best clothes, often hand-me-downs from their masters, altered with an African flair. They borrowed swords, guns and even horses from their masters." After the parade, marchers socialized and celebrated by electioneering and voting in an open space for several hours. The newly elected king then announced his court, and a victory party followed at the slave quarters of the winner. During the following year, the Black king dealt with enslaved persons accused of petty crimes.[52] This became one small way that the enslaved people could bind themselves into a community and exercise a modicum of control over its members.

John Adams visited Salem in 1771 and stayed at the King's Arms tavern. He recorded a revealing glimpse of enslavement in his diary when he described a fellow traveler saying, "I overtook Judge Cushing, in his old curricle, and two lean horses, and Dick, his negro, at his right hand, driving the curricle." Adams observed that "This is the way of travelling in 1771; a Judge of Circuits, a judge of the Superior Court, a judge of the King's Bench, Common Pleas, and Exchequer for the Province, travels with a pair of wretched old jades of horses in a wretched old hung-cart of a curricle, and a negro on the same seat with him driving." After arriving at the King's Arms, Adams stated, "The negro that took my horse soon began to open his heart; he did not like the people of Salem; wanted to be sold to Capt. John Dean of Boston; he earned two dollars in a forenoon, and did all he could to give satisfaction, but his Mistress was cross, and said he did not earn salt to his porridge, etc."[53]

Jacob knew when enslaved persons ran away and may have secretly cheered for them. For example, on February 19, 1774, twenty-five-year-old

Obed ran away from Richard Derby, one of Salem's leading men. The notice described Obed as having very black skin and a "nose more in the shape of a white person's than a Negro's." Derby chose not to describe what Obed was wearing because he took a considerable variety of clothing.[54]

Public executions had been infrequent, but on January 16, 1772, twelve thousand people witnessed the hanging on January 16, 1772 of thirty-nine-year-old Irish-born Bryan Sheehen convicted of rape in Marblehead. Such public executions were infrequent. The witnesses heard Sheehen exhort them to avoid bad company. After the execution, George Stewart, a bi-racial man referred to in the *Essex Gazette* as a mulatto, convicted of participating in a riot at Gloucester, sat for one hour on the gallows with a rope around his neck. Ultimately, he was not hanged but suffered twenty lashes.[55] Recently turned eighteen, Jacob may well have observed this event, although he may have been at some distance with so many people present. One wonders how he felt about the mental torture and then the whipping of the bi-racial man.

—

While Jacob adapted to his new life in Salem, Governor Thomas Hutchinson and the British government created mounting concern by enacting laws in opposition to the wishes of the colonists, and Jacob must have been very aware that tensions were rising.

And whereas Benjamin Daland, Truckman, has shewn his Readiness in transporting these Goods from Place to Place, contrary to the general Desire of the good People of this Town, we do further agree, that we will not, on any Account, employ him for the future. - Essex Gazette, October 2, 1770

4

Surrounded by Growing Revolution

THE EVENTS LEADING UP TO THE OUTBREAK OF WAR AND THE DECLARATION of Independence surrounded Jacob in Salem. He could not help hearing the debates about freedom and witnessing protest events. When Jacob arrived in town in 1768, disagreements over how to deal with the acts of Parliament strained interpersonal relationships among the citizens and the radically changing town leadership. By the end of that year, a group of men representing up-and-coming voices protesting British actions had taken over leadership from those belonging to long-standing families of influence who benefited from their royal government contacts. Everyone in Salem constantly had to evaluate whether to support those people who steadfastly supported British policies, the Tories, or those who sought to challenge the Royal government actions, the Whigs. Throughout Jacob's time in Salem, this ongoing struggle involved two very well-known and generally well-liked men, William Browne, representing the old elite families, and Timothy Pickering, Jr., representing the upcoming new elite unaccustomed to government and Royal favors. Pickering lived just to the south of the Deland residence, and Jacob probably encountered him.[1]

Jacob interacted in various ways with all these people while they sorted out their feelings about the critical but confusing political power challenges taking place in the town. Lawyers and judges tended to support British policies, although some wavered. Clergy members were divided, with several leaning towards loyalty to the royal government. Merchants were also divided, but most supported the developing protests, as did the common people. Benjamin Deland strongly endorsed the protests, even though people questioned that support at one point. However, the Salem community showed enough political division for other towns to suspect it did not fully support the protests. But, those suspicions were unfounded. Salem town meetings always supported Whig policies and punished individuals who broke the town rules sustaining them.[2]

Several of the ascending leaders brought 27-year-old printer Samuel Hall to town, expecting him to advocate for the merchants protesting the acts of Parliament. He opened a printing office in April 1768, a few months before Jacob's arrival, and on August 2, began publishing the *Essex Gazette* as the first Massachusetts newspaper not printed in Boston and kept the *Gazette* attuned to Whig feelings. He hired a rider to come out from Boston the day before each issue went to press so the news would be up to date. Hall supported the non-importation agreements so strongly that opponents attempted to put him out of business. They failed, only succeeding in increasing the *Gazette's* circulation.[3] He also began publishing his *Essex Almanack* in 1769. It offered various writings, including poems by Black female poet Phillis Wheatley in 1770. Whether Jacob was aware of Wheatley's work and that White people read it, or heard comments about it, is unknown.[4]

Tory feelings remained strong in many people. To compete with the pro-Whig *Essex Gazette*, Ezekiel Russell began publishing the *Salem Gazette and Newbury and Marblehead Advertiser* on Friday, July 1, 1774, promising to be politically neutral; under the motto – "Influenced neither by Court nor Country." However, he only published his paper until the following April, and the editor's obvious Tory bias probably caused its demise.[5]

—

Three months before Jacob arrived, town merchants and traders met at the King's Arms Tavern and unanimously voted not to order goods from Great Britain. They adopted this agreement in response to the Townshend Acts, which Parliament had passed following the repeal of the Stamp Act in March 1766. During the year from January 1, 1769 to January 1, 1770, they would not "import, nor purchase of others, any kind of merchandize from Great Britain, except coal, salt, and some articles necessary to the fishery."

Very specifically, they would not import "any tea, glass, paper, or painter's colors, until the acts imposing duties on these articles are repealed."[6] This non-importation resolution failed to succeed over time, but the disagreements it engendered kept passions strong.

Anger increased when British troops began landing in Boston near the end of September 1768. While leaders sought to keep the peace, the common people became more violent in their protests.[7] A large number of sailors in Salem's population lived up to their unruly-when-ashore stereotype. They "formed the nucleus of the mob which enforced the will of the majority by extra-legal methods" as the anti-British protests increased and graduated to "threats of tarring and feathering, breaking of windows, and placing live coals against front doors."[8]

In those times of contention, disagreements over appropriate actions threatened to break down the community. On May 27, 1769, the town instructed its representatives to the colonial Assembly to seek repeal of the tea tax to resolve the conflict between the colonies and the mother country.[9] Even supporters of the protests against British measures could find themselves in trouble. During August, October, and November in 1769, the town held a series of meetings "on business of importance" at the King's Arms Tavern for "gentlemen in general" and merchants and traders importing British manufactures in violation of the town agreement.[10]

On January 31, 1770, the Boston women took a stand when 536 signed a pledge not to consume foreign teas until Parliament repealed its taxes. Women in Salem also swore abstinence, as did women throughout the colonies.[11] Reflecting the protests against tea, on January 22, 1771, the *Essex Gazette* carried an advertisement for Robert Bartlett, notifying the people of Salem that, as a substitute for the forbidden tea, he had choice Labrador tea for sale. Native Americans used this herbal tea, said to bring relief from "rheumatism, spleen, and many other disorders." People also used other tea substitutes, including one called Liberty Tea, made from the medicinal herb loosestrife, consumed to fight dysentery, among other disorders.[12] However, not everyone abstained, and the importation and purchase of tea continued throughout the colony.

At the annual town meeting on March 12, 1770, the inhabitants agreed to continue the non-importation agreement and not purchase any goods imported "contrary to the agreement of the merchants in this town."[13] Before that meeting, town leaders wanted to review the original non-importation agreement and searched for the document. Merchant Peter Frye had accepted possession of it for safekeeping and was the last person seen with it. However, he did not produce it when approached, suspiciously claiming he had not seen it and did not know who had it.

Six months later, on September 25, the Salem Committee of Inspection, established to enforce non-importation, met to consider the actions of four prominent citizens. Before March, and perhaps even before January, these merchants had ordered boycotted goods from England in violation of the town agreement. The four accused included the forgetful Peter Frye, John Appleton, and two widows, Abigail Eppes and Elizabeth Higginson, who owned the businesses of their late husbands. The contraband tea, paper, and glass arrived in May, and the four merchants agreed with the Committee of Inspection to lock the items up in several locations, with the Committee holding the keys. However, soon after, the four merchants asked the Committee to release their goods to them. The Committee refused because the non-importation agreement remained in effect. In response, after threatening violence, the merchants obtained a court order and, assisted by the Tory Under-Sheriff of Essex County, "with force and violence broke open the stores" on September 22, retrieved their goods, and put them up for sale.

The Committee of Inspection ruled that the four had violated a measure that had been judged lawful, prudent, and necessary. The non-importation agreement had been "the only peaceable measure by which Americans could hope to obtain a redress of their grievances." By violating the "solemn, voluntary agreements," the accused had "taken an ungenerous advantage of their neighbours" who were adhering to the agreements and paying "due deference to the sentiments of a whole continent." The Committee judged the case to be one "concerning the liberty or slavery of America." Demonstrating women's reduced condition in eighteenth-century Massachusetts, the question arose as to how much to hold the two widows accountable for the men who had advised them.[14] Townspeople agreed to cease purchasing goods from these four merchants or anyone purchasing items from them for resale. They also agreed to "withhold all marks of respect, that would otherwise have been due to them" until they made amends. In other words, the community would shun them for violating the expected resistance to the actions of Parliament.

Sixteen-year-old Jacob became very aware of this case because truck man Benjamin Deland reportedly had transported the forbidden items for the four merchants. The Committee felt townspeople should no longer hire Deland and placed a statement to that effect in the *Essex Gazette*. Whether or not Benjamin understood just what he did wrong when working for these merchants, who were undoubtedly longtime regular customers, he and his business were in trouble. However, subsequent events show that he wholly and quickly regained his reputation, unlike the accused merchants. But, this incident during those stressful times demonstrates how strongly feelings could quickly turn against a person if people misconstrued their words or actions.[15]

—

The Boston Massacre on March 5, 1770, accelerated the rising concerns of the people of Salem for their freedoms and safety. On the event's first anniversary, Rev. Whitaker delivered a sermon on "The Fatal Tragedy in King Street."[16] Hearing about the massacre, Jacob learned about the death of Crispus Attucks, a mixed-race man described as mulatto in newspaper accounts of the incident. Jacob understood that men like him were involved in the protest activities associated with a fight for human freedom. The bloody event sharpened the debates between those supporting the Crown and Parliament and those opposing the British methods chosen to control the colonies, especially the use of troops. Even when the British government removed most of its troops from Boston in response to the uproar, a garrison remained.

Responding to the troop placements and the massacre, Massachusetts leaders began talking and writing about reforming the colonial militia. From its beginning, the colony established this local, part-time, self-defense military force. The original colonial militia system drew on the concept that citizens had a civic responsibility to defend their homes, family, and community from foreign invaders, outlaw gangs, the indigenous peoples living nearby (whose land they had taken), and others. In times of peace, these militia companies could become lax when more essential concerns, such as farming, dominated their attention.[17] Only in anticipation of imminent danger did the militiamen take their responsibility more seriously and, by then, it wasn't easy to get organized, equipped, and effectively trained. Now, fearing they would need to protect their communities from the troops of their mother country, to undergo additional military training some men organized military companies outside the colonial militia system.[18]

—

On December 1, 1773, the Tea Act went into effect, and just a month away from Jacob's twentieth birthday, a rowdy group of men destroyed a shipment of tea in Boston harbor on December 16, 1773. The *Essex Gazette* carried accounts describing the removal and destruction of tea from the cargo holds of three vessels, and the ensuing debates about the incident echoed throughout Salem.[19] To punish Boston, the British government imposed the Coercive Acts following the tea's destruction. These acts also directly affected Salem and its people.[20]

Whig supporting colonists like the Delands became even more incensed by this legislation. Their anger and fear increased. As Jacob entered the final year of his indenture, he must have wondered how these events would affect his prospects for a free life upon reaching age twenty-one. After the tea incident, the British increased the number of troops stationed at Boston, producing discussions in Massachusetts among leaders perceiving a need for military preparations. They initiated actions to reform the militia and increase the frequency and seriousness of training. Many older, higher-ranking militia officers had served the King during the French and Indian War and leaned toward the Tory side in the disputes. Those officers faced removal and replacement by men more in tune with the protest sentiment. As interest in building up the militia increased, so did concern over obtaining military supplies.[21] In this time of unrest, the militia was undergoing transformation from a colonial government entity to an arm of the opposition to that government. Since the militia could not be both entities at the same time, the officers and men in it became conflicted.

Debates also surrounded Jacob concerning actions proposed by the newly created Continental Congress that met in September 1774 in Philadelphia. Those actions aimed to coordinate and lead efforts to change the British approach to dealing with its colonies.

Jacob perhaps heard the mobs threatening Crown officials in Salem in reaction to Parliament's punishments of Boston. On March 17, 1774, 48-year-old Massachusetts Supreme Court Judge Nathaniel Ropes lay in bed, near death from smallpox, when disorderly crowds assembled around his house. They were angry even though Ropes had already stated that he would not accept any of his crown salaries and more recently had resigned his office.

Although Ropes held a reputation as an honorable man, members of the crowd proceeded to break windows and threatened to drag him out. He died the morning after this needless violence against him.[22]

People who did not publicly oppose the Royal colonial government also came under attack. Prominent lawyer William Pynchon had signed an address favorable to Governor Hutchinson in May 1774. While a mob demanded that he recant, they broke the windows of his house on the highway to Marblehead, not far from the Deland house. Pynchon was a Tory, but unlike many others, did not leave town. As a continuing symbol of the stark lawlessness of the times, he only boarded up the broken windows rather than repair them.[23]

Up to this point, the major protests against the acts of Parliament had centered at Boston, but the damaging effects of the Coercive Acts made Salem another focal point of unrest. Everyone expected activity at the port of Salem to increase after the port of Boston closed. On March 31, 1774, the British Treasury Board directed the Commissioners of the Customs at Boston to immediately prepare offices and accommodations in Salem and remove there to carry out their duties until receiving further orders.[24] As a member of Benjamin Deland's household, Jacob found himself in the middle of this political turmoil.

—

Preceded by the High Sheriff of Essex County and two deputies on horseback, Royal Governor Thomas Hutchinson entered Salem on the afternoon of April 26, 1774. Prominent Cambridge Tory General William Brattle, Royal Secretary for Massachusetts Thomas Flucker, and several other dignitaries accompanied him. Many "the principal gentlemen of the place" followed them "in their carriages." The following morning, the First Essex County Regiment of militia, commanded by Colonel William Browne, mustered on the plains between Salem and Danvers, not far from the Deland house. The regimental officers resigned in protest because Tory Colonel Browne would not resign from the Governor's council, forcing Browne to leave his militia command.

At noon, led by ubiquitous Tory leaning merchant, judge, forgetful keeper of the non-importation documents, and militia Lieutenant Colonel Peter Frye, the regiment marched through town to the Common. At about 1:00 pm, the governor reviewed the troop. Then, after the traditional musket firings, the militiamen were dismissed, and local gentlemen escorted the governor to "an elegant entertainment." That evening Hutchinson attended a ball at the Assembly Hall still owned then by Benjamin Deland, "where a great number of ladies shone with their usual brilliancy, and where his Excellency honoured the company with his presence."[25] Even though it produced some income, Deland may have found this event unpleasant, given his political preferences. But, 20-year-old Jacob, who likely worked at the ball, must have found this event fascinating with all its pageantry. The event signaled the end of Governor Hutchinson's tenure as the last civilian royal governor, soon to be replaced by General Thomas Gage. The governor returned to Boston on April 28 by way of Marblehead and departed for England on June 1.

As part of Parliament's punishing Massachusetts Government Act, one of the despised Coercive Acts, the General Court, the colonial legislature, would relocate to Salem beginning with its June meeting. As early as May 17, 1774, after General Thomas Gage replaced Hutchinson, the *Essex Gazette* reported the rumor that he would remove the seat of government from Boston to Salem.[26] Along with this move, Gage established his residence in Danvers at the mansion of prominent merchant Robert "King" Hooper, about four miles out of Salem. The day this story broke, a town meeting in Salem appointed a Committee of Correspondence to work with the other colonies on a proposed multi-colony non-importation agreement.[27]

The port of Boston closed on June 1 and the custom-house officers now residing at Salem opened their business there.[28] General Gage, accompanied by "a retinue of gentlemen in carriages," came to Salem on June 2. Many leading townsmen, predominantly government supporters including various civil and military officers, "went out on horseback to meet him, and escorted him hither in grand procession." Colonel Browne entertained Gage at his elegant mansion, and the following evening Gage was the guest of honor at "a brilliant reception and ball" in Deland's Assembly Hall. King George III's birthday fell on June 4 and was celebrated "with suitable demonstrations of the most affectionate Loyalty and Joy." Tory-leaning citizens hastened to introduce themselves to the new governor at these events.[29] Jacob probably took part as a servant at both the celebration of Governor Gage's arrival and the king's birthday.

The General Court met on June 7 in the Salem Town House.[30] Salem built its Town House in 1718 in the middle of School Street, standing fifty feet long by thirty feet wide and two stories (twenty feet) high. The upper floor served as the courthouse, while the lower accommodated town functions. The building had a cellar and was one of the few painted structures in town. Other than that, the Town House displayed no architectural elegance. However, it was welcoming and became a gathering place for leisure socializing and business conversations. Wide wooden benches in front of the building, extending on each side of the door, created a comfortable gathering place for older men and others to gossip and dissect the news. The nearby area was known as "The Exchange." The bell in the Town House turret called citizens together for town meetings and signaled alarms.[31] Jacob became very familiar with the sound of that bell because it rang just one block away from the Deland house.

By mid-century, Salem's Town House Square had become the town civic center containing the eclectic combination of the Town House, a Congregational meeting house, a school, and the town whipping post.[32]

—

The Whig organized extralegal Provincial Assembly also met in Salem on June 7. It adopted a resolution proposing a General Congress of the Colonies to meet at Philadelphia, later known as the First Continental Congress. It then elected five delegates to attend, including John and Samuel Adams. Governor Gage became alarmed by this action and decided to dissolve the Assembly. However, when Gage sent his secretary, Thomas Flucker, to the Assembly with the order to dismiss, the delegates locked him out so that he had to shout the order, which they ignored.[33]

The tall and slender Gage had lived in America for twenty years and married an American woman. He was very popular, mild-mannered, and known for his integrity. Gage's previous work in America had earned him friendly nicknames, including "Quiet Tommy," "Honest Tom," and the "Mild General," from friends who believed he had a strong sense of fair play. Gage received a welcoming message from the Tory-leaning citizens of Salem on June 11 in which they expressed that, "We are deeply sensible of his Majesty's paternal care and affection to this province, in the appointment of a person of your Excellency's experience, wisdom, and moderation, in these troublesome and difficult times." They pointed out to Gage that Salem "is graciously distinguished for that spirit, loyalty, and reverence for the laws, which is equally our glory and happiness."

In expressing their hopes for his tenure, the signers said, "We beg leave to commend to your Excellency's patronage the trade and commerce of this place, which, from a full protection of the liberties, persons and properties of individuals, cannot but flourish." Finally, they promised to "make it our constant endeavors by peace, good order, and a regard for the laws, as far as in us lies, to render your station and residence easy and happy." Forty-eight men signed this letter, including the ubiquitous Peter Frye.[34]

On June 18, 1774, a Whig leaning group of merchants and freeholders of Salem presented a similar address to Governor Gage. They expressed support for the protests against Parliament and, after conveying their "respects" on his appointment, commented that "the wisdom, mildness, and exact regularity of your conduct in another command" gave them great expectations "that this Province will enjoy the happy fruits of your benignity." Then they expressed their concern about the troubles in Boston and hope that Gage would prevent further evils. While Massachusetts citizens generally expected Salem to benefit from the closure of the Boston port, these local men noted that the limiting "formation of our harbour" would preclude it rivaling that of Boston. They also had no desire to "seize on wealth and raise our fortunes on the ruin of our suffering neighbours." Instead of benefitting Salem, they noted that closing Boston's harbor also injured Salem because "it deprives us of a market for much the largest part of our West India imports," most of which they sent to Boston by coastal vessels rather than overland.

Every town in Massachusetts would suffer from the Coercive Acts enacted to punish Boston. Like those who signed the Tory letter, these Whigs commented on the town's long history of loyalty to the crown and its efforts in North America and expressed, "A happy union with Great Britain is the wish of all the Colonies." They promised to adopt "every measure compatible with the dignity and safety of British subjects" as they endeavored to "preserve the peace and promote the welfare of the Province" and advance the King's best interests. Their letter expressed a polite and subtle warning that they would not blindly accept without protest any acts of Parliament that impinged on their rights as British subjects. They wished Gage success and that his efforts "may be crowned with the noblest reward, the voluntary, disinterested applause of a whole free people." One hundred and twenty-five persons signed this letter, including Benjamin Deland.[35]

Gage replied to the 125 supporters of the protest with gratitude but also with a polite warning of his own. He acknowledged Boston's sufferings, but justified the actions taken against the "repeated provocations to the King and the British Nation" those citizens had made. He hoped that all the citizens of Massachusetts would support Britain's rights "as the supreme head of her extended Empire" and reminded them that it was Britain's aim "to inculcate that due obedience to the King, in his Parliament, which your fathers acknowledge."[36] Jacob probably overheard Deland and other signers of these two letters express their thoughts and fears.

While these political events commanded the attention of everyone in Salem, daily life continued as usual in most ways. Benjamin Deland took up an ox chain and wanted to notify its unknown owner to come to claim it. He used the same newspaper notice about it to advertise his desire to purchase four or five "good chaise and saddle horses."[37]

—

On July 21, 1774, two companies of the British 64th Regiment of Foot, commanded by Colonel Alexander Leslie, arrived at Salem by ship from Castle William in Boston Harbor. The following day they disembarked and marched through town and then to the "King" Hooper property in Danvers, where they established their headquarters with Governor Gage.[38] Two weeks later, on August 6, the British 59th Regiment of Foot under Lieutenant Colonel Ortho Hamilton arrived at Boston from Halifax and proceeded to Salem. They made camp on Salem Neck to keep an eye on any rebellious activities taking place in town.[39] These British soldiers remained at these encampments until the Governor left the area and returned to Boston in early September. Just six months away from his twenty-first birthday, Jacob saw these red-coated soldiers frequently and perhaps felt the same combination of anger and fear about them as Benjamin Deland and others did.

Other than the annual meeting to elect local officials in March, the Massachusetts Government Act forbade town meetings without the Governor's permission. Despite this, the Salem Committee of Correspondence posted notifications on Saturday, August 20, 1774, calling for merchants, freeholders, and other inhabitants to attend a meeting at the Town House the following Wednesday at 9:00 am. Attendees would choose deputies to meet at Ipswich on September 6 with deputies from other Essex County towns in a county convention to determine what measures to take in response to recent acts of Parliament and other grievances.

Governor Gage prohibited attendance at that meeting in a Tuesday, August 22 proclamation. He also readied his troops. He called the Committee of Correspondence to meet with him at 8:00 am Wednesday, before the county meeting, at which time he asked if it was they who had put up the notices. After confirming that they had, he ordered them to disperse the meeting or face the consequences. Declining to call off the meeting, they told him the people would decide what they wanted to do. Although the Governor declared the meeting to be seditious and unlawful, the Committee and the assembled inhabitants believed the meeting was legal, despite the recent act of Parliament, and clearly within the laws of the Province. The Governor refused to argue the point with them, threatened to have the sheriff disband them, and if they continued to meet, he would use troops to break up the assembled residents.

Gage then summoned troops from the 59th Regiment of Foot. They left their encampment, each man armed with 18 rounds of ammunition, marched in the pouring rain to the entrance to Salem, halted, loaded their muskets, and about 80 of them advanced to "within an eighth of a mile from the Town House." The town meeting had adjourned before the troops arrived, having completed the election of six convention delegates. Finding no meeting to disband, the troops returned to camp.

The Governor had Tory Judge Peter Frye issue warrants for the arrest of the Committee members. Several Committee members posted bail and agreed to appear in court, while others refused. In the face of growing public outcry, Judge Frye wisely and quickly released them all without bail. Gage issued an ultimatum to the accused men to post bail by 4:00 pm Thursday. They ignored him. Gage finally backed down when faced by over 3,000 angry armed men that night. Judge Frye withdrew the arrest warrants when confronted with being shunned, or worse, by his fellow townsmen. He then resigned from his government office, promising not to publicly or privately support the Massachusetts Government Act. Even though Gage backed down, things were heating up.[40]

Gage returned to Boston. Two weeks later, the two regiments followed him. About 5:00 am on September 10, the 59th Regiment on Salem Neck marched through town to the music of fifes and drums on their way to Boston. Their heavy baggage had been transported to Boston the previous day by ship.[41] All this activity around him had to have given maturing Jacob deeper insights into the political situation. He also got a good look at the British soldiers whom the colonists felt were imposing, or threatening to impose, slavery upon them by force.

—

In September 1774, calls began circulating advocating the creation of an "Army of Observation" in the British colonies that would keep its troops in "constant exercise and discipline," ready for either "defensive or offensive operations." The mere existence of such an army might prevent the British government from ordering military actions against the colonists. If not, should British soldiers strike, this army would be ready to go into action without having to collect forces from throughout the colonies.[42] However, at this time, the Continental Congress voted down the proposal of Richard Henry Lee of Virginia to create a joint militia for the colonies. Instead, it created a non-military plan, the Continental Association, for an economic protest that included a boycott of British goods and created local committees to enforce it.[43] Everyone hoped that this action aimed at the British economy would bring authorities to their senses and remove threats of military action.

On October 26, 1774, the Massachusetts Provincial Congress began acting as an extralegal government, parallel to the royal colonial government, and adopted detailed instructions to strengthen the colonial militia now under its control. This Provincial Congress created an executive Committee of Safety, empowered to order the militia to turn out in an emergency, and a Committee of Supplies, to equip and support it. It called for obtaining £20,000 worth of muskets, cannon*, shot, and gunpowder; enough to supply five thousand men. It ordered militia officers to reorganize and create more efficient units, hold new officer elections, drill troops using the current British manual, and organize one-quarter of the militia into "minute companies." These "minutemen" would be special units that received additional training and held themselves ready to turn out on a moment's notice.[44]

—

As the conclusion of his indenture approached, Jacob wondered what he would do next. He had matured to adulthood in Salem and knew what to expect there. But, he may have longed to know the situation back in his native New Jersey, especially whether or not his mother was still alive and could tell him his family surname. Critical elements for him to evaluate were his prospects for a successful future as a young free Black man living within the constraints imposed by the White-dominated New England culture. The developing Revolution could only complicate whatever options he considered.

**The word "cannon" can be either singular or plural. While "cannons" is also correct for plural, the author has chosen to use "cannon" consistently.*

I lived and served in Salem until my time was out which was in January 1775. I lived in Salem & worked for different persons till the fall of 1775. In the spring of that year the war had commenced and the Battles of Bunker Hill & Lexington had taken place. About the last of October I enlisted as a soldier of in the United States service for one year. - Jacob Francis

5

Freedom From Indenture in Salem

JACOB'S LIFE ACQUIRED NEW MEANING FOR HIM ON JANUARY 15, 1775, WHEN his indenture time expired. We can only imagine what this freedom must have felt like for a 21-year-old Black man after living his young life controlled by White men who "owned his time." However, although never enslaved himself, he now had much in common with a formerly enslaved person in the way society viewed him.

For the first time in his life, Jacob was free to make his own decisions about how to live his life, within the scope of his abilities and the restrictions imposed by White culture. Would he have the motivation and talent to achieve success? We can only guess how Benjamin Deland had prepared Jacob for his freedom and what "freedom dues" he gave Jacob in the way of money, clothing, or other items to help get him started in life. Jacob struggled with his life's direction choices amid the institutionalized, although slowly changing, prejudices of eighteenth-century New England, complicated by military preparedness activities and the outbreak of hostilities increasing all around him. From the evidence seen throughout his life, Jacob had developed admirable and robust qualities of vision, hard work, focus, patience, and persistence. He was not interested in wealth beyond that needed to comfortably support himself and anyone he became responsible for, such as a wife and family. His mother, and perhaps to some degree Benjamin Deland and the other men who had owned part of Jacob's indenture time, may have been his models, along with other free Black men in Salem who influenced him.

—

It is hard to know whether Jacob wanted to remain in Salem or considered returning to New Jersey with its distant memory of his childhood frozen in time. He had lost contact with his mother for at least the past eight years since neither of them could write and did not know how life had changed for her and other people he had known in early childhood. Was his mother even still alive? On the other hand, Salem held some attractions for him. He certainly knew the Salem area well, had established relationships with local people, and was at least reasonably comfortable after spending almost one-third of his life there. From comments made about him later in life, people who came in contact with Jacob always liked and respected him.

Like other free Black men in Massachusetts, Jacob would live in a status inferior to Whites. However, if he broke the law, his legal punishment would essentially be the same as for a White person. By law, he could not vote, serve on juries, or serve in the militia during peacetime. Instead of performing a soldier's duty, a Massachusetts law of 1707 required free Black men to do menial labor on the militia parade ground and the town roads.[1]

But, what direction in life should he take? Indeed, what were the possibilities for a Black man exiting indenture? His options contrasted sharply with those available to a White man ending indenture. An enslaved or indentured Black man practiced whatever occupation his owner required and trained him to perform. However, free Black men pursuing a particular job in the free market often faced competition from free White men who expected preference. He might do reasonably well if he had obtained a skill, such as blacksmithing, during his indenture, but Jacob had not developed one. Most people in Jacob's situation found themselves limited mainly to employment in domestic service. Many White people would expect him to be just a laborer living on the margins of society for the rest of his life. What choice should he make? Compete with White men and seek work as a farmer? Try to enter an apprenticeship to learn a marketable skill? Or, go to sea as other Black and Native American men had done in Salem?

No matter the choice, he could easily find himself subject to insults and beatings from men who believed he was competing with them for work. He also faced social discrimination. If he did not continue to dwell with the Deland family, he could find his housing choices restricted to marginal places, perhaps in alleys near the wharves. He might be forbidden to appear in specific public locations and would face segregation at church services. Yet, he knew that some free Black individuals had risen above the restrictions of racism and succeeded in various ways. An example was poet Phillis Wheatley whose work appeared in Salem journals while Jacob lived there, and many White people throughout the colonies read her poetry, including eventually George Washington.[2]

—

By his own account, Jacob stayed in Salem. His only comment about his first ten months of freedom was that he took several short-term jobs working "for different persons till the fall of 1775." He does not indicate a change in residence, so perhaps he did continue to live with the Deland family while hiring himself out to Mr. Deland, as well as other men.

One job Deland may well have hired Jacob to work on that commenced shortly after Jacob's freedom from indenture involved remodeling the Assembly Hall into a church. Deland had sold the Assembly Hall to the church in November, and the church leaders organized on February 14. They then began removing the building's massive chimneys and opening up the interior by removing a partition and the second-level flooring. These modifications necessitated disassembling and cleaning 10,750 bricks, some of them reused to support a new porch. In March, members of the congregation purchased pew rights. Church leaders had arranged the pews creating two aisles and designating pews as wall or floor pews. Benjamin Deland likely purchased pew number four, one of the more expensive wall pews, which he owned in 1790.[3]

We do not know just how often during his indenture and then as a free man Jacob had to defend himself against racist attacks from people who mistakenly assumed that he was a slave or a runaway slave because he was Black. He may also have encountered distrust in his interactions with enslaved people because, unlike them, he was free. He was neither enslaved nor a White man. He had "freedom" but was a second-class citizen considered by many White people to lack important human attributes simply because he was Black. He could not help observing the hypocrisy of the White enslavers who argued so strongly against the Coercive Acts, which they felt Parliament had passed to enslave them. Living with restricted freedom while indentured and then as a free Black man must have been a catalyst for developing Jacob's belief in the natural equality of humans of all colors who should also have equal rights in society.

Gun carriages at Salem. Twelve pieces of brass cannon mounted, are at Salem, & lodged near the North River on the back of the Town. – British intelligence report, February 21, 1775

6

War Almost Ignites in Salem

MASSACHUSETTS COLONISTS PREPARED TO DEFEND THEMSELVES BECAUSE the British army maintained a garrison in the Boston area during 1774 and 1775. Securing artillery was a primary objective since it would give them a greater chance to defeat any British attack on their towns. Over the years of the French and Indian War, privateers operating on the coast of New England had removed cannon from captured French and other ships. However, they only took the cannon barrels because the gun carriages designed for shipboard conditions could not be used to transport them on the land. Therefore, towns like Salem employed local men to construct proper gun carriages to mount the seized barrels and the horse-drawn limbers to attach them to for transport.

Massachusetts Governor, and British General, Thomas Gage received mounting intelligence identifying these artillery pieces, just around Jacob's freedom date, and began making plans to capture the military supplies the colonists had stored at various towns around Boston. Just the day before Jacob's freedom began, Gage wrote to Colonel Alexander Leslie about preparing for actions in the vicinity of Marblehead and Salem. Leslie had commanded the troops accompanying Gage when he had set up his government headquarters at Danvers the past summer, so he knew the area.[1]

In addition to obtaining and securing artillery pieces, the colonists made other efforts to strengthen the militia. A letter to the Salem militia company officers dated February 2, 1775, referring to a Provincial Congress resolve of

October 26, 1774, stated, "we hereby recommend to you forthwith to endeavor to enlist one-quarter at least of the number of training soldiers in your company and cause them to be equipt with arms, ammunition and accoutrements fit for actual military service." The men who enlisted should be formed into fifty-man companies and "hold themselves in readiness to march at the shortest notice under the command of such officers as they shall choose." These enlistees would be the famous minutemen. The letter also ordered officers to provide the Provincial Congress with a report before March 17 stating the number of their militiamen and their equipment condition.[2]

The Second Provincial Congress of Massachusetts met at Cambridge during the first two weeks of February to address means for collecting military stores required to equip men called into service if the British initiated military actions. Forty-nine company-level officers of the First Regiment of Essex County militia met on February 13 at the house of Lieutenant Francis Symonds in Danvers. They elected regimental field officers, including Captain Timothy Pickering, Jr., the Deland's near neighbor and likely acquaintance of Jacob, as colonel.[3]

Pickering belonged to a prominent Salem family and had graduated from Harvard College in 1763. He held significant elective offices several times in Salem, such as selectman and town clerk, and was a leading Whig who wrote pamphlets supporting the Revolutionary cause. Commissioned a lieutenant in the Essex County militia in 1766, he studied military history and tactics, and in July 1775, published *An Easy Plan of Discipline for a Militia.* Some New England militia and some Continental units used Pickering's manual as an alternative to the more complex 1764 British Army drill manual. However, the British manual of arms remained primary in American regiments until 1778.[4]

—

The heating up of the Revolution was a daily concern to Jacob as he tried to establish his free life. As February unfolded, Salem nearly became the site of the first exchange of musket fire between New England militiamen and British regulars. Jacob experienced these tense events along with those people he knew in Salem. The previous November, Salem resident David Mason, known as Colonel from his service in the Seven Years War, had been named Engineer by the Massachusetts Committee of Safety and was very actively, and covertly, collecting military stores at Salem including several iron and brass cannon barrels. Blacksmith Robert Foster, living just over the North Bridge at the North Fields, agreed to make the carriages and limbers and employed several men to construct and paint them. Mason also used his daughters and his ill mother to make flannel bags for 5,000 artillery powder charges.[5]

Artillery was considered a critical weapon in eighteenth-century warfare. In places like Boston, where narrow necks of land connected the town to the mainland, artillery could clear attacking troops presenting a narrow front while crossing the neck. In other situations, artillery pieces could cause heavy material damage while raising the morale of the troops they supported and damaging that of the soldiers receiving their fire.

General Gage knew the colonials could raise more men than he had. Although inferior in military skills, if these opponents could employ sufficient artillery, they might well defeat him. On the other hand, if Gage had superior numbers of artillery pieces, he could overcome his manpower disadvantage. His need to deny the New England colonials any artillery they had accumulated led him to take actions that ultimately produced the encounters at Lexington and Concord in April. A similar encounter came close to occurring earlier at Salem in late February.[6]

One or more Torys who became aware of Mason's artillery collection provided General Gage with information about those cannon. Gage received an intelligence report dated February 21 stating, "Gun carriages making at Salem. Twelve pieces of brass cannon mounted, are at Salem, & lodged near the North River, on the back of the Town." Another report stated, "There are eight field pieces in an old store, or barn, near the landing place at Salem, they are to be removed in a few days, the seizure of them would greatly disconcert their schemes."[7]

After failing to prevent the Salem town meeting the previous August, Gage now acted quickly and secretly. By way of Marblehead, he sent a British force of about 250 men under Colonel Alexander Leslie to Salem to take or destroy the military hardware and gunpowder.[8] They arrived at Marblehead by ship on Sunday, February 26, keeping most troops below deck and out of sight. While people attended afternoon church meetings, Leslie mustered his soldiers between 2:00 and 3:00 pm and marched them through Marblehead.

With the British troops exposed to view, local men turned out, and several hastened to Salem to warn its residents. As the word spread, bells rang, drums beat, and alarm guns fired.

Upon learning of the British approach, Benjamin Deland immediately mounted his horse and rode off at a gallop for Danvers to spread the alarm. He found a local militia light-horse company there whose troopers reacted to the news by riding off in every direction to spread the alarm more widely.[9] At Salem, the town selectmen quickly gathered at Colonel Mason's house with John Pedrick, a messenger from Marblehead. After a brief exchange of information, Pedrick rode horseback north and over the North Bridge to alert more of Essex County. Colonel Mason immediately mounted his horse and rode across the North Bridge to Robert Foster's, followed by men he had gathered to remove and scatter the cannon to other locations.

When moving the endangered artillery, cannon barrels not yet mounted on carriages could be slung under farm wagons and taken away in multiple directions, while barrels mounted on carriages could be fastened to limbers hitched to horses and taken to safety. So many people helped move the cannon that they had safely dispersed all of them by the time the British entered Salem from the south.

Jacob must have heard the early warnings along with Benjamin and could have been one of Mason's helpers, but there is no record of his activity. If he did not go north with Mason, because the entire town was alerted he certainly became one of the Salem people who turned out to observe the approaching regulars and, if needed, to help slow down or stop the British advance toward Foster's shop.

The Town House and church bells brought people into the streets as the British approached Salem. It was a frigid day, and the British lacked overcoats. They had to pause at the bridge at the South Mills, whose wooden deck a local carpenter and his apprentices had made impassable just before the British arrival. Leslie ordered some men to repair the bridge and then led his troops across and marched up School Street, pausing at the Town House. A crowd formed, composed mostly of Patriots but also a few Tories. As the British marched with fifes and drums playing *Yankee Doodle*, a local Massachusetts militia drummer joined in beating a different rhythm, which, combined with the ringing church bells, created a cacophony of sounds.

After Mason and his helpers rushed north to disperse the cannon, other men proceeded north and assembled a diverse crowd of North Fields farm boys, sailors, women, and minutemen from Salem and other towns. As Colonel Leslie approached the bridge at North River, men raised the north draw span, perhaps on the order of Colonel Mason, to prevent the British from crossing. Several men, prominently including blacksmith Robert Foster, climbed onto the raised draw span to mock the British. The halted soldiers, heated and sweaty from their rapid five-mile march from Marblehead, were freezing and shivering in their light clothing in the late afternoon February cold. One man shouted at them that they looked like fiddlers because they "shake so!"[10]

Several leading men of the town, including Whig John Felt and Tory John Sargent, joined Leslie. Leslie ordered the draw bridge span lowered and the cannon surrendered to him. To which, one of the local men sarcastically told him that if he could find the cannon, he could have them. While the boisterous crowd collecting about Leslie at the bridge was threatening, no one resorted to throwing objects at the British soldiers. Not inclined to accept defeat, Leslie ordered a captain to face his company toward the crowd across the river and prepare to fire on them, even though they were not armed and no organized militia company had formed up in his path. Someone warned Leslie that, "You had better not fire; you have no right to fire without further orders, and if you do fire, you will all be dead men." The townsmen were out in force, with Jacob likely among them in some way. Leslie withdrew and consulted with his officers and then came back to forcefully announce they would cross the bridge even if it took a month. In response, he heard someone yell that he could stay as long as he pleased; no one would object.

Leslie ordered his men to take control of some of the many fishermen's dories, pirogues, and scows resting on the river bank, but their owners began to scuttle them. Attempting to get possession of the boats, British soldiers wounded several men slightly with their bayonets. When Rev. Thomas Barnard advised Leslie that it would be wrong to injure innocent men, Leslie announced it was a great insult to his troops to be stopped on the King's Highway. However, someone informed him that the highway was not the King's but belonged to several proprietors of land in the North Fields, including blacksmith Robert Foster, former shipmaster John Felt, and Salem truck man Benjamin Deland.[11]

Now late in the day, Leslie announced that if the people lowered the draw bridge and permitted his men to cross, the troops would only proceed a very short distance beyond it into the North Fields, then countermarch, re-cross the bridge, and depart the area. The local men agreed. Timothy Pickering's Salem militiamen, who had now formed on the north side of the river, marked a spot, probably less than 300 yards from the riverbank, and set up a guard.

A Massachusetts minuteman rider galloped up to the British just as they turned around to march back to their ship at Marblehead. This minuteman was none other than Benjamin Deland returning from Danvers. He mockingly warned Leslie, whom he had previously met, that the Danvers militia company had arrived in Salem with more men than Leslie's regulars "had lice in their hair." Unlike the unarmed crowd in town, these minutemen were armed, and supported by militia companies from other nearby areas that had also arrived.

The British troops performed as promised and marched back through town to the music of fife and drum. However, Leslie was not amused. He had not succeeded in his mission but had only raised a great deal of unease and anger. He had avoided another Boston Massacre-type incident but had failed in his mission when confronted by determined local people protecting their essential defensive firepower from the British regulars.[12]

Jacob had been at least an observer of this incident and perhaps had participated actively in some aspect of it. This event must undoubtedly have caused him to think deeply about how he would participate in subsequent events. As a free man, he would have more options than if still indentured, but his choices would be somewhat limited as a Black man.

You are not to enlist any deserter from the Ministerial Army, nor any stroller, negro, or vagabond, or person suspected of being an enemy to the liberty of American, not any under eighteen years of age. – General Horatio Gates, July 19, 1775

7

Creating an American Army

THROUGHOUT JACOB'S FIRST TEN MONTHS OF FREEDOM, MILITARY organizations in New England became increasingly prominent and complex. The long-standing militia, now under the Provincial Congress, first became the backup for a full-time New England army and then the Continental army that replaced it. On the day Jacob became free, an open military engagement between the colonial militia and British troops had not yet occurred. However, over the next six months there would be a near battle at Salem in February, actual day-long fighting beginning at Lexington and Concord in April, and a significant battle on the Charlestown peninsula at Bunker Hill* in June. During those months, the Continental Congress formed the Continental Army with George Washington as commander-in-chief. It was formed from militiamen besieging Boston who were exchanging fire almost daily with the British troops it had trapped there. Throughout all these changes and events, politicians and military leaders debated whether or not they wanted Black men like Jacob to serve in their military units.

—

After reaching age sixteen, although indentured, Jacob had been subject to some type of connection to the militia, most likely as a laborer since the

**The battle was actually fought on adjacent Breed's Hill but has always be known by the name Bunker Hill, so that term will be used in this work.*

law prohibited Black men from serving as soldiers. Now, as a free Black man, Jacob may have become involved with the Salem militia, especially after the events at Lexington and Concord in April. Black men were sometimes taken into the militia in Massachusetts even though technically excluded from it by law in times of peace. After requiring in 1652 that Black men, either settlers or servants, between the ages of sixteen and sixty, train as members of companies, Massachusetts had excluded all Black men and Indians from military duty in 1656 and repeated that ruling in 1693.[1] While forbidden to bear arms in peacetime, upon any alarm, free Black men turned out on the parade ground to perform any service in support of the militia ordered by the senior commissioned militia officer present. Failure to report for this duty resulted in a twenty shilling fine or eighty days of labor. In place of militia service in peacetime, the law required free Black men to work maintaining streets and highways for a number of days each year determined by the local town selectmen and comparable to days of militia duty for White men. Failure to serve resulted in a five-shilling fine.[2]

Throughout the French and Indian wars, Black men served in the military to compensate for the unwillingness of White men to sign up, and they valued the opportunity to serve and potentially improve their civil status. The Black recruits in these wars appear to have received the same pay as White men and served in integrated companies. No charges of cowardice or treason against Black soldiers appeared during those wars.[3]

—

The Salem news column in the *Essex Gazette* on March 7 notified all men subject to militia service under the law to "appear" in School Street at 9:00 am the following Tuesday with their "arms, ammunition and accoutrements." Each man should have "A well fixed firelock and bayonet --- A pouch that will hold 20 or 30 rounds of cartridges --- Half a dozen flints --- Thirty rounds of cartridges with balls, or a pound of powder and thirty balls --- A knapsack – A screw-driver and priming-wire [to make minor musket repairs]."

Anticipating that some men would only obey the call because it was the law and not because they whole-heartedly supported the cause, the notice stated "It is hoped that every friend to his Country, every man who has a respect for the recommendation of the Provincial Congress, or regards the safety of his life, liberty or property, will prepare himself to defend them against every invader; and appear thus prepared in School Street at the time abovementioned."[4]

As a free Black man, Jacob may well have felt subject to this order as conditions moved from peace toward war. The Massachusetts militia officers needed every man they could get and militia units had included both free and enslaved Black men from their colonial beginnings.[5] Laws were not always clear, especially regarding free Black men, and officers used personal discretion when they needed to fill the ranks. Jacob must have been torn as to whether or not to join one of the military units forming up knowing that people disagreed over whether or not he should even be allowed to enlist as a Black man. Jacob does say whether he turned out or even had the proper gear. Benjamin Deland may have helped outfit him if he did turn out.

By March 23, people in Salem, and as far away as Virginia, believed hostilities could break out in New England at any moment. When Virginia's Patrick Henry delivered his famous "give me liberty or give me death" speech that day before the Second Virginia Convention meeting in Richmond he said, "Gentlemen may cry, Peace, Peace but there is no peace. The war is actually begun! The next gale that sweeps from the north will bring to our ears the clash of resounding arms! Our [New England] brethren are already in the field!" On March 25, Salem voted to raise two companies of minutemen who would train a half-day every week and receive pay. The town's action did not mention Black men, an indication they could join.[6]

In April, the Massachusetts Provincial Congress, anticipating a greater need for more professional soldiers, resolved to raise a volunteer New England army consisting of men from all the New England colonies. It sent delegates to each colony to urge its participation. On April 14, the Committee of Safety began organizing the Massachusetts contingent for this army. The Congress then adjourned, just five days before the encounters at Lexington and Concord.[7]

—

On April 14, General Gage received orders from Secretary of State Lord Dartmouth authorizing the use of troops if necessary to enforce the Coercive Acts and other acts of Parliament. Five days later, the war commenced at Lexington and Concord when Gage sent troops to collect military stores reported to be at Concord, much like he had sent Colonel Leslie to Salem in February. When patriot riders such as Paul Revere and William Dawes aroused minutemen across the Massachusetts countryside, both White and Black men responded.[8] Late in the day, the British troops arrived back in Boston after those two encounters and the bloody, fighting retreat they suffered the rest of that long day at the hands of militiamen.

Several Salem and Danvers militiamen rode horseback out toward Lexington. Salem resident Benjamin Pierce and Danvers resident Benjamin Deland, Jr., a relative of Jacob's former indenture-time owner, were killed during the daylong fighting. Almost 300 militiamen under Colonel Pickering marched rapidly to the area. But, they did not arrive until the retreating British troops were reaching safety in Boston and Pickering chose not to engage them. It would have been natural for Jacob to march with Pickering, although he did not mention it later in life, perhaps because they saw no action.

Immediately after the day-long series of battles and skirmishes, conversations each day involved listening to and retelling stories identifying the British troops as the instigators and aggressors at Lexington. While the Salem men received criticism for apparently turning out slowly, a General Court on August 10 cleared them from any censure.[9] The owner of Salem's King's Arms Tavern renamed it The Sun in reaction to the widespread belief that the regulars had initiated the musket fire.[10]

—

Responding to the events of April 19, on April 21 the Committee of Safety began creating the New England army from the militia units that had massed around Boston. Instead of using the traditional colonial method of having each town supply a quota of men, the Committee told officers rather to seek recruits from the men on the Boston siege lines. The plan called for 30,000 men, with Massachusetts committed to furnishing 13,600. The Committee began enlisting the first 8,000 men to serve in newly created Provincial regiments for eight months, until December 31. Hopefully, the war would be over by then.

Over the next few weeks, New Hampshire, Rhode Island, and Connecticut responded to the call for province regiments in various ways. Immediately after learning of Lexington and Concord, men from New Hampshire responded as individuals and small groups. Expecting a more formal response from New Hampshire, the Massachusetts Committee directed Salem native Paul Dudley Sargent, then living in Hillsborough County, New Hampshire, to raise a regiment of men from that area. Since New Hampshire itself was also forming regiments, it declined to sponsor this one, so Massachusetts adopted

Sargent's regiment, ultimately containing men from New Hampshire and Massachusetts.[11] During the remainder of April and into early May, the New England army formed in fits and starts.

The Second Continental Congress convened on May 10 in Philadelphia and took steps to create a "national" military force. This action would require abandoning colonial period precedents and finding new methods to create an army of men from all thirteen colonies. The news that Ethan Allen and Benedict Arnold had captured Fort Ticonderoga in New York revealed the expanding nature of the war and left only faint hope of resolving the issues with Britain peacefully. The New England delegates defended the need for the expanded army, arguing that their troops were actually defending all thirteen colonies from British aggression. The delegates wanted the Continental Congress to adopt the troops at Boston, declare that the war involved all the colonies, and expect each colony to support the common actions.[12]

The Continental Congress formed itself into a Committee of the Whole to debate the current "State of America." Its first action was to act on a May 16 motion by Virginia's Richard Henry Lee that Congress raise an army. However, despite significant support, there was enough opposition to prevent quick action. The discussion considered the need for a military force at New York to defend it against a British force thought to be heading there. By May 21, John Adams believed the armies required at Boston and New York should exist at Continental expense. Additionally, during this time, the expedition against Canada became fully engaged in combat with British forces.[13]

—

Although an insufficient number of White men responded to fill the army, the Massachusetts Committee of Safety recommended on May 20 that no enslaved man should be enlisted into the Massachusetts regiments "upon any consideration whatever." Free Black men were another matter though, requiring Jacob to struggle with whether or not to enlist. A period of enlistment must have looked to Jacob very much like another period of indenture. The army would "own" his time. So recently freed from his indenture, he may not have wanted to give up control over his life again. He also may not have wanted to enlist into an army that did not openly welcome men like him.

On June 10, John Adams formally proposed that Congress adopt the various colonial troops besieging the British in Boston as its all-inclusive

Continental army. The delegates agreed to this on June 14, after reaching an agreement in the Committee of the Whole. Congress then resolved to raise ten rifle companies to send to Boston; six in Pennsylvania, two in Maryland, and two in Virginia. These would join the "New England army" troops and the forces needed to defend New York. They were the first troops raised explicitly for the Continental Army. Congress also established a committee to write up common rules and regulations for this force.

Recognizing that the new army must have a commander-in-chief, New Englander John Adams strongly hinted it should be Virginian George Washington, and Washington received a unanimous vote on June 15. On June 22, the Continental Congress asked Pennsylvania to raise two additional companies and form its eight rifle companies into a battalion*. Between June 17 and 19, Congress also named several generals to serve directly under Washington, including Artemas Ward of Massachusetts and Danvers born Israel Putnam now of Connecticut.

While Congress established its Continental Army, the New England army fought the Battle of Bunker Hill* on June 17. Militiamen from Salem, although called out, once again did not participate in that fighting. Congress spent several weeks organizing and selecting additional line and staff officers for various leadership roles in its Continental Army.[14] Jacob became involved in the discussions among Salem citizens about all these developments, especially the Battle of Bunker Hill.

—

Massachusetts men now entering the Continental Army enlisted for the remainder of the year. But, even that short, six-month enlistment led many men to rethink things and decide to go home to take care of their farms during the late summer and fall planting and harvesting seasons. They could serve in the part-time militia while taking care of their land and families and leave service in the full-time army to others. Therefore, men enlisting in the Continental regiments were more likely to be young and possess little property. Some young men saw better prospects in the army to begin building their lives if their families could spare them. Some young men simply sought adventure. Because many mature farmers with families did not enlist in the full-time Continental Army,

**A battalion was normally a collection of companies from several regiments or several companies from a regiment. The word was also often a synonym for regiment.*

recruiting officers made exceptions to fill the ranks. A widespread concern soon arose that too many recruits were young boys, older men, or Black men. Again, Jacob may have heard that men like him were considered incapable of possessing the necessary qualities required by the military.

Proposals for attacking Boston circulated while the new army was taking shape and seeking suitable adult White volunteers with less than hoped for success. As a slave-owning southerner, when Washington took command at Cambridge, he wanted to exclude Black men from the army. But, he badly needed men and was troubled that finding recruits was proving so difficult. Washington noted on July 10 that, "from the number of boys, deserters, & negroes which have been listed in the troops of this province [Massachusetts], I entertain some doubts whether the number [of qualified men] required can be raised here…."[15]

The creation of an army representing all thirteen colonies raised the issue of Black men participating as armed soldiers in regiments recruited outside of New England. In New England, both common white soldiers and officers appear to have generally accepted Black men. Black enlistments would be less acceptable in southern colonies. On July 10, General Horatio Gates published an order in various newspapers entitled "Instructions for the officers of the several regiments of the Massachusetts-Bay Forces, who are immediately to go upon the recruiting service." It ordered, "You are not to enlist any deserter from the Ministerial Army, nor any stroller, negro, or vagabond, or person suspected of being an enemy to the liberty of America, not any under eighteen years of age." Furthermore, only men who display "courage and principle" should be enlisted and they "must be provided with good and complete arms." At this point in the struggle, he optimistically believed that because "the cause is the best that can engage men of courage and principle to take up arms," and the "pay, provisions, &c., being so ample, it is not doubted but the officers sent upon this service will, without delay, compete their respective corps, and march the men forthwith to camp." That expectation proved impossible to achieve.[16]

Optimism that further combat should be minimal continued to grow from reports that the British suffered severely in Boston. A note from Cambridge dated July 13 commented, "We have undoubted intelligence that General Gage's troops are much dispirited; that they are very sickly, and are heartily disposed to leave off dancing any more" to the satirical, mocking tune of *Yankee Doodle*.[17]

By the end of the summer, colonial legislatures had taken measures to halt Black enlistment for several stated reasons. A significant negative was that some "Black freedmen" who had enlisted were actually runaway slaves whose masters could come looking for them. Black enslavement was part of the agricultural economy in New England, although not to the extent as in the south, and owners tended to value their enslaved labor. There also remained old fears about groups of Black men with guns causing civil unrest and slave revolts.[18]

The Continental Army continued to fail to develop as envisioned for several reasons. Pennsylvania Captain Alexander Graydon painted a word picture in his memoir describing the army forming at Cambridge. He wrote, "The appearance of things was not much calculated to excite sanguine expectations in the mind of a sober observer." While:

> *great numbers of people were indeed to be seen ... those who are not accustomed to the sight of bodies under arms, are always prone to exaggerate them. But this propensity to swell the mass, had not an equal tendency to convert it into soldiery; and the irregularity, want of discipline, bad arms, and defective equipment in all respects, of this multitudinous assemblage, gave no favorable impression of its prowess.*

Graydon singled out the officers for criticism noting:

> *I speak particularly of the officers, who were in no single respect distinguishable from their men, other than the colored cockades, which, for this very purpose, had been prescribed in general orders; a different color being assigned to the officers of each grade. So far from aiming at a deportment which might raise them above their privates, and thence prompt them to due respect and obedience to their commands, the object was, by humility, to preserve the existing blessing of quality.*

Focusing on Colonel Rufus Putnam, Graydon repeated a story of Putnam carrying a piece of meat in his hand and meeting a person who commented, "carrying home your rations yourself, colonel!" to which Putnam replied, "Yes, and I do it to set the officers a good example." Graydon also observed that it was not uncommon "for a colonel to make drummers and fifers of his sons, thereby, not only being enabled to form a very snug, economical mess, but to aid also considerably the revenues of the family chest. In short, it appeared, that the sordid spirit of gain was the vital principle of this greater part of the army."

Graydon then noted that the New England troops of Colonel John Glover's regiment raised primarily at Marblehead were an exception to what he had described. Graydon commented favorably that:

> *There was an appearance of discipline in this corps; the officers seemed to have mixed with the world, and to understand what belonged to their stations. Though deficient, perhaps, in polish, it possessed an apparent aptitude for the purpose of its institution, and gave a confidence that myriads of its meek and lowly brethren were incompetent to inspire.*

However, Graydon saw a problem with Glover's otherwise fine unit because, "even in this regiment there were a number of negroes, which, to persons unaccustomed to such associations, had a disagreeable, degrading effect."[19]

—

On September 14, Jacob may have seen and certainly heard about a detachment of New England troops from General Benedict Arnold's force, headed for Canada by way of the Maine woods, who marched through the area and camped for the night at Danvers. The next day, General Arnold came to Salem, where he dined and purchased 200 pounds of ginger and received 270 blankets from the Committee of Safety by order of Quartermaster General Thomas Mifflin. He hired a teamster to transport the ginger and blankets to Newburyport, where he arrived at 10:00 pm.[20] That teamster could well have been Benjamin Deland or someone else Jacob knew.

—

As a 21-year-old man, Jacob observed all the encouragements given to White men to enlist. At the same time, while he may have received some encouragement, he was generally not encouraged, or even expected by many, to do so. He needed a steady job, and the army could provide it, at least for a few months. Beyond employment and monetary considerations, Jacob must have developed strong positive feelings about the goals of the rising tide of revolution but wondered whether it would genuinely result in liberty for all people. But, while Jacob contemplated enlistment and worked at odd jobs, the debate over Black enlistments grew increasingly negative.

On September 26, Congressional delegate Edward Rutledge of South Carolina moved that General Washington "shall discharge all the Negroes as well slaves as freemen in his army." However, although strongly supported by delegates from southern colonies, Rutledge's motion lost.[21]

On October 5, John Adams wrote to Major General William Heath, under whom Jacob would later serve for a time, about concerns he and others had. Adams continued to hear the negative opinion about the Massachusetts regiments that "there are great numbers of boys, old men, and Negroes, such as are unsuitable for the service, and therefore that the Continent is paying for a much greater number of men, than are fit for action or any service." Adams asked Heath to inform him whether there was any truth in that observation or if this situation was more common in Massachusetts regiments than in those of other states, especially in New England. He was also concerned about the criticisms leveled at Massachusetts officers and hoped they were at least equal in numbers and quality to those from other states.[22] He would not receive a reply from Heath for several weeks.

By October, the war increasingly dominated Jacob's thoughts. He heard cannon fire on October 4 that broke out after a Beverly-based privateer running from the British Navy vessel *Nautilus* ran aground. The 16-gun *Nautilus* opened fire on the privateer and received retaliatory artillery fire from batteries at Salem and Beverly for several hours supporting the grounded ship. The privateer ultimately refloated and escaped before men from the *Nautilus* could board her.[23] People became convinced that British Navy ships would shell coastal towns in retaliation.

Along with all the citizens of Salem, Jacob anticipated such a British bombardment. As the month neared its close, Jacob heard that the General Court, fearing that the enemy would take measures to destroy Salem, had ordered adjacent towns to lend the sea port a sufficient quantity of ammunition to defend itself. After the British bombarded Falmouth on October 18, other towns and harbors, including Salem, employed large numbers of men for several days to build defenses because, as a newspaper reported, "no mercy is to be expected from our savage enemies!" Not having a full-time job, Jacob may have been one of those men employed. These activities were all occurring about the time that Jacob decided to enlist.[24]

—

After the Continental Army had kept British troops confined to Boston for six months, both sides contemplated their options. The British officers considered whether their troops should break out and attempt to disperse the American army. The Americans debated whether they should attack Boston and try to drive the British out.

During October, Washington considered an attack on Boston, anticipating that the enormous costs of a winter encampment and the dispiriting inactivity of his men would greatly diminish reenlistments in January. However, after meeting with his generals on October 5 to discuss what advice to give Congress regarding the new version of the army it had called for, whose enlistments would begin on January 1, Washington followed up with a letter to Robert Carter Nicholas in Virginia.

Washington told Nicholas, "The enemy in Boston and on the heights of Charlestown are so strongly fortified, as to render it almost impossible to force their lines, thrown up at the head of each neck." He predicted that a successful attack would end either in "great slaughter on our side, or cowardice on theirs." Washington believed that it only made sense to "keep them besieged, which they are [now] to all intents and purposes, as closely as any troops upon earth can be, that have an opening to the sea. Our advanced works and theirs are within musket-shot. We daily undergo a cannonade, which has done no injury to our works, and very little hurt to our men."

Even so, Washington admitted that due to a severe lack of gunpowder, his troops had to restrain themselves from continually trading shots, "being obliged, except now and then giving them a shot, to reserve what we have for closer work than cannon distance."[25] The military situation was a frustrating stalemate.

As Jacob contemplated enlistment, Washington again discussed with his generals on October 18 the possibility of an attack on Boston, but they unanimously rejected the idea. Between October 18 and 22, Washington met with a Congressional committee about the organization of the new army, set to begin January 1, and how many men were needed to continue the siege. The new army would consist of 26 regiments rather than 38. This reduction produced many expected and unexpected issues, resulting in misunderstandings, jealousies, and misrepresentation. The decrease in officer billets generated controversy and charges of prejudice or partiality towards individuals and their colonies. Amid all the debate, leaders expressed the hope and expectation that most of the expiring army's veterans would reenlist and the anticipated problems efficiently solved. However, after a month of effort, only 5,000 recruits had joined, leaving Washington very troubled by the recruiting issues they were encountering.[26]

—

Massachusetts agreed to raise 20,000 men, or more if necessary, by far the most from any New England colony. It would provide the same enlistment incentives offered when raising the present army - a coat, 40 shillings a month, and one month's pay in advance. Even though recruits were urgently needed, officers continued to debate "Whether it will be advisable to re-enlist any negroes in the new army - or whether there be a distinction between such as are slaves & those who are free?" When the Continental Congress had appointed Washington commander-in-chief, it had required him to always make decisions in consultation with his chief subordinates in a council of war. During such a council on October 8, Washington and eight of his officers, including several from New England, considered a recruitment policy proposed by British-born General Horatio Gates and "agreed unanimously to reject all slaves, & by a great majority to reject negroes altogether."[27]

Washington raised the same question with the Congressional committee visiting him at Cambridge and noted that his council of officers believed the army should exclude both slaves and free Blacks. The committee concurred on October 23. No Black men should be encouraged to join, or enlisted if they volunteered. Currently enlisted Black men causing the army to be considered defective, would be expelled.[28] This decision came while Jacob pondered his future and whether it would involve military service.

While Congress created the Continental Army to unify the thirteen colonies, Congress and its army took steps to decide which types of men would contribute to an appropriate sense of a united community and which would not. In effect, by establishing who could serve in the army, they would determine who belonged in society and who did not. The debate over the inclusion of Black men in the army exemplified that aspect of the Revolution. Who was an American and deserved to share in the rights being fought for to secure?[29]

Washington was increasingly fearful because enlistments in the original Continental regiments were due to expire by the end of the year, and enlistments in the new army were going slowly. In his October 22 general orders, Washington began another push to recruit men for the 1776 version of the Continental Army. Those men already in the army and agreeing to continue to serve should consider themselves enlisted to December 3, 1776, unless discharged sooner. All officers and men intending to stay should make it known by the following Wednesday.[30] The constantly changing situation of the reorganizing army made it difficult to know just how many recruits were needed.

General Heath finally replied on October 23 to his October 5 letter from John Adams describing the condition of the army, saying, "It is not surprising that jealousies do subsist, and that misrepresentations have been made, respecting our colony by some. But such will be despised, by the wise the generous and brave, who will be rightly informed before they censure." Heath admitted that the Massachusetts Regiments did contain "some few lads and old men, and in several regiments, some Negroes." However, he noted that Massachusetts was not alone in this regard, and "Rhode Island has a number of Negroes and Indians, Connecticut has fewer Negroes but a number of Indians. The New Hampshire regiments have less of both. The men from Connecticut I think in general are rather stouter [physically strong] than those of either of the other colonies, but the troops of our colony are robust, agile, and as fine fellows in general as I ever would wish to see in the field."[31] Presumably, these quality troops included the Black soldiers.

In an October 24 letter to John Adams from the camp at Roxbury, Massachusetts, General John Thomas mentioned that he regretted the Southern lack of respect for the necessarily quickly raised New England troops. He commented that in "the regiments at Roxbury, the privates are equal to any that I served with last war, very few old men, and in the ranks very few boys, our fifers are many of them boys." He acknowledged that "we have some Negros, but I look on them in general equally serviceable with other men, for fatigue [labor] and in action; many of them have proved themselves brave."[32] General Thomas's positive observations on the equality of Black and White men in the army were more robust than most White men would accept. One wonders if the feelings he expressed about equality extended to life outside the military.

Washington met with his officers again on October 23 and 24 to consider an all-out attack on Boston or simply punishing the British soldiers there with an artillery bombardment. However, because the artillery would also inflict damage on civilians, and the prospect of destroying Boston was so sensitive, Congress needed to approve. While the debates over military action around Boston continued, Americans equipped sundry vessels for privateering. Some of these vessels successfully captured British ships with badly needed military supplies for the developing army.[33]

—

Independence had become a hot topic in the army even though the military goal continued to be the redress of grievances.[34] Some officers also knew that France seriously wanted to hurt England by supporting the colonists, but they would do this openly only after the colonies declared independence.[35] As Jacob internally debated whether to attempt enlisting, it must have been difficult to know whether or not the army he sought to join would continue the fight to redress grievances with Parliament or would switch to fighting to secure independence.

—

As October drew to a close, Jacob decided to enlist for a year. Several factors must have worked in concert to bring about that difficult decision. While he never suggests that he simply needed a job, this could have been a factor; it certainly was for some White men. As a young man accustomed to authority, tired of odd jobs, and who sought adventure, he may have been fascinated by and curious about the life of a soldier, imagining it to be more romantic than it was in reality. However, he was finally free from the indentured servitude which had controlled his life experiences. Why would he give up that new freedom and have the army control his life in much the same way the owners of his indenture time had?

The army Jacob joined was being used as a tool for achieving political change, greater freedom for the White colonists of British North America. However, it could also showcase another revolution involving cultural changes, such as how society treated Black people. For some men at the time, enlisting in military service held the prospect of greater participation in a new political structure and community of its citizens. The questions pursued in developing that new structure would involve determining the qualifications for full participatory citizenship.[36]

Although he does not mention anyone specifically, Jacob probably knew other Black men who wanted to enlist. Discussions among young men in

Salem included sharing their desire, or perceived obligation, to join one or another form of military unit. Army recruiters who came to Salem may have told him about regiments containing men with ties to Salem and Danvers.

Some young White men around Jacob enlisted to prove that they were true men and worthy of respect. They especially wanted to impress family, other young men, and for some, young women. It may be that Jacob also wanted to prove his qualities as a man. In addition, enlisting gave him a chance to show White people that he was equal to them in human traits and skills. It was not uncommon for Black men to hope that by fighting for a common cause with White men and sharing in the credit for their victories, those White men would hold them in higher respect and treat them with justice.[37]

For six years, Jacob had lived surrounded by the growing revolutionary spirit of the Deland family and other strong Salem patriots. Whether Jacob was motivated primarily by enthusiasm or need, he would enlist to serve a cause, a combination of his own and the cause promoted by the people around him.[38] He would enlist at least partly to participate in the revolutionary struggle for freedom, even while he was not equally free with White men. Many years later, one of Jacob's sons became highly active in the movement to abolish enslavement and wrote a eulogy upon the death of John Quincy Adams in 1841. He wrote:

> *And now I should like to have the world know that the same principles of '76, which led the great mind of John Q. Adams to energetic action, to advise in behalf of his country to throw off the British yoke, actuated my father to shoulder his musket and serve through a bloody contest. And not only my father's but the blood of colored men was freely shed in that struggle for national independence.*[39]

That concept of freedom, however, must have been complex and confusing to Jacob. His life had been lived in the eighteenth-century world in which people experienced various degrees of freedom in their lives. While the White male leaders of the Revolution against Great Britain sought the highest degree of freedom for themselves, they relegated all others in society, women, poor Whites, apprentices, indentured servants, Indians, free Black people, and enslaved Black people to various gradations of servitude and lack of rights.[40] Jacob may well have kept hearing the words of freedom as a potential promise for greater freedom in the future for all. Just as Abigail

Adams reminded John to remember "the ladies," Jacob could have hoped the White political leaders would remember those people of African ancestry, fighting alongside White men for freedom, when it came to establishing full rights of citizenship.

Military life was dangerous, and Jacob knew that if the army accepted him, enemy musket balls, cannonballs, and exploding artillery shells would make no racial discrimination. Neither would smallpox and other diseases and discomforts that killed or debilitated large numbers of soldiers, as well as civilians. He would also suffer equally with the men in his regiment from whatever discomforts the weather inflicted on them. Still, he decided to enlist.

Part II

Fighting for Rights in the Revolution

Boston, Massachusetts Area of Inman Farm

From: *A plan of Boston in New England with its environs, including Milton, Dorchester, Roxbury, Brooklin, Cambridge, Medford, Charlestown, parts of Malden and Chelsea with the military works constructed in those places in the years 1775 and 1776.*
By Henry Pelham and Francis Jukes - 1777.

Library of Congress, Geography and Map Division

"... the same principles of '76, which led the great mind of John Q. Adams to energetic action, to advise in behalf of his country to throw off the British yoke, actuated my father to shoulder his musket and serve through a bloody contest." – Abner H. Francis

8

Enlistment in the Continental Army October-December 1775

WITH NOT MUCH MORE THAN THE CLOTHES ON HIS BACK, JACOB SET OUT from Salem sometime during the last days of October 1775, heading for Continental Army headquarters at Cambridge, located across the Charles River from Boston, some fifteen miles distant. He knew that although the army badly needed recruits, it did not openly encourage free Black men to enlist and often rejected them. However, he just might succeed in enlisting.

Jacob had to be careful and alert on his journey to Cambridge because a Black man on the road could raise suspicions just because of his color. For example, army General Orders for October 9, also distributed to civilians, had stated, "If any Negroe is found straggling after *taptoo* beating about the camp, or about any of the roads or villages, near the encampments at Roxbury, or Cambridge, they are to be seized and confined until sunrise, in the Guard, nearest to the place where such Negroe is taken up."[1] Jacob was probably not the only man from Salem seeking to enlist at that time, so perhaps he traveled with one or more White potential recruits who could vouch for him.

Upon arriving at Cambridge, Jacob sought out the Massachusetts regiment that he specifically wanted to join, possibly due to ties he had to men already serving in it. He learned the regiment's men had encamped on Ralph Inman's farm just outside the town. Inman was a Tory who had fled to Boston, and the Whigs had confiscated his farm. Jacob would be joining the army during a period of cold and disagreeable weather that continued for several days as a precursor to the onset of winter.[2]

—

The regiment Jacob sought was Colonel Paul Dudley Sargent's regiment, the unit Massachusetts had asked Sargent to raise. It had been established on April 23, 1775, and assigned to the Main Army outside Boston when the Continental army began forming on June 14. Thirty-year-old Colonel Sargent was born in Gloucester, Massachusetts, in 1745, nine years before Jacob, and spent his youth and early manhood in Salem, where his family relocated.[3] His Tory brother, John Sargent, had assisted Colonel Leslie at Salem when his troops encountered the opened North River drawbridge while searching for rebel cannon in February. So, Jacob was well aware of the Sargent family. The other field officers of the regiment were Lieutenant Colonel Michael Jackson of Newton, Massachusetts, and Major Jonathan Williams Austin of Chelmsford, Massachusetts.

When the Continental Congress had established its army the previous June and named Washington its commander-in-chief, efforts immediately began to adopt the troops around Boston and recruit additional men to create an army for the remainder of 1775. Initially, the Continental Army required only short enlistments because leaders expected Britain to back down from its oppressive actions when the colonists demonstrated their willingness to risk death in combat to maintain their rights. When Britain did not back down, it became clear that winning the war would require full-time soldiers serving for a long term, in addition to the part-time state militias.

The Continental Congress now wanted to give its army a Continental character rather than being a collection of colony or province-oriented regiments. Along with disbanding some of the 1775 regiments and authorizing others to continue as part of the new army, Congress authorized several new regiments for the 1776 army. Whether a man enlisted in the 1775 or the 1776 version, he understood he was fighting for the defense of liberty within the British Empire, not to gain independence from it. Sargent's regiment would continue as part of the new 1776 army, but its designation would change from the 28th Massachusetts Regiment to the 16th Continental Regiment. The Continental army would serve the purposes of the colonies sending delegates to the Continental Congress, and as such, it became "a manifestation of an imagined continental community."[4]

To build the new version of the army, officers urged men already serving to reenlist for an additional year and form a veteran base for the many recruits that would bring regiments to full strength. One-year enlistments for all recruits would begin January 1, 1776. Jacob must have become aware of all this reorganization when he heard during 1775 about local men enlisting in one or the other version of the army and comparing it with the several forms of militia duty in Massachusetts. He became one of those recruits supplementing to the veteran base reenlisting in Sargent's Regiment. He would join men from Massachusetts and New Hampshire who had enlisted only until the end of 1775, about two months away and who now faced the choice to either depart the army at the end of 1775 or commit to a new, one-year enlistment.[5]

Sargent's regiment consisted of ten companies numbered following the seniority of their captain. Using his adopted surname Gulick, Jacob enlisted into Captain John Wiley's company, designated number 10 because Wiley was the junior captain in the regiment, recently commissioned on August 25.[6] Captain Wiley's brother, Aldridge, served as the second lieutenant, and one of the captain's sons, also named John, served as a sergeant while another son, Samuel, was a drummer. This company strongly displayed the family connections that Washington and others found objectionable in New England regiments. Jacob agreed to serve for two months to help bolster the soon-to-be disbanded army for the remainder of the year and receive two months' pay for his service in November and December. He would then begin a one-year enlistment on January 1, 1776, in the new establishment of the army. He would serve a total of fourteen months.

How Washington's recruitment orders affected the practices of recruiting officers is not clear. The generality of the concepts "young boys" and "older men" gave recruiters leeway to use judgment. Was a particular young boy big enough and mature enough to serve well? Was an older man still fit enough to serve? However, there was no leeway allowed for Black men. None should be accepted. However, recruiters may have also used their judgment.

The prejudice against enlisting free Black men was unfounded. No one had claimed that Black men who had participated in combat had proven incompetent or in any way unable to carry out a soldier's duties. There is no evidence that White Soldiers or officers who had served with Black soldiers from Lexington through the summer at Cambridge made any complaints about them. No records exist to indicate disciplinary problems caused by racial diversity. Washington was so adamant about not wanting Black men in the army that he would have cited and highlighted any evidence of problems in his correspondence with officers and Congress as grounds for his exclusion policy.[7]

The officer enlisting Jacob acted counter to Washington's current policy regarding Black men. Jacob must have impressed the officer with his desire to enlist and his positive bearing and skills. He may have sought personal recommendations from soldiers in the regiment who knew him. To even be considered, Jacob had to convince the officer that he would not weaken the regiment due to any inability to perform his duties consistently and well. If Jacob impressed those men around him and did not cause trouble, it minimized the risk of criticism the enlisting officer faced for accepting a Black man.

The officer may have accepted Jacob simply because it was proving difficult to find recruits and persuade current soldiers to reenlist in the new version of the army. While the army veterans had been enthusiastic, confident patriots when they first enlisted, after months of army life, they now saw themselves as citizen-soldiers who had only contracted to serve for a set length of time. They would live up to their contract despite the adversities of army life but felt no further obligation. They had performed their duty for the cause, and now other men could perform theirs. Therefore, regardless of race, the army needed physically and constitutionally strong men with the character to work hard, obey orders, and support each other.

—

Upon his acceptance, initiating the enlistment process, Jacob declared the Continental Congress specified oath that "I, Jacob Gulick, have, this day, voluntarily enlisted myself, as a soldier, in the American continental army, for one year, unless sooner discharged: And I do bind myself to conform, in all instances, to such rules and regulations, as are, or shall be, established for the government of the said Army." The Continental Congress had passed those rules and regulations, the Articles of War, on June 30, 1775.[8]

As the process unfolded, Jacob learned that the army would pay him forty shillings each month, provide ample provisions, and grant him a furlough* to visit family for a time during the winter at the army's convenience. The last item

Known today as leave, a furlough was a specified leave of absence for personal business, rather than army business.

would not be a natural attraction for Jacob because he was so geographically removed from his mother. The recruiting officer asked if Jacob had brought a musket. If not, Jacob learned that six shillings would be deducted from his pay when the army could supply him with one. Later documents indicate that Jacob took up his musket, so he may have brought one with him, perhaps provided by Benjamin Deland.

At some point, he would receive new clothing from the army for a monthly fee of ten shillings withheld from his pay until completing payment for it. If Jacob had brought a blanket, he received a two-dollar allowance and learned he could keep the blanket at the end of the campaign, assuming he still had it.[9] However, as Jacob soon learned, even though he fulfilled his part of the enlistment contract diligently and without exception over its complete duration, the army would not always fulfill its promises of pay, ample food, and clothing.

Jacob's enlistment must have brought back memories of his indenture. The army owned his time for fourteen months in exchange for supporting him with clothing, food, and other necessary items. The one big difference was that the army would also pay him a set wage, when it could. While the army had accepted Jacob due to the urgent need for soldiers, this did not mean he would be fully integrated into it or accepted by all those White men he encountered, although it appears that he was. He might be tolerated while in the army, in the process of creating a colonial union, but that toleration could quickly disappear when he left the army. Although many White New Englanders positively accepted Black people, to varying degrees, others held extreme racist beliefs that could pose a danger to them. The army could not wholly shield Jacob from other soldiers' racist views and actions unless those actions interfered with army discipline and order.

Jacob would get to know best the other men in his mess, a group of six men who ate together and shared cooking responsibilities, and those with whom he shared quarters. Since mess squads were commonly composed of men who knew each other, he may have already known one or more men in his. As he settled into military life, Jacob knew that on any day, he might experience summary discharge just because he was Black. The army "owned" his time and could dismiss him at its discretion.

—

Jacob quickly found that the men in his company, like the rest of the army at Cambridge, occupied hastily and poorly built shelters connected by dirt lanes. Some lucky men lived in private homes, while the less fortunate sheltered in tents with either canvas or boarded sides. Many men crowded into crude, often poorly designed huts or makeshift semi-enclosures thrown together from wood, stones, and soil. As soon as Washington had taken command of the army in June, construction began on wooden barracks for the troops. However, work progressed very slowly because the army needed tremendous quantities of wood for other necessities, such as cooking and heat. To what degree Jacob's company occupied barracks space is not known. The camp also accommodated many horses and oxen that required space and personnel to keep them in shape for their essential work hauling wagons, artillery, and other items. Cattle brought to camp for food needed space and care, as well as slaughtering areas.

Benjamin Thompson, later Count Rumford, commented on the condition of the soldiers in a statement of observations from Boston on November 4, 1775. He noted, "They have no women in the camp to do washing for the men, and they in general not being used to doing things of this sort, and thinking it rather a disparagement to them, choose rather to let their linen, etc., rot upon their backs than to be at the trouble of cleaning 'em themselves." Also contributing to their "nasty way of life" was "the change of their diet from milk, vegetables, etc., to living almost intirely upon flesh" which had led to "those putrid, malignant and infectious disorders which broke among them soon after their taking the field, and which have prevailed with unabating fury during the whole summer."[10]

—

Jacob frequently heard discussions circulating through the army about the growing desire to declare independence from Great Britain. Just two weeks before his enlistment, a visitor to camp noted: "that the plan of independence was become a favorite point in the army, and that it was offensive to pray for the king." About a week before Jacob enlisted, General Nathanael Greene had argued for a declaration of independence in a letter, which may well have reflected the thoughts of many soldiers, stating that "we have no alternative but to fight it out, or be slaves."[11] For a free Black man like Jacob and enslaved and formerly enslaved men in the army, this kind of language must have had much more complex meanings than it did for White men. However, for at least some White men, the idea of fighting to prevent their own "enslavement" raised questions they pondered about their humanity as members of an enslaving society.

Also, the soldiers, like many of their leaders, seeing daily the difficulties in raising their army to full strength, may have seen declaring independence as the only avenue to obtaining significant military assistance from other countries.

—

The public areas of the camp could be very messy, and cleanliness was always a problem that Jacob faced. About three months before Jacob enlisted, Washington had ordered each company to appoint a private as its Camp Colorman to work with the Quarter Master sergeant. They would sweep encampment streets, fill up old latrines and dig new ones, and "bury all offal, filth, and nastiness, that may poison or infect the health of the troops." This cleaning needed to be done regularly and completely in order to "remove that odious reputation, which (with but too much reason) has stigmatized the character of the American troops." Despite those efforts, the men often did not even use the latrines.[12]

Sickness, often, but not always, a product of camp uncleanliness, surrounded Jacob during the better part of the nine months he spent with Captain Wiley's company in the Boston area. While a problem in warm weather, diseases increased dramatically during the cold months that were just beginning when Jacob arrived in camp. The available records do not show that Jacob was ever sick enough to need hospitalization, so he must have had a strong constitution.[13]

James Thacher, a doctor with another Massachusetts regiment, noted that in November, the army hospitals were "considerably crowded with sick soldiers from camp; the prevailing diseases are autumnal fevers and dysenteric complaints, which have proved fatal in a considerable number of instances." While Thacher felt the men received the best care available, he was concerned about how well the soldiers trusted the doctors. He noted that, not long after Jacob enlisted, a soldier's body was removed from his grave, probably for medical study by dissection, and the coffin left exposed in plain view. This oversight caused quite an uproar among the soldiers who felt it showed that the soldier's body "is held in no estimation after death," a feeling that Thacher believed could lead to severe problems in army morale.[14]

—

Jacob engaged in the same activities as the other men of his company and regiment when off duty. The men rotated cooking for their six-man mess unless one or two men were happy to do the cooking and volunteered to do it consistently. Jacob does not mention cooking, so his mess may have contained one or two such volunteers. When available, he could draw clothing items from the military stores and hire men with the various skills needed to make or repair clothing, shoes, boots, and other things. He could wash his clothes. He could visit friends in other units or purchase food in bulk from local people to consume or sell to other men in the regiment. On Sundays, he could attend church services and hear powerful Whig sermons.

Men who lived near Cambridge could visit home or receive visitors from home. Jacob probably did not do this unless he had friends from Salem who stopped by camp to see him or someone else. Soldiers wrote letters to and received messages from family and friends, but Jacob could not enjoy this contact. Not only was he unable to write, but even if he dictated a letter, he did not know just where to send it unless he corresponded with someone in Salem. Jacob had not seen his mother for at least eight years, and throughout his young life, he had been moved from one group of people to another in separate locations.[15]

"A view of the country from the town of Boston extending to Phipp's Farm, taken from the epaulement of the citadel at CharlesTown. 4th Janry 1776"

Archibald Robertson: his diaries and sketches in America, 1762-1780.

The New York Public Library, Spencer Collection, MS 66

Neither Negroes, boys unable to bear arms, nor old men unfit to endure the fatigues of the campaign, are to be enlisted.
– George Washington, November 12, 1775

9

Rebuilding the Continental Army

DURING JACOB'S FIRST TWO MONTHS IN SARGENT'S REGIMENT, THE ARMY carried out Washington's authorized army rebuilding efforts concurrently with conducting the siege of British-held Boston. Jacob must have quickly observed that his company and regiment lacked the full complement of men required for the developing 1776 army. Congress envisioned its army to consist of "at least" 20,000 men divided into 26 infantry regiments, each containing eight companies, in addition to riflemen and artillery units. Each company should have a captain, two lieutenants, an ensign, four sergeants, four corporals, a fifer, a drummer, and 76 privates. Full-strength regiments, if ever achieved, would consist of 728 officers and men. Like other regiments, Sargent's was essentially complete in terms of commissioned and non-commissioned officers*, fifers and drummers, but woefully deficient in the number of privates.

As a new enlistee expecting to serve beyond 1775, Jacob served beside men reenlisting for the coming year and others just waiting for their enlistments to expire so they could leave. Some did not even want to wait but decided to depart early, often taking their muskets with them and defying army efforts to retain those weapons because muskets were so scarce and hard to obtain. Serving in a Massachusetts regiment, Jacob undoubtedly heard men express

**Commissioned officers held the rank of ensign and above while non-commissioned officers were corporals and sergeants.*

the feeling that they, and other New England men, had carried the military burden for all thirteen colonies. They could use some help from the other colonies, as well as other countries.[1]

As the army renewed and built itself while simultaneously besieging the British army in Boston, General Washington needed recruits immediately because many enlistments ended on the rapidly approaching December 1. Most others expired before or on December 31. Washington's General Orders for November 12 ordered virtually all commissioned officers to recruit soldiers to serve until the end of December. However, those orders pointedly instructed that no officer should enlist "any person suspected of being unfriendly to the liberties of America, or any abandoned vagabond, to whom all causes and countries are equal and alike indifferent." Washington believed there were sufficient numbers of men available who supported "the rights of mankind and the freedom of America ... without resorting to such wretched assistance." Then he made an erroneous stereotypical reference to the British army when he commented, "Let those who wish to put shackles upon freemen fill their ranks with such miscreants, and place their confidence in them." Immediately following this, he instructed recruiting officers that "neither Negroes, boys unable to bear arms, nor old men unfit to endure the fatigues of the campaign, are to be enlisted."[2] But, what about those Black men like Jacob already serving?

—

Reenlistments and recruiting both suffered due to deep colonial provincialism. For example, Massachusetts men demonstrated a strong desire to serve only with fellow Massachusetts men and especially wanted all their officers to come from Massachusetts. Some crossover with Massachusetts and New Hampshire might be acceptable, as in Sargent's regiment. The same was true throughout the army because men from each of the thirteen colonies held various prejudices about men from the others.[3] Thus, rather than a united country, thirteen colonies cooperated to varying degrees in fighting the British.

—

Washington's vision for a higher quality army proved challenging to make a reality. By late November, even civilians outside the army heard that many soldiers had not been encouraged by the new army regulations and were determined not to reenlist.[4] Washington was worried by late November because the army had enlisted only about 3,500 men. To achieve even that number, he offered incentives, such as allowing men to spend time away on furlough. He noted that he had "been obliged to allow furloughs as far as fifty men a regiment, and the officers I am persuaded indulge as many more." Connecticut troop enlistments expired in early December, and efforts to convince the men to extend just a few weeks until the end of the year had proved unsuccessful. Making the continuing siege difficult, most of those men who had reenlisted for the 1776 campaign were absent on furlough.

Evaluating his situation as November drew to a close, Washington could only comment that:

> *such a dirty, mercenary spirit pervades the whole [army], that I should not be at all surprised at any disaster that may happen. In short, after the last of this month our lines will be so weakened, that the minutemen and militia must be called in for their defense; these, being under no kind of government themselves, will destroy the little subordination I have been laboring to establish, and run me into one evil while I am endeavoring to avoid another; but the lesser must be chosen.*[5]

Consequently, Washington needed more recruits than earlier anticipated. Recruiters continued trying to convince current soldiers to reenlist in their regiment or in another regiment if theirs was being dissolved. Recruiters also looked for civilian men to enlist in the new structure for one year. Men came and went almost every day, making an accurate accounting of army personnel impossible. This situation led to concern that the British might take advantage of any weakness by exiting Boston to attack the Continentals.

The raw, cold weather persisted into early December while Washington continued his efforts to maintain the necessary number of troops while simultaneously building his new one-year army for 1776. He received a severe blow on December 1, when his Connecticut troops insisted that they were departing because their enlistments were up. One of those regiments, the Third Connecticut, served in Jacob's brigade. He must have heard disparaging remarks about them from other New England soldiers who argued against their leaving. Over the next week, Washington made great efforts to convince the Connecticut men to stay for at least ten days.[6]

However, General John Sullivan reported on December 3 that "the cowardly traitors begin to leave us in companies & regiments & that even six or 7 days before their time is expired - what has possessed these vile poltroons remains yet a secret."[7]

—

During these months of concern over reenlistments, the controversy over recruiting Black men into the army coincided with an official recognition by some White officers of the valuable services that Black men could perform and the excellent soldiers they could be. On December 5, some thirteen Continental Army officers from five Massachusetts regiments, and a brigade surgeon, petitioned their Provincial Congress to reward Black private Salem Poor for his heroism at Bunker Hill on June 17. None of Jacob's officers signed the petition because they had not reached the battlefield until the fighting had ended, so they could not have observed Salem Poor's heroic actions. The petition noted that private Poor:

> *behaved like an experienced officer, as well as an excellent soldier, to set forth particulars of his conduct would be tedious, we would only beg leave to say in the person of this said Negro centers a brave & gallant soldier. The reward due to so great and distinguished a character, we submit to the Congress.*

This praise of Salem Poor was an extraordinary statement for these fourteen officers to make about a Black soldier. Comparing him to an officer equated him to a gentleman, a social class that most people believed a Black man could never enter. As a formerly enslaved man who had purchased his freedom six years previously, no one expected Salem to ever rise above being a poor laborer or, at best, a modest farmer. However, the timing of this tribute, six months after the battle, could not have been better, and perhaps this was not a coincidence.

The officers composed their statement just three weeks after Washington ordered his officers not to reenlist Black soldiers. These officers believed that Salem Poor was not the only valuable Black soldier at Bunker Hill or currently serving with the army. Could this have been an effort on their part to influence the Provincial Congress and Washington to view Black soldiers in general, not just Salem Poor, more favorably? The Provincial Congress would ultimately reject the petition on January 2, but in the meantime, it may have positively influenced Washington's thinking while dealing with December's many recruiting problems.[8]

—

Despite the strong recruitment efforts, by December 8, word circulated that only about 5,000 men had enlisted during the past month. The expectation that most men in the current army would reenlist into the new one had proven unfounded.[9] Recruitment was going so slowly that, even with recruiting officers working throughout New England, word spread through the army that men were unwilling to sign up unless, among other things, wages improved. The spirit of patriotism as a stimulus to enlist seemed to have subsided.[10]

All but one Connecticut regiment left camp by December 12, despite the many efforts to convince the men to stay.[11] To replace them in the defense lines around Boston, up to 5,000 Massachusetts and New Hampshire militiamen had been called out and began arriving in camp by December 10. Referring to them, Samuel Haws of Colonel Joseph Read's Massachusetts Battalion sarcastically noted, "This day the long-faced people arrived here from Wrentham and other places."[12] New enlistees and short-term militiamen were frequently referred to as "long-faced," presumably because their faces could not hide their inner fears about joining an army actively involved in siege warfare and not knowing just what to expect.

On the other hand, General Nathanael Greene, hoping to increase morale, commented from Cambridge on December 18, "The Connecticut troops are gone home; the militia from this province and New Hampshire are come in to take their places. Upon this occasion they have discovered a zeal that does them the highest honor. New Hampshire behaves nobly." Although recruiting continued, so many of the recruits lacked muskets that it became even more critical to collect the muskets from men departing at the end of their enlistment, by force if necessary, although paying for the arms taken.[13]

Sermons worked in combination with speeches and songs, salutes and standards, arms, accouterments, and uniforms and ultimately battles to imprint all of those belonging to the army.
- Holly A. Mayer, *Congress's Own*, 123.

10

Improving the Continental Army

IN ADDITION TO REBUILDING HIS ARMY, WASHINGTON WANTED TO IMPROVE its effectiveness dramatically. Washington issued an order about the time Jacob arrived in Cambridge stating that "as many officers, and others, have begun to enlist men for the Continental army, without orders from Head Quarters; the General desires, that an immediate stop be put thereto; that the enlistments be returned." His observations convinced him that he lacked qualified officers who were properly "authorized and instructed in what manner to proceed" to enlist men for his army. Jacob's enlistment represented one example of what Washington especially sought to avoid, enlisting Black men, young boys, or older men.[1]

His officers' behavior, in general, troubled him, believing they were too close to their men. He planned to weed out the worst of them and only commission officers in the future who demonstrated proper command behavior with their subordinates. However, he recognized this would prove difficult given New England's relative egalitarianism. To obtain the quality of officers he desired, Washington sought authority to commission the officers for the Massachusetts regiments, but the colony maintained control of officer selection.

—

Jacob enlisted in the army amidst Washington's efforts to improve it by making the men appear more uniform in their clothing. While Jacob may have received a coat, he continued wearing whatever clothing he had when he enlisted. The other men in his company and regiment wore a wide variety of clothing styles and colors. The proper use of uniforms communicated a common visual identity that might help break down barriers among men from different backgrounds working together. That unifying visual identity could help enhance a feeling of community and common cause. Although Washington wanted clothing uniformity, many factors kept undermining that goal throughout the war. As a result, Jacob must have fit in with the soldiers, often distinguished by raggedness, missing components, and lack of uniformity in their clothing.[2]

At one point, Washington had ordered all his soldiers to wear a hunting shirt, but the different colonies could not find enough material. Because the army had no consistent uniforms in its early days, Washington established "badges of distinction" to distinguish the officers. Washington was determined to develop a hierarchy of authority and subordination in the army to replace its egalitarian feelings, especially among the New England troops. When Jacob saw a yellow or buff cockade on a man's hat, he knew the man was a captain, while a green cockade identified a lieutenant or ensign. He also knew that a stripe of red cloth worn as an epaulet on the right shoulder signified a sergeant and green cloth a corporal.[3]

But, Washington hoped a more proper, uniform appearance was imminent. General Orders for October 28 recommended that non-commissioned officers and private soldiers planning to reenlist in the new 1776 army should only purchase shirts, shoes, stockings and a good pair of leather breeches, but not coats or waistcoats, "as it is intended that the new army shall be clothed in uniform." Washington also told his officers on November 1 to delay procuring coats or waistcoats "until they are arranged into proper corps and the uniforms of the regiment they belong to ascertained; which will probably be in a few days."[4]

On November 4, the Continental Congress voted to provide clothing for the army, charging each man one and two-thirds dollars per month. To achieve this, Congress planned to purchase material as inexpensively as possible and sell it to the troops at cost. Enlisted men trained as civilian tailors would then make up the waistcoats and coats from brown dyed material. Regimental distinctions would show in the color of the facings; the collar, cuffs, and lapels. Taking payment for uniform cloth from each man's salary became complicated when the fabric did not arrive, and neither did the money to pay the men.[5]

—

During his first two months in the army, while the enlistments of many men around him approached expiration, Jacob found himself surrounded by the many problems Washington constantly communicated to Congress. Washington noted:

> *as the time approaches for their discharge they grow careless of their arms, ammunition, camp utensils &ca. nay even the barracks themselves have felt uncommon marks of wanton depredation, and lays us under fresh trouble, and additional expense, in providing for every fresh sett; when we find it next to impossible to procure such articles, as are absolutely necessary in the first instance.*

Discipline also suffered as the men with only a limited enlistment time remaining could "have the officers too much in their power" because the officers needed "to obtain a degree of popularity, in order to induce a second enlistment." As a result, Washington observed:

> *a kind of familiarity takes place which brings on a relaxation of discipline, unlicensed furloughs, and other indulgences, incompatible with order and good government, by which means, the latter part of the time for which the soldier was engaged, is spent in undoing what you were aiming to inculcate in the first.*[6]

Although still having a long way to go, the army was changing in a positive direction. A correspondent wrote to a relative in England on November 3 and compared the current Continental army to the troops who had fought at Bunker Hill the past June. He noted the revised officer corps and that everything in the army was now "carried on with regularity, and the men supplied with every necessary both for clothing & provisions." Good beef was so plentiful that large numbers of cattle brought in daily by local farmers returned to their farms. The correspondent lived on a main road and, on some days, saw up to 300 wagons pass by carrying supplies for the army from as far away as Connecticut and Philadelphia. Regarding clothing, he noted that the Continental Congress had ordered the purchase of "a very large quantity of coarse goods" to be sent to the army so the men could be dressed "in uniform."[7] This somewhat optimistic report from a civilian might have drawn some sarcastic laughter among the soldiers in camp if they heard it.

Soldiers' living conditions still left much to be desired. Rhode Island Quaker Moses Brown visited the camp in late December, during one of the coldest years in recent years, seeking ways to help Boston's poor civilians suffering under the British occupation. He observed that:

> *All around the encampment is one scene of desolation, fruit, range and other trees, fences &c. Some buildings taken smooth away, the town of Cambridge so crowded no lodgings to be had, that we were obliged to lay by the fire, uncovered but with our own clothes, partly on the floor and partly on an underbed of straw. This trial, (new to me), seemed necessary to fit us for our journey, by giving a sympathy with those we had to visit who had not the comforts of life.*[8]

General Greene likewise noted on December 31 that:

> *We have suffered prodigiously for want of wood. Many regiments have been obliged to eat their provision raw, for want of fuel to cook it; and notwithstanding we have burnt up all the fences, and cut down all the trees, for a mile round the camp, our sufferings have been inconceivable. The barracks have been greatly delayed for want of stuff. Many of the troops are yet in their tents, and will be for some time, especially the officers. The fatigues of the campaign, the suffering for want of food and clothing, have made a multitude of soldiers heartily sick of service.*[9]

Washington noted on December 24 that the army "had suffered much for want of fire-wood and hay." Food, though, he seemed to believe was more plentiful. He optimistically ordered that meat rations for the men were to be corned beef and pork, four days a week, salt fish one day, and fresh beef two days. Because the army could not procure milk during the winter season, the men were to have one pound and a half of beef, or eighteen ounces of pork, per day. To supplement the meat, men should receive a half-pint of rice or a pint of Indian meal per week, three pints of peas or beans per man per week, or a vegetable equivalent. Each man should receive one pound of flour each day, but hard bread to be dealt out one day each week, in place of the flour. Each man should receive six ounces of butter, or nine ounces of hog's lard, per week. Liquids included one quart of spruce beer per day or nine gallons of molasses to one hundred men per week.[10] However, this was only a goal, and reality proved to be quite different.

At the time I was enlisted the British army lay in Boston, after that I remained with the regiment at Cambridge and in the neighborhood of Boston until the British were driven out of Boston.
– Jacob Francis

11

The Siege of Boston November-December 1775

SARGENT'S REGIMENT BELONGED TO FIFTY-SEVEN-YEAR-OLD MAJOR GENERAL Israel Putnam's Division of troops stationed in the siege lines around Boston. Washington established his headquarters at the confiscated Cambridge home of Tory Henry Vassal. Danvers born Putnam was a legendary hero of the French and Indian War, although many of the tales about him were more myth than reality. Jacob had no doubt heard some of them and was probably pleased to be under his command.[1] Putnam's division, stationed around the army headquarters, held the central portion of the American line facing Boston and also served as the reserve force. General Putnam used Ralph Inman's confiscated stately, three-story house for his headquarters during the siege. The men in Putnam's Division camped on the surrounding farmland, among the crop and grazing fields, and a dwindling collection of trees, including fruit trees.[2]

The regiments of Putnam's Division were divided into two brigades. Brigadier General William Heath commanded one while the other brigade, including Colonel Sargent's regiment, had no brigadier general commanding it. Brigades took the name of their commander, and because the man nominated to command this brigade had declined to serve, it was known as the "vacant" brigade until a suitable commander could be installed. This situation required that division commander Putnam also commanded the vacant brigade.

All the regiments in Putnam's division came from Massachusetts, except for one from Connecticut.

Another division commanded by Major General Artemas Ward formed the army's southern, or right-wing opposite Boston Neck around Roxbury and contained brigades commanded by Brigadier Generals John Thomas and Joseph Spencer. Major General Charles Lee's Division formed the left-wing, opposite Charlestown and consisted of Brigadier General John Sullivan's and Brigadier General Nathanael Greene's brigades.[3]

Part of the reason for this organization of forces was Washington had to deal with "the irascibility and pettiness" of his top generals in reorganizing the army. Washington had found a way as much as possible to "put disgruntled brigadier generals in service under major generals with whom they had no personal squabble."[4]

—

Upon joining the men in Captain Wiley's company, Jacob quickly heard about the frequent rain and almost daily artillery fire from the enemy that had characterized the days leading up to his arrival at Cambridge. Other topics of conversation included the constant rumors and expectations that British troops would exit Boston to attack Washington's army. Jacob must have also heard the dispiriting revelation that well-known patriot leader Dr. Benjamin Church was actually a British spy. His case had been unfolding during October and continued into the first weeks of November.[5]

Jacob began on-the-job training immediately upon joining his company at the Ralph Inman farm. Unlike in well-established armies, there had been no "basic training" program to prepare Jacob before assignment to a regiment.

Captain Wiley assigned Jacob to quarters and a mess, and Jacob immediately began adjusting to camp routines. Beating drums awoke him at first light, signaling the troops to occupy defensive works in readiness to repel any surprise attack. After sunrise, he marched with the men to prayers. During the day, if not assigned to a work detail, he joined with men being drilled on soldiering skills by the sergeants and junior officers. Orders advised regimental commanders to pay strict attention to their men's discipline and "learning them to march & performing all the different evolutions & maneuvers, which is of more essential service than dwelling too long upon the manual exercise," that is, loading, firing, and handling the musket.[6]

Jacob thus learned a soldier's skills gradually as he performed his duties. Roughly every fourth day, Jacob took a turn on guard duty. Each day orders assigned some men to work details, known as fatigue duty, and Jacob performed this duty frequently. Much of the fatigue work involved building and strengthening the extensive defensive positions constructed of earth, stone, and wood. These works never seemed to reach completion; there was always something to repair or add to them. While some men worked on construction projects, others did necessary camp jobs such as gathering firewood and cutting it up to be burned for cooking or warmth.[7]

Even if he had some limited Salem militia experience before enlisting, Jacob was probably one of the many recruits who notoriously knew very little, if anything, about how to load, fire, and care for a musket properly. The scarcity and poor condition of muskets among Washington's troops greatly delayed developing proficiency in their use. Orders instructed officers to give any muskets they had or acquired to men they judged to be healthy and capable of quickly learning to use them properly. The extensive lack of experience and training in handling muskets resulted in frequent, sometimes lethal, misfires in the camp. The lack of muskets also led the army to create supplies of wooden spears, kept at guard posts and various points in the defensive works, for use by men without muskets.

Jacob never mentions being without a musket, so he must have had one all or at least most of the time. What kind and condition of musket Jacob brought with him or was issued is unknown. He may have brought a musket and then at some point required a replacement. We don't know if being Black ever delayed his receiving a good musket or if he ever received one quickly because his officers considered him a skillful man. Throughout his enlistment, when not drilling, standing guard, or on a work detail, either from his initiative or at the direction of his officers, Jacob regularly took time to keep his musket clean and adjusted.

—

Information, often mostly rumors, circulated freely through the camp by word of mouth and in letters, printed tracts, pamphlets, and newspapers. One day the men might hear that the British were considering making accommodations and the King had received a petition from the Continental Congress. Then, a few days later, the story would change and confirm the British determination to put down the rebellion forcefully. In early November, the contents of George III's August 23, 1775 proclamation for suppressing the rebellion arrived in Cambridge, convincing Washington that reconciliation was hopeless. Rumors about the wording in the King's statement convinced soldiers like Jacob and the men in his regiment that an extended war was inevitable and independence might be the only sane objective. The King was not going to give in and their army service would not be cut short.[8]

About a week after Jacob enlisted, Washington admonished his troops in General Orders to immediately desist from a plan he had heard about to observe Guy Fawkes Day, including that "ridiculous and childish custom of burning the effigy of the Pope," an old New England custom that Jacob must have encountered in Salem. Washington felt that mocking celebration would counteract the efforts to encourage the Canadians to join in the struggle as the fourteenth colony. Washington felt his soldiers should be acting in ways to help the Canadians know they were "Brethren embarked in the same cause" and encouraging them to join the fight, rather than "insulting their religion."[9]

The ever-present rumors continued through rain and some snow in the cold, nasty weather of mid-November. Around November 10, news circulated through the camp that American forces had captured the British fort at Chambly in Canada. Then, joyful word spread by November 29 that General Montgomery had taken Montreal and the British were falling back to Quebec. The men also shared contradictory rumors about the British sending more troops to Boston. Stories touting ship captures by American privateers circulated almost daily and raised morale to some degree. One day word would spread that the British had burned houses at a coastal town and the next day that they had not. Even rain, hail, and snow on November 26 could not suppress the ever-popular stories about privateers. All of these rumors put Jacob and his fellow soldiers under the stress of constantly changing negative and positive expectations [10]

Jacob may have heard through the camp rumor mill when Colonel Henry Knox departed Cambridge on November 15 headed for Fort Ticonderoga on Lake Champlain in New York. Knox had presented an ambitious plan to Washington, and, recognizing its quality, Washington approved it and promoted the young Knox to colonel. Knox was just 25 years old, with little military experience. He had been a bookseller in Boston and had read voraciously, especially military tracts. His wife, Lucy, was the daughter of Thomas Flucker, the secretary to the Royal Governor and a Tory. Jacob probably saw Flucker when he attended events in Salem with the Royal Governor, especially those held at the Deland owned Assembly Hall.

Knox planned to take possession of as many of Ticonderoga's useable artillery pieces as he could and transport them to Cambridge to augment Washington's firepower and make it possible to bombard Boston from Dorchester Heights. Knox arrived at Ticonderoga on December 5 and immediately began selecting the items he wanted and preparing them for transport. For that arduous task, he needed sleds, oxen, and horses to transport the heavy cannon to Boston. When he had everything ready, Knox anticipated it would take him 15 days to get the artillery to Cambridge. However, due to several factors, including the terrain and winter weather, it would ultimately take him 40 days.[11]

—

Jacob had joined an army in the process of conducting a siege of Boston. Ever since the battle of Bunker Hill in June, the American troops had constantly been digging in and constructing earthwork defenses around the city to discourage the British from sending troops out to drive them away. Early defense works included a redoubt* on Cobble Hill, which became known as Putnam's Impregnable Battery**.[12] A significant defensive work on Prospect Hill became known as Fort Putnam. Both were named for Jacob's division commander, who had initiated and overseen their construction. When Jacob joined Sargent's regiment, the seemingly eternal construction continued to extend and improve these defensive positions.

A Tory spy visited the Continental camps at Roxbury and Cambridge about the time Jacob enlisted to assess the military qualities of the defensive works for the British. The Tory judged them to be suitable for about 20,000 men, impregnable, and ready for battle in all respects. He estimated the defensive lines to be about 20 miles in total length and to consist of forts, redoubts, and breastworks of the proper height up to 17 feet thick. The works had wide and deep trenches before them, fronted by "forked impediments" pointing toward attackers to impede and slow their advance. He noted it looked like the army had been at work for seven years instead of just seven months. These compliments preceded statements describing high-quality Continental Army

---

* *A redoubt was a small fort, often detached from and supporting a large fort.*

***A battery was a position containing several artillery pieces.*

officers and men enjoying good living conditions. He expressed his judgment that everyone was in high spirits.[13] The men serving in the camp, and even Washington, might have questioned those last observations.

The siege was six months old when Jacob enlisted and elements from both armies exchanged fire almost daily. Detachments of men frequently moved about doing their duties and drew the attention of observers from the other side who then had them targeted.[14] Sentries and fatigue parties from both sides often drew enemy fire. The American goal was to make life so difficult for the British in Boston that they would evacuate the town by ship so that the American forces could secure it.

On November 3, just a few days after Jacob's arrival, British ships fired an estimated twenty-five cannon shots at the American defenses. Six days later, there was an alarm when the British tried to round up and take some cattle from Phipp's farm on the Lechmere Point peninsula, less than a mile to the east of the Inman farm. In this attack, British light infantry came over from Boston in boats, landed on Lechmere Point, and drove back the sentinels. The retreating sentinels gave the alarm, and American soldiers turned out so that, as one man wrote in his journal:

> *the world seemed to be full of men, and the cannon roaring on both sides, and the small arms a cracking and the cannon balls would whistle through the air, and we could see them strike in the water and make it fly as high as the houses, and the regulars landed about 500 to get some of our cattle, and the riflemen way-laid them and fired on them and the regulars ran, and our men whorawed [hurrahed] and fired and the regulars pulled on their oars and went off.*

Several hundred Americans forded through at least two feet of water in the causeway to face the British, who retreated to their boats. A British ship and floating artillery battery maintained a brisk fire but caused no serious damage. However, the regulars lost two men while taking away ten cows. Three or four Americans received wounds, one mortal. Although not involved in this skirmish, Jacob heard it and learned details of it through the rumor mill.[15]

—

All this activity took place while General William Howe, who had replaced Gage, struggled with orders from England to evacuate his troops from Boston before winter set in. Explaining his delay in following those orders, he had to inform his superiors that he did not have enough ships to remove everything and everyone. Howe could not possibly evacuate before spring and really hoped that Washington would attack him in Boston. That way, his troops could defeat the Americans in battle on his terms. He had no desire to attack their impressively strong defensive positions around Boston. However, remaining in Boston created conditions that made the lives of his soldiers, not to mention the civilian population, miserable and unsafe. Smallpox, dysentery, and other diseases were one big problem, but so was the lack of food and firewood.[16]

Still, his fellow soldiers probably expressed to Jacob their wonder that the British just seemed to settle more completely into Boston rather than try to defeat them. The fighting from both sides amounted more to harassment than full-scale combat operations designed to defeat the enemy definitively. General Howe resisted attacking the Americans with his army because he feared a repeat of the heavy casualties the British had suffered at Bunker Hill. His army had suffered those immense casualties in June when attacking a foe defended by only quickly dug, unfinished defensive works, and fighting with inadequate supplies of ammunition and little artillery support. What would his troops suffer if they attacked the Americans behind their much more extensive, well-prepared defensive positions supported by substantial artillery?

However, there was little expectation the Americans would launch an attack. Jacob probably learned from his new comrades that the British were improving their defensive works at Bunker Hill and Boston Neck and settling in for the winter. The Continental army's constantly changing conditions during its transition made an assault on Boston too risky. It was also undesirable to inflict damage on the town and its people. Much better to encourage the British to leave town by the sea without a full-blown battle.[17] Another reason not to attack Boston in force, was Washington's continuing worry about his major problem of supplying his troops with enough munitions to keep the fight going.

—

Good news on that subject came on November 29 when John Manly, commanding one of several privateers operating around New England, captured the brig *Nancy* during a streak of bad weather that prevented other British ships from protecting her. After the capture, a prize crew brought the *Nancy* into Gloucester, where workers unloaded her cargo over several days.

That cargo included valuable military items badly needed by the army, and included 2,000 muskets, bayonets, and ramrods, cartridge boxes, more than 100,000 flints, 30 tons of musket shot, 10,000 tons of iron balls for 6- and 12-pounder cannon, 20,000 one-pound balls, 3,000 case shot, 11 gun carriages, and 7 ammunition wagons. A standout item was a 13-inch brass mortar. Other supplies included dozens of lanterns and frying pans, 150 camp kettles, over 100,000 nails, and 20,000 spikes, plus watch coats, horse harnesses, and other valuable items.[18]

Colonel Stephen Moylan, a secretary to Washington, described the joy aroused by the military stores brought in from the *Nancy*, writing, "such universal joy ran through the whole [camp] as if each grasped victory in his hand." Information about this valuable capture spread throughout the camp and encouraged some, but not many, soldiers to reenlist.

Moylan noted that on December 2, to celebrate the *Nancy* event and try to convince the Connecticut men to extend their enlistments to the end of the year, one raucous and "truly ludicrous" ceremony occurred. General Putnam, whom Moylan referred to as "old PUT," mounted the captured 13-inch brass mortar, "with a bottle of rum in his hand, standing parson to christen, while god-father [General Thomas] Mifflin gave it the name of Congress. The huzzas on the occasion I dare say were heard through all the territories of our most gracious sovereign in this Province." Jacob very possibly witnessed this scene, and if not, he certainly heard much about it. American soldiers took to patting the *Congress* for good luck.[19]

On December 11, the news of the *Nancy's* capture and her military stores appeared in the *Boston Gazette*, but it was ancient news in the camp by then. However, reports that the enemy had captured a privateer tempered that good news. Like all rumors, some men believed the report was accurate while others discounted it. This discouraging report turned out to be true.[20] Also, while the *Nancy* items made up a significant and very welcome haul to improve the American army, in the days following, nearly 2,000 soldiers in the army around Boston still lacked muskets or rifles, some of them likely in Jacob's company.

—

Throughout November, British artillery peppered the rebel lines every day, with modest effect. By one tally, enemy guns fired more than two thousand rounds during the six months after the Battle of Bunker Hill in June, but they killed only seven Americans in Cambridge and a dozen in Roxbury.

In his journal, a young Continental fifer wrote that shells arced overhead at night, "moving like stars in the heavens."[21] As winter approached, mortar shells sometimes struck on frozen ground and bounded up again; others plopped into the marshes without detonating, to be dug out by scavengers eager to extract the much-needed gun powder.

In mid-December, Jacob served on fatigue parties constructing an artillery position on Lechmere Point. The British did not fire on the work crew, leading Washington to expect Howe might come out from Boston and attack his troops. Everyone anticipated an attack, and Jacob had to work each day with that expectation in mind. The winter weather slowed construction by producing conditions that made digging difficult. Troops under General Putnam had broken ground on November 22 for a series of earthworks on Cobble Hill and had completed many of them by December 11. But, fortifying Lechmere Point became a difficult winter challenge for Continental Army engineers and officers, not to mention the men on the fatigue parties.

Beginning on December 12, the work included constructing a causeway over swampy, low ground and then a covered way onto Lechmere Hill to protect the troops by concealing their movements. Three hundred men, including some from Jacob's regiment, took up work on the Lechmere Point defenses on the foggy morning of December 17. However, the Royal Navy and Royal Artillery initiated an artillery barrage from less than half a mile away, forcing the men to take cover. This barrage resulted in only minor damage, but one man received a leg wound. General William Heath led a second team of 300 men from the other brigade of Putnam's division to the same location the next day, expecting a "bloody day."[22]

Jacob served many days on fatigue duties, and at some point, was part of a group of 500 men working at Lechmere. The soldiers worked in small squads of eight or ten men overseen by a corporal or sergeant. Throughout his life, Jacob recalled that one day while on fatigue duty at Lechmere Point:

> *General Putnam came riding along in uniform as an officer to look at the work. They had dug up from the frozen ground a pretty large stone which lay on the side of the ditch. The General spoke to the corporal who was standing looking at the men at work & said to him 'my lad throw that stone upon the middle of the breast work,' the corporal touching his hat with his hand said to the General 'Sir I am a corporal.' – 'Oh' (said the General) 'I ask your pardon sir' and*

> *immediately got off his horse and took up the stone and threw it up on the breastwork himself & then mounted his horse & rode on, giving directions.*[23]

Putnam's action was yet another example of the problem Washington and others felt the New England officers and men exhibited due to their egalitarian attitudes. Putnam demonstrated the reality that there was little or no difference between commissioned or non-commissioned officers and enlisted men when there was work to be done. Washington wanted officers to instill obedience and discipline in their men and believed Putnam should have admitted his identification error and instructed the corporal to order one of his men to lift and position the stone.

For fatigue parties at Lechmere Point, two sentinels took posts to watch the British artillery batteries across the Charles River and yell out "a shot!" when they saw one fired. The incoming shots could be either solid iron cannonballs or hollow iron balls filled with gunpowder and fused to explode, preferably just above a body of troops to inflict multiple casualties. Orders instructed the fatigue party to respond to that signal by dropping to the ground and staying down until the solid shot struck the ground or the gunpowder-filled shell burst, when they should get back up and continue their work.

One day, very soon after beginning work, the sentinels observed a shot fired. It proved to be a howitzer or mortar shell that fell and burst a few feet from some men, throwing up dirt among them. A piece of the shell hit a soldier's hat. Shortly after, several discharges came close together. A shell burst in the air, followed by several heavy cannonballs that hit the face of the earthworks. The British appeared to have hoped that the men would return to work after a shell burst and be vulnerable to the solid shots. The next shot was another shell that exploded in the air about 60 or 70 feet high and had little effect on the working soldiers. This intermittent artillery fire continued through the morning hours. The officers later learned that a British artillery officer had watched to gauge the effect of the fire and reported to his general that it did little but strengthen the resolve of the workmen. He unsuccessfully recommended that the firing cease.[24]

Work constructing defenses in the hard ground continued for several frigid days amid sporadic British artillery fire. Solid shot from 24-pounders

---

**An abatis was a barrier serving the purpose of later barbed wire.*

often embedded in the breastwork while shells exploded in the air. On a freezing and snowy December 24, the men cut down an orchard and laid the trees around the works with the branches pointing toward any attackers, thus forming an abatis* in case of a British landing and infantry attack.

On December 26, engineer Jeduthan Baldwin "laid a platform" for the large 13-inch *Congress* mortar.[25] It had taken about a month to enable the defensive works to accommodate large artillery pieces. Baldwin would continue to work on the site through late February, directing fatigue parties from Sargent's and the other Putnam's division regiments.[26]

The American commanders understood the immense value of this battery situated so close to Boston. On a cold December 29, David How of Sargent's regiment went out on fatigue duty to Lechmere Point, where he worked on the strong redoubt. They laid a platform for a mortar in the lower bastion and a cannon platform in the upper bastion*.[27]

On January 2, 1776, General Washington informed Joseph Reed in Philadelphia, "It will be possible to bombard Boston from Lechmere's Point." However, to do that he required both much larger amounts of powder and authority from Congress. As soon as those needs were satisfied, "Boston can be set in flames."[28]

During these weeks, fatigue parties also worked on the other Cambridge area defensive works, including the batteries, redoubts, and forts. This work often involved ox carting, laying sod on the earthworks, and creating abatis from felled trees. The ground was frozen a foot deep on January 12.

—

Jacob must have heard about Colonel James Frye's Tenth Massachusetts Regiment from Jacob's brigade leading about 1,200 men to Cobble Hill during the night on December 28 to try to cross over the millpond ice and surprise the British outposts on Charlestown Neck. However, the ice proved to be too thin, ending the attempt. Another impediment to success may have been a man slipping and firing his musket, inadvertently warning the British.[29]

—

In late December, Washington became increasingly concerned about his incomplete army. Once again, his orders barring Black men from joining the

---

**A bastion projected from the corner of a fort. Constructed at an angle to the line of a wall, it allowed defensive fire in several directions.*

Continental army came into question. For two months, Jacob and other Black enlistees had lived with the fear that the army would summarily dismiss them. Washington knew of the British attempts to recruit Black men, especially in Virginia, where Lord Dunmore actively encouraged Black enlistments. Washington even heard reports that numbers of Black men had earlier responded to General Gage's offer to serve in the British army.[30] Washington wrote to Henry Lee on December 20 that victory in the war might depend on "which side can arm the Negroes faster."[31] Perhaps the petition from the fourteen Massachusetts officers to reward Salem Poor for his exemplary and heroic performance at Bunker Hill was playing an influential role in Washington's contemplations to allow for free Black enlistments.[32]

Black poet Phillis Wheatley may also have influenced Washington's thinking. Wheatley wrote a poem honoring Washington that she sent him on October 26, 1775, when he was ordering that no Black men should be enlisted. It may be that Wheatley had heard about the policy and attempted to help Washington realize that all people should be equal. Washington did not see her letter and poem until December, at the time he was considering his policy.[33]

Adding to the debate at its highest point, free Black enlistees, possibly including Jacob, who had been told they must leave the army, protested in some manner to their officers, and this had gotten to Washington. The result of all these threads coming together at a time when Washington needed to do all he could to create and establish his army for the 1776 campaign was significant for Jacob. On December 30, Washington's General Orders read, "As the General is informed, that numbers of free negroes are desirous of enlisting, he gives leave to the recruiting officers, to entertain them, and promises to lay the matter before the Congress, who he doubts not will approve of it."[34]

Washington did not have to admit that his desperate need for troops had caused his reevaluation of Black men in his army. He just was granting the wishes of a group of men who had served him well, despite his vociferous efforts to remove them from the army and prevent others like them from joining. Washington's order allowing Black enlistments appeared as the army went through its major reorganization on December 30 and 31 as enlistments expired. If not for this order, Jacob might have been discharged involuntarily on December 31 simply because he was Black.

Recognizing the issue to be political as well as military, Washington followed up with a letter to John Hancock on December 31 stating that:

> *It has been represented to me that the free negroes who have served in this army, are very much dissatisfied at being discarded – as it is to be apprehended, that they may seek employ in the ministerial army – I have presumed to depart from the resolution respecting them, & have given license for their being enlisted, if this is disapproved of by Congress, I will put a stop to it.*[35]

His action raises the question of whether he made this decision because the Black soldiers' protest moved him as evidence of their humanity or whether it was primarily from his fear that they would join with the British if expelled. In any event, it may have been the first time in his life that Washington responded positively to an appeal from free Black men.[36]

On December 30, Jacob paraded with Sargent's regiment, and Major Austin took muskets from the men who had not reenlisted. If they had brought the firearm with them when they enlisted, army officers evaluated the musket to determine a fair price and then purchased it into Continental service, forcefully if necessary. This action caused immediate discontent among the men who wanted to keep their muskets or disagreed with the offered price and considered the compensated confiscation unjust and tyrannical.

On December 31, those men who had enlisted only for 1775 packed up to go home by the "hundreds and by thousands" and departed on Monday, January 1, the day Jacob began his one-year enlistment.[37] In the words of retired General William E. Rapp, this inability to convince so many men to reenlist demonstrated that "the modern notion of patriotism in the face of great national peril is very different from the detached individualism of 1775. New Englanders had a sense of personal liberty and independence that allowed them to walk away without qualms or sense of abandonment when their voluntary enlistment period ended."[38] Strong Patriot and early historian of the American Revolution, Rev. William Gordon wrote in the spring of 1776 that "'tis the cast of the New Englanders to enlist for a certain time, and when the time is expired to quit the service and return home, let the call for their continuance be ever so urgent."[39]

By the end of 1775, in addition to Washington tentatively permitting the enlistment of free Black men, "public opinion had virtually emancipated the slaves of Massachusetts. Some took their freedom, departed their enslavers, and were not forced to return. Others received their freedom when they asked for it. Some towns voted that no bondage should exist among them and that no man should be answerable for the support of his manumitted servants."[40] However, efforts to officially end slavery in Massachusetts had to continue until the end of the Revolution.[41]

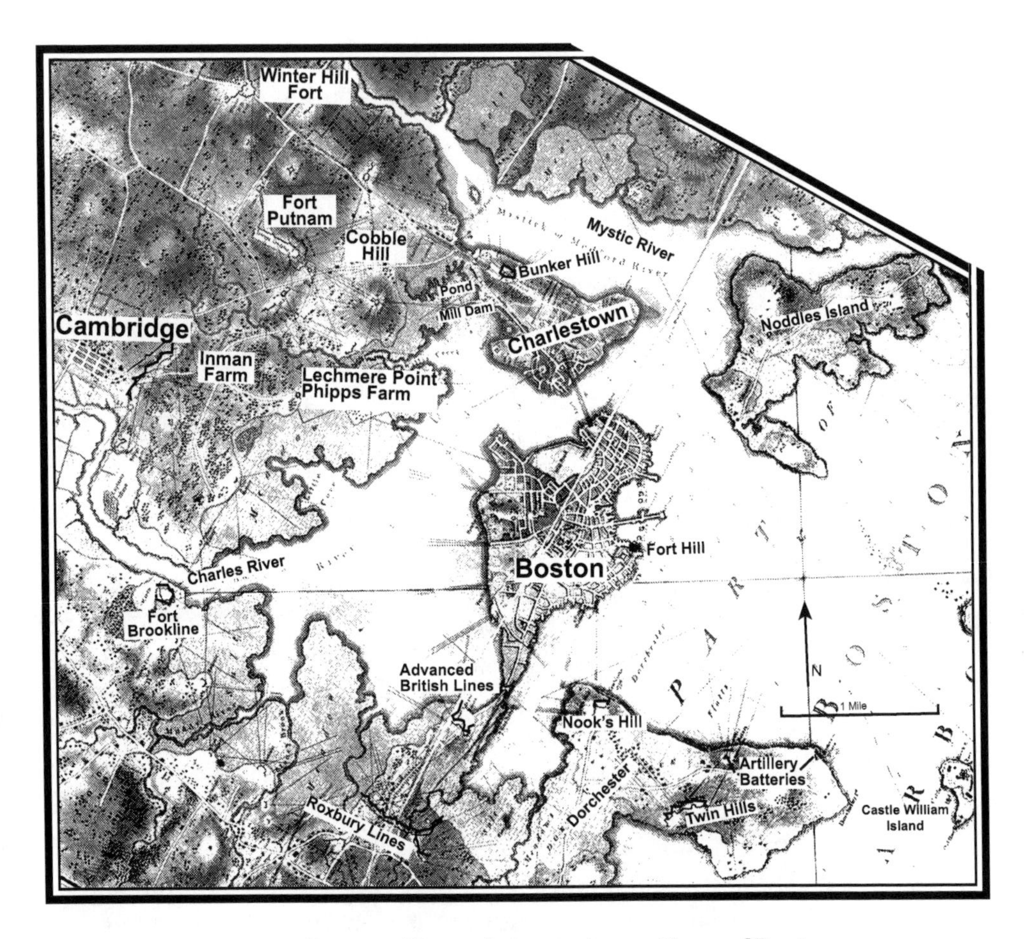

Boston, Massachusetts Area - Siege of Boston

From: *A plan of Boston in New England with its environs, including Milton, Dorchester, Roxbury, Brooklin, Cambridge, Medford, Charlestown, parts of Malden and Chelsea with the military works constructed in those places in the years 1775 and 1776.*
By Henry Pelham and Francis Jukes - 1777.

Library of Congress, Geography and Map Division

It is not in the pages of History perhaps, to furnish a case like ours; to maintain a post within Musket Shot of the Enemy for Six months together, without powder and at the same time to disband one Army and recruit another, within that distance, of Twenty odd British regiments, is more probably than ever was attempted; But if we succeed as well in the last, as we have heretofore in the first, I shall think it the most fortunate event of my whole life.

– George Washington to John Hancock, January 4, 1776

12

The Siege of Boston
January – March 1776

EARLY ON THE MORNING OF JANUARY 1, 21-YEAR-OLD JACOB HEARD GENERAL Washington's announcement that the day marked the "commencement to the new army, which, in every point of view is entirely Continental." The full announcement combined a motivational oration with a review of expectations. The original Continental army that had been somewhat impromptu was now to be an organized regular army.

The original regiments of the army raised by individual colonies and given province names, would now carry the name Continental. Jacob's regiment officially became the Sixteenth Continental Regiment, although still popularly known as Sargent's Regiment. But, while the name might change, its identity with Massachusetts remained predominant even though it also contained men from New Hampshire. Likewise, his fellow soldiers still tended to think of themselves as Massachusetts or New Hampshire citizens rather than Continental. How Jacob, a New Jersey native who had spent six critical years leading to his adulthood and freedom in Massachusetts, identified himself is unknown. Did he think of himself as American, a New Jerseyan, or did he identify first with Massachusetts?

During the day, a British officer came out from Boston under a flag of truce and brought copies of the King's speech to Parliament the previous October 27 that denounced the "rebellious war" as an attempt by rebels to establish an independent empire. The Patriots already knew the wording in that speech from a copy captured from an Irish ship by a privateer in November. Instead of convincing colonists to give up the fight, as the King expected, this speech enraged the Patriots, including their soldiers.[1]

Washington ordered the red, white, and blue British Union Flag raised on a tall flagpole, formerly a schooner's mast, mounted at Fort Putnam on Prospect Hill to celebrate the New Year and promote unity among the colonies. This flag replaced a large red flag previously flown there by General Putnam. While the British Union flag symbolized the unity of England and Scotland. It had also come to symbolize colonial unity in opposition to the British government acts the colonists found oppressive. The flag rose up the pole, accompanied by thirteen guns firing and an equal number of cheers. However, British officers misinterpreted the meaning of this flag-raising, believing that it signified rebel surrender rather than the rebels demonstrating their unity.

This flag confusion highlight the need to find better ways to unite the colonies functionally and symbolically to ensure success. The cause needed a completely new flag design to identify it as consisting of unified Americans and not just a collection of provincials identifying first with their colonies.[2] Arguments promoting the need for a declaration of independence also continued to make the rounds. Again, Nathanael Greene encouraged this idea within days, telling Rhode Island delegate to Congress Samuel Ward, "Permit me to recommend, from the sincerity of my heart, ready at all times to bleed in my country's cause, a declaration of independence; and call upon the world, and the great God which governs it, to witness the necessity, propriety, and rectitude thereof." Such were the sentiments and the spirit that continued to permeate the American camp and surround Jacob.[3]

—

While Jacob performed his regular duties associated with the siege of Boston, the tasks involved with army reorganization took place around him. January 1 may have been the official first day of the new army structure, but the reorganization process was still incomplete. Sargent's regiment followed orders to draw up a list of its officers to receive commissions in the new army and to create a return, or report, of the regiment's strength as soon as possible

– distinguishing any militia or one-month hold-overs from the old regiment.[4] Jacob knew the regiment still needed additional recruits to be complete.

The men present for duty included some veterans from 1775 who had not reenlisted and whose remaining service commitment would expire long before the year ended. The army was not yet stable in the number, much less the quality, of men that Washington needed to plan actions against the enemy.

Sargent's regiment reorganized internally into eight companies, the new standard, and Jacob continued in Captain Wiley's company, now designated as company number eight in accordance with Wiley's junior standing among the captains.[5] The regiment still encamped at Inman's farm as part of General Putnam's brigade and division.[6]

As his army's new structure took shape, an anxious Washington wrote to the Continental Congress that, "It is not in the pages of history perhaps, to furnish a case like ours." He was simultaneously disbanding one army and recruiting its replacement (at least in part) while maintaining a defensive position within musket shot of "twenty odd" British regiments for six months without adequate gunpowder. But, should it achieve a successful outcome, Washington admitted, "I shall think it the most fortunate event of my whole life."[7]

Inadequate gunpowder supplies continued to raise significant concerns, and there were still not enough muskets to arm every man with one. Wood, needed in large quantities for warmth and cooking fires, and to reinforce tents or build barracks and earthworks, was another item continually in short supply. Providing soldiers with adequate food would continue to be a concern all winter, as would illnesses, including typhus, malaria, jaundice, respiratory infections, dysentery, and smallpox.[8]

As the army reorganized during the first week of January, General Putnam learned that the British planned to present the premiere performance of a derisive play penned by British General John Burgoyne about *The Blockade of Boston*, at the converted Faneuil Hall on the night of January 8. General Putnam ordered some 200 American troops over to Charlestown under Battle of Bunker Hill veteran Major Thomas Knowlton to destroy about a dozen houses that had survived that battle intact and now housed sutlers*, mechanics, and camp women with the British army. The Americans moved out from Cobble Hill about 9:00 pm. They crossed the millpond dam quietly, avoiding talking or fife and drum music, and with about thirty or forty men

---

**Sutlers were civilian merchants who attached themselves to the army to serve the soldiers.*

carrying large bundles of wood chips soaked in brimstone and turpentine. This force surprised the British sentries, took five men and one woman prisoner, and then ignited their bundles to set fires to the houses.[9] While Jacob was probably not part of this attacking group, he saw the burning houses not far from his location and soon heard stories of the successful results.[10]

So many personnel changes took place daily that Washington had to inform the Massachusetts legislature on January 10 that he could not provide an accurate accounting of his army's strength. What he distressingly knew from the number of men leaving, though, was that the army was "weaker than I had any idea of," and it was weaker than it had been at any point since its founding the previous June. In addition, the new organization modifications caused a great deal of confusion for those continuing to serve. Feelings of discontent with army life spread widely with the many men heading home upon their enlistment expiration.[11] Washington resorted to calling out militiamen to fill the remaining holes in the ranks because, "I am more and more convinced, that we shall never raise the army to the New Establishment by voluntary enlistments."[12]

—

Given the manpower shortage and lack of recruits, along with growing fears that free Black men would enlist with the British, Congress supported Washington's December 30 order regarding recruitment of free Black men. It resolved on January 16, 1776, the day after Jacob turned 22, that "the free negroes who have served faithfully in the army at Cambridge, may be re-enlisted therein, but not others."[13] While accepting Black men like Jacob currently serving in the army, this order did not authorize recruiting additional Black men; even though they had proven their worth and White men were not enlisting in the required numbers.

As a result of the continually ongoing recruitment efforts, new enlistees did occasionally join Jacob's regiment. Caleb Leach enlisted at Inman's Farm in Captain James Keith's company, and Leach indicates he also got to know men in Captain James Perry's and Captain Wiley's companies. David How enlisted on January 22, 1776, in Captain Keith's company. How had left the army in December at the end of his first enlistment and now returned, enlisting to serve until the end of the year. As a veteran, he settled in quickly and the next day cooked for his company and received from Colonel Sargent one month's pay and 12s for the blanket he brought with him. During the following week, using his local connections, How bought and sold several items, including a wild turkey that his mess had for supper. How also purchased quantities of cider and chestnuts, expecting to profit by reselling them, which he did throughout the week. Caleb Leach was also close to home, and his brother visited him, informing him of the death from a fever of a family friend at Roxbury. Leach visited the army hospital at Cambridge to see a friend in the regiment who was sick with a fever.[14]

—

The army established a "laboratory" at Cambridge. Skilled artificers, including carpenters, blacksmiths, wheelwrights, turners, and tinsmiths, assembled and repaired military items there. The army also rotated soldiers to the laboratory to prepare musket cartridges and other munitions. Men from Sargent's regiment prepared munitions for various periods at the laboratory until the British left Boston in March. Several new enlistees who joined Jacob's regiment in January spent time there, and it is likely that Jacob also worked there at some point. One young man, 16-year-old Isaac Huse, later stated that upon joining Captain Keith's company, he and about 20 other men made up a detachment under Lieutenant David Chandler to work in the laboratory at Cambridge. Their work involved "running balls," their term for casting lead bullets, and combining them with gunpowder in a paper tube to make up cartridges.[15]

Maintaining an adequate supply of ammunition was a constant concern. On February 1, the laboratory moved to Harvard College, and the next day the men working there assembled cartridges all day.[16] Throughout the following month, they cast lead bullets and made up cartridges. The needless expenditure of ammunition reduced the supply of this essential that the men assigned to the laboratory worked hard to increase. Washington took steps to reduce wastage and ordered his men to only fire their muskets in combat and under orders. Jacob heard the order on February 16 to fine soldiers for every cartridge they lost.[17]

—

Army morale significantly improved on January 18, when Colonel Henry Knox's impressive and critical train of 58 artillery pieces began arriving from Fort Ticonderoga. This outstanding success, overcoming tremendous odds to bring the crucial artillery to Boston, justified Washington's promotion of 25-year-old Knox to the rank of colonel on the eve of the expedition to Ticonderoga. The Lechmere Point defensive earthworks Jacob had been helping to construct would mount some of the arriving cannon.

On January 19, the ground was frozen rock-hard 22 inches deep, and army engineer Jeduthan Baldwin wrote, "in one night it froze in the trench 8 inches deep so that we pried up cakes of frozen earth 9 feet long & 3 feet broad." The next day the sod in the hard frozen marsh simply could not be dug out. When General Washington and several other officers came to view the works on January 22, the ground was frozen excessively hard up to two feet deep. Men continued to serve on fatigue parties constructing defensive positions as best they could. On February 12, men picked up bullets fired by the regulars toward Lechmere that lay on the ice. Engineer Baldwin saw that many men found large numbers of British bullets, up to eighty.

Construction soon began on a guardhouse at Lechmere. On February 20, the fatigue party with engineer Baldwin at Lechmere Point "dug round & undermined large pieces of frozen earth which we rolled out on skids of several tons weight each, in digging for the guard house." They constructed the wooden guard house structure over the next few days.[18]

—

On January 24, 1776, Sargent's regiment switched its brigade assignment to General William Heath's Brigade, still in the Third Division under General Putnam.[19] In Heath's Brigade, they joined Colonel William Prescott's Seventh Continental Regiment, Colonel Edmund Phinney's Eighteenth Continental Regiment, Colonel John Greaton's Twenty-fourth Continental Regiment, and Colonel Loammi Baldwin's Twenty-sixth Continental Regiment. These were all Massachusetts regiments. A report created that day showed a total of 17,633 men in the army and where they were living. Jacob was one of the 3,400 men quartered at different places just outside Cambridge, including Fort No. 1, the Inman house and farm, and other nearby locations.[20]

—

Sickness continued to be a severe problem, debilitating many soldiers. A new enlistee in Sargent's regiment, Obadiah Brown, went to the army hospital on February 4 to help care for the sick and found eighty men there.[21] When men in the regiment sought medical aid, the medical officer, following the medical practices of that time, usually bled them or gave them medicine that often simply made them throw up. Regimental funerals were all too common as men died in the army hospitals from illness in significantly greater numbers than from wounds suffered in combat.[22]

—

Jacob had minimal time for relaxation and not many options when he did. Orders in February forbade all non-commissioned officers and soldiers from playing cards or other games of chance, because "at this time of public distress, men may find enough to do in the service of their God and their Country without abandoning themselves to vice and immorality."[23]

However, poor camp conditions and monotonous routines sometimes led men to indulge in undesirable excesses. Even while the American and British forces engaged in daily long-range harassing combat, some soldiers got themselves drunk or into other kinds of trouble. On February 7, private Obadiah Brown noted in his journal that "two soldiers drank 33 glasses of brandy & gin. One died." Two women, likely prostitutes, were drummed out of camp the morning of February 10.[24] Fighting among the men was common due to the conditions of camp life and the often tedious, repetitive work. Food was always an issue – never enough and seldom appetizing when available.[25]

—

Jacob heard about and probably saw when some of the men stationed on Winter Hill marched toward Charlestown and burned down a tide-mill on the evening of February 8.[26] While conducting minor harassments like this, Washington found himself concealing the actual condition of his army, even from his own officers. On February 9, though, he had to acknowledge that 2,000 men still did not have muskets, even though he had "tried every method I can think of to procure arms for our men." On top of everything else requiring attention, he said, "I have sent officers into the country with money to purchase arms in the different towns, some have returned and brought in a few, many are still out, what their success will be I cannot determine." He advised Congress that the regiments were "very incomplete" and recruiting "goes on very slow" partly because men could receive more money in other services, such as privateering or the militia.[27]

While Jacob could readily recognize the lack of men and firearms in his regiment and the army in general, he could also directly see the vast differences in the degree of training and discipline among the men around him. He also recognized his improving depth of understanding and level of skill in performing the duties assigned to him. However, Washington unloaded to Congress on February 9 his frustration with the inability to train his army adequately. His words describe his situation and the process that Jacob was going through with great insight.

> *To bring men well acquainted with the duties of a soldier, requires time; to bring them under proper discipline and subordination, not only requires time, but is a work of great difficulty; and in this Army, where there is so little distinction between the officers and soldiers, requires an uncommon degree of attention. To expect then the same service from raw, and undisciplined recruits as from veteran soldiers, is to expect what never did, and perhaps never will happen. Men who are familiarized to danger, meet it without shrinking, whereas those who have never seen service often apprehend danger where no danger is. Three things prompt men to a regular discharge of their duty in time of action: natural bravery, hope of reward, and fear of punishment. The two first are common to the untutored, and the disciplined soldiers; but the latter, most obviously distinguishes the one from the other. A coward when taught to believe, that if he breaks his ranks, and abandons his colors, will be punished with death by his own party, will take his chance against the enemy; but the man who thinks little of the one, and is fearful of the other, acts from present feelings regardless of consequences.*[28]

A few days later, the situation markedly improved when ten regiments of New England militia arrived in camp carrying needed ammunition supplies for the army. These men significantly increased the size of Washington's army, encouraging him to call a council of his officers on February 16 to explore once again an attack on Boston. However, his officers still did not support such an attack, even though the Continentals, combined with the militia, greatly outnumbered General Howe's forces.[29]

—

Recognizing that discipline needed significant improvement, on February 14, orders noted a "great neglect" in reading the general orders to the men. This omission gave the men an excuse to disobey those orders, so the neglect had to stop. The orders also reminded company captains to read the "Rules &

Regulations of the Army" to their men at least once every two weeks. The men were "generally unacquainted" with their contents, and hearing them frequently "would benefit the service, by learning the troops their proper line of duty and save many from punishment."[30]

Despite such orders, discipline continued to be a stubborn problem. On February 23, Washington confirmed the court-martial sentence calling for James McCormick of Captain Thomas Farrington's Company in Colonel Sargent's regiment to receive lashes.[31] Regimental commanders oversaw the details of all court-martial punishments. Jacob turned out with the men of his regiment, often accompanied by other regiments, to witness the all too frequent floggings and the occasional military execution by firing squad or hanging.

—

On February 14, about 4:00 am, 600 British troops from Boston and Castle William landed at Dorchester Hill to surprise the American guard near the south end of the American lines. They burned four or five houses and took one older man and two boys prisoner. The Americans turned out and drove them back, but only fired one musket.[32] While he may not have heard this action, Jacob certainly learned about it in camp the next day.

Washington held his last council of war at Cambridge on February 16 to once more consider an attack on Boston. Again his officers rejected such an attack, although Washington had argued strongly that a well-aimed stroke against the enemy at that time could end the war favorably for the Americans.[33] Learning of the colonial army's progress in Canada helped calm the perceived need for a victory at Boston felt by those who supported an attack. The men working on the lines with Jacob did not know about the councils of war Washington held with his officers to plan the future. They just responded to their daily orders without knowing why specific work was needed or what would come next. They could only wonder how many more months the seemingly never-ending siege activities would continue and what would bring them to a close.

—

Along with the men in all regiments, on February 17, Jacob received 24 rounds of musket ammunition. Captain Wiley checked Jacob and the other men in his company to make sure each man got the exact number and no more. Jacob also learned that later he would have to account for these cartridges or pay four pence for any he lost or fired without orders. Captain Wiley also inspected the entrenching tools of every kind currently carried by men in the company and did what he could to put any deficiencies in good order by working with the quarter masters.[34]

Orders went out to the colonels on February 17 to immediately and indelibly mark the regimental number on the muskets carried in their regiments. Those marks would identify muskets purchased by the army and prevent their theft and resale back to it.[35] Engraving the regimental number on the gun stock was one way to do this. Assuming Jacob had a musket at this point, it became marked as belonging to the 16th Regiment. Also, due to supply issues, that same day, orders went out to the militia to use powder horns and shot bags instead of cartridge boxes that were also in short supply.[36]

The army also lacked sufficient entrenching tools. On February 18, Jacob's regimental quartermaster examined his quarters while going through all the soldiers' quarters to collect "all the entrenching tools of every kind whether broken or whole & deliver them to the Clark of the Market immediately." After that time, any person found possessing such tools would be subject to trial as a defrauder of the Continental stores. The following week, Colonel Sargent sent all axes, pickaxes, spades, shovels, and other entrenching tools possessed by his regiment to the Quarter Master General in Cambridge.[37] If any soldier were alert and interested enough to wonder why it was necessary to collect all these tools, the answer would reveal itself in a few days.

—

While uniform clothing could build regimental identity among the men, a unique flag identifying their regiment could also give them a symbol to rally around. On February 20, orders went out to furnish each regiment with a unique, small, and light flag whose "colours should if it can be done, bear some kind of similitude of the Regt to which they belong" and display the regiment's number. Colonels were to consult about the design without delay so that the Quartermaster General could provide them quickly. At the same time, the colonels and Quartermaster General should also confer about any shortages in camp equipment so replacements could be secured without loss of time, "as the season is fast approaching for taking the field."[38]

As part of the ongoing concern over filling army manpower vacancies, on February 21, each colonel received orders to send an officer from each company into the country to recruit, while continuing to recruit in camp among short-term militiamen and visitors. Even though recruits were urgently needed, officers were forbidden to enlist "any boys, old men or Slaves," but the orders did not mention the free Black men that Congress wanted to discourage. Because muskets were still lacking, these recruiting officers should also obtain any good arms they came across. Several days later, further orders reminded officers to only purchase arms that were "good and fit for immediate use," preferably British army "Brown Bess" muskets complete with bayonets. Also, because each county in Massachusetts had formed a committee to purchase arms, the officers should not get into bidding wars with those civilians.[39]

—

Jacob's regiment at Inman's farm received orders to prepare to support a picket of 60 men ordered to Lechmere Point on February 21 should the British attack, a strong possibility according to information recently obtained. Jacob and his comrades in Sargent's regiment spent another day anticipating a bloody battle that did not occur.[40]

By February 24, Jacob heard rumors spreading through the camp that the British had prepared ships for sea and were preparing to embark and leave Boston.[41] As with many rumors, this information proved premature, and there would be some intense fighting before the regulars left.

In late February, concerns spread regarding the shortage of qualified doctors to care for the sick and wounded, along with insufficient instruments, medicines, and bandages. To evaluate the knowledge and skills of regimental surgeons and surgeon's mates, including surgeon Parker Cleaveland of Sargent's Regiment, the Director-General of the Hospital received orders to set up an examination system and present certificates to those medical men found qualified.[42] Combat could break out at any time and increase the need for medical men. The same day, troops mounted several heavy cannon at Lechmere Point, and four days later, the British fired artillery at the Point and its defenses.[43] All of this activity certainly put into question the rumor that the British were on the verge of abandoning Boston.

The following day at morning quarters, Jacob heard once again that the army might soon be in major combat, and he should prepare his mind and all necessary equipment for it. Jacob may have felt this was just another false alarm. However, he heard the added encouragement that "it is a noble cause we are engaged in, it is the cause of virtue and mankind." Every "temporal advantage & comfort" he valued for himself and his posterity now depended on his vigilance and exertions. The officer reading these orders stated bluntly, "in short[,] slavery or freedom must be ye result of our conduct." Jacob must have reacted internally to this statement about the future of White men in America. Those words held a different meaning for Jacob, who could only hope that a military victory would also mean full liberty and equality for him and other free Black men, as well as for enslaved Black people.

Orders reminded Jacob and his fellow soldiers that the cleanliness of both their person and weapons was crucial because unless "their arms are kept clean and in good firing order, it is impossible to vanquish ye enemy." These strong words neglected to consider that not every soldier had a musket and that many officers were concerned about the number of guns in disrepair and unfit for use. The orders also reminded the men that "cleanliness of the person gives health & a soldier like appearance that no confusion may ensue when the troops are called to action."[44]

With combat seemingly imminent, fatigue work at Lechmere Point continued for Jacob and the other men in his company and regiment. Private Obadiah Brown mentioned this duty in his diary on February 6, February 20, when they received fire from Boston all day, and February 27. On February 25, the army brought two 18-pounders to Lechmere Point, and at night four more cannon arrived there.[45]

"We have," Washington wrote on February 26, "under many difficulties, on account of hard frozen ground, completed our work on Lechmere's Point. We have got some heavy pieces of ordnance placed there, two platforms fixed for mortars, and everything for any offensive operation. Strong guards are now mounted there, and at Cobble Hill." Ten militia regiments had arrived to strengthen the lines. Washington could now set a date to extend the lines and take possession of Dorchester Heights at their south end.[46]

Jacob and the men of Sargent's regiment stood guard duty at Lechmere Point about every fourth night during the remainder of February. It was a leap year, and, on February 29, Obadiah Brown stood sentry duty for ten hours. Guard duty continued to generate criticism about discipline, and at the end of February, officers were concerned about noise problems and the inattentiveness of men at various guard posts. Due to the continuing musket shortage, orders came for the wooden spears that had long been gathered at various posts and redoubts to be checked over, cleaned, and collected together at the proper locations, ready to be used by the men lacking muskets.[47]

—

Late February was a confusing time for individual soldiers such as Jacob. Battle preparations were clearly underway, but at the same time, it was evident that the British were preparing to leave Boston. American troops could see the British "watering & fitting up their vessels for the reception of the crew" and "actually put some of their heavy ordnance on board." However, this could just be a deception to conceal an oncoming attack. Just like his commander in chief, Jacob could only contemplate whether what he saw and heard was the prelude to a battle. As Washington wrote, "time only can show."[48]

By the beginning of March, the defense works that Jacob had exerted himself to help construct during fatigue duty had become impressively extensive, consisting of artillery emplacements, redoubts, and earthen breastworks up to 17 feet thick. Camp activity continued to anticipate heavy action. On March 2, Jacob marched with Colonel Sargent's regiment to Cobble Hill to occupy the north, middle, and south redoubts until receipt of further orders. Sargent, along with other colonels, received orders to immediately have each non-commissioned officer and soldier create one good fascine and gather them all under a sentry with the quarter-guard of the regiment.[49]

Responding to this order, Jacob gathered up a bundle of long sticks and bound them together to make his fascine. It was just one of thousands that would help strengthen new defensive earthworks under construction. In addition to the fascines, some men put together wooden frames known as chandeliers to hold the fascines in place, while others collected quantities of hay to be "screwed" into large bundles for use in the defenses. When in place, the men covered the fascines in the chandeliers as much as possible with earth to form strengthened earthwork defenses. The men had become skilled at making fascines while on fatigue duty constructing all the defensive positions. Work continued at Lechmere Point that day, and David How noted in his diary that other Americans had been carrying mortars down to it.[50]

Other preparations indicating imminent engagement with the regulars included preparing 2,000 bandages to dress broken limbs,

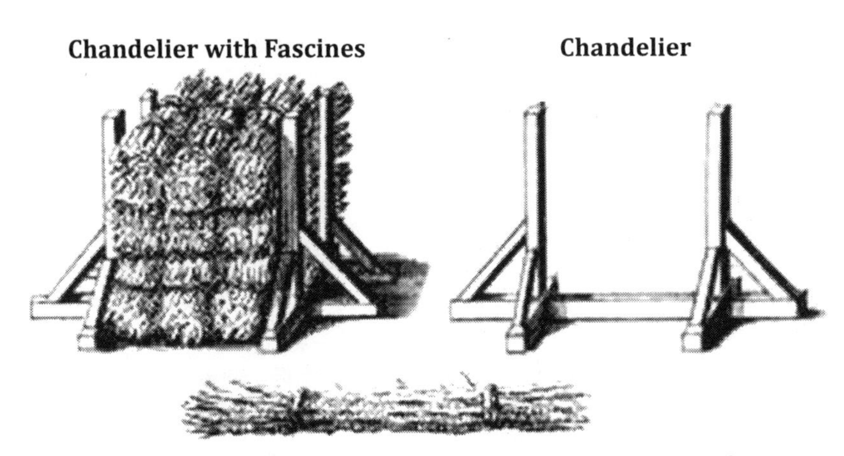

A fascine is a bundle of sticks about six feet long and bound by two or three ties.
The Military Engineer, M. LeBlond.

collecting 45 bateaux* capable of carrying 80 men each, and two floating batteries on the Charles River. Militiamen from towns near Roxbury that Washington had requested on February 26 increased the army's manpower as they arrived. All of these preparations supported Washington's plan to take possession of Dorchester Heights and fortify it, as well as send troops into Boston itself if events over the next few days made such a move reasonable.[51]

On the night of March 2-3, both armies fired cannon and mortars at each other almost all night. Obadiah Brown stood sentry that night when the bombs flew thick. A shell fired from Boston toward Prospect Hill that morning fell on a platform at Fort Putnam, creating unspecified damage. Three regiments carried field pieces from Cambridge to Roxbury, and others moved cannon to Lechmere Point. Disappointingly, when American troops fired the famous 13-inch mortar Congress for the third time, it split apart and became useless. Two 10-inch mortars also burst. These mortars may have been overly stressed by not being correctly bedded on the hard frozen ground.[52]

After the all-night artillery exchange, Jacob heard in the March 3 orders that men should not travel back and forth between camp and Roxbury, except when necessary, because of the possibility that the British might make a foray out of Boston in that direction. Jacob then found the officers of his brigade

---

**Bateaux were wooden, flat bottomed boats with raked bow and stern and flaring sides used by the military to transport troops, equipment, and supplies.*

were checking the men to make sure that the healthiest carried the scarce muskets. He also saw those men without muskets or found to have defective ones were given spears as a substitute.[53]

Orders on March 4 said to prepare the hospital for receiving more patients and that Harvard College was now designated also to receive the sick and wounded. The barracks on Prospect Hill or any other part of the camp were to immediately be made ready to receive at least 100 wounded and to designate a sufficient number of men to assist in carrying wounded men to the hospital and provide barrows or other means for their use.[54]

Obadiah Brown saw the "balls and shots flew like hailstones" while standing sentry duty at Lechmere Point that day. At about 10:00 pm, word spread that the regulars were loading into boats opposite Lechmere Point. Jacob and the other men took up their arms and attended their alarm posts for two hours upon hearing the alarm. Seeing the Americans in readiness to receive them, the regulars chose not to cross the river. Artillery fired from both sides all night. Three bombs fell into the fort at Lechmere Point, with a bursting shell killing one "Indian" in the regiment. The troops at Lechmere fired thirty-two 24-pound shots, fourteen 18-pound shots, and two 10-inch shells while the men at Cobble Hill fired eighteen 18-pound shots. These were part of an artillery barrage of 144 solid iron cannonballs and 13 exploding artillery shells fired that night of March 4 from Roxbury, Lechmere Point, and Cobble Hill. That was a much higher concentration than previously fired in a day.[55]

At some point, Jacob heard the report going through the ranks that General Thomas, leading some 2,000 troops accompanied by 350 oxcarts pulled by 700 oxen, had taken possession of the frozen ground on Dorchester Heights. The troops spent the whole night vigorously constructing defensive works using the fascines, chandeliers, wooden barrels filled with dirt and stones, and other items Jacob and nearly every soldier had made during the previous days.[56] Overnight, Thomas's troops emplaced these items to form a wall and cut down many fruit trees to create an abatis in front of it. Men placed the wooden barrels in locations to strengthen the defenses and where they could become makeshift offensive weapons if sent rolling down the hill to smash into attacking troops, killing some and disrupting the others.[57]

Colonel Sargent served as a duty field officer on March 5 when the British fired at Dorchester Heights almost all day. When an alarm sounded to prepare for action, the Third Division troops at Cambridge paraded near

Fort No. 2 and remained there throughout the day.[58] If the British moved to attack Dorchester Heights, these 4,000 troops would attack the British forces in Boston by crossing the wide Charles River in the 45 large bateaux.[59]

Preparing to attack Dorchester Heights, General Howe ordered 2,400 men to Castle William, from where they could cross over the water and attack Dorchester during the night. However, a severe gale blew up, preventing the transports from reaching the island. Jacob and the Third Division men thus never had to cross the Charles River and fight what would have been a very bloody battle in Boston. Two nights later, the Castle William guns fired on the American forces at Nook's Hill, also known as Foster's Hill, on Dorchester, where the Americans continued constructing earthworks. The British also fired from Boston Neck. The Americans counter-fired from Cobble Hill, Lechmere Point, Cambridge, and Roxbury. This artillery duel lasted until daylight with no definitive results.[60]

On March 6, Jacob heard about the 500 hogsheads filled with sand for the Dorchester Heights defenses that soldiers could send rolling down the hill to disrupt and kill advancing regulars. Jacob also heard that one man was found dead in the fort, supposedly a murder victim, and that a man stationed on Winter Hill burned to death after falling into a fire. The Continental Congress ordered Americans to fast on March 7, and General Orders announced this to the troops. The men made up cartridges in the morning and went to religious service in the afternoon. Jacob heard in a camp conversation that "Captain Spalding's Negro" died.[61]

Colonel Sargent again served as a Field Officer of the Day on March 8.[62] The night of March 9, American troops went to Dorchester Neck, where they opened fire on Boston and ships in the harbor. Hot return artillery fire from Boston killed four Americans at Nook Hill with one ball. The Americans received orders to fire at Boston and kept firing all night from Lechmere Point, Cobble Hill, and Roxbury.[63] Amid this fighting, orders went out to regiments that had not drawn clothing from the Quartermaster General to do so immediately and to all regiments to hold themselves in readiness to march with an hour warning.[64]

Washington, however, went on with his preparations. To annoy the British shipping, he planted a battery at the northeast of Bird's Hill, near the water at Dorchester Neck. Nook's Hill, nearer to Boston and completely commanding it, was especially dreaded by the British commander. Its possession by the Americans would place Howe entirely at their mercy. A strong American detachment set off at night to plant a battery there and act as circumstances required. Some of the men imprudently kindled a fire behind the hill, revealing their purpose to the British, who commenced to cannonade them. "More than eight hundred shot were fired during the night. Five Americans were killed, and the works at Nook's Hill were suspended."[65]

—

On March 10, the news ran through camp that 25 ships left Boston and the British regulars seemed to be in great confusion putting all kinds of military stores and baggage on transports.[66] However, Jacob heard more brisk firing originating from Boston the night of March 11, and the Americans returned fire from Roxbury.[67] Obadiah Brown noted that two men, one of which he knew, died where he was, and the army drummed one man out of the camp for some offense.[68] Some officers raised concerns about providing sufficient clothing so that their troops could form up quickly. They also felt that officers and soldiers should keep their belongings to a minimum to prevent encumbering the supply wagons. It was costly and not always possible to get the teams of horses required to transport just the essentials.

Washington announced the forming of his Life Guard and that he sought appropriate men from the various regiments. Men selected should be well-made and between five-feet-eight and five-feet-ten inches tall. Personal cleanliness was also important. Nominated men were to meet at headquarters at noon the next day without uniforms or arms, and officers should only send men willing to serve Washington. No inexperienced men should be nominated, only men who knew the manual of arms. Given Washington's feelings about Black soldiers, Jacob was probably not even considered.[69]

Colonel Sargent was again a field officer of the day on March 12. Word came out from Boston that the British continued preparations for leaving the town. British soldiers broke down many gun carriages, wagons, and other large items and threw the pieces from the wharves into the harbor to prevent the Americans from using them. Arming the Continental soldiers was still a problem, and some of the identification numbers put on muskets had been defaced to prevent the discovery of illegal sales. Concerns about company officer quality and their inadequate disciplining of their men still abounded, and there continued to be too many vacancies in the regiments.[70] From his camp in Cambridge, Jacob probably heard about one regiment of men marched to Roxbury from Cambridge that day and saw flashes of cannons off at sea that night.[71]

While the British appeared to be preparing to evacuate Boston on March 13, Jacob heard the orders that no officer or soldier should go into Boston without authorization because the enemy had spread smallpox throughout the town. Also, once in town, soldiers must refrain from pillaging because the people of Boston already had suffered significantly during the British occupation.[72] The following day a man died who shared a barracks room with Obadiah Brown.[73]

On March 15, Lieutenant David Thomas came up to stay with recently promoted Corporal David How's company (Captain James Keith's) in place of the deceased Lieutenant David Chandler, who had died of smallpox on February 21 at about 1:00 pm at the pest house.[74] In the evening, a fire broke out in Patterson's regimental barracks at Cambridge. The fire destroyed six rooms, some musket cartridges, and other items. That day, one regiment of riflemen, with some young women from Cambridge, marched off for New York. Two regulars deserted from Boston. And fifteen prisoners taken at sea by Captain John Manly came under guard to the college at Cambridge.[75]

Because there had mostly been artillery exchanges, many Americans let down their guard even though many anticipated a British surprise ground attack. General Orders on March 16 noted that officers of all ranks had been making unnecessary visits to Cambridge at all hours, creating an unsafe situation since they were not with their troops if there should be an alarm.[76] Obadiah Brown had a bad cold.[77] Washington sent a strong detachment to fortify Nook's Hill and brought matters to a crisis when the British discovered this move. The British cannonaded Nook's Hill during the night, but the Americans did not respond, just maintained their ground while expecting more action.[78]

—

So far in his military service, Jacob had performed a lot of physical labor building defensive works and survived the frequent cannonades from Boston. Perhaps equally important, he had avoided severe illness. Jacob suffered from but survived the various unpleasant aspects of soldier life, including deficiencies in quality food, clothing, and equipment. But, so far, he had served in an army that had not suffered a battlefield defeat. How long that would continue, Jacob could not predict. Presumably, he was now fully immersed into his company and regiment and knew who he could trust and who to avoid.

Sketch of the burning & destroying of Castle William in Boston Harbour

Archibald Robertson: his diaries and sketches in America, 1762-1780.

From The New York Public Library, Spencer Collection, MS 66

After the British left Boston the army with our regiment and myself along with them marched by way of Roxbury (that way we could go by land) over a cause way into Boston. Lay there two or three days then were ordered out to Bunker Hill. We marched out & encamped there, and lay there some time then our regiment was ordered to an island at that time called Castle William.

– Jacob Francis

13

Boston After the British Evacuation March-July, 1776

RATHER THAN ATTACK THE AMERICAN DEFENSIVE POSITIONS, THE BRITISH began to evacuate Boston on March 17. Word spread through the ranks that at about 9:00 am, American troops had embarked on boats to cross over the Charles River to Boston, and General Sullivan, with a party of soldiers, took possession of the evacuated British fort at Bunker Hill. Someone from Sullivan's troops wrote on the barracks wall to signify the American retaking of it, "brother Jonathan's room[,] welcome to Bunker Hill."[1]

Although the British fleet lingered in sight for several days, Washington prepared to take control of Boston. Greatly fearing for the health of his troops, Washington wanted to ensure he occupied the town safely, making every effort to keep his men from catching smallpox. He positively forbade all officers and soldiers to go into Boston without a pass or for any reason other than to carry out orders. Patrols would inspect the town and clean out any smallpox contamination before permitting troops to enter it.[2]

During the day, Jacob learned that one man in Sargent's regiment died, and one of Sargent's officers killed "a Tory's Negro." He probably also witnessed a man of the regiment receive 30 lashes for a recent offense.[3]

The British left a few troops at Castle William, preparing explosive charges to destroy the fort. At about 8:30 pm, Jacob heard 87 detonations. He then saw the ministerial troops burn down the Castle William barracks before abandoning the island at 9:00 pm. Dr. John Warren, the younger brother of Dr. Joseph Warren, killed at the Battle of Bunker Hill, noted that the British did not leave a building standing.[4] The following day, American troops went to the island and began to construct new fortifications.[5]

Washington continued to be worried about the traps he understood the British had laid to infect his men with smallpox and decreed on March 20 that the first thousand men into town must be smallpox survivors who would be safe from the disease.[6] He ordered two regiments to march into Boston, guard the city, and perform such duties as the officer-in-charge he had designated there should think proper.[7] The same day, General Heath's brigade, except for Sargent's regiment, departed Boston and began the march to the New York City area to join the troops stationed there.[8] Washington believed that the British forces leaving Boston would reappear at New York. Many men from the departing regiments remained behind in the hospital, and one man died there that day.[9] It is unclear why Sargent's Regiment was detached from the brigade and remained at Boston.

—

On March 22, the men who had been "on command"* making cartridges and running balls at the laboratory rejoined the regiment. Jacob recalled that Sargent's regiment then "marched by way of Roxbury (that way we could go by land) over a causeway into Boston and lay there two or three days." Marching into the town, Jacob traversed marshland marked by the remains of several burned buildings. He then crossed the moat cut across the neck of land connecting Boston to the mainland. He passed through the massive British defensive works at the neck, including substantial earthwork defenses and lines of felled trees, creating an abatis with sharpened branches pointed out to impede any assault. Jacob must have been relieved that Washington had never ordered his troops to attack those works.

The departing regulars had driven iron spikes into the firing holes on cannon barrels left behind, rendering them useless, and had broken apart

Soldiers were designated to be "on command" when absent from their company temporarily performing some essential duty. Some soldiers on command could still be with their regiment but performing jobs that took them out of the usual fatigue, guard, and other regular duties performed by their company.

many artillery carriages. Jacob had to avoid stepping on the many caltrops scattered about the town. These devices, known as crow's feet, were iron balls with four, one-inch-long sharp points arranged so that no matter how the caltrop fell, one point was in a position to penetrate a foot or hoof and obstruct an enemy advance.[10]

Marching through Boston, Jacob saw the terrible "havoc, waste, and destruction of the houses, fences, and trees" resulting from the extended British military occupation and the Continental Army siege. A returning Bostonian saw how people had been deprived not only of "the comforts, but many of the necessaries, of life" and had "become thin, and their flesh wasted, but yet in good spirits" at the British departure. They were more determined than ever to support their rights and liberties. In contrast, the few remaining Tories displayed looks of guilt on their "thin visages."[11]

Another returning resident saw things somewhat more positively. Just hours after the British departed, Dr. John Warren found the houses:

> *to be considerably abused inside, where they had been inhabited by the common soldiery, but the external parts of the houses made a tolerable appearance. The streets were clean, and, upon the whole, the town looks much better than I expected. Several hundred houses were pulled down, but these were very old ones.*[12]

Dr. Warren saw the forts throughout the town just as the enemy left them. He described some as being very strong, while others were relatively weak and apparently only meant to give an impression of strength from a distance. Fort Hill on the Boston Harbor waterfront, where Jacob's regiment stopped on their first day in Boston, had only five lines of barrels filled with earth as a defensive work.[13]

Dr. James Thacher, whose regiment entered the town along with Jacob's, noted, "the inhabitants appeared at their doors and windows" and "though they manifested a lively joy on being liberated from a long imprisonment, they were not altogether free from a melancholy gloom which ten tedious months' siege has spread over their countenances." Altogether, he thought the conditions of the streets and buildings displayed "deplorable desolation and wretchedness."[14]

Jacob may have seen one or more of the churches the regulars had abused. They had destroyed the Old North Church and converted the Old South Meetinghouse into a riding school for the dragoons. Other churches and public buildings had become barracks or hospitals. The Green Dragon Tavern was a hospital, and the town hall, Faneuil Hall, had become an "immoral theater."[15] He probably encountered desperate inhabitants picking through the large quantities of coal, food, and drink that the British had denied to them during the winter, as well as military stores. Jacob and his fellow soldiers shared with the liberated people of Boston the glorious feeling resulting from forcing the British to retreat from the area. He also could not help but notice that while the idea of independence had previously been somewhat controversial or uncomfortable, residents and soldiers now talked about it freely. It now appeared to them that Britain could not subjugate the colonies and prevent their independence.[16]

Washington also felt the rising tide of support for independence after the British retreat. He wrote to Joseph Reed that:

> *My countrymen I know, from their form of Government, & steady attachment heretofore to Royalty, will come reluctantly into the Idea of Independancy; but time, & persecution, brings many wonderful things to pass; & by private letters which I have lately received from Virginia, I find common sense is working a powerful change there in the minds of many men.*[17]

When employing the phrase "common sense," Washington referred to the widely read popular pamphlet of that title written by Thomas Paine that made the strong case for independence. A declaration of Independence was only some ninety days away.

—

Sargent's regiment occupied the barracks at Fort Hill that night.[18] Immediately, Washington's troops began taking measures to fortify the town against any further British attempts to occupy it, including the defenses at Fort Hill. Detachments also worked on other positions. Captain Perry's company occupied the barracks on Bunker Hill and built a fort on land between Chelsea and Charlestown.[19]

However, these actions to improve defenses could not dismiss the fear persisting among the soldiers and residents that the British might return and attack Boston. The British fleet remained nearby on March 24 even though the weather had been favorable for its departure. Therefore, Jacob heard orders that there should be no straggling and that regiments should be ready for action at a moment's warning with their arms and ammunition in good order.[20] No attack materialized, and 25 British ships sailed off on March 25. The next day there was some desultory cannon fire from the last few British ships still in the area.[21]

In many ways, after the British departure, life in Sargent's regiment went on as usual, but maintaining discipline became even more of a challenge with the danger of imminent combat removed. During the day on March 27, Jacob and the entire regiment witnessed four men from Captain Wiley's company receive corporal punishment. One man suffered 15 lashes for neglect of duty, one endured 39 for stealing and deserting, one took 10 for neglect of duty and getting drunk, and the fourth received 20 lashes for both neglecting duty and getting drunk. Two days later, Colonel Sargent was appointed president of a court-martial to try additional offenders.[22]

Men continued to come and go from the regiment. Fifteen-year-old Samuel Capen appeared at muster one day in March. He had not enlisted but had come to camp to begin service as a substitute for his father, Christopher Capen, who had enlisted in Captain Frederick Pope's Company for one year. However, like many Minutemen, Christopher had a large farm and family that required his care and attention. The family solved this problem by sending young Samuel to camp to substitute unofficially for Christopher, allowing him to return home. Samuel began answering to his father's name. While he was obviously not Christopher Capen, the company officers understood his situation and did not officially object. Samuel, consistently identified as Christopher, served with the company through the year. Samuel proved to be a good soldier but was perhaps one of those young "boys" that people saw and judged detrimental to the effectiveness of the still-developing Continental Army.[23]

—

On the last day of March, Major General Artemas Ward took command of all troops in the Boston area. He ordered Sargent's and one other regiment to take station in Boston.[24]

On April 4, Sargent's regiment was officially assigned to the Eastern Department, comprising the forces stationed in New England.[25] Army life remained unpleasant, and Jacob and his companions must have welcomed spring weather after the hard winter. Private Obadiah Brown saw some barn swallows on April 9, which pleased his fancy.[26]

However, Jacob's pay, and that of his fellow soldiers, was in arrears. Colonel Sargent received orders on April 5 to submit February pay abstracts for his regiment as soon as possible.[27] Among the news and rumors spreading through the camp, Obadiah Brown heard erroneous information on April 10 that the Americans had taken Quebec, losing 800 men. But, there had been no American victory, and the illness-decimated American army at Quebec would be in full retreat the next month.[28]

Warmer weather did not bring relief from rampant illness. During the spring and early summer, men died almost daily at the army's hospital. Private Obadiah Brown frequently worked at the hospital between stints at several posts on fatigue and guard duty. He saw men die at the hospital almost daily, mostly from illness but also from wounds. On April 7, a man had his leg badly cut with "one good stout piece cut out." On April 12, a young man had his leg amputated close to his knee while a man pushed him down over a chest to hold him steady for the surgeon. Brown spent April 16 at the hospital and watched over another man with an amputated leg. Two days later, the man died; as Brown says, much resigned to the will of God. The following day Brown helped bury him.[29] Not all deaths occurred in the hospital. For example, one man drowned on May 5. Jacob no doubt heard about the deaths of these men in his regiment whom he knew in various ways.

The sicknesses removing men from active duty made keeping a count of the army's effective strength difficult. Orders to help remedy this problem went out on April 10 to regimental surgeons to provide the brigade major every Friday with a weekly return of all the sick and unfit men.[30]

—

Even after the enemy departed Boston, soldiers still had to prepare for a possible attack by returning ministerial forces. Washington ordered General Artemas Ward to employ his troops in strengthening Boston's various defensive works. Sargent's regiment received orders on April 2 to march to Charlestown and garrison Breed's and Bunker's Hill.[31] That night Jacob marched to Bunker Hill, recalling, "We marched out & assembled there, and lay there some time."[32] They found extensive and complex earthworks with trenches, parapets, bastions, blockhouses, lookout posts, and redoubts built by the British.[33] After staying overnight in these fortifications, some men returned to Boston and spent several days making up cartridges and packing them up along with buckshot, powder horns, lead balls, and other items to send out to the troops at New York.[34]

Colonel Sargent's regiment, stationed in the town, received orders on April 6 to parade immediately with proper officers, march to Fort Hill, and take directions from the works' superintendent.[35] Captain Keith's company, and possibly others, marched to Bunker Hill from Fort Hill on April 12 and then to Cambridge to pack cartridges. Then they marched to Norwich, Connecticut, to guard several loads of powder and ball heading for New York. They returned to Bunker Hill by April 28.[36] In addition to supplying the troops at New York with ammunition, regimental commanders received orders on April 28 to determine immediately the number of cartridges required to provide each man with 24 rounds. One of his officers checked Jacob's cartridges and recorded any deficiencies to be corrected as soon as possible.[37]

To accomplish all the physical labor urgently needed to improve the forts protecting the harbor, General Ward ordered on April 20 that all men not on a necessary military duty must turn out for fatigue every day. No men should be held back as extra cooks or waiters or any non-essential duties. As usual, this type of order aimed to change current negative behavior rather than prevent it from developing.[38]

—

Washington had ordered General Ward to keep regiments together as much as possible to maintain discipline. Even with no immediate threat, Ward should grant no furloughs and keep both officers and men strictly at their duty. To improve discipline, officers received frequent reminders about the proper way to carry out even their repetitive, daily responsibilities. Regimental adjutants received orders on April 10 to personally bring their men detailed for guard duty to the grand parade precisely at 9:00 am, when the guards were relieved. The adjutants must first have their men drawn up on the regimental parade, then examine their arms and ammunition, see that the men are shaved, clean, and as neat as the condition of their clothes will admit.

Regimental commanding officers received orders to exert themselves to provide their men with suitable clothing as soon as possible. They should require orderly sergeants not to bring a soldier onto the regimental parade in slovenly condition and to confine any soldier refusing to comply with this order. The field officer of the day must attend on the grand parade to see the guard march off to their post.[39] The need for these orders revealed several widespread problems among the officers in consistently carrying out their responsibilities.

Washington had warned General Ward to pay particular attention to reducing the frequent cases of improper discipline among both officers and enlisted men, resulting in frequent court-martials and troops drawn up to observe floggings. During the day on April 2, Jacob witnessed one of Captain Thomas Farrington's men receive 30 lashes for stealing a cheese.[40] Several days later, a court-martial presided over by Colonel Sargent, with Captain William Scott serving as judge advocate, sentenced Amos Brown to 15 lashes for profane swearing, being drunk, and using insulting language. Jacob observed Brown's punishment at 5:00 pm that afternoon.[41]

Jacob also witnessed men from other regiments receive punishment. On April 16, a court-marital found 23 men of Colonel Israel Hutchinson's regiment guilty of mutiny and disobedience of orders, assaulting and entering the main guard. One man received a sentence of 39 lashes for mutiny, another 39 lashes for disobedience of orders, 39 lashes for snapping his gun at an officer, and one week's imprisonment in the dungeon. Several men were acquitted, and others given various combinations of 39 lashes and imprisonment. Several suffered the death penalty. Some of these penalties would be carried out at Dorchester Point in front of their regiment. Other men were to be whipped on Wednesday at 6:00 am on the Boston Common before the regiments in town assembled for that purpose, weather permitting. The executions were yet to be scheduled.[42]

On Saturday, April 27, six men from Jacob's regiment were found guilty of desertion and sentenced to receive 20 lashes on their bare backs. One man was to be reprimanded in front of the regiment when the others received their whipping at 6:00 am on the regimental parade two days later.[43]

Because alcohol continued to contribute to disorders, the commissary received orders on April 28 not to supply any guards with rum without specific orders. It became well-known that men assigned to fatigue duty drank their rum as soon as they received it each morning, "whereby their health is impaired and other bad consequences follow." Orders directed the officers commanding fatigue parties "to see the rum drawn for the men be properly mixed with water, and served to them at such time as will do them most good; they may draw pails for that use of the commissary, and return them at night."[44] While Jacob undoubtedly did consume his rum ration, there is no record that he ever got in trouble due to alcohol. He seems to have been a man who always wanted to stay in control of himself.

—

The regiment continued to gain and lose men regularly, and recruiting efforts were inconsistent. On May 1, Lieutenant Thomas came in with ten men he had enlisted for Captain Keith's company.[45] But, on May 24, orders read that no officer was to leave camp on recruiting, and anyone currently out on that duty must return immediately.[46]

—

The expected return of a British army, or at least a raid from one, overshadowed daily life. The general orders for May 3 reported the "intelligence that sixty sail of British ships, with 12,000 troops on board, are on their way to Boston, and may soon be expected." Therefore, all officers and men received orders to be prepared and expect to undertake "extraordinary duty at this critical time. The salvation of this town, this colony, and the continent is now eminently depending: therefore, duty, honor, the love of God and our country call upon every man for his utmost exertion." General Ward could later report that he had "directed all the Officers to turn out with their men upon the Works, which they chearfully complyed with and are constantly upon fatigue with their Men."[47] The constant false expectations of enemy activity must have been stressful for the men and the officers. It also led to increased difficulty in taking seriously the so far baseless alarms.

On May 4, Sargent's regiment went from Boston to Noddles Island for fatigue duty to build a fort and stayed for several days.[48] The regiment recorded 331 men present and fit for duty and 26 men present, although ill, out of a total paper strength of 516. Fourteen men were absent due to illness, 126 men were absent "on command" performing duties that took them away from the regiment, and 20 were away on furlough. Sixteen men had enlisted the past week, and one man deserted.[49] This muster states the regiment to be 124 men short of full strength.

The fortifications on Fort Hill, Charlestown Point, and Castle Point were almost completed, with several heavy cannon mounted in each fort. A detachment continued work repairing the artillery batteries on Castle Island. General Ward wrote to Washington on May 9, that "six companies of Colonel Sargent's regiment have been employed in demolishing the enemy's works on Bunker's Hill, and building the fort on Charlestown Point, until these were nearly completed: since, the greatest part of them have been at work on Noddle's Island."[50]

Major Jonathan Austin received orders the next day to garrison Castle Island with Captain Keith's, Captain Farrington's, and Captain Wiley's companies to maintain its security while working on the island's fortifications. Jacob and the other men landed on the island with all their baggage before nightfall on May 11, and the next day, several British warships came in sight and fired 24 cannon shots at them.[51] Jacob later recalled that:

> *our regiment was ordered to an island at that time called Castle William. The island contained about 10 acres. It was about 3 leagues or 9 miles from Boston. The channel for vessels passed close under it. The island had had a fortification in the shape of a half-moon but it was badly much destroyed by the British before they left. The British fleet then lay about 9 miles farther out.*[52]

Fatigue parties turned out to work at 7:00 am and 2:00 pm for four hours each.[53]

General Orders for May 12 instructed Lieutenant Colonel Jackson, who had been sent to Charlestown with another part of Sargent's regiment, to use the troops there to complete the fort at Charlestown Point "with all expedition." Major Austin at Castle Island received orders to use his men to provide the security for that post and "assist the committee of the [Massachusetts] General Court with the men off duty in completing the works there." He would be augmented by 100 men, with their officers, from Colonel Hutchinson's regiment to assist him. The orders that day also specified that the men should "be supplied with milk and other provisions in the same proportion and manner they were last summer." The Continental Congress had designated May 17 as a day of fasting, humiliation, prayer, and abstaining from "servile labor" to undertake confession of sins and prayers for a successful prosecution of the war if Britain continued to press it and deny the rights of the colonists. Therefore, General Ward canceled all fatigue duties for that day, and "all ranks should show suitable deportment."[54]

—

In between his fatigue and guard duties at Castle Island, Jacob heard almost daily about the activities of privateers seeking to capture British ships, both to deny their cargoes to the British and to bring in badly needed military supplies for the American army. He learned of a privateer capturing a British transport within sight of Boston on May 14.[55] During the fasting day of May 17, privateer schooner *Franklin,* commanded by James Mugford, Jr., the ship's Master, captured the *HMS Hope*. She carried 1,500 barrels of gunpowder in addition to a large number of other badly needed military items, and Mugford brought his prize into Boston Harbor. The troops saw a reported 60 ships off Boston in the bay.[56]

The next day was very rainy with no fatigue duties. Obadiah Brown had guard duty, during which he read several letters from home and heard cannon fire out to sea at night. On May 20, the British sent five boats out, each carrying 20 regulars, attempting to capture the *Franklin*. In the ensuing battle, Mugford received a fatal lance thrust while defending his ship by wielding an ax to wound the hands and arms of British soldiers attempting to board his vessel. While Brown heard inaccurate accounts of casualties, he did comment accurately to his diary that some "regulars left there with their hands and arms behind." Jacob must have heard the same accounts as Brown. In addition to local happenings, by May 21, the news and rumor mill dismally informed Jacob of the American army defeat at Quebec and its May 6 withdrawal.[57]

—

Throughout the month, Jacob witnessed more punishments while paraded with his regiment. In the first days of May, one of Captain Farrington's men received 20 lashes for being absent from roll call without leave.[58] A court-martial tried John McCoy of Colonel Sargent's regiment for striking the corporal of the guard while in the execution of his office and sentenced him to 15 lashes on his naked back. However, upon recommendation by Colonel Sargent and other officers of the regiment, he was pardoned. During mid-May, three men from Sargent's regiment received 39 lashes each for deserting.[59]

Later that month, Michael Barry, a Black soldier from Captain Farrington's company, received 39 lashes for being absent at roll call.[60] Compare this with the lighter punishment given the White soldier from the same company for the same offense. Was this an instance of racism, or had Michael Barry been on warning for other minor offenses? When Jacob observed the punishment, he would have known the reason and probably knew Barry well as one of the few Black men in the regiment. Farrington's company often acted together with Wiley's.

On off-duty days, Jacob and the others used their time for "brightening their guns and bayonets, preparing their accoutrements, cleaning and mending their clothes, shaving, &c." Overnight, the regimental adjutant examined the men's arms to make sure they were operational and looking good. No impaired muskets would be accepted on parade. Men were to have their own muskets, and there was to be no borrowing or lending of arms for guard duty.[61] As usual, these orders reflected existing problems, not just potential ones.

To improve morale and discipline and provide a modicum of relief from the constant round of fatigue duty, orders given on June 1 stated that beginning on the following Monday, one company from every regiment would be exempt from all regimental duties each day. This "day off" would rotate through the companies with the "oldest company first," that is, the company with the most senior captain. Captain Wiley's company would, therefore, go last.[62] Fatigue and guard duty continued into the warm weather, and soldiers could find relief by going swimming after a hard day of work or standing guard in the heat. The heavy physical labor in the heat produced fear that the men's clothing had become unhealthy and hurtful. On June 21, a company officer checked the cleanliness of Jacob's living space and clothing.[63] The long-overdue pay owed to the men created another morale problem. When money arrived at camp on June 25, officers could apply for payments due in March and April, leaving accounts still about two months behind.[64]

Maintaining arms and ammunition in good condition was a constant concern. About June 1, Jacob had his cartridges examined by an officer who collected any damaged or worn ones to return them to the commissary for replacement. Then, on June 13, he paraded with his regiment when the officers inspected their muskets. Again, on June 23, he turned out at 7:00 pm with the regiment for inspection of his musket and cartridges, and his officers told him to be ready to turn out on short notice.[65]

Many muskets were in poor condition, and men received orders to give them to the armorer for repair and then not neglect to retrieve them, which some men had previously done. The army had increased the number of armorers to get the muskets of the brigade in good repair. Also, everyone knew that it was against orders to discharge their muskets for sport or any unauthorized purpose. Still, some did. A one-dollar reward was offered on June 25 for information on such unauthorized firings and the conviction of the offenders. The offered reward increased to two dollars just four days later. Since a missing round in a man's cartridge box would be evidence of disobeying orders, stealing a round from another soldier's box could remove the pressure while putting another man under suspicion. Jacob had to watch out that men in his regiment did not put him at risk for punishment. [66]

Discipline suffered in other ways as well. On June 5, John Love from Sargent's regiment received 20 lashes for desertion. Late in June, Thomas Summer of the regiment received 39 lashes for disobedience and insulting his captain.[67]

—

In addition to the everyday camp illnesses debilitating men and taking the lives of some, there was constant concern over the deadly smallpox. Captain Keith of Sargent's regiment broke out with smallpox on June 4 and went to the hospital, where he stayed two weeks until June 19.[68] Inoculation posed an issue, though, because while an inoculated man suffered through a milder case of the disease, he could infect others around him with the full illness. Therefore, the army kept inoculated men isolated until they recovered. Orders on June 16 addressed less controlled private inoculations stating, "As it has been repeatedly suggested to the General that some officers and men have been privately inoculated for the small-pox, whereby the lives of others are endangered, and the public service injured, the General once more therefore positively forbids all [private] inoculation." Officers and men violating this order would be punished and "if an officer, his name shall be published with the infamy due to so ruinous a crime."[69] The numbers of men involved were still confusing, so the June 29 general orders required regiment commanders to submit a report the following Monday to the brigade major listing the number of men who had had smallpox and the number who then had it.[70]

—

As morning broke on June 14, some dozen British ships lay within sight from Castle Island. Adam Nichols of Captain Perry's company went with a party bringing two 18-pounders, two 9-pounder field pieces, and one 13-inch mortar sent to Long Island at Nantasket Roads to attack and drive the British fleet away. They arrived at about 10:00 pm. Men from Sargent's regiment provided a guard while others went to work preparing the artillery positions. Upon receiving fire and observing the American gun emplacements, the British weighed anchor and pushed off. But, before they sailed away, they sent a boat to the lighthouse and set a timed charge that blew it up. The Americans returned with their artillery feeling a sense of accomplishment. Over the next few days, American privateers took several British ships, capturing the regulars aboard them and the news swept joyfully through the camp.[71]

The companies of Colonel Sargent's regiment not yet at Castle Island received orders on July 2, the day Congress voted for independence, to join the three companies already there with all expedition.[72] However, heavy rain turned back their leading boats. They made it to the island the following day and encamped in tents.[73]

On July 4, when Congress accepted the text of the Declaration of Independence, smallpox was so rampant in Boston that orders went out to officers at the out-of-town areas, such as Castle Island, to allow only smallpox survivors to come into town. There was great concern that the disease would become rampant at other posts. Orders again warned officers to isolate any man who came down with the pox and punish anyone involved with self-inoculation.

Orders for dealing with contagious men and those who had not yet had the virus became confused at times. The army would inoculate soldiers in Boston, along with the inhabitants, but men outside of Boston should not be inoculated until ordered.[74] The July 5 orders told officers in Boston to send any man who did not want to be inoculated to Dorchester to work on the defenses there. However, inoculation of every man remained the goal so "that the town may be cleansed as soon as possible." No man would be inoculated in Boston after July 6, so inoculations needed to be completed expeditiously.

Instructions went out for dealing with men suffering the full disease as well as those recovering from inoculation. The commissary received orders to supply smallpox sufferers with Indian meal, rice, and other necessaries instead of the regular fare.

During their isolation recovering from inoculation, officers were to:

> *turn out their men every morning before sunrise for exercise: this must not be neglected, as their health greatly depends upon their taking the morning air and moderate exercise. All the officers are to take the best care of their men, and see that they do not go into any practice injurious to their health whilst under the operation of the small-pox. They must not sleep in their barracks in the daytime,*

> *expose themselves in the hot sun, nor to the fire, or any hot place, heat being very injurious, but keep themselves clean and cool, and attend carefully to the directions given them by their surgeon.*[75]

Even with these precautions, deaths from smallpox continued to occur. Jacob does not say anything about being inoculated himself or of suffering from the disease. But, he was surely inoculated at some point if he had not suffered and recovered from the illness before joining the army.

The ubiquitous rumors and fragments of news about the army at New York and successful privateers on the coast continued to circulate in camp. Spring rain fell on the Castle Island camp on July 5.[76] Men also continued to run afoul of regulations whether or not they knew them. Although Washington had given explicit orders not to pillage in Boston, two men from Captain Farrington's company received 39 lashes for breaking into a house in Boston and stealing some items.[77]

—

Orders given on July 11 relieved Sargent's regiment from the Eastern Department and assigned it back to the Main Army, then at New York preparing defenses against an expected British expeditionary force.[78] At first, some of Sargent's men believed their destination to be Fort Ticonderoga, where some other troops had been ordered.[79] The regiment received orders on July 15 to use the next two days preparing for departure and then begin the march to New York.[80]

During the day on July 18, just as the regiment finished its departure preparations, Jacob heard the Declaration of Independence read in Boston. Sargent's and Whitcomb's regiments paraded under arms in King Street at the State House (today the Old State House) formed into three lines in 13 divisions on the north side of the street. On their right stood a detachment from the Massachusetts regiment of artillery with two cannon. Many influential people assembled in the State House, including the Council, members of the House of Representatives, magistrates, ministers, selectmen, military officers, and other dignitaries from Boston and neighboring towns. A large crowd assembled in King Street and the nearby area.

Artillery Colonel Thomas Crafts used his strong voice to enthusiastically read the Declaration from the State House balcony at 1:00 pm, standing next to Sheriff William Greenleaf. Greenleaf was the designated reader but did not trust his voice to carry, so he had asked Crafts to read it to the crowd.

When Crafts concluded, the assembled crowd gave three cheers followed by fire from 13 cannon at various locations such as Fort Hill, Castle Island, and Dorchester Neck. The two cannon on King Street then fired 13 times, followed by 13 musket volleys fired by the two infantry regiments. The men stood in 13 groups, and each fired in succession. Jacob fired his musket in one of those groups to celebrate independence and perhaps wondered what independence would mean for a free Black man like himself and for those Black people currently enslaved. Bells rang throughout the town. After the ceremony, any sign or object on nearby buildings relating to the King and his government was taken down and burned in a large bonfire on King Street.[81]

One wonders just how much Jacob, and the other men, could envision the many changes that the Declaration would bring about, both to the army and the newly declared States, if they defeated the Ministerial troops. The army's mission changed immediately from fighting for the common rights and strengthening the loose community known as the United Colonies to securing the independence of the various colonial communities evolving into a continental community that would become the United States. The Continental Army made the appropriate changes to oaths, the Articles of War, and its organization. Whereas up to this point, debates among colonies cooperating to achieve common goals had determined army actions; actions would now be the product of debates among States moving toward greater unity. As Jacob's military community, Wiley's company was now part of "the even-greater emerging community of the developing nation."[82]

—

The regiment continued losing men to smallpox and left behind several men too sick to travel when it marched for New York. For example, Jacob Hayden of Captain John Vinton's Company remained at Castle William and later showed up in Stamford, Connecticut, around the beginning of November. When challenged to rejoin his company, he was able to show them his discharge from the army, given to him at the hospital. Caleb Leach of Keith's company had smallpox and was left at Brookline hospital when the regiment went to New York.[83]

After spending the night camped at Dorchester, Sargent's regiment set off for New York, passing through Roxbury and Jamaica Plains into Dedham, where they spent the night. The men must have still been talking about the

Declaration and that they were now really fighting for independence and not just a redress of grievances. They must have also speculated about what they would encounter in New York when they united with the Main Army preparing to oppose the British forces assembling there.

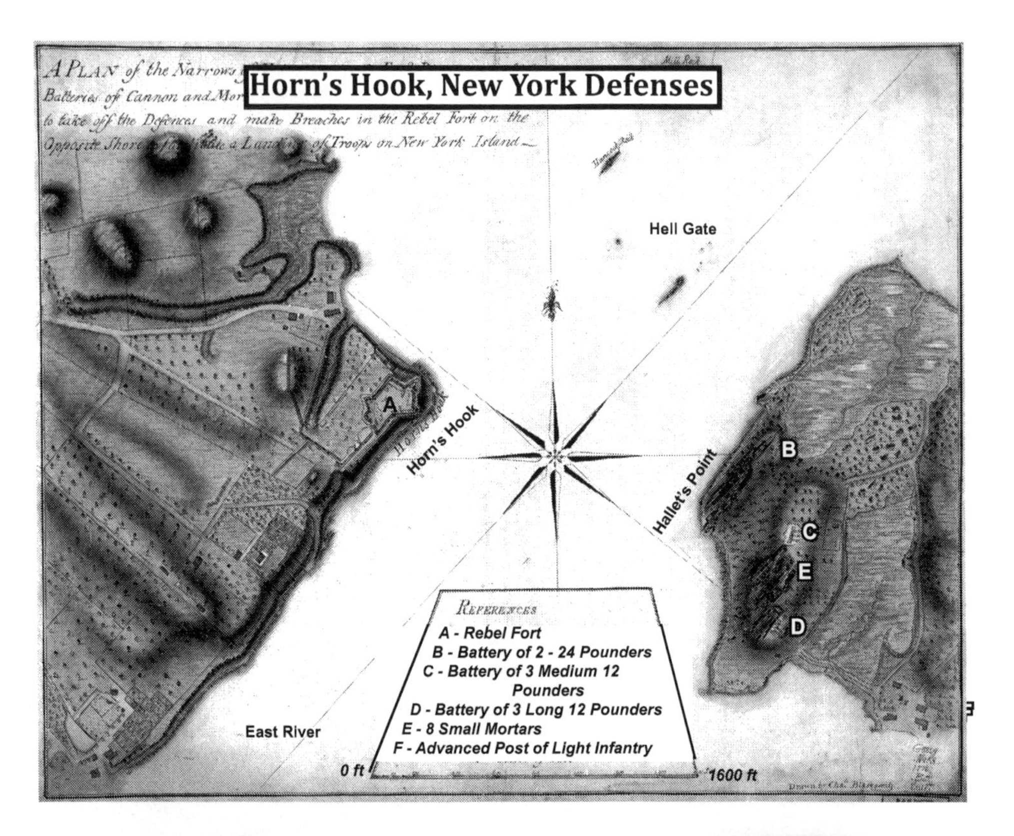

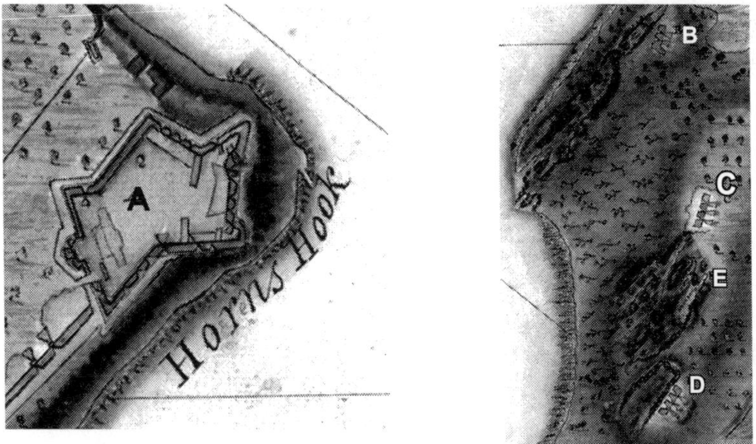

A plan of the Narrows of Hells-gate in the East River, near which batteries of cannon and mortars were erected on Long Island with a view to take off the defences and make breaches in the rebel fort on the opposite shore to facilitate a landing of troops on New York Island.
By: Charles Blaskowitz- 1776

Library of Congress, Geography and Map Division

We lay on that island til about harvest time then we left the island & was ordered to New York...We staid a day or two in New York there were no other troops but our regiment with us. After a day or two we marched out to a place called Hell Gate on the north side of the East river where we threw up breast works; and the British threw up breast works on Long Island on the opposite side of the East River & used to fire across. We lay there some time.

– Jacob Francis

14

New York Campaign July-August 1776

JACOB ALWAYS REMEMBERED THAT "WE LAY ON THAT ISLAND [CASTLE ISLAND] til about harvest time then we left the island & was ordered to New York." After spending the night at Dedham, Jacob says, "from the island we crossed the river[,] left Boston on our right hand and marched to New London," Connecticut. They spent nights at several towns along the way, including Attleboro, Providence, and Coventry. At Norwich, Jacob and the regiment put their baggage on board a brig tied up to a wharf in the harbor, and some of the men also boarded it, but most marched on to New London.[1]

The rest of the men embarked on the brig when they arrived at New London on July 25, and it set sail the next day for New York, going as far as the lighthouse where they spent the night. Their journey continued on July 27, but they only sailed about 60 or 70 miles on Long Island Sound due to weak, intermittent winds. Jacob recalled that upon nearing New York, they finally "came down the East river, left Long Island on our left, ... at that time the people were cutting oats." The ship arrived at Hell Gate and the East River on July 28 and lay at anchor all night. A Dutch explorer had originally named the water confluence Hellegat, meaning "bright strait" or "clear opening." However, the name later became Anglicized to Hell Gate partly because of dangerous rocks and whirlpools that made navigation very dangerous due to the confluence of tide-driven currents from Long Island Sound and several rivers.[2]

The ship sailed down the East River the next day, anchored until late afternoon, returned to Hell Gate, and finally landed at Horn's Hook on Manhattan Island. Dutchman Sybout Claesen had named this point of land in honor of his birthplace, Hoorn, Holland. Claesen was a carpenter in lower Manhattan and used this land as a farm. In 1770, Jacob Walton purchased eleven acres of Horn's Hook, about six miles from the present city hall in New York. Walton built a mansion for his bride that he named Belview on the site of today's Gracie Mansion, the official residence of the Mayor of New York City. As the Revolution developed, Walton remained a Loyalist.

When Jacob landed at Horn's Hook, there was a small fort called Thompson's Battery near Walton's mansion. Some 200 Westchester County, New York minutemen under Colonel Samuel Drake had built it there in February. The star-shaped fort with nine artillery positions was now part of a developing system of defenses planned by General Charles Lee on the East River in anticipation of British movements to take possession of New York. Located across from Hell Gate and Ward's Island (today's Randall's Island), this fort could prevent enemy ship passage through Hell Gate and secure American passage between Long Island and Manhattan.

Before his soldiers departed the ship, Colonel Sargent ordered them to venture no more than eight rods (132 feet) from the fort.[3] Sargent later recalled, "Genl Washington ... was pleased to note to Congress... my arrival and fine appearance of the Regt, he gave me the command of Horn's Hook opposite the British on Long Isle."[4]

However, what Washington actually reported to Congress on July 29 was, "Yesterday evening Hutchinson's and Serjeants Regiments from Boston arrived ... I am fearful the troops have not got entirely clear of the small pox. I shall use every possible precaution to prevent the infection spreading, and for that purpose have ordered them to an encampment separate and detached from the rest." In a letter to Artemas Ward, he was more precise, indicating that just one man in the two regiments had smallpox, and he hoped to prevent it from spreading.[5]

—

Jacob must have heard the news when 45 British ships arrived at New York on August 1 carrying 3,000 troops led by Generals Henry Clinton and Charles Cornwallis. Over the next twelve days, an additional 3,000 British and 8,000 Hessian troops arrived, bringing the total number of British ships at New York to 400, including 73 men-of-war. The enemy troops encamped on Staten Island now numbered 32,000, poised to attack the American defensive works on Manhattan and Long Island. Jacob heard a distant exchange of naval cannon fire on the North (today's Hudson) River between American row-galleys and British warships about noon on August 3.[6]

—

Sargent's regiment exercised and got used to its new surroundings during the first week of August. However, discipline continued to be a problem even in a rapidly developing combat zone, and punishments continued, including 39 lashes simply for swearing oaths. On August 4, a court-martial found Thomas Herbert of Captain Wiley's company guilty of theft and sentenced him to 39 lashes. Herbert appealed to a general court-martial and was acquitted. William McIlvaine of Captain Wiley's company and Samuel Weaver of Captain Farrington's company each received 30 lashes for desertion. Daniel McGuire of Captain Scott's company received 39 lashes for desertion and enlisting in another regiment for a second enlistment bounty.[7] On August 6, three men were whipped for desertion, followed by three whippings on August 8, two for desertion and one for refusing to do duty.[8] Four men, including James McCormick of Captain Farrington's company and Thomas Williams of Captain Asa Barnes' company, received 39 lashes each for desertion. McCormick was unstable and would attempt to desert again in the future.[9]

The random musket firing continued to be a problem that wasted ammunition. Jacob heard in General Orders on August 7 that many soldiers were discharging their muskets on the pretense of ignorance of the orders against it. Others claimed orders from their officers to do so when they could not safely extract an unfired cartridge. Commanding officers received orders to inspect firearms daily and assemble men unable to remove unfired cartridges on the regimental parade or another designated location. Upon the drumbeat for evening retreat, the men should all discharge their muskets together. Washington expected colonels to pay special attention to this to achieve and maintain a high regimental reputation for their high quality of musket readiness.[10]

The various camp illnesses and disorders also continued. Among the news and rumors, word passed that 45 men had died in New York.[11] General Heath believed the number of sick to be about 10,000, and it was impossible to provide proper hospital care for that many men.[12] Because the musket shortage still prevailed, orders went out to regiments to take muskets from the sick and give them to healthy soldiers who lacked them.[13]

—

During their first week at Horn's Hook, Jacob and the men of his regiment engaged in "immense labour" to strengthen the fort.[14] Jacob heard orders on August 9 for every man to have his equipment in readiness at a moment's notice and have a half-pint of rum to take with him. Everyone anticipated contact with the British to commence at any time.[15]

A man in Sargent's regiment died on August 12 as illness continued to take its toll. The following day, word spread that additional ships had joined the British fleet at the New York harbor. Jacob and his fellow soldiers heard cannon fire from across Manhattan Island on the North River, which they supposed was directed toward some British ships. Captain Keith's company marched to Norwich the following day to guard a load of powder on its way to the troops at New York by ship. They would be gone from Horn's Hook for two weeks.[16]

Colonels received orders on August 13 to send their quartermasters to the Laboratory to collect a cart containing spare ammunition. They should post that cart, along with a horse and driver, at a safe and proper location near the regiment. Jacob heard that Washington expected, "Every good soldier will be silent and attentive, wait for orders and reserve his fire, 'till he is sure of doing execution." Also, that "if any infamous rascal, in time of action, shall attempt to skulk, hide himself or retreat from the enemy without orders of his commanding officer; he will instantly be shot down as an example of cowardice." However, men who "distinguish themselves, by brave and noble actions" will be rewarded and officers should be attentive to notice such men.[17]

The British might initiate action at any time. Regimental commanders received orders on August 14 to have three days of provisions cooked immediately, ensure full canteens, remember that the rum allowance was half a pint per day, and ensure that their men were ready to meet the enemy on short notice. Orders noted that to supplement the continuing inadequate number of muskets, "There are a number of spears, at the Laboratory, which will be of great use at the posts, and are waiting to be distributed." All units received orders to turn out the following morning, march to their alarm posts ready for action, and stay until 9:00 am or until further orders.[18] General Heath rode out to inspect conditions at Horn's Hook and then rode to Kingsbridge at the northern end of Manhattan Island.[19]

Temperatures naturally became hot in the middle of August while American troops kept arriving in large numbers. Sickness continued raging, and another man in Jacob's regiment died on August 16. A credible rumor spread through the camp that there were currently 15,000 men unfit for duty in New York.[20]

On August 18, Jacob heard more cannon fire directed against British ships in the North River. A sergeant in his regiment died on August 19, and he knew men with the camp disorder and other ailments, such as rheumatism, who drank concoctions such as brandy and sugar to achieve some relief. A terrible storm producing great thunder and lightning came through the region on August 21, and word spread that lightning killed seven men in New York.

News spread on August 22 that the regulars had landed on Long Island. Jacob heard cannon fire over the following few days but no concrete information about it in the rumor mill. Camp life continued with its usual sickness and discipline problems. One man received 39 lashes on August 23.[21] About this time, Caleb Leach of Captain Keith's company, who had remained in Boston with smallpox, rejoined the regiment at Horn's Hook.[22]

—

Jacob and his fellow soldiers continued their exhausting work constructing breastworks at Horn's Hook while the British landed troops on Long Island.[23] After several days of maneuvering and skirmishes, Jacob says, "While we lay there (Horn's Hook) the battle of Long Island took place" on August 27. At some point during the following three days of fighting, Jacob recalled, "there was a number of men detailed from our regiment, so many from each company, to go over & join the American army[,] perhaps 200 men. I was one." For Jacob to be selected, he must have been one of the individuals fully-equipped with a good musket and accouterments, recognized as a solid, reliable soldier, and have been in good health.

He recalled,

> *We crossed the river at Hell Gate & marched on to the Island in the direction we was ordered but did not get to join the army til the battle had commenced & our army was on retreat. We had to cross a creek [Gowanus Creek] to get to our army who had engaged the enemy on the other side [and] lost[.] before we got to that creek our army was repulsed & retreating & many of them were driven into the creek & some drowned. The British came in sight & the balls flew round us & our officers finding we could do no good ordered us to retreat[,] which we did under the fire of the enemy. We retreated back to Hell Gate & recrossed to our fortifications.*

Sargent's detachment had no men killed in this encounter, but private Barnes of Captain Wiley's company was captured.[24] Several men in the regiment died at the hospital from diseases that day. Obadiah Brown jotted in his diary, "I think it is sober times."[25]

Lieutenant Ephraim Cleveland of Captain Barnes's company went over to Long Island with some men on August 30 and brought off some cows and horses. While there, the regulars came in sight with some light horse, infantry, and Loyalists. Cleveland's men got away but had to leave some of the cattle behind.[26]

Jacob continued to hear occasional single gunshots in camp despite the repeated orders forbidding it. Washington came to believe that almost every day, someone accidentally shot a soldier in his own regiment. Orders came out once again that firelocks with loads unable to be drawn out by a wire configured for that purpose must be discharged together by command of an officer at the beating of Retreat. Jacob paraded with his regiment at 5:00 pm when his officers examined his ammunition and musket conditions. As the officers inspected their men, they took any damaged cartridges they found to be turned in and replaced with fresh ones. Officers counted the men to make a return of the regiment. Washington ordered General Peleg Wadsworth to reinforce Colonel Sargent at Horn's Hook with two regiments from his brigade as soon as possible. Tension mounted as Jacob knew his officers anticipated an alarm due to the proximity of the enemy who had occupied Hallet's Point across the East River from Horn's Hook.[27]

—

On August 31, 1776, Sargent's regiment detached from Mifflin's Brigade and joined a newly created brigade commanded by Colonel Sargent, who also kept command of his regiment. Sargent thus took on the responsibilities, although not the rank, of a brigadier general. His brigade would be assigned to the Main Army for the remainder of the year.[28]

"View of Rebel Works Around Walton's House"
Archibald Robertson: his diaries and sketches in America, 1762-1780.

The New York Public Library, Spencer Collection, MS 66

"View of Part of the Rebel Works round Walton's House with the situation of our Batterys on Long Island - taken from N. York Island 8th Octr. 1776"
Archibald Robertson: his diaries and sketches in America, 1762-1780.

The New York Public Library, Spencer Collection, MS 66

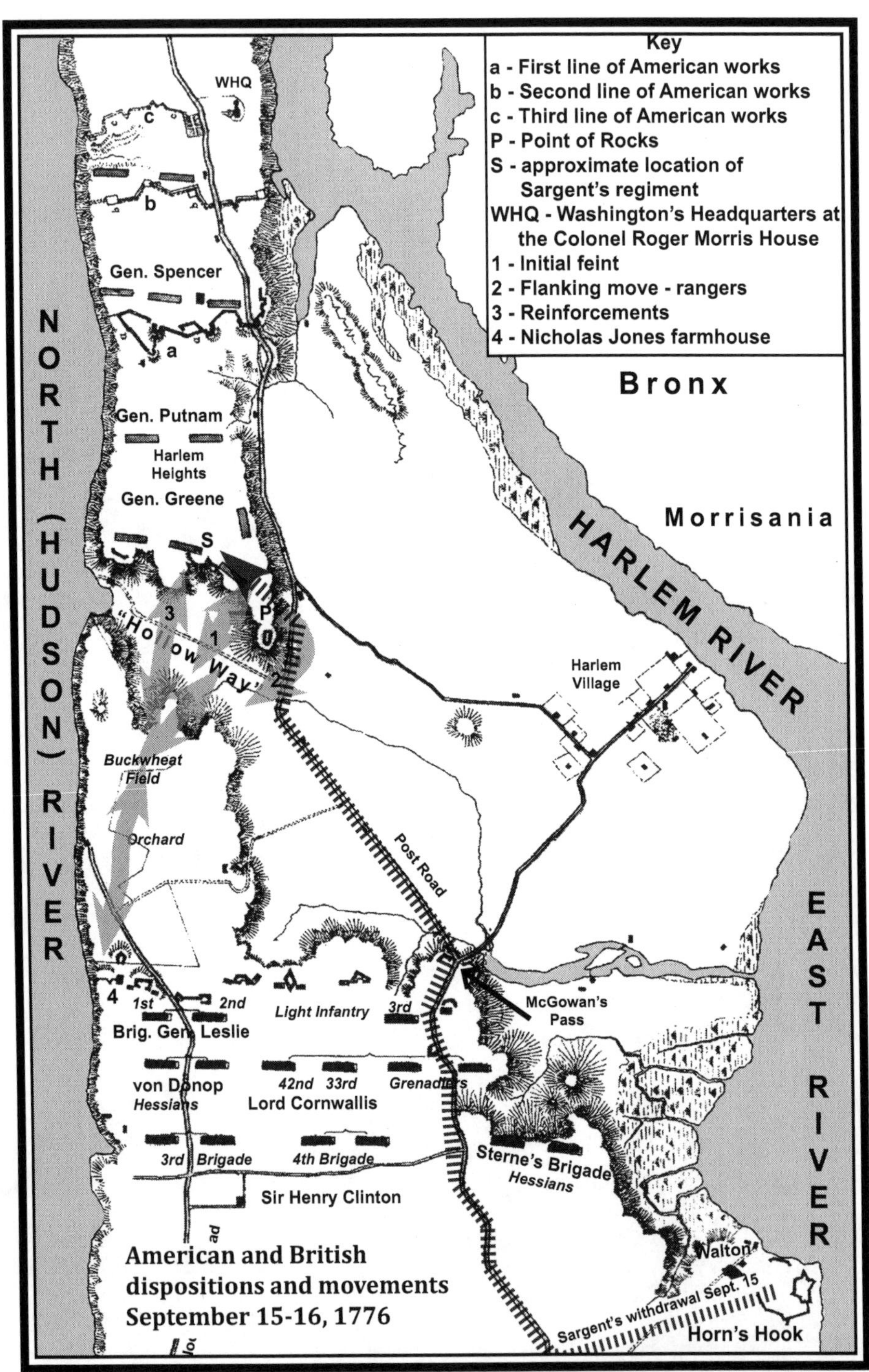

Based on maps between pages 50 and 51 and 258 and 259 of Johnston, The Battle of Harlem Heights.

We had orders to leave that place & marched to West Chester by way of King's bridge --- we lay there some time and every night we had a guard stationed out 2 or 3 miles from where the regiment lay at a place called Morrisania. I mounted guard there every time it came to my turn. – Jacob Francis

15

New York Campaign September 1776

WITHIN DAYS AFTER THE AUGUST 27 BATTLE ON LONG ISLAND, JACOB became aware of a party of British engineers surveying the land about 500 yards across the East River from Horn's Hook at Hallet's Point.[1] Their survey was part of British actions being taken to stretch out their troops along the East River from Red Hook in Brooklyn northward to Hell Gate. When completely positioned, the British troops would be a threat to cross to Manhattan at any point between the Battery at the island's southern tip and Kingsbridge at the northern end, a stretch of fourteen-and-a-half miles.[2] On Manhattan, Washington dispersed his troops to protect the island from enemy crossings between. Combat for the control of New York had only begun. Sargent's Regiment and Brigade belonged to Spencer's six brigade division guarding the line stretching from today's Fifteenth Street north to Horn's Hook and Harlem.[3]

Soldiers like Jacob suffered a growing feeling that they were becoming trapped on Manhattan Island. Jacob may have heard comments among his officers about whether or not the army should try to hold Manhattan or abandon it. Noting the lack of excitement and sharing the concerns he heard from the men around him, Jacob must have wondered what lay ahead.

Washington advised General Heath to procure as many boats as possible for the Harlem River to help provide a means for men and supplies on Manhattan to connect with Westchester County across that river. On September 1, Corporal David How participated in this effort and wrote in his diary, "We have been down the River after all the boats we could find & brought them here this night." This measure responded to the belief that the British planned to land at Harlem. General Orders that day required the troops of General Joseph Spencer's Division, including those at Horn's Hook, to be ready at any moment to march to Harlem to prevent a British landing.[4] Amid the heightened activity and expectations for battle, Jacob realized militia units were departing the army in large numbers and this must have added to his apprehensions, as it did for many others.

With everyone anticipating imminent British action, additional construction on the Horn's Hook fort commenced on September 2 and 3, beginning with building a breastwork in advance of the regiment tents. General Washington visited the fort on September 2, the day he ordered commanding officers to ensure that their men had at least two days rations on hand and were ready for any emergency. If commanders could not get baked bread, they must give their men flour to bake it themselves or to use in some other manner. General Spencer's regiments were to be ready to march "at the shortest notice."[5]

To remedy a problem he observed whenever his troops marched, Washington ordered regimental officers to "see that the men take their tent-poles in their hands – All their tin-camp-kettles, and see the tents tied up carefully, and a sufficient guard left to take care of them."[6] With things heating up, Jacob may have been like Obadiah Brown, who philosophically recorded in his journal during this week, "I said but little but thought the more." The recent defeat on Long Island had severely damaged the spirits of the men. The British and Americans exchanged artillery fire on September 4 and 5, and Brown noted it was "warm between the enemy and our people." Sargent's men kept under arms, prepared for any attack across the East River.[7]

Despite the need for each soldier to maintain vigilance, Jacob undoubtedly saw, as General Washington certainly did, how discipline among some of his comrades deteriorated, resulting in various forms of misconduct.[8]

—

Overnight on September 4, between 9:30 pm and 5:00 am, the British worked on constructing platforms for two artillery batteries at Hallet's Point positioned to fire across the river at Walton's House and the Horn's Hook fortifications. By September 6, one fully constructed battery had three 24-pounders, and the other had three 12-pounders, along with ten small brass Coehorn and Royal mortars. While ordered not to open fire yet, the Americans were concerned because the British batteries were so near them.[9] General Spencer's orders for the day urged Colonel Sargent to vigorously push forward the work on the Horn's Hook fortifications.[10]

Several men from Sargent's regiment, including Obadiah Brown, Lieutenant William Scott and several privates from Jacob's company departed on September 5 to join the new company of rangers. They were not transferred from Sargent's regiment but continued to be listed in regiment musters as "on command" with the rangers. The rangers were an experimental collection of volunteers drawn from their regiments to form a unit similar to Rogers's Rangers from the French and Indian War. It was considered an honor to be accepted. Washington revisited Horn's Hook on September 6, and some American rangers "drove off the guard on Long Island and took a number of guns and a glass worth eighteen dollars." Obadiah Brown noted in his diary that the rangers moved up to Harlem on September 8. Over the following days, it was clear to Jacob and the others that the regulars were "in great preparation for battle."[11]

The British cut down trees and brush on Hallet's Point on September 7, clearing a field of fire for their artillery and the next day commenced firing at the American fort very early in the morning, and "shots and shells flew very thick." The Americans fired only three guns in response. Corporal Hathaway of Captain Perry's company took an enemy ball in the breast that killed him. Two other men were wounded. The artillery fire remained brisk all day, beginning an intense and destructive cannonade that would continue until September 15.[12] This was reminiscent of the siege of Boston except that the artillery fire was closer and engagement with enemy infantry seemed more certain.

Continental Artillery Captain Eliphalet Howell informed Colonel Knox about this action. He reported that, "The enemy has opened two three gun batterys and have at least four Royals and have very much damaged two platforms and the breast works are very much shattered. They have also broke our Limbers. They have sent a shot through one of our large carriages." Regarding human casualties, Howell wrote, "One of Col Sargent's regt is killed and two or three wounded. But we [the artillerymen] have none lost or wounded." He concluded with, "They continue to keep up a very severe bombardment and cannonade. Their ordnance is 12 and 24 pounders.

I should think it necessary that there should be carpenters sent here to repair platforms. P.S. we can bring but two guns to bear upon them."[13]

The army had outfitted Jacob and his fellow soldiers only for the summer campaign. Their clothes, shoes, and blankets now showed extensive wear and would soon be unfit for the approaching fall and winter weather. Available tents, many old and worn out, could only accommodate two-thirds of the men. Those inadequate tents would not provide the necessary protection when the weather got colder in the fall and winter. Returns showed that at least one-fourth of the army was sick and lacked comfortable accommodations to recover more quickly.

More immediately, the men at Horn's Hook knew that their position on low ground put them in great danger. The river was so narrow that fire from the British artillery across from them, combined with that from British ships in the river, could pound them severely.[14]

—

On September 9, both sides exchanged shots in a "brisk cannonade," and General Heath commented that "the American artillery was so well plied that the British ceased firing."[15] Colonel Sargent reported by express rider that about 4,000 British troops along with many wagons had marched down to the place where they had embarked that morning to head for Barnes, or Buchannan/Montresor's Island (today's Randall's Island), where they were currently landing. This troop movement created concern that the British would try to gain possession of the heights on "this side" of the Harlem River and cut off communication.[16] Washington later reported he expected the British to land at Harlem or Morrisania opposite to it on the Harlem River.[17]

Sargent's men knew that Horn's Hook was one possible point where the British might focus their landing when attacking Manhattan. Their fort's artillery prevented British ships from passing north on the East River, which was why they received so much fire from the British batteries established opposite them. Washington recognized the importance of the men and fortifications at Horn's Hook and noted that thankfully the British guns "have not materially damaged them."[18]

The British actions led the Americans to believe they intended to land troops near Walton's House, and Sargent's men worked hard on September 10 building breastworks on the East River shore.[19] As he worked, Jacob felt the earth trembling to the sound of cannon fire. He knew the regulars had landed on Buchannan and Montresor's Islands, possibly in preparation for crossing above them to cut off a retreat of the American army from the city, including Horn's Hook. Obadiah Brown recorded that, "A boy took up a shell to git the powder out and another boy struck on it to get the fuse out. It went off. Tore ones thies [thighs] all to pieces. Alarm at night."[20] During the multiple-day cannonade, Private Solomon Bryant of Captain Pope's company was wounded and carried to the hospital, where he remained for several weeks.[21]

On September 11, the cannon again played very hotly, but the men heard no significant news.[22] The British and Americans held a peace conference at the Billopp house at the southern end of Staten Island, attended by John Adams, Benjamin Franklin, and Edward Rutledge. Following that unsuccessful effort, at a council of war on September 12, Washington and his generals again debated defending or evacuating the city. The council voted to evacuate, bring the troops north, and form them at Harlem Heights, just northwest of Horn's Hook. The troops began the complicated process of removing the many troops and their military stores and the sick to Harlem Heights. Washington left the city and set up his headquarters at the Morris Mansion, well to the north of Horn's Hook. That day, the quartermasters impressed into Continental service every available team and wagon to remove all troops and supplies from the city. At the same time, the British appeared to be preparing to cross the East River to Manhattan from Montressor's Island.[23]

The American and British batteries at Hell Gate continued to exchange fire on September 12. Isaac Fowls of Captain Keith's company was killed during the morning by a cannonball fired from the British 32 gun frigate *Rose* in the East River that took off his head.[24] The muster return for Sargent's regiment that day showed 36 fewer men than on May 4. The number of sick had significantly increased to 63 men present although sick, while 71 were absent due to illness, making a total of 134 sick, much worse than the 40 on May 4. Just one surgeon and one surgeon's mate had to care for them all. Ninety-eight men were on command, a number with the rangers and some at the laboratory. Isaac Huse recalled that about then, "I was detached under Sargent Noyes to the Laboratory and remained there two or three weeks."[25] Two men had deserted since the last return. The regiment still required 113 men to be complete.[26]

Caring for the large numbers of sick was becoming overwhelming. Washington ordered that each brigade appoint an officer of captain's rank or higher empowered to procure the necessary items for the sick and wounded. Simply finding nurses for the hospital proved nearly impossible, requiring that infantrymen be assigned to care for the sick, removing them from their companies on command.[27] Removing supplies and the sick from the potential paths of British landings and taking them to Harlem Heights was proving very difficult, lacking sufficient horses and wagons, compounded by the heat of that September.

General Howe decided on September 13 to land troops on Manhattan in two places, Horn's Hook and Kip's Bay. However, his officers advised him to consider "the situation and construction" of the Horn's Hook fort that made it "extremely difficult to destroy it effectually."[28] The bombardments from Hallet's Point had failed to force out the American infantry and artillery. Combining this factor with the treacherous waters of Hell Gate, Howe decided only to land troops at Kip's Bay.[29]

—

Captain Farrington lost three men captured on Saturday, September 14.[30] The cannon roared all day, and about sunset, six enemy ships, including two warships, passed between Governor's Island and Red Hook and proceeded up the East River. Jacob and the men in his regiment could tell that the regulars kept in continual motion that night, convincing them to expect an attack in the morning.[31]

Jacob and his regiment turned out before dawn on what would be the bright, clear, breezy Sunday morning of September 15, fearfully anticipating that the British would try to land at Horn's Hook. Colonel Sargent had lost three men to British cannon fire the week before. The men stayed alert, unaware that the British were instead preparing to land further south at Kip's Bay. Just before 11:00 am, Jacob heard the first shots of an hour-long naval bombardment at Kip's Bay. Seventy heavy cannon, augmented by smaller weapons, carried out the heavy attack that Admiral Howe's secretary, Ambrose Serle, described as "so terrible and so incessant a roar of guns few even in the Army & Navy had ever heard before."[32]

It must have sounded very ominous to Jacob and the men just up the river at Horn's Hook. Sargent's Brigade continued to receive cannon fire from across the river even after becoming aware that the British had crossed at Kip's Bay. Jacob Walton's house at the fort burned down after being hit by a British shell.

The American forces at Kip's Bay retreated quickly in a disastrous rout. As word of the rout spread, Jacob's regiment abandoned the Horn's Hook fort and retreated inland and north toward Harlem Heights to avoid entrapment at Horn's Hook.[33]

During the orderly retreat, Captain Keith commanded the covering party that departed the fort last. He soon saw a soldier intercept private James McCormick of Captain Farrington's company when he left the line of march and headed toward the British. The two men exchanged strong words. McCormick raised his tomahawk, and the two men were faced off and arguing when Ensign Fish of Wiley's company approached them and ordered McCormick to return to his company. McCormick shouted that he would not, that he wanted to go to see his wife. Ensign Ebenezer Fish did not believe he was married. Even when told the enemy was nearby and advancing, McCormick insisted on leaving. Then, upon being strongly ordered again to rejoin his company, McCormick appeared to obey. However, Lieutenant Jonathan Brown of Captain Perry's company saw McCormick stray away from his company again by more than twenty rods. At this point, Colonel Sargent personally intercepted him and brought McCormick back at gunpoint. McCormick had a reputation as a trouble maker who often sought a fight and had previously received lashes for desertion.

Later that day, Captain Keith encountered McCormick as he once more appeared to be deserting to the enemy. Keith ordered a squad to take him into custody, but McCormick swore he would not return to his company. Keith repeated the order, but McCormick loudly swore he would kill someone in the regiment and would rather be with the regulars. Keith arrested McCormick to face a court-martial for desertion and mutiny, as well as firing on his own regiment.[34]

In addition to disciplinary incidents such as McCormick's, as Jacob's regiment marched for Harlem Heights the day became quite hot and dusty, and British scouting detachments captured two men from Jacob's company. To cover the troops retreating toward Harlem Heights, Colonel William Smallwood's Maryland regiment had earlier set up a post on advantageous high ground, half a mile south of McGowan's Pass, ahead of the advancing enemy on the Post Road. They remained there most of the day.

Still protecting its baggage, Sargent's brigade was the last unit to reach Smallwood's post as the British approached the area. The regulars divided into two columns, with one headed for the North River attempting to flank and surround the Americans. Ordered to retreat in good order, Smallwood, now with Sargent's brigade, withdrew to the American lines forming on the rocky southern edge of Harlem Heights at a depression in the terrain known as the Hollow Way. They arrived a little after dusk, and that night, Jacob and his fellow soldiers lay in a Harlem Heights field above the Hollow Way on the left front of the American lines with the earth for their bed and "covered only by the clouds of an uncomfortable sky." Like the other men of his company, Jacob felt his "blood chilled by the cold wind that produced a sudden change in the temperature of the air."[35]

—

The following morning, British engineer Archibald Robertson visited the abandoned American works at Horn's Hook and noted that the British artillery fire had significantly damaged the Walton house. He complimented the eleven-foot thick parapet that Jacob and his fellow soldiers had constructed because it had stood up well to the British 24-pounder artillery fire from a distance of just 710 yards. However, Robertson felt the British troops could have easily attacked the position if the Americans had not abandoned it.[36]

At Harlem Heights that morning, Sargent's regiment formed up with General Greene's three brigades forming the southernmost of three lines that featured three small redoubts. Jacob was one of about 10,000 men who took up positions in those lines stretching across the bluffs of Harlem Heights between the Hudson and Harlem Rivers. The British front line encampment took shape less than two miles away across the Hollow Way. However, because of dense woods on its southern side, the Americans could not see how the British troops arranged themselves.

Before dawn, orders went out to Major Thomas Knowlton's newly formed rangers to reconnoiter across the Hollow Way towards the hidden enemy. They came into contact with about 400 regulars near the Nicholas Jones stone farmhouse, forcing them to retreat. Ranger Obadiah Brown from Sargent's regiment, felt that "about a hundred of us engaged 2000 of enemy. ... I was shot through my arm." The next day Brown, who had exaggerated the size of the enemy force, went to the hospital in great pain and noted that two men died there. Brown's wound prevented his return to duty for the remainder of the campaign while he suffered a long recovery.[37]

As the rangers retreated, Jacob heard the blare of British hunting horns sounding the call for a fox chase to insult, intimidate, and dismiss the retreating Americans. Adjutant General Joseph Reed writing to his wife, noted, "I never felt such a sensation before; it seemed to crown our disgrace" at Kip's Bay.[38]

A group of 150 volunteers from Greene's Division "scrambled down the bluff to a salt marsh." As the British rushed towards them, they retreated several hundred yards while still firing. They had been a decoy, and now an additional 900 men were sent in to stop the British advance. Men sent as a flanking attack on these British were unsuccessful, and Major Knowlton was mortally wounded. The men fought well, and Washington responded by expanding his goal to achieve a more significant victory. and sending additional troops to support them.

Soon 1,800 men fought the British soldiers at a buckwheat field on the hilltop. The troops sent out to support this small group included Sargent's regiment, probably operating on the right side of the American force. The fighting became intense as both sides sent in troops, including artillery.[39]

When the firing began, Jacob and the others must have felt like Lieutenant David Dimock of Colonel Comfort Sage's Connecticut battalion, who wrote in his journal:

> *I could not help feeling an involuntary tremor, as though me knees were giving away, as I was obliged to stand still and listen to the steady 'tramp tramp' of the approaching foe, but as soon as we received their fire and the man at my right hand side fell forward shot through the heart, the blood spouting in a stream from his bosom, at the sight of that blood all the tremor was gone in an instant, and vengeance was the only feeling. We returned the fire, and then ran backward down the heights and formed at the foot. Our orders were not to fire until we could see the feet of the pursuing British through the smoke of battle. We did so. The British kept firing, but not seeing our men they shot over their heads. In this way our men kept on till they crossed a little brook, when they formed on the bank and made a stand. The British finally retreated with great loss, the waters of the little brook running red for many miles with British blood.*[40]

The Americans stood in line up to four deep, instructed not to fire until ordered. Jacob saw the British Highlanders in their kilts, the blue-coated, brass-helmeted Hessian grenadiers, and green-coated Hessian Jäger light infantry among the enemy. He may also have seen one or more of the high-ranking American officers, including Israel Putnam, Nathanael Greene,

George Clinton, Joseph Reed, and other members of Washington's staff who joined in the battle.

The British also received reinforcements. After fighting in the buckwheat field between noon and 2:00 pm, the British retreated into an orchard and then to the vicinity of the Jones house, where the fighting had begun. As the British sent forward more reinforcements, orders came for the Americans to withdraw. They did so, but only after giving a great "Hurrah!" before departing in good order. Colonel Reed later recalled that "they were recalled with difficulty, so new to them was the experience of putting the British soldier to flight." The British did not continue the battle, but the American soldiers remained ready to reengage until near sunset.[41] In the aftermath of the fighting, Jacob, along with each soldier involved, dealt with his thoughts about escaping death when others nearby him had been killed or wounded. Exhaustion, hunger, and thirst complicated those thoughts while they took action to care for the wounded and bury the dead.

—

At the close of the day's combat, Washington established strong picket guards of 800 rank and file, plus officers, including two colonels. However, Jacob must have been pleased when Sargent's regiment, along with others that had been heavily engaged in the fighting , was ordered to "retire and refresh themselves." Jacob knew though, that their orders included instructions to "hold themselves in readiness to turn out at a minute's warning" should the British renew the fighting.[42]

The following day, Washington described the very intense battle saying:

> *They advanced in sight yesterday in several large bodies, but attempted nothing of a general nature; tho' in the forenoon there were some smart skirmishes between some of their parties and detachments sent out by me; in which I have the pleasure to inform you our men behaved with bravery and intrepidity, putting them to flight when in open ground and forcing them from posts they had seized, two or three times.*

Washington estimated the extent of enemy losses considering evidence, "from some of their wounded men which fell into our hands, the appearance of blood in every place where they made their stand and on the fences as they passed, we have reason to believe that they had a good many killed and wounded, though they did not leave many on the ground." Three men from Captain Farrington's company had been captured, one man from Captain Keith's company killed, and a corporal and private from Captain Perry's company killed. Records of the Sargent's Brigade wounded are incomplete but estimated at 40 to 50, indicating their significant involvement in the action.[43]

The success of this encounter with regulars, highlanders, and Hessians at a mere 40 yards for over an hour greatly inspired the troops to feel more confident in a future that had looked very bleak just the day before.[44] However, the renewed spirit did not significantly improve army discipline and order.

Brigade Major Daniel Box saw many men plundering on Harlem Plain about 2:00 pm the day after the battle. He took a squad down and caught up with Ensign Matthew Macumber, of Captain Barnes's company, leading more than twenty men, "all loaded with plunder, such as house furniture, table linen, and kitchen utensils, China and delft ware." Major Box ordered the booty to be laid down or carried back to where they had found it. Macumber responded by claiming, "he had his Colonel's order for what he had done, and that he would defend the plunder as long as he had life."

Box asked Macumber if he knew who he was and that the General's orders forbade plundering. Then, when Macumber ordered his party to "make ready" their muskets, Box jumped over a fence followed by his small party and told Macumber his men would fire at them if they did not deliver up the booty. Macumber and his men replied that "they would die by the plunder." Box, having fewer men, withdrew to assemble a larger squad. When Macumber saw Box returning with reinforcements, he left his party and ran away across the fields carrying many items. Major Box followed and succeeded in capturing and disarming Macumber and his men.[45]

Because of that incident and others like it, the General Orders for September 18 stated:

> *Commanding Officers of regiments, and all other officers are charged in the strictest manner to prevent all plundering, and to seize every soldier carrying plunder, whether belonging to the same regiment or not, or on whatever pretence it is taken; and the General positively commands that such plunderer be immediately carried to the next Brigadier, or Commanding officer of a regiment, who is instantly to have the offender whipped on the spot.*

Washington feared that men had committed significant irregularities and excesses under the pretense of ranging or scouting. He forbade any patrolling or scouting parties unless he or the Brigadier General of the day approved them, and they must always have an officer in charge. He stated, "The General does not mean to discourage patrolling and scouting parties, when properly regulated; on the other hand, he will be pleased with and accept the services of any good officers who are desirous of being thus employed, and will distinguish them."[46]

—

Colonel Sargent's Brigade joined General Heath's Division and was ordered to march up to Kingsbridge and follow General Heath's orders for encamping. Colonel Ward's Connecticut regiment was annexed to Sargent's Brigade for the present.[47]

Sargent's Brigade marched over King's Bridge and encamped all night about a mile and a half northeast on Valentine's Hill.[48] Jacob says, "Soon after that we had orders to leave that place & marched to West Chester by way of Kings Bridge. We lay there [Valentine's Hill] some time and every night we had a guard stationed out 2 or 3 miles from where the regiment lay at a place called Morrisania. I mounted guard there every time it came to my turn." Morrisania, where Jacob stood some guard duty, was a sizeable rural manor, one of four in the Bronx, owned by the Morris family whose member Lewis Morris signed the Declaration of Independence. His half-brother, Gouverneur Morris, was another important political figure of the time. The manor contained many small farms, dairies, and cattle yards leased by farmers from the Morris family. Some of the farmers held small numbers of enslaved persons in bondage.

—

At the Macumber plundering court-martial held at Harlem Heights on September 19, several men confirmed the account of Major Box. However, several men from Macumber's company testified that the ensign had expressly told them not to plunder and broke up the plundering by his men. One man said the items they were carrying when confronted by Major Box were items Macumber had told his men to take to Colonel Sargent. The court found Macumber not guilty of plundering, robbery, or mutiny. But they did find him guilty of "offering violence to and disobeying Major Box." His sentence was to ask Major Box's pardon and "receive a severe reprimand from Colonel Sargent." As usual, Washington reviewed the court proceedings could not help recognizing that "the men who defended Macumber were among those who were to share in the plunder."[49] Dissatisfied with the court's decision, Washington ordered the court to reconvene on September 21 and reconsider the sentence.

When the court reconvened, Maryland Captain Nathaniel Ramsay, who had also intercepted Macumber's men and their loot, after being sworn as an additional witness, gave his version of what had happened. Ramsey noted that:

> *Ensign Macumber had at this time a knapsack full on his shoulder, out of which stuck two waxen toys, which I took hold of, and jested with him on his having such a pretty sort of plunder; he made me no reply, but ordered them to proceed with what things they had; they had a large chair full, consisting of poultry and some house furniture; some were loaded with kettles and kitchen furniture.*

Ramsey repeated to Macumber that orders forbade plundering.

Ramsey then gave his version of the encounter with Major Box, which elevated the seriousness of the violence Macumber and his men had threatened. He concluded with, "I have no doubt but if any attempt had been made to disarm the prisoner [Macumber], his party would have fired; and I was so apprehensive of this, that I stood on my guard."

Ensign Macumber offered no evidence on his behalf. After thoroughly reconsidering the evidence for and against the prisoner, the court reversed its verdict and found him guilty of plundering and mutiny. It annulled the previous light sentence and ordered Macumber "to be cowhided," lashed with a leather whip, and immediately cashiered from the army.[50] On September 25, General Orders stated that "Colonel Sargent is to send to the Provost Guard the soldiers who were with Ensign Macumber, and charged with plundering at Harlem."[51]

—

While Washington continued to debate abandoning Manhattan Island over the next month, Jacob must have felt like he was in a trap just waiting to be sprung by the British. Everyone, especially Washington and his generals, wondered what General Howe would do next. While they speculated whether

Howe planned to drive the Americans completely off of Manhattan Island or not, they also pondered whether Washington would order the island's evacuation before Howe took action. This inaction left both the British and the American forces facing each other in their armed camps with the soldiers anticipating renewed combat.

However, in the continuing absence of serious combat, life in the American camp reverted to the usual monotonous round of duties and restricted free time that often brought out the worst in some men. The everyday problems of camp life, cleanliness, the weather, and illness became the focus for men like Jacob. As the days stretched into weeks, morale deteriorated along with discipline. Colonel Joseph Reed described this problem writing, "A spirit of desertion, cowardice, plunder and shrinking from duty, when attended with fatigue or danger, prevailed too generally throughout the whole army."[52]

On the morning of September 21, the soldiers saw the light from a large fire to the south that proved to be the city of New York burning disastrously.[53]

—

A September 21 muster return shows Colonel Sargent's four regiment brigade contained only 618 rank and file present and fit for duty, making it only about the size of a regiment. Sargent's regiment itself was missing one captain, three first lieutenants, six second lieutenants, and one ensign. Only 298 men were present and fit for duty, just three more than on September 12. The number of men present although sick, was down by 19, while those absent due to sickness were up by eight. Ninety men were on command. Since the last muster, one man had deserted.[54]

Jacob saw that he and the men around him already needed new clothing and other necessities before fall turned into winter. General Orders for this day noted that need and authorized regimental commanders to send out officers to purchase needed items. How they would be able to do this under the always uncertain circumstances was not clear. Joseph Allen had joined as paymaster for Sargent's regiment, but Sargent had sent him out as the proper person to procure clothing, leaving the paymaster position open.[55]

Proper care for the sick continued to be a concern, along with the issue of plundering. General Orders commented that:

> *The many complaints that are hourly made of plundering both public and private property, induces the General to direct that every regiment be paraded at five o'clock this evening, the knapsacks and*

> *tents of the whole to be examined under the inspection of the field officers, and all articles, not the proper baggage and accoutrements of a soldier, set apart, and kept by the Colonel, or commanding officer, 'till inquiry can be made, how they came possessed of them.*

Jacob had to undergo that inspection of his personal possessions. Other discipline infractions continued unabated, including the wasting of ammunition.[56] Among all the uncertainty during the remainder of the month, the men continued building huts in preparation for the winter.[57]

—

Some skirmishes did take place while both sides contemplated how to proceed with the campaign. Jacob recalled, "There was an island [Montresor's] near there the tide made up round it. The British had a station on the island and a British ship lay there." On September 12, General Heath at Kingsbridge ordered Lieutenant Colonel Michael Jackson of Sargent's regiment to dislodge the enemy that night from Montresor's Island, also known to the men as Hospital Island. Jackson should parade his troops at "the new bridge" at 11:00 pm, load them onto flat-bottomed boats, and float with the tide to Morrisania. When the tide allowed, the boats were to proceed to Montresor's Island. Upon landing at the island they should leave a small party with the boats, then surround the enemy troops and kill or capture them. Any prisoners taken should not be abused, and troops should not burn any buildings unless necessary to achieve their goal. To achieve success these actions would have to be conducted in secrecy, silence, and with dispatch.[58]

General Heath's newly appointed aide-de-camp, Major Thomas Henly, a well-respected officer, volunteered to go with Jackson. Due to tidal problems, or hesitancy by the other two boats, only the lead boat landed on the island. Although the attack had been revealed due to incomplete security, the attackers forced the first British troops to retreat, but when reinforcements came up, they made the Americans withdraw. During this brief encounter, Major Henly "received the fatal ball through the heart." In addition, Captain Hubbard, the recently appointed temporary paymaster of Colonel Sargent's Regiment,[59] was killed, and Lieutenant Colonel Jackson received a bullet wound in the leg. Altogether, about 14 men were killed, wounded, or missing. Whether or not Jacob participated in this action is unclear, but he still remembered late in life that "in an attack on that island one night Col Jackson was wounded." Officers on the two boats that failed to land on the island in support found themselves indicted for "cowardice and misbehavior in the attack made upon Montresor's Island on the morning of the 23rd instant," and one, Captain John Weisner, was cashiered.[60] Captain William Scott of Sargent's regiment was the other man indicted, but he was not mentioned in the court report and was ultimately not charged.

—

How Jacob felt at this point about the army he served in we do not know. But on September 23, after the uncoordinated attack on Montressor's Island took place, General Knox wrote to his brother that General Washington:

> *is as worthy a man as breathes, but he cannot do everything[,] not be everywhere. He wants good assistants. There is a radical evil in our army – the lack of officers. We ought to have men of merit in the most extensive and unlimited sense of the word. Instead of which, the bulk of the officers of the army are a parcel of ignorant, stupid men, who might make tolerable soldiers, but are bad officers; and until Congress forms an establishment to induce men proper for the purpose to leave their usual employments and enter the service, it is ten to one they will be beat till they are heartily tired of it.*

He recognized that the officers did not have professional training, and "as the army now stands, it is only a receptacle for ragamuffins."[61] Jacob knew that several Sargent's regiment officers became subject to court-martial. However, Captain Wiley seems to have been a good officer and was promoted to major in 1779 and served until 1781.[62]

By September 24, Washington felt growing concern about the approaching dissolution of his army at the end of the year. The similar problem he had experienced the previous year at Boston was repeating itself. For a variety of reasons, he did not expect many men presently in service to reenlist. He told Congress, "A soldier reasoned with upon the goodness of the cause he is engaged in, and the inestimable rights he is contending for, hears you with patience, and acknowledges the truth of your observations, but adds, that it is of no more importance to him than others." Washington encouraged Congress to take substantive actions to make enlistment attractive. Among other factors, he believed Congress had to raise soldier pay, not to mention providing it regularly, and enlist men for the "continuance of the war." The essential elements of providing proper food and clothing, sufficient muskets and ammunition, and care when sick also needed significant improvement.[63]

Just how Jacob felt at this time about reenlisting at the end of the year is not known. Was he one of the few who would reenlist simply "upon principles of disinterestedness," or was he one of the men so discouraged by life in the army, struggling both on the battlefield and in areas of general discipline, who would leave? The question of reenlisting would directly confront him in just a few months when Washington would plead with men to extend their enlistments at another critical point in the war. But, for the present he just had to keep doing his duty faithfully.

Desertion had always been a problem but it increased after the battle on Long Island in late August. The army took a number of measures to stop it. Captain Wiley sat on a court-martial at Kingsbridge on September 25 investigating the charge of desertion brought against Lieutenant Henry Drake of Captain Joab Houghton's Company of the regiment commanded by Lieutenant Colonel Joseph Phillips of the New Jersey five-month militia levies serving with the Continentals.

Lieutenant Drake's story highlights the varied and sometimes loose nature of service commitments among the state troops serving under Washington. Drake had never signed on officially, but he knew Colonel Phillips from previous militia service. He had voluntarily agreed to join him for just two months, receiving no pay or rations. He had made it clear that he was not signing on for five months like everyone else in the regiment and expected to leave as a free agent after two months. Drake got caught up in the desperate efforts to prevent desertions after the disaster at Long Island but was quickly acquitted and returned to his home in Trenton and the inn he operated there.[64]

Captain Wiley also sat on the court-martial, along with Major Austin and Captain Barnes, for Ensign Benjamin Snow of Captain Perry's company charged with "leaving his guard and absenting himself from the camp and duty without leave." There was no written accusation, and no accuser appeared, so the court ordered him discharged from arrest. However, the court's action did not remove the possibility of Snow being tried later.[65]

Along with desertion, the other familiar breaches in discipline continued to be seen. Robert Higgins received 20 lashes on September 27 for getting drunk and denying duty, Thomas Brimblecom 10 lashes for getting drunk, and the regiment drum major 15 lashes for theft.[66] Also on September 27,

Captains Wiley and Scott sat on the court-martial at Harlem Heights for William Higgins of Captain Alexander Hamilton's artillery company, accused of "breaking open a chest and stealing a number of articles out of it, in the room of the Provost Guard." Robert Wilson testified that "A person came into a room where I was, and told me that some men up in the Provost Room had broke open a chest and were plundering it. I went up and found the prisoner, Higgins, with another, tucking a gown and cloak into his bosom. I took them away from him. He said that others were concerned as well as him, and denied that he broke open the chest." Peter Lynch confirmed the testimony. The court found him guilty and sentenced him to receive 39 lashes on his bare back.[67]

—

At this time, Jacob's company consisted of just Captain Wiley and Ensign Fish, one sergeant and two fife and drum musicians, 52 privates present and fit for duty, 8 men sick present and 1 man absent sick, and 8 men on command. This total of 74 officers and men, including Jacob, left 11 men needed to complete the company. The eight men on command included one with the rangers, two with the wagon train, three officer's waiters, one camp "colorman" on camp cleaning detail, and one man assigned somewhere else not indicated.[68]

—

Jacob faithfully performed his duties surrounded by conditions that demoralized many weaker men. Unlike many others, though, he kept his head straight and continued to act in accordance with expectations. The future for him and those he served with still looked very unclear except that everyone anticipated combat to be renewed at some point.

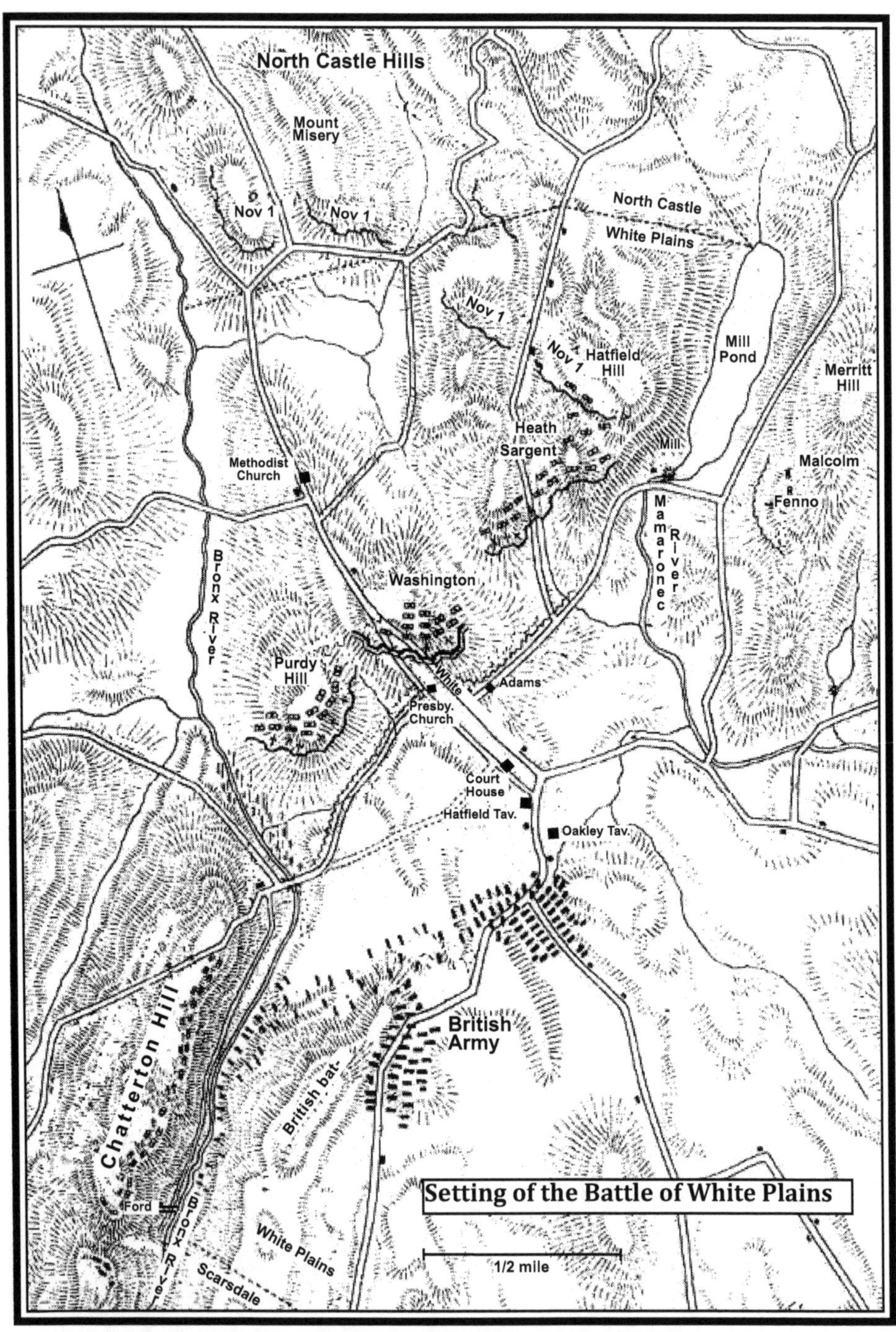

Based on Topographical Map of the Battle of White Plains, October 28, 1776 in Hufeland, *Westchester County during the American Revolution : 1775-1783*, between pages 130 and 131.

"After some time we were ordered to march to the White Plains. We marched there and then joined General Washington's army. We lay some time at the White Plains. While we lay there the British landed and attacked some of our troops & had a brush there."
- Jacob Francis

16

New York Campaign October 1776

OCTOBER BEGAN WITH EVERYONE STILL WONDERING JUST WHAT GENERAL Howe was planning as a follow-up to the Harlem Heights battle and struggling with continuing concerns about the discipline of the Continental troops. Joseph Allen returned on October 1 from procuring clothing for Sargent's Regiment. He assumed his office as regimental paymaster, and during the day, a man from Captain Farrington's company suffered 20 lashes for drunkenness, and the drum major again received 20 lashes. James McCormick of Captain Farrington's company, sentenced to death for desertion and mutiny during the retreat from Horn's Hook to Harlem Heights on September 15, was ordered to be hanged on October 2 at 11:00 am. All men not on duty would be paraded on the Grand Parade at that time to witness it.[1]

That night, the General Orders read to the regiment acknowledged the army's discipline problems. A frustrated Washington stated, "It is with much concern the General is informed that though the new rules for the government of the Army have been out some time, they have not been generally read to the soldiers. Surely gentlemen do not reflect what prejudice it is to the service to omit so material a point of duty." Jacob no doubt heard the new rules read soon after if he had not heard them before.[2]

—

Sargent's regiment at Kingsbridge on October 4, 1776, reflected the army's overall incomplete and worsening condition. While Colonel Sargent and Major Austin were fit for duty, Lieutenant Colonel Michael Jackson was present, although wounded. Only Captain Pope and Captain Farrington had their full complement of company officers. Ensign Cleveland commanded Captain William Scott's company as the only officer present. Other companies were missing one or more officers who were sick or on command. In Jacob's company, Captain Wiley and his lieutenant son were fit for duty, and Ensign Fish was present but sick. Lieutenant Scott was on command with the rangers.[3]

While not at full strength, Captain Wiley's company was the largest and most complete of the regiment's eight companies. In all, the regiment had 250 men present and fit for duty out of 503, and lacked 137 privates to be complete. Wiley's company had its full complement of three sergeants and two musicians, but only 51 men out of 70 were present and fit for duty, while 7 were present ill and 6 were absent due to illness. Six men were on command, including two with the rangers. Even just on paper, the company was short ten men.[4]

Ensign Benjamin Snow of Captain Perry's company was rearrested to face the charge of leaving his guard while on duty and absenting himself from camp without leave and tried by court-martial on October 4. Lieutenant Woody Dustin of Captain Farrington's company testified "that Ensign Snow came to his tent, and told him that he had some friends he wanted to visit, and asked him to go with him." Dustin then asked Snow whether he was on guard duty. Snow said he was, but that he had secured Ensign Fish of Wiley's company to serve it for him. They departed about 3:00 pm and returned about dark, having gone about two miles from camp, possibly too far away to hear drums beating to arms. Several men testified about this exchange of duty, including Captain Wiley and Lieutenant Wiley. Lieutenant Wiley stated that Ensign Snow had made the exchange in the manner frequently used in his regiment. The court found Ensign Snow not guilty.[5] This route to duty modification was just one example of how men worked around official procedures to satisfy personal situations. It was also an example of why Washington continued to criticize the quality of many officers who did not strictly follow standard army procedures.

—

Jacob was immersed in an army incompetently supplied with necessities and containing few officers of merit, especially at the regimental and company level. In early October, Washington believed that without decisive action from Congress, the war would fail. He told John Hancock that Congress did not fully understand the severity of the situation, and pleaded, "Give me leave to say, Sir; I say it with due deference and respect, (and my knowledge of the facts, added to the importance of the Cause and the stake I hold in it, must justify the freedom) that your affairs are in a more unpromising way than you seem to apprehend." The army was just three months away from disbanding at the end of the calendar year, and while Congress had voted to raise another army to replace it, time was running short. Washington pointed out to Hancock that there was "a material difference between voting of battalions and raising of men." In terms of recruiting men for the new force, he warned, "there are more difficulties than Congress are aware of."[6]

Washington continued to worry about unsanitary camp conditions. Jacob heard in General Orders on October 4 that, "The shameful inattention in some of the camps to decency and cleanliness, in providing necessaries, and picking up the offal and filth of the camp, having been taken notice of before in general." Washington declared he would publicly state the names of specific regiments that fell short of expectations in future General Orders.[7] But, would public humiliation solve the problem? Physical punishments did not seem to be solving other discipline problems.

The next day, one of Captain Farrington's men and one of Captain Wiley's each received 20 lashes for being drunk. Jacob also watched as two fellow members of Captain Wiley's company had to painfully ride a wooden horse for 15 minutes for being absent at roll call without leave.[8] The "wooden horse" held the victim, who painfully straddled it with his legs dangling. The legs were pulled down by weights so that all weight was on the crotch, often leading to permanent disfigurement. The Continental Congress articles of war officially limited punishments to "degrading, cashiering, drumming out of the army, whipping not exceeding thirty-nine lashes, fine not exceeding two months' pay of the offender, imprisonment not exceeding one month."[9] Although not officially authorized, riding the wooden horse was not an unusual punishment.

—

Washington prepared to spend the winter in the Harlem Heights and Kingsbridge area unless Howe made further moves. The October 9 General Orders told Jacob's officers to prevent their men from covering their tent floors with earth. Earlier, orders had told them to use what wooden boards they had for tent floors rather than sidewalls. Even so, tents would not provide adequate protection during the winter, and brigade commanders received orders to apply to the Quartermaster General for lumber and have their men, in their spare time, build barracks or huts "fit for winter use." However, no specifications for the huts were given. It was also clearly ordered that constructing winter shelters should not be allowed to interfere with work on military defenses.[10]

British actions on October 9 made it a very long day for Jacob. Three British warships and their tenders sailed up the North River that morning, successfully passing between Fort Washington on the New York side and Fort Lee on the New Jersey side, despite hot fire from the American forts. This action on the western side of the American positions on Manhattan Island caused leaders to question British intentions on the eastern side positions. General Heath ordered Sargent's regiment to march down to the guard post at Morrisania, between three and four miles south of Kingsbridge and across the Harlem River. The British proceeded to inflict a series of damages along the North River on both land and water on the west side of Manhattan. One vessel they sank carried David Bushnell's experimental submarine *Turtle* on board, ending his efforts to use it to sink British ships.[11]

Late in the day, with no indication of British activity on the eastern side of the island, General Heath ordered Colonel Sargent march in the opposite direction some twelve miles north of Kingsbridge to Dobb's Ferry on the North River to dislodge the large number of regulars reported to have landed there. Sargent took 500 men, 40 light-horse, one Continental Artillery Regiment howitzer and crew under Captain Edward Crafts, and a detachment of artillery under Captain Jotham Horton with two 12-pounders, currently at Phillip's Mills. Sargent's orders told him to make sure to defend the howitzer properly and "dislodge the enemy; killing or taking prisoners, as occasion may require." He should notify General Heath if the enemy troops re-embarked on their ships, as well as about any other noteworthy occurrences.[12]

After the long day of marching, Sargent found the report of the British landing to be erroneous. He wrote to General Heath at 2:30 am, "I have just arrived at Dobbs's Ferry. Very peaceable here; can see nothing of the enemy. There is not any of the enemy landed. We have no ammunition on the road for the small arms. The ships are about three miles above this place, where I shall order a party immediately." Heath replied from Kingsbridge that, unless things changed, Sargent should leave at least Captain Christopher Darrow's 10th Continental Regiment company, along with some ammunition and provisions, to reinforce the guard there and return immediately with the remainder of his detachment to Kingsbridge. Sargent and his men did not get back to Kingsbridge until that night after a long day of seemingly inconsequential activity. The following day was raw and cold, and militia were coming in every day.[13]

—

On the morning of October 12, the enemy landed in large numbers at Throgs Neck on the eastern side of the American positions. They were attempting to attack the American fortifications around Kingsbridge on their left flank and pin the American army against the Hudson River. However, Throgs Neck was more an island than a peninsula and American troops guarded its two narrow approaches, making movement onto the mainland difficult. The British held off pushing their attack for six days while waiting for baggage and supplies to arrive from New York.

At some point, Sargent's regiment received orders to march down near the enemy troops that had landed. The British did not proceed any distance from their ships, and Sargent's regiment did not get involved in any action.[14] While the British waited, Colonel Sargent received orders not to "march over to support the regiments near Frog's Point [Throgs Neck] without further orders, as this post [Kingsbridge] may be left too bare." Information circulated through the camp that "a large number of boats were seen off Willsett's Point about sunset, full of men, and were standing eastward."[15] Willsett's Point is today's Willet's Point opposite Throgs Neck near the entrance to the East River from Long Island Sound.

On October 15, Sargent's, Ward's, and Colonel John Chester's regiments, and the regiment commanded by Lieutenant-Colonel Storrs, formed a brigade under the command of Colonel Sargent to be part of Major General Sullivan's division. Washington continued to demand his officers keep their men informed of what was expected from them. The officers must be "particularly attentive to the men's arms and ammunition, that there may be no deficiency or application for cartridges when we are called into the field."[16]

British troops remained at Throgs Neck the next day, while Washington held a council of war that decided to abandon the camp at Harlem Heights but maintain the garrison at Fort Washington. To prepare for any British advance, they would station portions of the army in Westchester County along the hills bordering the west side of the Bronx River and fortify both Valentine's Hill and Miles Square in the Kingsbridge area.[17]

On October 18, Howe's troops left Throgs Neck and moved to Pell's Point, where landing and advancing would be much easier. General Glover's Brigade delayed them upon their landing, and Howe stayed in the area of Eastchester and New Rochelle until October 22. Learning that the British appeared to be moving toward White Plains, where only about 300 militiamen guarded large amounts of military stores, Washington initiated efforts to advance the army there before the regulars could take it. Stirling's Brigade moved out ahead of the main army on October 18 to take and hold positions at White Plains.

Leaving a garrison of 2,000 men at Fort Washington on Manhattan, Washington began assembling about 13,000 men at White Plains, complete with artillery, baggage, and supplies. The troops and supplies reached White Plains slowly due to a lack of horses and wagons. This massive movement had to be accomplished in short stages so supply wagons could make multiple trips. Soldiers dragged the artillery normally pulled by horses. This slow transport took four exhausting days to complete a routine one-day trip. American troops created a series of entrenched outposts along the west side of the Bronx River, and Spencer's division occupied that line.

Jacob went with Sargent's regiment to Throgs Neck on October 20 and a party went out at night to gather up all the oxen and horses they could find, returning at daybreak. The next day they marched just a mile and were ordered back to camp. Jacob recalled, "The regiment did guard duty on Throggs Neck where the British threatened to land and on October 22 set out for White Plains." They took all their baggage and arrived, more rapidly than most other units, on October 23.[18]

—

General Heath placed his division on the left of the American line. They built only modest defensive works suitable for infantry, on the high, strong ground north of the White Plains courthouse on the west slope of Hatfield Hill. To their left front was "a deep hollow through which ran a small brook [Mamaroneck River], which came from a mill-pond a little above." To the right, the ground gave way gradually toward army headquarters on the plain near the crossroads and then ascended to higher ground at Purdy Hill and eventually Chatterton's Hill. Across the millpond, troops stationed on Merritt Hill under New York militia Colonel William Malcolm and Continental Artillery Second Lieutenant Ephraim Fenno secured the American left flank.[19]

By October 24, Sargent's Regiment had increased by 20 to 270 men present and fit for duty. Captain Wiley's Company was down from 51 to 46.[20]

Upon arrival at White Plains, concern immediately arose about "straggling," that is, wandering, from camp. Jacob heard General Orders on October 24, reminding officers and men of the need for them to be together upon an alarm.[21]

Sargent's regiment did some uneventful marching the next day and returned to camp. The following day they moved their tents to the top of Hatfield Hill. Sergeant Hooper of Captain Pope's company went missing on October 27.[22] The same day, John Cooper of Captain Keith's company was imprisoned in the courthouse at White Plains by Brigade Major Benjamin Fish for one night. Cooper had stolen two muskets and other things from Colonel William Malcolm's New York militiamen.[23] In late morning they heard a heavy cannonade from the distant area of Fort Washington.[24]

—

The enemy's main body advanced as far as White Plains on October 28. As they marched up two main roads paralleling the Bronx River to within one mile of the American camp, the Americans engaged them, and both sides took many casualties.[25] The British marched toward Washington's position located in the center of the American lines. During the march, Howe became more interested in taking Chatterton's Hill, located on the American right flank and occupied by various American troops who had built some defenses and were using its many stone walls as defensive positions. Howe assigned about 4,000 men to cross the Bronx River under artillery cover. These included the von Donop, Rall, and von Lossberg Hessian regiments.

These troops met destructive fire from the Americans on the hill but tried again while Colonel Rall's Regiment moved to their left and attacked from a smaller hill to the south. Both sides took significant casualties, and the Americans fell back escaping to the right side of the American lines and leaving the British in control of the hill.[26] This partial victory meant that Howe held the high ground on the American flank, in position to make a decisive move. However, he let that potential victory slip away by not following up immediately with a flank attack and deciding to await reinforcements before renewing combat.

Upon the commencement of battle that day, Heath's Division troops occupied their defensive lines. Jacob says, during the battle, "our regiment & I with them marched by General Washington's order toward a hill [Chatterton's] where the engagement was but the British got possession of the hill and we retreated back to the camp. The British established a garrison on this hill." Young substitute Samuel Capen recalled, "The battle with small arms was on our right wing & much more in front than we were and our men retreated but where I was, the battle was with field pieces."[27] Colonel Sargent received a severe wound to his knee during the fighting, which incapacitated him for several weeks. This was his second wound of the war; the first had occurred at Bunker Hill.[28]

One participant described the battle, saying:

> *The scene was grand and solemn; all the adjacent hills smoked as though on fire, and bellowed and trembled with a perpetual cannonade, and fire of field-pieces, howitz[ers], and mortars. The air groaned with streams of cannon and musket shot; the air and hills smoked and echoed terribly with the bursting of shells; the fences and walls were knocked down, and torn to pieces, and men's legs, arms, and bodies, mangled with cannon and grape-shot all around us. I was in the action, and under as good advantages as any one man, perhaps, to observe all that passed, and write these particulars of the action from my own observation. No general action was designed on our part, and I believe one thousand men were never engaged at any time with the enemy. They came on to the hills opposite our lines and halted; and after cannonading some time part of the lines, in a short time they became very still and quiet.*[29]

—

After the terror and physical activity of battle, ordinary hardships and routines of camp life once again took over while expectations for renewed combat persisted. Hunger and thirst added to the suffering resulting from the cold, wet weather. The men could only do the best they could to find comfort, utilizing the few resources available and their ingenuity.[30] Jacob recalled he "stood sentinel that night in a thicket between the American camp and the hill so near the British lines that I could hear the Hessians in the garrison which was between ¼ and ½ mile from me."

Heath's Division acted on orders the next day to fall back to a position on high ground. The British remained on the ground they had won, and Howe waited for reinforcements rather than renew the attack. Then, "A rain of uncommon violence, during the whole night, made the ground so slippery that it was thought it could not be possible to mount the face of the hill." Howe postponed his intended renewal of combat. When the weather cleared about noon on October 31, Howe still "did not think proper to put his former intentions in execution." Even though reinforced, he knew the Americans had strengthened their lines during the delay and were in a proper position to defend themselves. Also, the heavy rain had created slippery mud in which his troops would find maneuver challenging.[31]

American forces observed on October 31 that the British had erected four or five artillery batteries and that hills overlooked the American lines near the town of White Plains. Therefore, they withdrew troops from the lines, and by 9:00 am that morning, "the guards and sentries burned the town, and forage all round it." General Heath described the burned structures and their contents as several barns, one house containing forage, and some military stores that they could not remove. The Americans removed their stores and withdrew about a mile and a half from the town, where they planted artillery on the hills. When some enemy advanced, the cannon "saluted them," and they stopped.

One officer noted, "Our men are in good spirits, and with much patience endure great hardships and fatigue." The sick and wounded were sent out about eight or ten miles from the camp. Just what the British planned to do next, no one knew.[32]

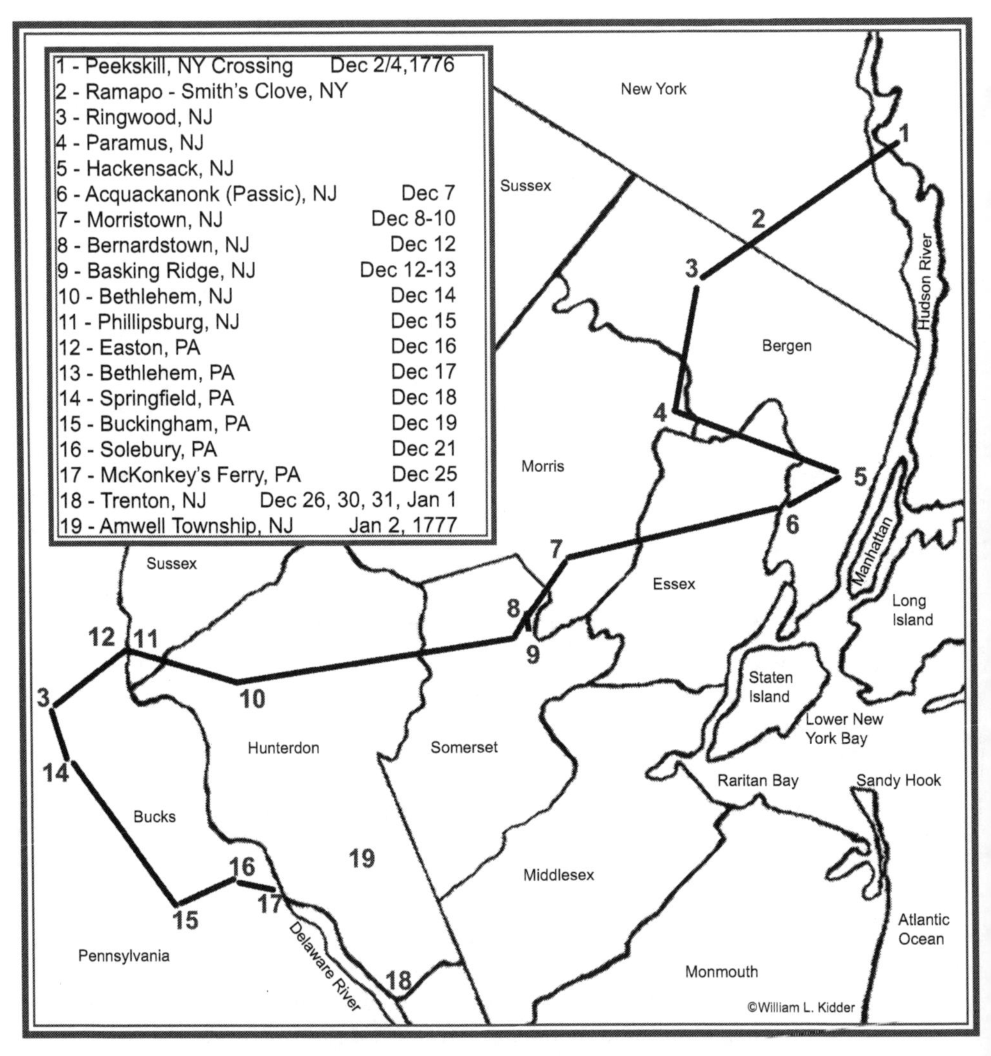

The Lee/Sullivan Route across New Jersey - December 1776

The Route followed by the 16th Continental Regiment from Peekskill, New York to Bucks County, Pennsylvania in December 1776 just prior to the Battle of Trenton.

The first part of the journey the regiment was under General Charles Lee and after his capture on December 13 command fell to General John Sullivan.

Then we received orders & marched to Peekskiln on the North river. We halted a day and night a little distance from the river and then crossed at Peekskiln to the west side of the river from whence we marched on & I do not recollect the names of places we passed thru til we got to Morristown New Jersey. We lay there one night the marched down near to Baskin ridge & lay there the next night. That night General Lee was taken in or about Baskin ridge. I heard the guns firing – the next morning we continued our march across Jersey. - Jacob Francis

17

New York Campaign November- December 1776

WASHINGTON WAS GREATLY CONCERNED ABOUT SOLDIERS WHO LEFT THE army "when there is the greatest necessity for their services." He forbade officers lower than brigadier general to discharge or give permission for a soldier to leave camp.[1] The muster return for November 3 revealed the depleted condition of Jacob's regiment, also typical of other regiments. Major Austin commanded the regiment since Colonel Sargent and Lieutenant Colonel Jackson remained absent due to their wounds. The only staff officers were the adjutant, surgeon, and surgeon's mate. Major Austin had just three captains, two first lieutenants, two second lieutenants, and five ensigns instead of the standard eight of each rank. There were just 17 sergeants, and 11 drums and fifes for the eight companies. The rank and file strength of the regiment on paper was 498, but there were now just 242, just about half, present and fit for duty. The regiment still needed 143 men to be complete.

Fifty men were sick but present, 106 were absent sick, and 100 were on command with the rangers, working at the laboratory, helping care for the sick, or performing other duties.[2]

—

The British began to withdraw from the White Plains area with their baggage the night of November 4. On November 6, the troops marched toward Dobb's Ferry, although many American soldiers thought they were heading back to Manhattan Island.[3] Samuel Capen optimistically and naively observed, "They appeared to be afraid to attempt to engage our main body and so they retreated."[4] Jacob recalled, "The British lay there a while and then left that place and our regiment marched after them about 3 or 4 miles farther east." Washington wanted to establish his position in the North Castle Hills containing defensible positions should the British return. Corporal David How says he left White Plains and marched to Mount Misery in those hills.[5] Even as the British withdrew, there was still danger while they were relatively near. Captain Farrington lost one man captured on November 5.[6]

Anticipating his men would inflict violence on area Loyalists after the battle, Washington's General Orders on November 2 had forbidden setting fire to any house or barn without special orders from a General Officer, and Jacob no doubt heard that order.[7] However, some men from Sargent's regiment did become involved in civilian property destruction. If he had not already heard it through the rumor mill, Jacob heard in Washington's General Orders on November 6 that, "It is with the utmost astonishment and abhorrence, the General is informed, that some base and cowardly wretches have, last night, set fire to the Court-House, and other Buildings which the enemy left. The army may rely on it that they shall be brought to justice, and meet with the punishment they deserve."

Two days later, Jacob heard orders that "The Court Martial of which Genl. McDougall is President, to sit immediately for the trial of Major William Austin in arrest, upon charge of Burning the houses at White-Plains, contrary to General orders."[8] Major Austin was twenty-five years old in 1776. He had graduated from Harvard, studied law under John Adams, and had served on the Chelmsford, Massachusetts Committee of Correspondence in 1774. He had helped write the Middlesex Resolves in August 1774 and had been prominent in many Chelmsford patriot activities.[9] He was currently the senior officer present in Jacob's regiment. The court found him guilty but only sentenced him to receive a reprimand. Major General Charles Lee found that sentence unacceptable and ordered a new court-martial, charging Austin with "wanton, barbarous conduct, unbecoming not only an officer, but a human creature."[10] The incident had personally upset Washington, and he wrote to Lee on November 12 that, "I hope the trial of Major Austin for burning the houses will not be forgot; publick justice requires that it should be brought on as soon as it can."[11]

A new court-martial met that day with Rhode Island Colonel Daniel Hitchcock as President. Austin pleaded not guilty. The first witness, Mrs. Adams, stated that a party of men came to her house the night of November 5. "They told her to get her things out of the house as quick as possible; that she attempted to take some things out of a bed-room, when some of the men told her to be gone or they would blow her through [shoot her]; that the party would not suffer her to dress her children, but drove them out of the doors naked" and then set the house on fire. When Mrs. Adams "asked Major Austin why he could not save her house, and burn the others; he replied, because you are all damned Tories, and there was a damned Tory taken out of your house this night." As she left it, "some of the men began to carry things out of the house, when she asked them why they took those things then Major Austin spake, and told her he should carry them to the General's, and alleged General Sullivan's orders for it."

Mrs. Adams continued that, "after some of her things were carried out of doors, some of the men insulted her with ill language, (in the presence of Major Austin,) such as damned Tories, &c, threatening to blow her through." She said her sister "took Major Austin by the arm crying," and he asked her why. She told him that he was an officer and could prevent the improper treatment. Mrs. Adams's mother "told Major Austin she hoped he would not burn her house too; on which he told her there was another house above that she might go into." Then Major Austin "told his men to go and set the other houses on fire as quick as they could." Private Elisha Dunham, who stood guard that night about a hundred yards from the burning houses, testified that he "heard the crying of women and children as he thought," and Private William Harrop corroborated his story.

On the trial's second day, Sergeant Churchill recounted the story using a very different tone when he testified that he had "been on a scouting party with Major Austin, and on their return the Major ordered him back with five men to the houses which they burnt, and told him to take good care of whatever things he got; to keep them safe, and bring them off to his markee [tent]." When Major Austin:

> *came to the house, he asked Mrs. Adams what time of night it was; he then asked her for a candle, &c., and told her he must burn the house and they must get their things and children out of the house, but told them not to be frighted, for he should not hurt them; and before the house was set on fire, he and his party did carry some of the things out of the house, such as bedding, wheat, &c.*

Major Austin then:

> *told the women they might go to a red house nearby, and if they would, his men should carry their things for them; that he heard no ill language towards the women from any of the party, neither in the house or out of doors, during the whole time they were there; that the women cried and seemed to be in great distress, but he told them they should not be hurt.*

Private Tilley How testified that:

> *When they came to Mrs. Adams's house, they asked the people what time of night it was, and asked them for a candle, and told them they must burn the house; that he immediately went to carrying things out of the house; that he waited for the aged woman to get up and dress herself; he then took both feather bed and straw bed on which she lay, and carried them out of doors; that he laid down the straw bed and the feather bed upon it, and told her to lie down on it; that he assisted in the carrying things out for about half an hour, as near as he could judge, before the house was set on fire, and then a straw bed was set on fire in the house by some of the men; that during the whole affair he heard no abusive language from any of the party towards the women or children.*

Tilley How further testified, "that what things were tied up in two blankets were carried to the Major's markee [tent], and all the rest were left with the women; that the house the aged woman desired her things might be carried to was on fire when the Major first came to Mrs. Adams's house." Private James Linzer corroborated Churchill's and How's testimony. Captain

Keith said he was present with Major Austin and agreed with the statements given by Sergeant Churchill and Tilley How.

The court then asked Major Austin whether he had orders to burn the houses, and he confessed he did not. However, he "alleged as an excuse his being in company with some of the General Officers just before the houses were burnt on the Plains, and heard General Putnam say he thought it would be best to burn all the houses, &c., and finding there was houses burnt on the Plains soon after, he thought it his duty to burn the said houses as he did."

This second court found Austin guilty of "behaving in a scandalous, infamous manner, such as is unbecoming the character of an officer and a gentleman," and sentenced him to be discharged from the service.[12] Since Major Austin, as the only field officer present in Jacob's regiment, had been running the regiment in the absence of Colonel Sargent and Lieutenant Colonel Jackson, his departure left the senior captain, Frederick Pope, to run the regiment.

—

Due to Sargent's debilitating wound, brigade command temporarily devolved onto Colonel John Chester, who commanded a Connecticut regiment in the brigade that was now part of Sullivan's Division under General Charles Lee. Lee took command of the troops at White Plains on November 10 with orders to defend against any British attack up the Hudson River or into Connecticut. However, if the British moved in force into New Jersey, he was to join up there with Washington, leaving his sick behind. On November 11, General Lee's daily orders gave his men the uplifting news that a force of Americans had defeated the Cherokee Indians in North Carolina and that the British army descending from Canada toward Fort Ticonderoga had returned north to end the campaign for the winter.[13] However, this news did not relieve the pressure felt by Washington's troops.

The muster return for November 16 continued to show manpower losses in Sargent's regiment that now had only 140 rank and file effective and present out of 488 men. That meant each of the eight companies averaged about 17 or 18 men rather than the 76 authorized. Captain Pope commanded the six captains, one first lieutenant, two second lieutenants, and two ensigns present with the regiment. There was also the adjutant and paymaster, but the quartermaster, surgeon, and his mate were missing. There were just ten sergeants and seven fifes and drums. Sixty-five men were present although sick, while 110 sick men were absent, and 173 were on command. The regiment lacked 152 men and one musician to be complete on paper. Since the last muster, one new enlistee had joined, and two men had been discharged.[14]

Jacob heard on November 17 that the day before, the British had captured Fort Washington and its garrison, including anyone he knew from the regiment on command there with the rangers. By that date, Washington had crossed the troops he had with him to New Jersey and several days later would begin his retreat across the State of New Jersey with British troops under General Cornwallis pressuring him.

—

During the period that had begun with the regiment leaving Horn's Hook on September 15, fifer Luther Cary lost his tent, blanket, overcoat, and shoes. Cary later recalled, "Exposed to the inclemency of the weather without any shelter I found my health so impaired that I was unable to do duty and my health continuing to decline about the middle of November applied to Capt Pope," then the senior captain commanding the regiment, to obtain "leave to retire from the camp and find some place better suited to my condition." Cary did not recover from his illness until sometime the following February after going to one of the hospitals in New York or Connecticut, where he was discharged.[15]

Washington had crossed his troops to the west side of the North River before November 20 and told Lee, "it would be advisable in you to remove the troops under your command on this side of the North River, and there wait for further orders."[16] Washington was beginning his long retreat across the State of New Jersey, keeping himself between the British and Philadelphia. He had hopes of bringing the British to battle at some advantageous position in New Jersey, but for that, he would need Lee's troops with him.

On November 24, Sargent's regimental muster showed 169 rank and file fit for duty, an improvement of 16 from the previous week, but still, the least of any regiment in the brigade. There were 41 men present but sick, a small improvement, and 139 absent sick, a significant negative change. One hundred men were on command. The regiment needed a sergeant, a musician, and 191 rank and file to be complete, at least on paper. Since the last muster, one recruit had joined, and three men had been discharged at the expiration of their enlistments.[17]

In addition to being low on men, the army was also short of other things. General Lee justified his reluctance to march and join Washington because "part of the troops are so ill furnished with shoes and stockings, blankets, etc., that they must inevitably perish in this wretched weather. Part of 'em are to be dismissed on Saturday next [when their enlistments expire] and this part is the best accoutered for service."[18]

Lee had been collecting blankets and shoes and begged the Massachusetts and Connecticut governments to send those items forward. He also begged them to send militia to replace his Continentals as they left when their enlistments expired. Jacob and the men in Sargent's regiment were still at Mount Misery when they received orders on November 27 to fix their packs and cook provisions for a march. They struck their tents the next morning and marched out at noon for Peekskill, although Lee had been unable to obtain enough blankets and shoes for them. They reached Crompond, located in the town of Yorktown, just east of Peekskill, and stayed the night of November 29.[19]

By then, Washington was nearing the completion of his retreat across New Jersey. During the retreat, he had ordered General Lee several times to bring his troops to join him. However, Lee had delayed, creating incredible frustration in Washington.

—

After failing to obtain two regiments from General Heath at Peekskill to attach to his division, Lee's 4,000 men crossed the North River between December 2 and 4 and began to march toward Morristown, New Jersey, leaving behind many sick men.[20] They left privates Thomas Powell and Titus Wood of Captain Barnes's company there, unable to do duty in their ill condition.[21] David Keith of Captain Keith's company was left behind and carried to the Stamford hospital by Joshua Strams of his regiment.[22] Caleb Leach of Keith's company says:

> *Towards the close of the year 1776 he was taken sick with the bilious fever in consequence of exposure and hardship, and was carried to the hospital in Stamford, Connecticut. Here he remained till an officer whose name he does not recollect came to the hospital and furnished him with money and a pass to get home. He was so frail that he often forgot the route to get home in Halifax, Massachusetts and had to ask directions.*[23]

The teenage substitute Samuel Capen says, "I was very healthy and never had any fault found of me. I always answered to roll call & to the name of [my father] Christopher Capen being a substitute for him." But in November, "my time was nearly out and then I had a number of large and painful boils and I went to what was called a recruiting hospital in a town called Rye and it was a Meeting House & went to another place for a short time & from there I was discharged with a number more and with an order to draw provision at several places on our way home." He got home towards the last of December or the beginning of January and rejoined his father and family.[24]

On November 30, Dr. Turner at Stamford, Connecticut, reported: "We are in a most crowded situation, with the sick of the army swarming as if there was no end to them for several days past, and continue so to do." He then listed men he felt should be given discharges because of their condition and asked for instructions on discharging others without obtaining permission from a higher authority. To quantify things, he noted, "There is not less than six or seven hundred invalids now in town, and I dare say not one quarter of them, if they were now in camp, would be of any further service this campaign."[25]

While Jacob, with Lee's troops, crossed the North River during the first week of December, Washington's troops crossed the Delaware River at Trenton to Bucks County, Pennsylvania to put a barrier between them and the advancing British. After crossing at Peekskill, Lee's troops encamped one night and then, according to Jacob, continued on to New Hampstead, now Ramapo, the Smith's Clove, Ringwood, Pompton, Hackensack, Paramus, and Acquackanonk. They reached Morristown on December 8, the day Washington completed crossing his troops to Pennsylvania and the British occupied the middle of the State to Trenton.[26] Jacob, of course, did not know this. He only knew that he was back in the former colony and now state, where he had been born but absent from for about a decade.

—

Colonel Sargent's wound had healed enough for him to rejoin his regiment in New Jersey on or about December 3, and the brigade again became Sargent's Brigade. But, upon arriving, he was greatly distressed to find his regiment reduced from the 727 officers and rank and file it contained when he had left Boston in July to just 197 now. He also found his lieutenant colonel crippled and his major sent home in disgrace. Four of his captains were deceased, and eight subordinate officers were disabled. Always looking out for his men, he proclaimed, "None but a parent can conceive of my feelings, my poor regiment had not received a cent of pay for four months." Therefore, once again, "I gave them a months pay for which I never received a cent for I never asked for it therefore could not expect it." He also collected 120 pairs of shoes, all he could obtain, and gave them to his men.

Years later, in 1819, former Corporal David How sent Sargent two pounds of apples in the autumn "as interest" for the shoes and promised to send two pounds "every year if he had an opportunity."[27] How was eternally grateful for the way Colonel Sargent had looked out for his men, as was Jacob and the other men of the regiment.

Orders went out the following day for "the whole Army to strike their tents to-morrow morning, at half past seven, and to parade in order to march by eight." Colonel Daniel Hitchcock's brigade would march in front, followed by Colonel Glover's brigade, then the wagons, and Colonel Sargent's brigade at the rear. General Alexander McDougal's brigade was annexed to Colonel Sargent's. Hitchcock's and Glover's brigades would form the first line of defense if the enemy attacked the front, Hitchcock on the right and Glover on the left. Sargent would form a second line in the rear, with the baggage wagons paraded in a line in front.[28]

Word reached Lee's camp on December 8 that Washington had completed crossing his army to Pennsylvania at Trenton. But, instead of rapidly proceeding to join up with Washington, Lee kept his troops at Morristown from December 8 to 11 while he contemplated whether to march to Washington's assistance, as Washington had ordered, or attack the British at Brunswick or Princeton. Lee considered his men were currently not in condition to move out because they lacked shoes. On December 10, Washington wrote to Lee telling him that General Howe was definitely planning to proceed against Philadelphia, and he needed him and his troops badly. Lee finally ordered General Sullivan on December 12 to depart with their forces and march to join Washington in Pennsylvania. They would march to Germantown on the road to Easton, Pennsylvania.

On December 12, Lee's troops marched to Bernardstown and stayed the night in the woods. Lee himself decided to spend the night, with a guard of about 15 men, at a tavern run by Widow White at Basking Ridge some three miles away. There, Lee became a British prisoner when captured the morning of December 13 by Lieutenant Colonel William Harcourt with about 25 troopers and four officers of his 16th Regiment of Light Dragoons.[29] Jacob heard the gunfire, and a group of men, including Corporal How, pursued the dragoons for eight miles but were too late to overtake the British and their important captive.[30]

—

Now commanded by Major General Sullivan, the division got into motion and marched to the New Jersey town of Bethlehem on December 14. The following day they marched to Phillipsburg, where they crossed the Delaware River to Easton, Pennsylvania, and got their baggage and wagons across the next day. They marched to the Pennsylvania town of Bethlehem on December 17, where they stayed in the woods, then marched to Springfield the next day and stayed the night. The following day they marched to Buckingham and camped out there over a very snowy night.

The men drew more stockings and shoes from Colonel Sargent on December 20 and then marched about seven miles the next day to Solebury, where they encamped in the woods.[31] Jacob recalled, "Our company lay off from the river a few miles below Coryell's Ferry & above Howell's Ferry."[32]

—

On September 16, at the time of the battle at Harlem Heights, Congress had authorized raising a new, three-year army to replace the one-year 1776 army. This change mirrored the changes taking place when Jacob had joined the army at the end of 1775; one army was dissolving while another was taking form to replace it. Again, just as in 1775, the army wanted to recruit as many veterans as possible for the new army. Jacob no doubt felt that pressure of the call to reenlist. Although Jacob's regiment had fought well, the men and officers had not always acted with the best discipline between actions. But, Jacob had demonstrated a high level of discipline.

As with his initial enlistment, this decision would have him consider a combination of need, a sense of duty, and a desire for recognition. However, this time he also considered whatever sense of fellowship he felt among his comrades-in-arms that had developed during the months of hardships they experienced together and how it extended to feelings of community or family in the army after a year in the same company and regiment. Did Jacob still feel separate due to race or other factors?

While political and military leaders preferred men to volunteer for the new army for ideological reasons, in reality, they understood that Continental military service represented an employment contract agreed to by the soldier and the Congress, supported by the province maintaining the regiment. Jacob had experienced ample evidence of the failures of Congress and Massachusetts to live up to that contract.

During the final months of his enlistment, the situation Jacob faced in the army is described well in a letter from North Carolina Congressional delegate William Hooper to fellow delegate Joseph Hewes. Hooper wrote it on November 5 while Jacob's regiment was recovering from the Battle of White Plains and wondering what would come next. Hooper's letter described things as:

> *We shall under the best of Circumstances find difficulty enough to reinlist our Army, without Blankets, without cloathing in an extreme cold country, without a probability of these difficulties being suddenly removed, Men will not easily be tempted to persevere in a service where they are to purchase honour at so dear a rate. The Enlistment of 9/10ths of our Army will expire before the last day of December, of great part of them in the middle of November & of very many in the beginning of December. The greatest number that are enlisted for a longer time and will be at the command of the Cont. in the beginning of January will not be above 2000, a handful to conflict with 25000 British troops. I find to my sincere mortification that no measures have yet taken place for recruiting in Camp. This has been entrusted to the respective states and has succeeded as I expected, What is everybodys is nobodys business. Already such a hatred to the Eastern troops exists in the Southern Corps, that it requires the utmost exertions of the Genl. Officers to prevent its breaking out into acts of violence and occasioning a general schism in the Army.*[33]

—

An army muster return dated December 22 showed Colonel Sargent's Brigade of six regiments, Sargent's, Ward's, Chester's, Reed's, McDougall's, and Ritzema's, now reduced to about the size of just one complete regiment with 672 rank and file present and fit for duty out of a possible 1,639. The six regiments ranged in size from just 36 to 221 men, with Sargent's about average. Sargent's eight companies only had six captains, three first lieutenants, no second lieutenants, four ensigns, eight sergeants, and just

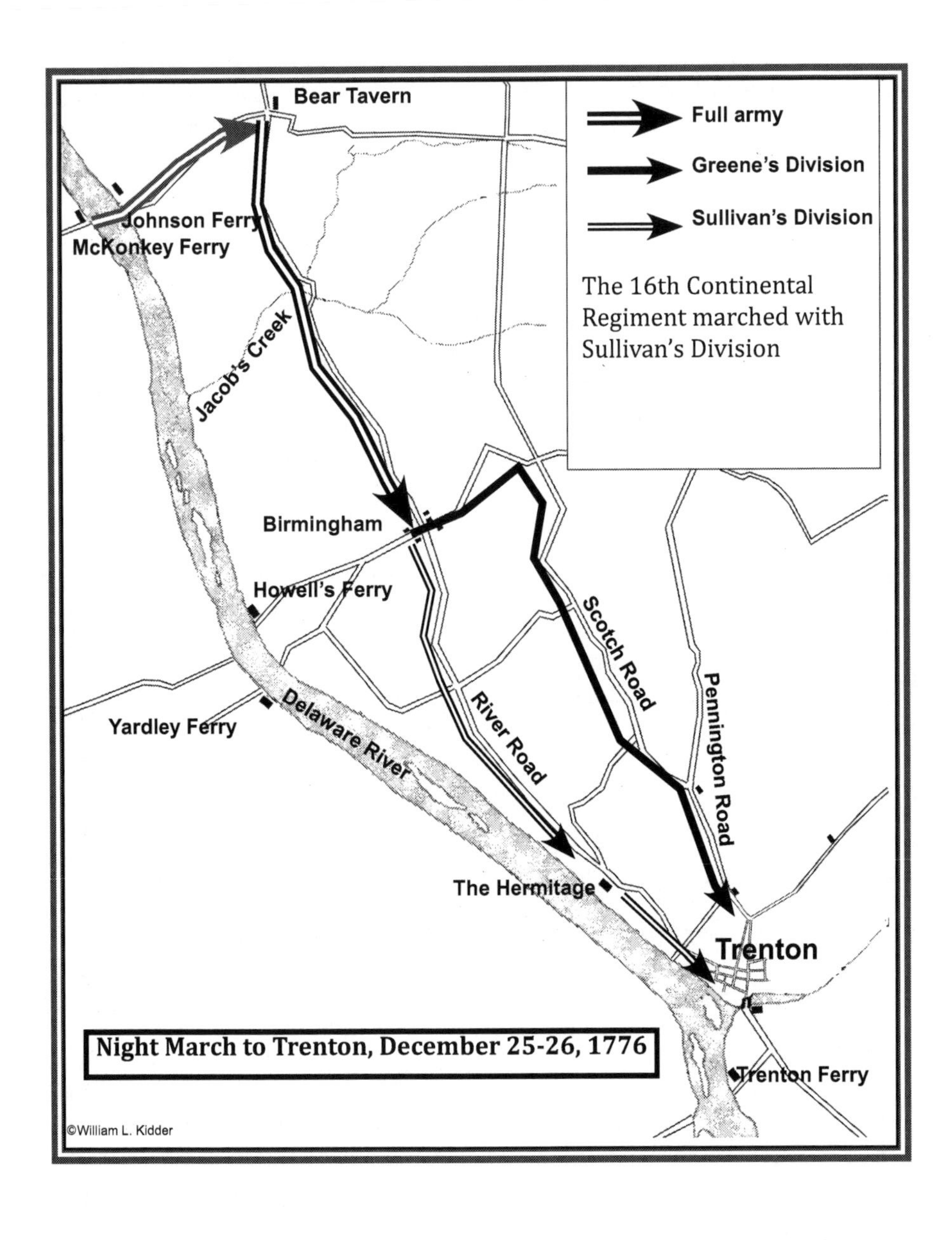

Night March to Trenton, December 25-26, 1776

five drummers and fifers, leading only 122 men present and fit for duty. The eight companies averaged just 15-16 men each. Six men were present, although sick, while a whopping 235 were absent sick. Seventy-two men were on command.[34]

Jacob's regimental remnant moved on from Solebury about four miles to shelter in houses on December 23 and drew cartridges and provisions on the 24th for a "scout" the following day.[35] Along with the other men surviving in his regiment, Jacob received 60 cartridges.

Colonel Sargent received orders at noon on December 25 to march about twelve miles down to the river at McConkey's Ferry. Upon arriving near the ferry, the men learned that Colonel Glover's 14th Massachusetts Regiment, containing many racially diverse men from Marblehead, supplied crews for the boats carrying troops over the river. They were assisted by local men who had strong ferry boat operation skills, some of them serving in the local militia for either Pennsylvania or New Jersey.

Two Hunterdon County, New Jersey militiamen who knew the area well joined Sargent's Brigade to accompany with them as guides on the march to Trenton. Colonel Knox assigned four artillery pieces and their crews to Sargent's Brigade. At sunset, it began to drizzle, and it was raining by the time they got to the river.

About 11:00 pm, a severe storm with high winds developed, making it even more challenging to get the soldiers across and safely ferry over the horses, artillery, and wagons.[36] Washington had chosen to cross at a ferry because it could provide the flat, barge-like ferry boats, attached to and guided by overhead lines stretching across the river. These boats were vitally needed to get the many horses, supply and ammunition wagons, and 18 artillery pieces across the river safely. The ferry boats were designed to take civilian horses, wagons, stagecoaches, and passengers on foot across the river, so it was easy to adapt them to military service. The weather presented the real problem.

Washington had also collected some sturdy Durham boats to get the troops across. These were 45- to 65-foot long boats, about eight feet wide, curving to a point at both ends like a canoe. They were strongly built and designed to carry heavy bulk cargoes up and down the river, not across it. While the conditions made use of the ferry boats difficult, getting the Durham boats safely across was perhaps equally challenging. Once out in the river, the crew had to fight the current pushing them downstream. This effort required pointing the boat partly upstream while rowing against the current and perhaps also using the long poles to push against the river bottom. The floating pieces of sheet ice just magnified the problems. It was exhausting work for the boat crews as each heavy, awkward vessel made several round trips across the river, transporting the approximately 2,400 troops.

—

Sargent's men were among those who had not been crossed by midnight, the planned time to complete the crossing.[37] They finally began their crossing river sometime after midnight. Jacob probably crossed in a Durham boat with Captain Wiley's company and several other Sargent's regiment companies that were now so decimated. He may have been among the men who wondered why the army was taking so much artillery across in the foul weather, including those pieces he saw crossing on the flat ferry boats. However, Jacob knew he would have difficulty keeping his gunpowder dry in the storm and may have been encouraged knowing that artillery was considered a foul weather weapon that the troops could fire successfully even when wet conditions reduced the reliability of muskets. During his crossing, Jacob no doubt heard Colonel Knox's deep bass, "stentorian" voice as he loudly directed the crossing maneuvers. That voice could be heard above the wind and crunch of the ice that filled the river with floating sheets and pieces.[38]

After he reached the New Jersey shore and clambered out of the boat, trying to avoid getting wet with freezing river water, Jacob helped to build fires to keep himself and others warm until the march to Trenton began, whenever that would be. Jacob could feel the storm increasing in strength, and "it rained, hailed, snowed, and froze, and at the same time blew a perfect hurricane," causing the fire to slice through "in a moment" the fence rails the men burned for warmth. To keep warm, like everyone else, he had to keep turning around before the fire. While finding little success keeping warm, Jacob may have found that the noises of the river crossing, the clearing away of the ice, the rattle of cannon wheels and wagon wheels on the frozen ground, and the general cheerfulness of the troops took away any fears and doubts he had about the imminent actions.[39]

It was not until about 2:00 am that all the infantrymen got across, and the artillery did not finish crossing until about 3:00 am. Sargent's regiment finally formed up with the other troops about 4:00 am, still suffering from the constant snow, rain, and hail, and began to march, four hours behind schedule. General Adam Stephen's Brigade of Virginia regiments led off the march, followed by the rest of General Greene's second division, led by General Mercer's Brigade, then General Stirling's, and then General Roche de Fermoy's. Each brigade marched with its assigned Hunterdon County militia guides and Continental artillery pieces.

General Sullivan's first division followed next, led by Colonel Sargent's Brigade with four artillery pieces, then Colonel Glover's Brigade with three, and finally General St. Clair's Brigade, as the reserve, with two. Each brigade had several local militiaman assigned as guides. The whole army stretched for at least a mile along the road.[40] One fifer remembered, "we began an apparently circuitous march, not advancing faster than a child ten years old could walk, and stopping frequently, though for what purpose I know not."[41]

Jacob marched through the storm with the way only lighted by torches secured to the artillery carriages that "sparkled & blazed in the storm all night."[42] He marched the first mile and half up a hill, rising about 200 feet, on a rough and icy road with the storm blowing in his face.[43] When the leading group reached the crossroads near the Bear Tavern, the New Jersey militia guides directed them to turn right onto the road that is today's Bear Tavern Road and continue marching in a more comfortable southeasterly direction with the storm now at Jacob's back. However, the road was still slippery and challenging to follow.

They marched through a combination of open fields and forested wood lots. The uneven roads were strewn with rocks and stumps and contained ruts and holes filled with slushy water. Farm crop fields alternated with stretches of trees to border the dirt road. No portion of the road could be traversed easily by the large group of men attempting to march eight abreast, with their officers on horseback and accompanied by horse-drawn cannon and supply and ammunition wagons, and parties of guards out on the flanks. The leading units experienced the best road conditions, which were still ugly. Each successive group found the road conditions progressively more difficult after previous units churned up the road even further.[44] Jacob's regiment, marching in about the middle of the column, suffered from the churned-up road conditions produced by the elements of the army preceding it while also making things even worse for those who followed.

After proceeding about a mile and a quarter, the leading troops came to a deep ravine containing Jacob's Creek. The men unhitched the horses pulling the artillery pieces. Although the road angled as it descended the ravine to reduce its steepness, they had to move the cannon slowly after attaching them to long ropes wrapped around trees as mooring posts. The men locked the carriage and limber wheels in place using tree branches run between them to jam the wheel spokes to prevent wheel rotation and a runaway object. At the bottom, they had to ford the ice-cold creek water churned up by the storm and the army's passage. After crossing the creek, they had to haul each cannon up to the more level ground, consuming a lot of time and contributing significantly to the fatigue of man and horse.[45]

After clearing the Jacob's Creek ravine, the road leveled out with only a gradual rise. However, the storm's fury increased amid alternating rain, snow, and hail driven by varying and often intense winds. Several soldiers froze to death when they sat down to rest and fell asleep. Jacob and the men in Wiley's company had to watch out for each other because many were ill or had trouble keeping up due to fatigue.[46]

Having joined with Washington's army so recently before this stormy night, Jacob and others in Sargent's regiment probably had little idea of just where they were going and why. By this point in his military experiences, though, Jacob probably found that situation pretty standard and believed that, as in the past, wherever they were going could not be any worse than where they had been. By keeping moving, he could at least hope for something better.[47]

Jacob did know that he was only a few miles from his place of birth, and he would like to be able to go there and search for his mother if she even still lived there. Apart from any such musings, during the march, Jacob probably heard Washington or another officer ordering the men in a loud voice above the storm to "keep by your officers for Gods sake keep by your officers."[48] Colonel Sargent recalled the march to Trenton as "one of the most boisterous nights ever experienced by man."[49]

After crossing a plateau, the road began to gently descend again for about a mile to the crossroads hamlet of Birmingham, about three-and-a-half miles from Bear Tavern. At Birmingham, the Bear Tavern road intersected the road leading west toward Howell's Ferry on the Delaware River and east to the Scotch Road.[50] They reached Birmingham, about halfway to Trenton, just about 6:00 am, a little before daylight.

—

At Birmingham, Washington had Greene and Sullivan, and other officers, synchronize their watches with his before the army split to follow two different routes to Trenton. Greene's division departed first, headed east toward the Scotch Road that would take them to the Pennington Road and bring them to the upper end of Trenton. Sullivan's division would have a slightly shorter route, so they delayed a bit before heading straight through Birmingham to take the River Road and attack Trenton at the opposite end of town from Greene's attack. At this point, Jacob's clothes, like everyone else's, froze to his back,[51] and although he had made every effort to protect his powder and musket firing mechanism from getting wet, those efforts had primarily been in vain. Bayonets would have to be relied upon, at least by those few men who had them.

Before reaching Trenton, Sargent's Brigade at the head of Sullivan's Division following the River Road caught up with a unit of about 40 men sent ahead of the crossing to set up roadblocks to maintain the secrecy of the attack. These men were raw recruits for the 1st New Jersey Regiment and led by experienced Captain John Flahaven.[52] These recruits joined in with the leading elements of Sargent's Brigade as the march continued toward Trenton.

About a mile outside the town of Trenton, within minutes of Greene's division opening fire at the Hessian guard post on the Pennington Road at the north end of town, Sullivan's Division engaged the Hessian Jäger picket posts near New Jersey militia General Philemon Dickinson's home, The Hermitage, on the River Road. Jacob may well have seen the Jäger in their green coats retreating hastily toward town while dodging a ten-round barrage of relatively ineffective artillery rounds fired by General Dickinson's militia troops stationed just across the river.[53]

When they got near the French and Indian War era stone barracks at Trenton, the 50 Jäger formed up and delivered just one volley before the Americans were upon them and they resumed their rapid retreat.[54] The Jäger hurried along Front Street, heading for the stone bridge over Assunpink Creek, still held by a Hessian picket, and escaped over it.[55] Their commander may well have thought that the other Hessians would join them on the high ground of Mill Hill just across the creek where they could defend themselves against the American attack. However, that never happened, so the Jäger headed south and then east to avoid capture and perhaps unite with other Hessian and British forces in the Bordentown area or Princeton.

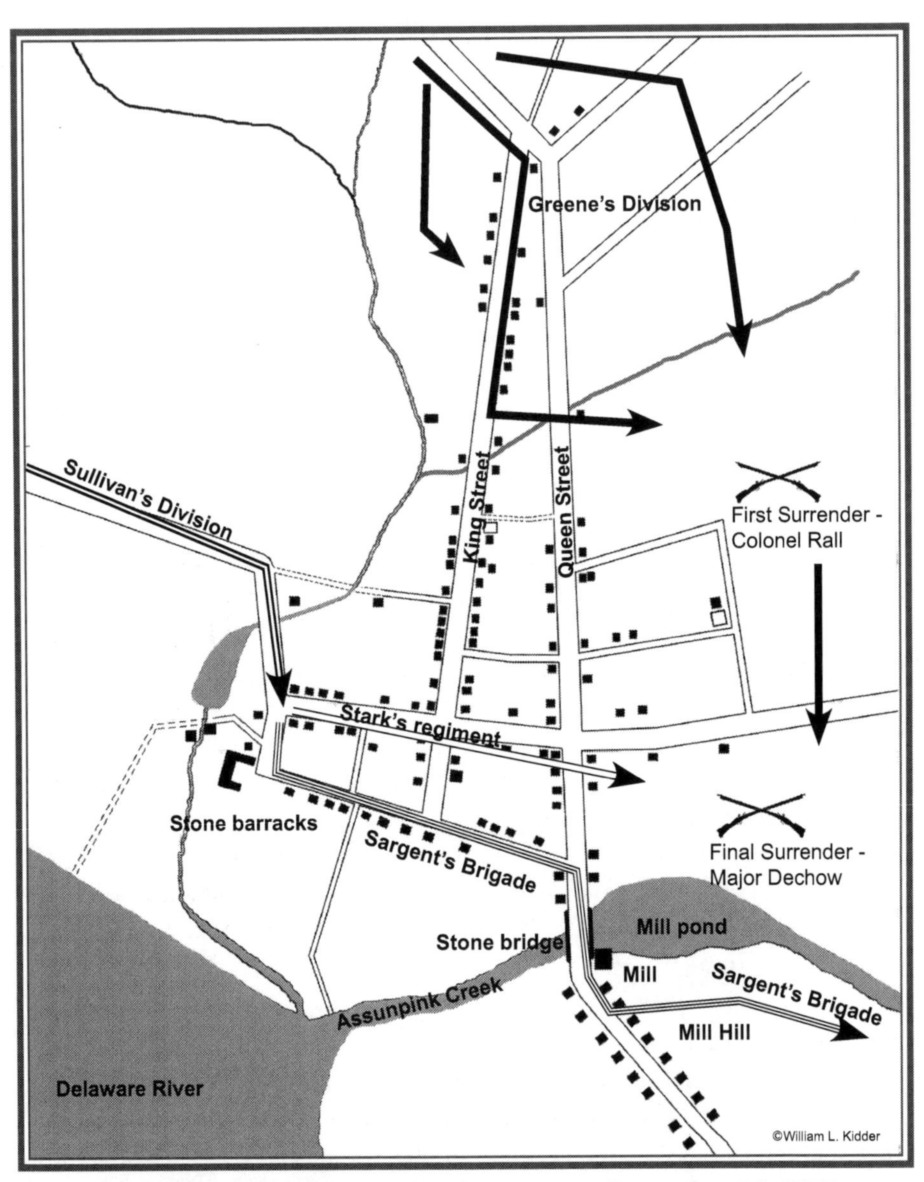

Conceptual Map of the Battle of Trenton on December 26, 1776.

After initial fighting in town, Colonel Rall moved his troops toward an apple orchard on the outskirts of the town where he was mortally wounded before surrendering. In the lower part of town, Sullivan's Division sent St. Clair's Brigade against the Hessian Knyphausen Regiment and Sargent's and Glover's brigades cut off access to the bridge on Assunpink Creek. They then took position on the Mill Hill side of the Assunpink Creek to prevent Hessian escape. The final surrender of the Knyphausen Regiment took place across the Assunpink from them.

Jacob entered Trenton on its southwest side and "marched down the street from the river road into the town to the corner where it crosses the street running out towards the Scotch road." That was King Street, where much of the early action was taking place. To his left, Jacob could see General Greene's troops engaged with the Hessians up King Street and hear the artillery fire and somewhat sporadic musket fire two forces exchanged. He also heard the shouts of Hessian officers trying to form up, and keep formed up, the men in their companies and regiments as they turned out in the streets but had to seek shelter from the American artillery fired down the street at them.

He may also have seen Colonel John Stark's New Hampshire regiment, accompanied by an artillery detachment, turn at the corner of Second Street and River Road to march toward the Hessian Knyphausen Regiment marching toward them from the Bull Head Tavern. A squad of Stark's regiment in the division advance captured some 60 Hessians. After about half an hour of fighting in the wind, sleet, and snow, Jacob recalled, "the firing ceased & some officers, among whom I recollect was General Lord Stirling, rode up to Col. Sargent & conversed with him[,] then we were ordered to follow."

Sargent's and Glover's brigades crossed the stone bridge that the fleeing Jäger had crossed at the grist mill and occupied ground along Assunpink Creek at the foot of Mill Hill while St. Clair's forces secured the bridge.[56] Some American troops used the stone grist mill by the bridge as a fortress while fighting any Hessians who tried to cross the creek.[57] Once across the bridge, Colonel Sargent deployed his artillery pieces and began firing back across the Assunpink at the Hessian Knyphausen Regiment. Jacob could see where a Hessian cannon had become stuck in some mud, delaying the Hessian troops as they struggled to free it. This delay allowed the Americans to secure the bridge and Mill Hill beyond it.[58]

Major Friedrich von Dechow, commander of the Knyphausen regiment, received a mortal wound and decided to surrender, seeing no possibility of escape for his troops. Dechow hobbled along toward Queen Street, aided by a corporal who tied a white handkerchief to his spontoon, a short pike carried by a non-commissioned officer, and held it high as they walked toward Joshua Newbold's house to give themselves up. Dechow surrendered to General Sullivan when he reached Queen Street.[59]

After Dechow departed the battlefield, men from his regiment decided to proceed up along the Assunpink to look for a ford they could use to escape the town but they ran into Colonel Glover's Brigade that had crossed back toward town at the ford the Hessians could have used. One group of Hessians attempted to negotiate the ice-cold water in the creek, and some men found themselves up to their necks in the frigid water, struggling for footing on the muddy creek bottom. At least one officer did get across. Several men drowned, while others found it too deep and turned back.

The panic of the Hessian troops increased from hearing the frantic noises made by their servants, women, and musicians who gathered by the creek with much of the brigade's baggage. While some of the Knyphausen men were trying to swim across the millpond, Stirling's brigade came marching up to within forty steps of them, where they formed into two columns, with two cannon in front.[60]

Now surrounded, the Knyphausen regiment faced Stephen's and Fermoy's brigades from Greene's Division on the north, Glover's Brigade on the east, Sargent's Brigade to the south, and St. Clair's Brigade guarding the bridge. Mercer's and Stirling's brigades of Greene's Division held the rest of the town. A mounted officer from Stirling's Brigade rode toward Captain Friedrich von Biesenrodt, now the senior Knyphausen officer, and negotiated the surrender.[61] Jacob always remembered vividly that, "we were formed in line and in view of the Hessians, who were paraded ... and grounded their arms and left them there."[62]

—

St. Clair agreed to allow the officers to keep their swords and baggage and the noncommissioned officers to retain their swords and knapsacks. However, about an hour after the surrender, American soldiers took their swords and knapsacks from them.[63] After the surrender, some American soldiers circulated among the prisoners, "and after satisfying their curiosity a little, they began to converse familiarly in broken English and German."[64] A number of the less disciplined men broke into buildings to find kegs of alcoholic beveridges and began celebrating, much to Washington's and other officers' despair and anger.

Jacob may have had similar observations and feelings as artillery Sergeant Joseph White, who ever after remembered:

> *my blood chill'd to see such horror and distress, blood mingling together – the dying groans, and 'garments rolled in blood.' The sight was too much to bear; I left it soon, and in returning I saw a field*

> *officer laying dead on the ground and his sword by him, I took it up and pulling the sheathe out of the belt, I carried it off. It was an elegant sword, and I wore it all the time I staid in the army.*[65]

Captain Oliver Pond of the 13th Continental Regiment picked up a Knyphausen Regiment brass plated fusilier cap as a souvenir.[66] Jacob does not mention taking any souvenirs, so he probably did not.

Washington wanted to transport the Hessian prisoners across the Delaware River at the Trenton ferries so he could continue military operations to force the British to retreat from more of New Jersey, which they firmly occupied. Jacob was one of several men from his regiment "detached to go down & ferry the Hessians across to Pennsylvania."[67] He recalled, "about noon it began to rain & rained very hard. We were engaged all the afternoon ferrying them across til it was quite dark when we quit." They only got a very few prisoners across due to the continuing river ice in the Trenton falls area that had prevented militia troops under General Ewing from crossing the night before. However, at least one wagon loaded with Hessian arms was brought to the ferry at Trenton and safely taken across along with six Hessians.[68] He "slept that night in an old mill house above the ferry on [the] Pennsylvania side."

Because trying to cross at Trenton was so laborious and dangerous, the army and its prisoners, including Hessian women and children dependents, marched back to Johnson's Ferry, across from McConkey's, to cross back to Pennsylvania throughout the evening and night. This movement also helped break up the alcoholic celebrations by the less disciplined soldiers. Sargent's regiment did not get back across until the following day.[69]

—

Just what Jacob did for the next two or three days after spending that night of December 26 at the old mill house, he does not say. He probably helped guard the prisoners and perhaps marched them to Newtown, from where the army conducted them to Philadelphia on December 29. At that point, Jacob needed to find his company and rejoin it.

After resting his troops for two days, Washington decided to cross them back to Trenton. About the morning of December 30, Jacob got back across the river at one of the several ferry crossings and rejoined his regiment "where I had left them ... up the Asanpink east of Trenton." He says, "we lay there a day or two & then the time of the year's men was out and our regiment received part of their pay."

Back in Trenton, Jacob found the town exhibiting the brutal effects of the Hessian occupation and the battle. He could also see that Washington's army was now larger than it had been at the Trenton battle, and there were many more militiamen alongside the Continentals. He may have experienced a flashback to the previous December when the 1775 army was dissolving while the 1776 army was forming and militiamen kept arriving and augmented the army. A number of Washington's troops temporarily sheltered in houses that the Hessians had taken possession of in December and then abandoned the day of their defeat.

Among the residents who had remained in Trenton despite the Hessian occupation were some enslaved Black people whose owners had left them behind in town to do what they could to protect their enslaver's property. Buildings showed damage from artillery and musket fire, and many windows had simply shattered. Fences had been torn down for firewood. Jacob does not mention if he knew that some badly wounded Hessians had been left behind in several buildings in town, along with several Hessian medical officers, on parole. Every day between December 26 and December 29, one or more of these wounded men died and were buried at the Presbyterian Church. More would die during January and February, while others recovered.[70]

—

Having only two days left on his enlistment and knowing that Washington greatly wanted men to extend their enlistments for six weeks, Jacob had many conflicting thoughts as he pondered Washington's request. From the day of his enlistment in October 1775, he had seen men leave the army as individuals and even as entire regiments when their enlistments expired. Washington and his officers had made pleas each time to convince men to stay, but had generally failed. However, other men had always come in to replace them, both from militia sent to the army for short periods of time and from new enlistees. Washington's army was now actually growing in size with the addition of large numbers of New Jersey militiamen and Pennsylvania Associators (volunteer militiamen) whose morale had been raised by the Trenton victory.

Jacob often heard his fellow New England soldiers describe their commitment to the army as a voluntary contract. After fulfilling their obligation, they should be free to leave, especially when Congress and their State had failed to completely fulfill their part of the contract by frequently failing to provide promised food, clothing, and pay. However, he also remembered that men agreeing to stay and those whose enlistments were not yet expiring often yelled and cursed at the departing men. If he left, he would probably hear heated words yelled at him, more than likely tinged with racial judgments. Would his leaving convince some White men that Black men were not trustworthy to the cause they were fighting to win?

Among Jacob's considerations was the feeling that the army had never entirely welcomed him due to his race. However, some individual officers and fellow soldiers indeed accepted him, and he must have felt loyalty to them. He was now part of a community in the army, but did that feeling extend to a "band of brothers?" As a free Black man in New Jersey in the dead of winter, he would have no guaranteed home, community, or job if he departed that military community. He would need to start a new life in a culture and society that did not respect or welcome people of color any more than the army did, and perhaps even less.

Jacob still believed in the cause of independence and freedom for which he had been fighting. But, he had done his duty - in a more intense and life-threatening way than many men who supported the cause - and other men were joining the army. Jacob now had a unique opportunity to achieve his personal goal of finding out who he was and building a life for himself in his personal struggle for freedom from racial prejudice. It had now been about a decade since he had seen his mother, and he was now just about fifteen miles from where he had last seen her. If he could find her alive, he could learn his family name and abandon the name Gulick.

Jacob was just one among the many men whom Washington tried to convince to extend their enlistments for six weeks. Jacob assembled with his regiment to be addressed by newly promoted General Henry Knox and heard his commanding voice urge them to stay just a few more days. General Thomas Mifflin came up to Trenton from Bordentown to do the same. Washington also addressed the men while mounted on his horse, alluding to the recent victory at Trenton and telling them the army could now do more for the country than at any future time.

When no one stepped forward to extend, Washington spoke up again and told the men:

> *My brave fellows, you have done all I asked you to do, and more than could be reasonably expected; but your country is at stake,*

> *your wives, your houses, and all that you hold dear. You have worn yourselves out with fatigues and hardships, but we know not how to spare you. If you will consent to stay only one month longer, you will render that service to the cause of liberty, and to your country, which you probably never can do under any other circumstances. The present is emphatically the crisis, which is to decide our destiny.*[71]

Neither Jacob nor any of the others knew just what would happen in those six weeks if they extended. However, several men in Captain Perry's company now agreed to extend their enlistments. Josiah A. Crossman later stated he had been in the regiment the entire year and "requested to stay six weeks longer" along with "most part of his company."[72] Adam Nichols of Perry's company had caught smallpox in Boston and did not rejoin the company until early October when he rejoined and fought in the Battle of White Plains and all subsequent actions. He also extended his enlistment for six weeks, fought at Princeton, and went to Morristown, where Colonel Sargent discharged him with the remainder of the company.[73]

—

Among those who did not extend their enlistments were the men too sick to continue in the army. Throughout Jacob's fourteen months in the army, he had seen many of his fellow soldiers, including his officers, suffer from various illnesses. Those with milder cases remained in camp during their recovery, while the medical staff sent men with more severe cases to military hospitals until able to resume their duties. These sicknesses had severely depleted Sargent's regiment over the year.

In addition to losing the men who died from disease, those who became incapacitated received early discharges. For example, Jacob Hayden had developed smallpox and remained at Boston's Castle William when the regiment left for New York. Subsequently sent to the hospital at Brookline, Massachusetts, he remained there for over three months before being moved to the Boston hospital, where he received his discharge in November. He was one of the few men to receive a written discharge, which came in handy later when charged as a deserter.[74] Lemuel Field had taken sick while the regiment was at Kingsbridge in October and went into the hospital for about two weeks. He tried to resume duty, but finding himself physically unable to perform it, returned to the hospital, where General Sullivan discharged him in November.[75]

Many men received their discharges the same day that Jacob's enlistment expired but at locations distant from Trenton, such as White Plains or Peekskill, New York, or Stamford, Connecticut, where they had gone for hospitalization. Among these were Captain Vinton's son John, who came down with smallpox in the summer and developed complications that kept him hospitalized until his discharge in January.[76] Other men also discharged from his company on January 1 included Samuel Bisbee and Joshua Stearns.[77] Fifer Hezekiah Packard of Captain Keith's company became hospitalized several weeks before the year's close and returned home verbally discharged without a regular discharge paper in January.[78] Jedidiah Russell says that on January 1, 1777 at the Peekskill hospital, more than twenty men were "drawn up in line & treated with some rum & were dismissed with good wishes for a safe return to our homes without any written discharge."[79]

—

Even though Black re-enlistment rates were strong during the war and Jacob did not express dissatisfaction with army life, he did not extend, even for the ten-dollar bounty Washington offered. Jacob recalled, "I had 7 ½ months pay due to me & I believe others had the same. I received 3 months pay & all the rest of the regiment received the same & and we were ordered after a certain time to come to Peekskiln on the North River and then we should receive our pay." He noted, "I was with the regiment & in service from the time of enlistment. At that time about 14 months and never left it until I had received the three months pay and had permission to return to the place of my nativity in Amwell about 15 miles from Trenton." He received only a verbal discharge and was told he would receive a written discharge when he reported to Peekskill for the remainder of his pay. Although he would now be free of the army, he had no concrete plans aside from finding his mother and learning his family name. However, he had not given up on the cause for which he had fought.

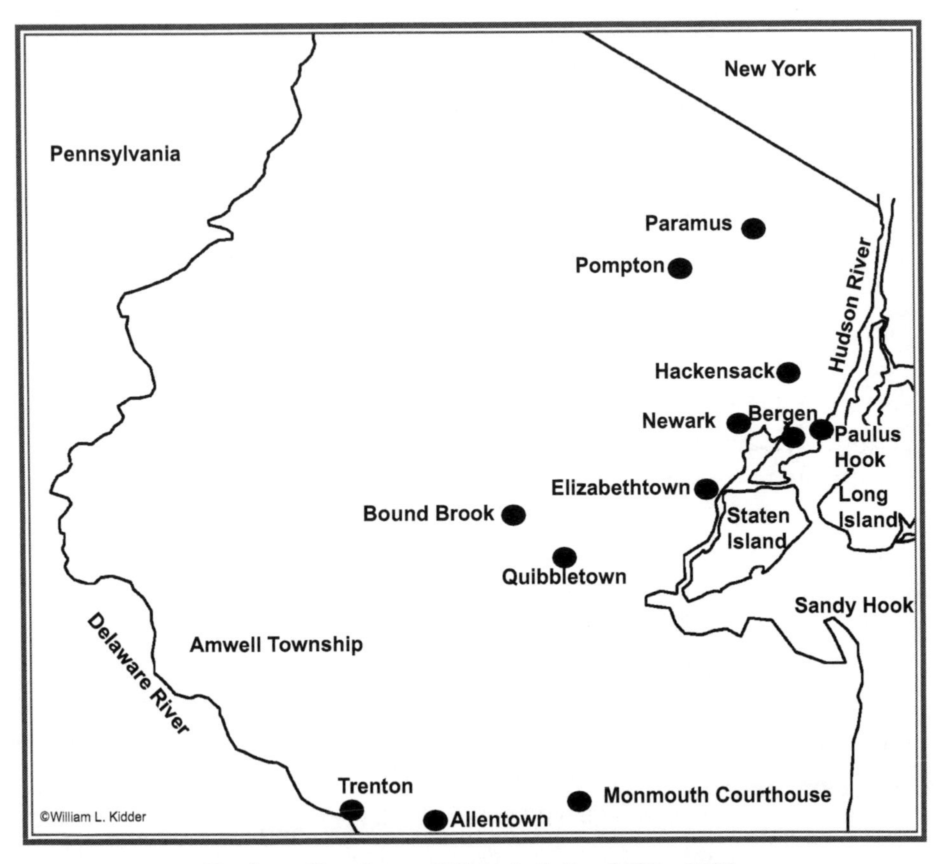

Northern New Jersey Militia Activity - 1777 - 1783

Map of north portion of New Jersey showing locations mentioned by Jacob Francis as places he served at during his one-month call-outs for active militia duty.

I immediately returned from Trenton to Amwell & found my mother living, but in ill health, I remained with her and when the time came to go to Peekskiln for my pay and discharge I gave up going and never received either my pay or a discharge in writing that pay 4 ½ months at 40/ a month £4.0.0 proc[lamation]:money equal to $24 as yet due to me from the United States. – Jacob Francis

18

New Jersey Militia Service 1777-1783

AFTER AWAKENING TO THE SOUND OF THE DRUM EARLY ON THE MORNING OF January 1, 1777, Jacob and the other men from his regiment who were not extending their enlistments prepared to depart the army from Trenton. During the morning, Jacob drew his incomplete pay and "Sase" [sauce] money to help purchase food on his trip home.

Jacob does not indicate hearing any negative comments or shouts from soldiers not departing. Rather than being seen as "sunshine patriots," these men were tough survivors who had stayed with the army through various dangers and terrible situations and, unlike others, had not deserted before the expiration of their enlistment. They had faithfully fulfilled their contract, and some were now in such terrible health that, although not hospitalized, they could not do much anyway. The large number of militiamen coming into camp and augmenting the army also lessened the concern over their departure on the verge of additional combat action.

Jacob was now a free man, neither indentured nor under the control of the army. He had personal goals but no definite plan lined out to achieve them. Jacob was stepping out into what was to him a largely unknown geography and culture. He must have had a strong sense of confidence in himself and his ability to deal with whatever life presented to him. One thing was definite, though, he had not given up on the cause for freedom and equality, especially for Black people, for which he had risked his life and fought to achieve side by side with White and Black men for fourteen months.

The day Jacob and the others whose enlistments had expired left the army, the new longer term version of the Continental Army became official. It contained the veterans who had reenlisted for three years or the duration of the war as an experienced nucleus to bolster the raw recruits, and for at least six weeks, it would include those men who had extended their previous enlistments. Changes to the army's structure included the reorganization of Sargent's regiment, now renamed Lieutenant Colonel Michael Jackson's Regiment, still composed of eight companies and assigned to Colonel Sargent's Brigade. Even as Washington looked to continue pressing the British, just like the 1776 army, his new army lacked its full complement of soldiers. Washington truly needed the many New Jersey and Pennsylvania militiamen who joined him at Trenton to participate in whatever actions he had planned for the next few weeks. Hopefully, the new Continental regiments could be brought up to full strength before the spring campaign began.

Corporal David How and others from Colonel Sargent's regiment who did not extend their enlistments departed in the afternoon, in all probability with Jacob among them, to begin their long walk to various points in New England. How noted in his diary that he was "about 500 miles from home"[1] and Noah Drake of Captain Pope's company set off wearing a "regimental coat with buttons marked or stamped on them No 20" rather than the number 16 for Sargent's regiment. He wore the coat for a different regiment because like everyone, including Jacob, he only had remnants of his army clothing supplemented with items acquired in various official and unofficial ways.[2]

Leaving their Trenton regimental camp, the men crossed the Assunpink Creek stone bridge and headed up King or Queen Street. They saw again the devastation from the Hessian occupation and the December 26 morning battle that had taken place among the houses and commercial and public buildings and on the somewhat more open orchard and farmland on the eastern outskirts of town.

When they got to the head of the street, they turned left onto Pennington Road to walk toward the hamlet of Pennington, then known as Penny Town, in Hopewell Township, located between Trenton and Amwell Townships. Using this indirect route, the men heading for New England avoided Princeton and the substantial British army then assembling there. Much of central New Jersey remained under British control, requiring the veterans returning home to make a wide detour around the British-occupied areas. The day was foggy and cloudy, with periods of rain and temperatures in the low forties climbing into the low fifties late in the day, melting the ice and snow and creating deep mud.[3] David How says they only went about four miles that day and then found a place to camp for the night.[4]

While Jacob made his homeward journey on January 1, Washington's army back at Trenton worked on their Mill Hill defenses, preparing for the British attack expected within a few days. Washington sent about 1000 troops up the main road toward Princeton to set up ambushes where streams crossed the road. He expected the British to approach Trenton by that road, and those ambushes would serve as harassment, not major actions, to delay the British army from reaching Trenton until late in the day. Jacob could identify with the uncertainties of those soldiers in Trenton anticipating a battle, much more readily than he could with the people he wanted to rejoin as he walked on his journey to an uncertain home and future life.

—

Jacob headed north into Amwell Township the following day, where How and the New England men bade him farewell. Leaving Jacob in Amwell, they marched northeast to Bridgewater, where they spent the night of January 2. They would continue on to Morristown for the night of January 3, then head for Ramapo and then Peekskill before heading to New England.

Jacob wore what remained of his tattered and filthy regimental uniform as he continued his journey and search for his mother. Having turned in his musket before leaving, he was unarmed. He could see how the area he walked through had suffered dramatically from British and Hessian plundering atrocities during their December occupation. The people still lived in fear, in contrast to their joy of several days before springing from Washington's December 26 victory because the British now had assembled an army at Princeton that it would use to seek revenge for that defeat at Trenton. Unless Washington could force the British stationed at and around Princeton to fall back toward New York, people still feared for the safety of their families and property.

Jacob had to be careful to avoid possible military patrols from both armies. In addition to possible British patrols from Princeton, local militiamen were also out in small scouting parties keeping an eye on any British foragers. People tended to interpret negatively any unknown Black man traveling alone. Therefore, any local inhabitant or militia patrol encountering an unfamiliar Black man in a ragged Continental Army uniform might suspect he was a deserter or a runaway enslaved man. Without a written discharge to identify him and his status as a veteran, those suspicions would multiply.

So, Jacob had to travel carefully, minimizing contact with other people while trying to locate his mother. He may have remembered particular farms and dirt roads from his childhood that could help him find his way to where he remembered she had lived. As Jacob walked, just two weeks short of his twenty-third birthday, he may have encountered people he had known during his first decade of life. Several of the farmers who had owned portions of his indenture time still lived in the area, as did other people he might remember. Henry Wambaugh was now in his late fifties and had two sons. Forty-eight-year-old Minne Gulick, whose family name Jacob had adopted, now had five girls and two boys, the oldest child about eight years old.[5]

—

At daybreak on January 2, the British began marching about 7,000 regulars and Hessians under General Charles Cornwallis from Princeton to Trenton on the deeply muddied road where the American harassment parties successfully delayed them at the stream crossings.

Very likely, Jacob found his mother alive that day. Finding her badly ill, he quickly decided to stay with and care for her for as long as she lived. While the two of them had much to tell each other about their lives over the past decade, Jacob was most curious about learning his family surname, feeling incomplete as a person without it. He soon learned that the family name was Francis, and from that day forward, he went by the name Jacob Francis. Unfortunately, he does not tell us the origin of the name. Was it the name of his biological father, whom he never even mentions existing? Was it the name of a former enslaver of his mother, if she ever had one? Was it just a name that his mother liked for some reason? Ironically, the surname's traditional origin comes from the Roman-Latin "Franciscus," which referred to the Franks and meant "a free man" around the fifth century.[6] Whatever the source, Jacob warmly accepted it and never again called himself Jacob Gulick.

—

While Jacob and his mother brought each other up to date on their lives, the few men still with Jacob's old regiment participated in the skillfully delayed late afternoon and evening battle across the Assunpink Creek at Trenton. Jacob and his mother may have faintly heard in the distance the concluding actions at dark that involved heavy cannon fire from both armies.

Jacob's former regiment mates weathered the cannonade and, after dark, kept their campfires burning. Shortly after midnight, upon stealthily receiving orders, they formed up quietly as the army very quietly departed Trenton and marched all night toward Princeton. Using several local militiamen as guides they avoiding the British night encampment by using a roundabout route and escaping the trap they appeared to be in there. Jacob and his mother knew nothing of this secretive march, which the British did become aware of but did not challenge, misinterpreting it as only preparation and repositioning for the resumption of fighting the following day. The mild daytime temperature plunged into the twenties at night, freezing the mud hard like concrete.

About dawn on January 3, the temperature measured only 21 degrees as Jacob and his mother awoke to start their day and as Washington's troops arrived near Princeton, ready to attack the roughly 1500 men the British had left there the day before. Jacob may have heard distant artillery fire near Princeton that morning and perhaps saw one or more American militia patrols out that day. British troops stationed at Princeton and marching south from town to reinforce the main army at Trenton, as ordered the night before, unexpectedly spotted part of Washington's army in the distance advancing towards Princeton. Washington's troops also unexpectedly spotted a few of the British troops. Neither side knew precisely what troops they had observed.

When each commander took steps to investigate the unknown troops, the Battle of Princeton began on farm fields south of the village. The Americans achieved a total victory and completed the encounter by mopping up British resistance in the village of Princeton. By evening, the Americans had commenced their march to Morristown, and the British at Trenton had rapidly marched to New Brunswick rather than follow them. Washington had achieved his goal of driving the British out of most of New Jersey and raised expectations for the Revolution's eventual success. The British no longer controlled the area where Jacob wanted to establish his free life.

Jacob had likewise achieved his goal of finding his mother and learning his family name. He was now free to pursue his life, while still having to fight through and around the systemic racism constraints of eighteenth-century

New Jersey. Jacob had proven to the army that he was a valuable soldier who did his job skillfully, stayed healthy, and kept out of trouble. Now, Jacob wanted to prove to the White-dominated New Jersey culture that he could overcome its racist obstacles to achieve success and raise a family who would carry on the fight for equal freedom for all that he had waged in the army.

—

Jacob immediately commenced his efforts to build a settled life for himself in New Jersey at a time when White inhabitants continued to debate their varied attitudes toward slavery and the humanity of Black people. Not wanting to leave his mother while she lived and deeply involved in settling down in Amwell, Jacob never went to Peekskill to receive his back-pay and written discharge.

Washington's leadership in the "ten crucial days," beginning with the Battle of Trenton and ending with the Battle of Princeton, had saved the Revolution by driving a significant portion of the occupying British army out of New Jersey, and the remainder would leave in the spring. For Patriots in general, this considerable change revitalized their faith in the success of the Revolution. For Jacob, it meant that he would be able to start his new life in the place of his birth without danger from a British army of occupation. Jacob had helped achieve all this with his service in the Continental Army; now, he would help maintain it by serving in the New Jersey militia for what turned out to be the next six and a half years.

Following the expectations for men under New Jersey law, Jacob signed into the local Amwell militia company commanded by Captain Philip Snook, brother-in-law of Jacob's former indenture time owner Henry Wambaugh. The modified New Jersey militia law passed on March 15, 1777, two months after Jacob's return, made no distinction of race but simply stated "all effective men between fifteen and fifty" should serve.[7] Throughout the remainder of the war, subsequent militia acts did not exclude men by race but did say or imply that they must be free. Jacob had been able to join the Continental army largely because it could not find enough White recruits. Now, so much was being asked of the New Jersey militia, and so many men took advantage of ways to avoid service that officers were more than willing to accept any men agreeing to serve for themselves or as substitutes for others.

However, Jacob was much more than just a man willing to serve. As a 14-month veteran of the Continental Army who had experienced months of siege warfare and several face-to-face battles with the British regulars and Hessians, Jacob brought highly valued military experience to his militia company. He used his military expertise skillfully and faithfully whenever called out for active duty. Fellow Amwell militiamen Jerome Waldron, John Manners, and Moses Stout remembered long after the war that when they served in the militia with Jacob, everyone knew he had served in a New England Continental regiment. They could readily see how that experience contributed to the high quality of his service. Jacob even used New England military jargon, such as referring to his knapsack as his "snap sack," the term he informed his amused New Jersey friends that the "Yankeys" called it. John Manners long recalled his many conversations with Jacob about his Continental service they had during their mutual militia service and continuing after the war.

—

Jacob turned out for his first one-month tour of active militia service in 1777 after the reduced British forces remaining in New Jersey after the battles of Trenton and Princeton had left the State. Later in life, Jacob gave an excellent description of how the New Jersey militia system worked by employing what he called "the months service." He said, "The militia took turns[,] one part went one month & then the other part went out a month & relieved them & then those that were out the first month went again[,] so that one half the militia in this part of Jersey was out at a time & this continued several years."[8]

During the remaining six years of the war, depending on current needs, captains periodically divided the men in each company into up to eight "classes." Each month orders called out one or more of those classes, as needed. The division into classes allowed the men in a family, and men living close to each other, to serve in different classes. This usually prevented all men in a family or neighborhood from being called out on active duty simultaneously. It also facilitated keeping the economy functioning.

The downside was that each month's call-out assembled men into make-shift companies that had not trained together. Because the officers also rotated duty, men often served under officers with whom they were unfamiliar, and captains seldom led a company of men they had trained together. In any given month, captains might command classes drawn from several companies joined together temporarily just for the month. Likewise, privates, non-commissioned officers, and subaltern officers might serve under a captain and field officers they did not know well.

Captain Snook's company belonged to the Third Hunterdon Regiment, composed of men living in Amwell Township. This regiment often worked closely with the First Hunterdon Regiment, consisting of men from Trenton, Hopewell, and Maidenhead townships.* The classes from both regiments called out each month combined into one make-shift regiment. The commanding officers of the two regiments alternated command each month. So, while Jacob signed into Captain Snook's company, he did not always serve his month-long tours of active duty under him. There were times when he had a different captain from either the Third or First Regiment. For example, under this system, around 1777 Jacob served at times with Captain John Phillips or Captain Charles Reading, in addition to sometimes with his regular company commander Captain Snook.

Because men often got called out every other month, especially early in the war, they found it very difficult to conduct other aspects of their life, including keeping their farms or businesses going. Consequently, men often paid a fine or hired a substitute for a month-long tour when they felt they just could not afford the time away from home or their business. However, only relatively well-off men could afford this option.

As a man trying to make his way toward a respected life, Jacob says, "I always went out when it came to my turn to the end of the war as one of the militia & went out once as a substitute for a person who was to go but could not and gave me $75 continental money to take his place and I did & served the month. The name of this person I am unable to recollect as I was not particularly acquainted with him."[9] Serving a month as a substitute did not give Jacob credit for his regular service. The month he substituted could well have been sandwiched between two months when he served his own call-outs so that he may have served three consecutive months.

Periodic incursions by British soldiers coming over from Staten Island into New Jersey to forage for supplies or harass the Patriots, in addition to dealing with Loyalist activities, created a constant need to call out western New Jersey militiamen to defend eastern New Jersey. Jacob mentions frequent tours at Elizabethtown, Newark, and other parts of East Jersey. During his first tour of duty in late spring 1777, Jacob says, "We marched first to Elizabeth Town & staid a month. We laid part of the time at a place near there called Hallstead's point," located on Staten Island Sound directly

---

**Today this would be part of the city of Trenton, Ewing Township, Hopewell Township, and Lawrence Township.*

across from the northwestern corner of Staten Island. Fellow militiaman Jerome Waldron later remembered, "Jacob Francis a colored man being in the same service." They served a month and marched down to Elizabethtown, to maintain picket guards at different places along the sound, such as Hallstead's Point and De Hart's Point, to watch the British and Loyalist "refugees" on Staten Island. Jerome Waldron recalled Sergeant Goffe mounting the guard and "Jacob being on guard and standing sentinel." He noted that Jacob "was a good soldier and always did his duty well."[10]

Jacob found that his so-called one-month tours of duty could vary in length and that travel time across the state on foot did not count as part of the assigned time. When called out on an alarm, the time out could vary wildly but was usually no more than a month, plus travel time, so long as the militiamen called out for the following month relieved them on time. This variable duty routine made it very difficult for a man to plan the other aspects of his life. However, for a single young man like Jacob, in addition to substituting in the militia for pay, short-term jobs were frequently available to cover for men out on militia service for a month. The rotating one-month tours to eastern New Jersey continued through the war, although the time gaps between the later tours might be longer than a month. Jacob describes several tours without stating their specific dates, although he goes into great descriptive detail about them.

Unless a militiaman kept a written record, he forgot some tours or the memory of one tour merged with another over time. Turning out so often made it challenging to keep things straight, and the differing personnel encountered on each tour resulted in confusion over who was where and when. Particularly memorable occurrences helped men to recall some individual tours. For example, John Manners recalled that he and Jacob served a one-month tour in the same company, commanded by Captain David Jones or John Phillips when they lay below Bound Brook and between there and Quibble Town. Samuel Corwine recalled seeing Jacob at Elizabeth Town serving in the militia in March 1778.[11]

—

One term of service that Jacob served appears to have been part of efforts to repulse a British foray under Sir Henry Clinton in mid-September 1777 that included the Battle of Second River at today's Bellville, New Jersey, just north of Newark. This tour may be the call-out that Jacob described as occurring at the time of the Battle of Brandywine, a much better-known battle. Jacob served a month under Captain Philip Snook and marched to Newark, where they stayed for a month and "lay in the building in Newark called an academy or schoolhouse."

They received an alarm that British and Hessian troops from Staten Island were attacking Elizabethtown, and:

> *one company marched out toward Elizabeth two miles or more along the road til we came to a piece of rising ground when the British came in sight. When we saw their numbers, we fired on them and then retreated & left the road to a place of low ground covered with bushes and lay on the west of the road. We turned into that. The Hessians I think came foremost.*

Jacob saw three columns of blue-coated Hessians, green-coated Hessian light infantry Jàger, and red-coated British regulars. He noted, those troops "got on the rising ground[,] fired on us & after we got off some distance some of us concluded to cross back toward the road and get a shot at them."

Jacob recalled that:

> *one Joseph Johnson belonging to the company & myself went. We separated and I crept along among the bushes til I got almost within gun shot when I heard a voice behind me and looked round & there was three Hessians near me that belonged to a flanking party and had got between me and the company. They took me prisoner. Johnson was some distance from me and was taken prisoner by another party.*

As a prisoner, Jacob says his captors "took me, out to the road, to the British army & [I] marched with them under guard through Newark and was carried some distance up the river called Second River. Night came on and sometime in the night we came to a creek that ran down into the river." At this point, Jacob recalled, "some of our militia, but I don't know who, expecting the British, had placed themselves in some bushes on the left of the road near the creek & fired on the British as we came up. This created some confusion & broke the ranks & the most of them left the road & turned off to the right toward the river."

Four Hessians guarded Jacob, and he says that when the militia fired the guards "turned on the alarm & left me." Now free but still in danger, Jacob recalled he "stood near a steep bank that ran down into some bushes toward the creek. Finding the men a little way from me. I stepped down the bank into the bushes and laid down. The militia that had fired retreated & I saw nothing of them. The British staid a few minutes, one of the captains was wounded, then they formed on the road again & marched on." Now ignored by his captors, Jacob says he "lay in the bushes some time til they were all gone then came out & pushed back to Newark & joined Captain Snook's company there about 2 o'clock in the morning." Despite all of that, Jacob could report, "I staid my month out." Captain Snook's brother, Peter, recalled the men received their usual verbal discharges at Passaic Falls at the end of their month. They were called out again shortly afterward, and Lieutenant Philip Service commanded the company because Captain Snook was ill.[12]

—

Along with his friend Moses Stout, Jacob served another one-month tour during which they went to Bound Brook and from there to Pompton. They remained there for a time, and the captain formed a scouting party of about sixty men, including Jacob and Moses, led by two subaltern officers.* The scouting party headed out toward the British lines by way of Paramus and Hackensack and "toward the English neighborhood as we called it down toward Bergen and Paulus Hook." Jacob recalled they went "a few miles to where there was an old guard house on the west side of the river that was unoccupied. And on the opposite side another which we supposed to be occupied by the British. We went to the guard house on the west of the river & staid an hour or two."

Across the river, the ground rose after a short distance. Jacob continues, "After waiting some time we saw some troops come over the rising ground at a distance & march down toward the river below us where they were obscured from our sight by an intervening road." The British appeared to outnumber them. Jacob says, "the subalterns who were with us apprehending they might cross the river below & come in on our rear ordered us to retreat & not to fire. We had not proceeded up the river far when a considerable party of the British troops we had seen below came in sight on the opposite side of the river and fired on us."

**Subalterns were the commissioned officers below the rank of captain and the term indicates lieutenants or ensigns.*

Now under fire:

> *The subalterns took the lead in the retreat & ordered us to carry on the march firing. We marched a little way. The British kept firing. I was behind the rest of our party and a bullet struck very near me upon which I suddenly turned around and fired. Then our whole party turned & fired on the British upon which they retreated. Again our subaltern officers had pushed on ahead and we saw no more of them. We marched on without them and joined the army at headquarters & I joined my company.*

—

Jacob "particularly" recalled being out on active duty for the Battle of Monmouth in June 1778. On that tour, Captain Snook's company was part of the composite First and Third New Jersey militia regiments commanded by Colonel Joseph Phillips of the First Hunterdon Regiment of General Philemon Dickinson's brigade. When called out, they marched to Trenton, then to Bordentown and Black Horse, then Allentown, and finally to near Craig's Mills between Englishtown and Monmouth Court House. Jacob and Captain Snook's company were part of the effort to shadow the British as they marched from Philadelphia across the State, heading for Sandy Hook. A significant battle interrupted the British march at Monmouth Court House on the exceedingly hot day of June 28.[13]

Jacob later said:

> *Our regiment & myself with it was on the battle ground & under arms all that day, but stationed on a piece of ground a little to the northwest of where the heat of the battle was, & were not actively engaged with the enemy but our Captain Snook, was permitted to go or went for the course of the day for some purpose, but what I am unable to recollect or state, to another part of the field, and received a wound from a musket shot through his thigh. After the battle was over we were discharged and returned home.*[14]

Jacob's friend Jerome Waldron recalled in more detail what happened to Captain Snook. He says that Snook was advancing when he received orders from a colonel to collect 50 or 60 militiamen, including Waldron. Waldron recalled:

> *We paraded some distance we came in sight of the British and about 200 of them advanced and fired on us and a party of British light horse got between us and the wood and charged us and wounded four of our men and one of the light horsemen got killed and we took his horse. Capt. Snook was shot thro his thigh. And we carried him back – the main body of the militia did not get engaged at that time.*[15]

Lieutenant Jacob Johnson took command of the company after Snook's wounding.

—

The 1779 militia act excluded enslaved persons from serving. However, free Black men were encouraged to serve because White men were not turning out in sufficient numbers. However, this did not mean that White men accepted Black men living in New Jersey as equals. New Jersey policies regarding Black people were "not intended to secure his betterment within the state." Instead, authorities designed policies "to discourage black immigration into New Jersey and to remove those Afro-Americans already living in the state."[16] Presbyterian Rev. Jacob Green of Morris County published a pamphlet in October 1779 stating, "can it be believed that a people contending for liberty should at the same time, be promoting and supporting slavery?" However, men like Green were merely objecting to hypocritical actions. They were not arguing from a belief in the human equality of Black people with White.[17]

During his militia service, Jacob served alongside and under the command of men who owned slaves. Militia General Philemon Dickinson of Trenton Township, commanding the New Jersey militia, held about half a dozen men and an unknown number of women and children. Several captains Jacob served under, including Charles Reading and David Jones, also owned enslaved men, and Jacob's friend and fellow private John Manners held one old enslaved man in 1780. There were no doubt other men he served with who supported enslavement while fighting for independence and freedom for White people. That irony could not have been lost on Jacob.[18]

—

Jacob was an industrious young man. He worked hard to establish himself as a farmer throughout the disruptions to life during the war, especially the frequent militia call-outs. Within three years of his Continental

Army discharge, by January 1780, he is listed as a "free negro" paying taxes on a house, 46 acres of land, including 36 acres improved for farming, and one hog. That hog was just one out of the 926 Amwell hogs in January and 1,576 hogs in June. While certainly not wealthy, given the systemic obstacles confronting Black people and the wartime economic disruptions, this was quite an accomplishment at that time. He was one of only two free Black men listed as owning land in the 1780 Amwell Township tax records. The other man, Omer Jupiter, paid taxes for 24 acres, 22 improved, along with two cows and two horses. No free landless Black men are listed as taxed for items other than land, such as houses, horses, businesses, and other things, although many landless White men are.

The records list enslaved men over the age of sixteen by quantity but not by name. Throughout the large Amwell Township, 54 enslaved men are listed in January and 57 in June. Most of the White men taxed for owning slaves owned just one, while six owned two. Nine enslaved men were labeled as old and two as lame. The list does not include enslaved females or male children under age sixteen.[19] After purchasing his land, Jacob continued to turn out for his militia tours and heard about the capture of Cornwallis at Yorktown while serving at Newark in 1781.

Amwell Township celebrated the end of the war on April 23, 1783, with a gathering at Snyder's tavern, the usual site for town meetings. The *New Jersey Gazette* reported that "a large number of the respectable inhabitants of the township of Amwell assembled." The statement "respectable inhabitants" no doubt meant White men, although Black people probably observed from the crowd's periphery. Although he never mentions it, Jacob may have attended the event in some formal fashion due to serving in the militia. A dinner at noon followed the discharge of thirteen cannon and the cheers of those assembled. After dinner, guests offered thirteen toasts, each accompanied by an artillery discharge.

Predictably, men made toasts to the peace and peace commissioners and the new nation on this occasion. They toasted America's European allies in addition to Washington, his generals, and army, and especially those who had died in combat. On a negative note, the twelfth toast stated, "May pretended neutrals during the late well fought contest be forever excluded from the councils of the United States." But, the thirteenth toast praised the state of New Jersey, "May she ever stand distinguished as a pattern of virtue, publick spirit and strict justice; and be always upon her guard against tyranny, in whatsoever garb she may appear." For Jacob and other Black men who fought for the ideals of freedom and independence, this probably wrang hollow. New Jersey was not prepared to "stand guard" against the tyranny of enslavement and systemic racism. However, the paper reported, "The whole was conducted with the greatest good order and decorum. Joy shone in every countenance; and in the evening the company retired."[20]

—

While Jacob spent six years building his life and serving in the militia, the enslaved people he lived among continued to seek personal freedom by escaping from their enslavers. In Amwell, the enslaved man Lun ran away from Isaac Johnson in June 1776, but Johnson did not advertise it until April 1778 and did not indicate the reason for the delay, which may have been war-related. Johnson did say it was probable that Lun would change his name and described him as "about 30 years of age, about five feet eight or nine inches high, a thick well set fellow, has a remarkable scar on his upper lip of a cut, and is thought to have a pass with him. He is the Negro that formerly belonged to John Severns." Johnson offered a thirty-dollar reward.[21]

In July 1780, Amwell Sheriff Joshua Corshon offered a four-hundred-dollar reward for the capture of a "new Negro man, that can scarcely speak a word of English." The term "new Negro" meant that he had recently been brought from Africa. This man had been confined in the Trenton jail and had been advertised to be sold on July 27. The runaway was about five feet nine or ten inches tall and took with him "two tow shirts, one pair tow trousers, one pair leather breeches, a white flannel jacket, an old blue cloth jacket, old shoes, and a leather furred cap."[22]

Toward the very end of the war, on February 1, 1783, John Laquear and Tunis Quick of Amwell offered a twenty-dollar reward to whoever apprehended and secured two Negro men who ran on January 26. "One named Elimas, 20 or 21 years old, about 5 feet 6 inches high, straight and stout built, has a lump on the second joint of one of his thumbs, lisps in his talk; had a light yellow broadcloth coat, and jacket of the same, leather breeches, and a small round hat; the rest of his clothes unknown." The other man named Ben was:

> *near of the same age with Elimas, about 5 feet 7 or 8 inches high, a good countenanced fellow, has a scar on the right side of his forehead, stoops in his walk; had on a lead coloured soiled linsey coat half*

> *worn, and an old jacket of the same colour, leather breeches, black stockings, an almost new felt hat, with a piece of yellow binding round the crown; but 'tis suspected they may change both their names and clothes.*[23]

It appears that Elimas, or Limas, was captured but ran away again on August 18, 1785, now having a scar on his right leg. He was suspected of having gone to Sussex County and was now 23 and described as five feet eight or nine inches high.[24]

Enslavers continued to sell people they no longer required in their service. Tanners Peter and Philip Case of Amwell, near Flemington, advertised for sale on April 10, 1780 "two valuable Negro men." Both were "well acquainted with the farming business, remarkably industrious & good tempered, and will be sold for no fault, but want of employ." The same day, Rachel White, living near Flemington in Amwell, offered for sale "a likely healthy Negro wench, about 24 years of age; she has had the measles and smallpox, and can do all kinds of house work, at which she is very handy, and will be sold for no fault."[25] On June 14, John Covenhoven near Tyson's Mills in Amwell advertised "a young Negro wench, about 15 years old" for sale.[26]

As one of the few free Black persons living among so many enslaved Black people, life for Jacob must have been psychologically complex. In both his private and public life, he was fighting for liberty for "all men," as stated in the Declaration of Independence. He was a living example proving the racist stereotype of the dangerous free Black man was utterly false. All the available sketchy evidence indicates that both the White and Black people Jacob lived among liked and respected him. However, whenever he met someone new, he had to overcome that false stereotype once again.

—

After the war ended with independence achieved in 1783, Jacob could give his full attention to establishing a productive life and eventually beginning a family. Life would still be difficult, but Jacob had survived even more challenging times.

Part III

Aftermath of War:

Life as a Black Veteran Seeking Equality

...at the time of her marriage it was not customary for white persons to perform the marriage ceremony for people of coulor, but that so far as she knows it was always done by persons of their own coulor.
- Mary Francis, Pension application

19

Creating a Life in Amwell 1783-1800

IN-BETWEEN MILITIA TOURS AND THEN AFTER THE WAR, JACOB WORKED HARD to establish his place in society before marrying and raising a family. He wanted to avoid becoming dependent on support from the township or becoming just another poor laborer that fit the White racist stereotype of a free Black man. Life was not easy in the erratic economic climate of that time, and tax records do not show him owning taxable land in 1784. While economic fluctuations and rampant inflation were obstacles to more substantial economic success, another factor was that his militia duty interfered with maintaining his farm since he had no wife, children, or relatives to maintain it when serving on a call-out. However, he did pay taxes for a house and two cattle. For some reason, this tax document did not identify him as a free Black man as would be expected.[1] He does not appear at all in the July/August 1786 tax ratables.[2]

As he struggled, Jacob may well have been aware when his former time owner Henry Wambaugh died in 1787. He may also have been aware that Minne Gulick served as a surveyor of the highways in neighboring Hopewell Township in 1785 and 1786.[3]

—

While seeking to establish himself, Jacob lived among Black people unable to visualize a better life due to enslavement. Their lives could abruptly change at any time their enslaver decided to sell them. Jacob would have been aware of those sales. In March 1785, William Frazer of Amwell advertised the sale of "a likely young Negro man, about 18 years old, is stout and well made, has had the small-pox and measles, and is remarkably healthy. He has been brought up to the farming business, and occasionally waiting at table."[4]

Many of the sales took place privately without announcement in the newspaper. On December 22, 1787, Mary Capner of Flemington noted in a personal letter that a Mr. Williams had recently sold a twelve-year-old girl, that "Lawyer Smith" had paid £100 for a Negro man, and that a neighboring farmer had bought himself a farm hand.[5] For owners of enslaved people, selling them resulted in pure monetary profit and no further responsibility for that human life. However, there was no financial profit for owners who manumitted an enslaved person, and the former owner still had some responsibility for the freed person not becoming a financial burden on the local government. The economics of manumission discouraged it.

White people opposed to the practice of enslavement sometimes raised their voices. A 1786 law contained an indictment of the institution in its preamble, indicating a growing reaction against enslavement among at least some State leaders. Law modifications in 1788 prohibited slave trading across state lines and provided punishments for cruelty to enslaved persons. The law seems to have missed the understanding that enslavement itself was inherently cruel. Another instance of legislative hypocrisy. Enslavers could free an enslaved person between the ages of 21 and 35 upon two township overseers of the poor attesting to their soundness of mind and body. Enslavers must arrange for enslaved persons to be taught to read, although enslavers did not always adhere to this law. While this law moderated some aspects of enslavement, the fundamental institution stood firm.[6]

Early advocates of abolition in New Jersey had failed to create a strong movement during and after the war for independence. Several factors contributed to this failure. One was the persisting raw racism of many White people who believed abolition would lead to a race war and destroy their civilization. These racist fears combined with the economic devastation resulting from the Revolution to retard interest in the movement, especially in the eastern part of the State, where the economy relied more heavily on enslaved labor.[7]

—

The 1789 United States Constitution that replaced the Articles of Confederation adopted during the war years did nothing to curtail the institution of enslavement. Neither did it expand equality for free Black people, many of whom, like Jacob, had risked their lives and fought for the freedoms of "all men." These issues would be left up to the States to determine individually. Both during and after the war, Jacob knew people who were first loyal to their State rather than the collection of States under the Articles. Under the nation-creating Constitution, the right of States to determine both slavery and the rights extended to Black citizens would spark the political division between those who believed in strong central government, initially the Federalists, and those who believed strongly in States rights, initially the Anti-Federalists.

—

When George Washington took his oath of office on April 30, 1789, Jacob was thirty-five years old and set to begin the next stage of his life. Still not taxed for land ownership, the tax records for 1789 show Jacob living with farmer John Reid.[8] Reid owned 100 acres of improved and 42 acres of unimproved land, four horses, and seven milking cattle at the time of the tax levy. While living with Reid, Jacob worked alongside an enslaved man owned by Reid. However, at this point in his life, Jacob wanted to be independent and start his family.

At some point, Jacob had met and fallen in love with a young girl named Mary, enslaved by prominent farmer Nathaniel Hunt. We can only conjecture the story of how Mary became enslaved and her life during enslavement. Nathaniel Hunt's son, Samuel, later stated that he had known Mary since childhood. Samuel was born about 1780 when Mary would have been fourteen or fifteen.[9] Hunt also enslaved another young girl, ten or eleven-year-old Phillis, and an elder adult man, Cato.

Jacob had undoubtedly participated in many interactions with enslaved people and their enslavers that heightened his desire to see an end to enslavement and changes to society to guarantee equal rights for all. While enslavement is never free from inhumane factors, circumstantial evidence hints that Nathaniel Hunt may have been a somewhat kindly master, although Mary left no statements describing her treatment. She appears to have been living in the Hunt family from a very early age, raising questions about the identity of her parents, whom she never mentions. Had Nathaniel Hunt enslaved her parents? Had they been sold? Had they died? Had Hunt purchased her as a young girl? Did she know who her father was? Was Mary the product of a rape? Was she of mixed race? And, very significantly, was Nathaniel her biological father as well as enslaver?

Mary later stated that she and Jacob met sometime after his military service ended. In 1789, twelve years after his Continental Army discharge, Jacob felt the time had come to marry her. One wonders why Jacob chose this year, especially since he had not yet established a farm. Mary was at the marriageable age of 23, twelve years younger than Jacob, so he may have feared losing her if he procrastinated. Also, he may have felt he did not want to be too advanced in age while his children were growing up. Although there is no marriage record, Mary later recalled the ceremony took place in September 1789. Jacob and Mary thus united their lives to begin their new family the same year the United States Constitution went into effect, uniting the thirteen states into a new country, and about five months after Washington's first inauguration as President.

A free Black man courting an enslaved woman raises questions about their courtship and decision to marry. The developing romance presented Jacob with obstacles for however many months or years it extended. Romance stories usually involve the young man seeking permission from his prospective bride's parents, especially her father. Seeking permission from an enslaver would be even more complex. This interaction leads to questions about the nature of their relationship with Nathaniel Hunt. Did Jacob get to know Mary because of some interactions with Nathaniel? To what degree did Nathaniel Hunt approve or disapprove of the developing romance? Did Hunt facilitate or impede the relationship?

Whatever the history of her enslavement, it seems clear that Mary and Jacob had positive feelings about their relationship with Nathaniel Hunt. It would certainly seem that Nathaniel Hunt approved the marriage and perhaps even encouraged it. No one providing an account of the wedding in later years indicates any tensions on that day. However, Jacob certainly did not want Mary to remain enslaved to Nathaniel after their marriage. We can only imagine the negotiations between Jacob and Nathaniel Hunt to facilitate the marriage and guarantee that Mary would no longer be Hunt's enslaved property at the end of the wedding day. However, we do know that Nathaniel agreed to sell Mary to Jacob on the celebratory wedding day.

The wedding was a Hunt family affair and celebration. As Mary Francis later said, "at the time of her marriage it was not customary for white persons to perform the marriage ceremony for people of coulor, but that so far as she knows it was always done by persons of their own coulor." Nathaniel Hunt's enslaved man Cato had previously been enslaved by "old Doctor Finley" and had conducted many area marriages for Black people. So, Cato performed the wedding ceremony, and both White and Black people, free and enslaved, attended the event. This leads one to wonder whether Nathaniel conducted himself more like the father or the enslaver of the bride during the ceremony.

In many ways, it appears that Nathaniel Hunt treated Mary emotionally more like she was his daughter rather than his enslaved servant. He allowed the wedding to be held at his house with his family attending and agreed to sell Mary to Jacob on their wedding day after the ceremony. However, had Nathaniel truly felt fatherly toward her, he could have freed Mary at any point in her life. The fact that he did not free her indicates that he was caught up in the cultural, economic, and legal morass of enslavement that discouraged manumission and abolition. As Nathaniel's slave, Mary could give birth to multiple children who would automatically be enslaved to Hunt for life without his need to purchase them. He could later sell them for a profit. However, if Nathaniel manumitted Mary, he would still be responsible for her economic support if she ever needed community assistance.

Selling Mary to Jacob removed any further legal requirement for Nathaniel to support her and made Jacob both her husband and enslaver regardless of the sale price. If Jacob freed her, he would be responsible for her if things did not work out economically. Jacob and Mary took a gamble on the good faith of Hunt and married before her sale to Jacob. If he did not sell Mary to Jacob after the wedding ceremony, or if he did not manumit her instead, their children would be born as the enslaved property of Hunt.

True to his word, after the ceremony, Hunt formally sold Mary to Jacob, and after a few days she departed Hunt's service. We do not know if Hunt demanded market price from Jacob or merely a token payment to make it a legal sale. At some point, probably almost immediately, Jacob freed Mary, although no manumission record has survived. Above and beyond his affection for Mary, it must have been a joy to Jacob to be able to free an enslaved person. He had fought for freedom and would instill in his children the commitment to fight for full equality. During their life together, Jacob and Mary had seven boys and one girl, all born free.[10] However, their children gradually encountered the restraints society imposed on free and enslaved Black people and learned from their mother about her personal experiences with enslavement.

An intriguing question about the marriage concerns a daughter of Mary's named Phebe. In his 1836 will, Jacob refers to Phebe, then grown up and married, as the "daughter of my beloved wife Mary" and bequeaths her ten dollars. However, he describes all of the other children listed as "my" son or daughter. This phrasing indicates that Mary was pregnant with Phebe at their marriage but that Jacob was not Phebe's biological father. Was Phebe's conception the result of a rape by a member of the Hunt family or someone else? We just do not know.

Jacob readily adopted Phebe, and she appears in Flemington store ledgers where Jacob and his family shopped and in her marriage record as Phebe Francis. Jacob and Mary's first recorded child together, John, was not born until two years after the marriage leaving a time gap in which Phebe could have been born. Mary makes no mention of Phebe in her later statements about the wedding or the birth of John. However, Mary estimated her wedding date based on its occurrence about two years before John was born on December 19, 1791, and she thought in September. While it is also possible that Mary already had young Phebe, perhaps born about 1788, the fact that no accounts of the wedding mention her would seem to preclude that. Also, Mary may have been early enough in her pregnancy that those attending were unaware of it, and she did not want to make it public. Importantly, if Phebe had been born before the wedding, Nathaniel Hunt would have had to sell her also to Jacob. Otherwise, Hunt would have continued to enslave Phebe. However, even though conceived of an enslaved woman, Phebe was born after Mary became free and therefore was born free.

The evidence for a good relationship between Nathaniel Hunt and Jacob and Mary Francis is indirect but telling. While no surviving statements describe the relationship, Jacob and Mary named a son after Nathaniel and used Hunt as the middle name for another son. When Hunt's other enslaved girl, Phillis, later wanted to marry a free Black man, she also became free. The elderly Cato apparently died enslaved. Mary maintained contact with the people among whom she grew up. Decades later, Nathaniel Hunt's son, Samuel, and his formerly enslaved girl Phillis helped Mary obtain her widow's pension based on Jacob's military service.

—

Life in Amwell Township seems to have been comfortable for Jacob and Mary. However, as the new United States of America began to develop in the later eighteenth century, a primary motivation driving political policies in New Jersey continued to be discouraging Black people from migrating into the state and removing those already residing in it.[11] Clearly, for many people, the idea of all men being created equal that Jacob had suffered and fought for did not apply to Black people in the new nation.

The 1790 census showed that among New Jersey's 184,139 total population, its 14,185 Black residents made up 7.7%. About 20% of the Black residents were free.[12] Hunterdon County* had a total population of 20,253, of which 1,492 residents, or 7.4 percent, were Black. The county population included 1,301 enslaved persons, and Jacob, Mary, and infant Phebe were among the just 191 free Black people. About one person in fifteen was enslaved.[13] Victory in the war for independence and writing a Constitution for the new nation did not change the inhumane system of enslavement. However, those events did stimulate some enslaved people to seek freedom. Wealthy Amwell farmer Abram Williamson offered £5 for a runaway enslaved man in November 1790. He described the escaped man Prime as "twenty-five years of age, about five feet eight inches high, well set, of a yellow complexion and impudent look, speaks English and low Dutch and is apt to boast." The following year, Gilbert Vancamp offered a ten-dollar reward for the capture of his runaway enslaved man Primus, who was "about 26 years old, 5 feet 10 inches high, pretty black; his front teeth somewhat defected; plays the fiddle and fife very well; he is a smart, active fellow, very ready in his answers."[14]

—

The Federal Militia Act of May 9, 1792, passed when Jacob was 38, required "male white citizens" between 18 and 45 years old to be enrolled in their state militia. It did not expressly forbid Black enlistment, and no discussion of race occurred during the legislative debate. New Jersey echoed this requirement in its 1792 militia law reiterating the words "white" and "citizen" for those who must participate and made no statement forbidding Black participation.

**During Jacob's lifespan and most of Mary's, Hunterdon County was more extensive than it is today. Several southern townships were detached in 1838/1839 to become part of the new Mercer County.*

However, no Black men can be identified in the militia units called up during the 1791-1794 Whiskey Rebellion or the War of 1812. Therefore, had 38-year-old Jacob wanted to participate in the militia, he would have been rejected because he was Black. This reality may have suited Jacob just fine since it removed one distraction to building a life for Mary and their young children. However, it must have been a slap in the face to a man who had served, and greatly suffered, with other Black men so willingly and ably during the Revolutionary War.[15]

Although Black men in New Jersey like Jacob had proven their value serving in the Continental Army and the State militia, racial discrimination remained rampant, as did the fear of arming Black men. A non-military factor behind the exclusion of Black men from the militia in those times of relative peace was that the militia became a social institution, more than a military one. When companies or entire regiments mustered for a quarterly drill day, the event became an opportunity for community gatherings and festivities. Politically ambitious men saw leadership in the militia as a path to local and state political office as well as social prominence. Militia musters became de facto political rallies. Just as in other political and social groupings at that time, White men did not permit Black men to participate with them.

Had Black men been needed as soldiers to fill out units lacking enough White men, they would have been welcome, but not for social occasions with political overtones.[16] This practice was clear evidence that life in New Jersey mirrored the perception of Alexis De Tocqueville in the 1830s that Black people experienced even worse discrimination in the north than in the south.[17]

The Flemington Volunteers militia company formed in September 1807, and members volunteered to be ready to march at a moment's notice when called by the Governor. Other early militia units, which Jacob and his family would have been very aware of, included the Uniform Infantry Company, Fifth Troop of the Hunterdon Squadron, and the Flemington Grays.[18] Like other Revolutionary War veterans, Jacob probably looked with some amusement upon these well-clad, properly uniformed, very much part-time, untried, soldier-like characterizations. Except for a few older officers, most of the men had never experienced the discomforts associated with military life, much less real and constant warfare.

—

Abolition remained controversial as the eighteenth century entered its final decade. Some New Jersey Quakers and Pennsylvania Abolition Society members founded The New Jersey Society for Promoting the Abolition of Slavery in 1793, with headquarters in Burlington. It would last only until 1812. This group advocated gradual abolition, feeling that this had a greater chance for limited acceptance than seeking outright immediate total abolition. Economic factors and the "property" rights of enslavers still took precedence over the human rights of enslaved persons in New Jersey.[19] The Hunterdon chapter met at the Friend's Meeting House in what is today Quakertown.

This relatively weak group remained essentially a West Jersey organization with a solid Quaker influence while inadvertently aggravating the racial tensions that divided eastern and western New Jersey. In the 1790s, the number of slaves in New Jersey increased by nine percent, due mainly to increases in eastern parts of the State where Quakers were a small minority. In Hunterdon County, the number of slaves actually decreased by six percent. However, many people continued to oppose abolition, feeling that free Black people threatened a stable society. For many who supported abolition, that concept only meant ending the institution of enslavement, not improving the lives of Black people, accepting them as equal human beings, or ensuring they had equal rights with whites.[20]

The year 1793 also produced the federal fugitive slave act. By essentially permitting bounty hunting men to seize "potential" runaway slaves, it increased the danger to free New Jersey Black people of being kidnapped and taken south to be sold into enslavement. Throughout the late eighteenth and early nineteenth centuries, free Black people in New Jersey had to be wary of getting caught up in an illegal coastal slave trade that kidnapped people and sent them south on ships to be sold.[21] Jacob and his family may have been more secure in Hunterdon County, where they were well-known, but not completely.

—

While these events of the 1790s were taking place, four children joined Jacob and Mary's family, beginning with Jacob, born on November 10, 1794. Jane, Abraham, and Isaac B. followed over the next several years. What the "B" in Isaac's name stood for is never indicated in available documents. As an adult, he is often referred to as I. B. The family now had six young children who kept Mary and Jacob busy as they continued to create a good life for them.

—

Toward the end of the century, a 1798 law that reaffirmed and modified previous state enslavement laws and laws pertaining to free Black people was one factor that kept low the number of Black people in New Jersey. Although the law raised the age to which an enslaver could manumit a person to 40, manumission now required two property owners to sign a bond for 100 dollars to guarantee that the freed man or woman would not become a public charge. While maintaining the practice of enslavement, it placed additional restrictions on enslaved people, beyond what their enslavers might inflict, by forbidding enslaved people from "meeting in large companies, from running about at nights, and from hunting or carrying a gun on the Lord's Day."[22]

In a significant restriction on the rights of free Black people in the state, it also ordered:

> *That no free negro or mulatto, of or belonging to this state, shall be permitted to travel or remain in any county in this state, other than in the county where his or her place of residence may lawfully be, without a certificate from two justices of the peace of the county in which he or she belonged, or from the clerk of the county, under the seal of the court, certifying that such negro or mulatto was set free, or deemed and taken to be free in such county.*

While the required pass could be defended as protection from kidnapping into slavery, it would only protect if introduced into court. This protection was doubtful in the case of kidnapping and destruction of the pass by the kidnapper.

As for free Black people from other states, the law restricted their interest in coming to New Jersey by decreeing, "no free negro or mulatto, of or belonging to any other state in the union shall be permitted to travel or reside in this state without a certificate from two justices of the peace of such other state, that such negro or mulatto was set free or deemed and taken to be free in that state."[23] By this law, all free Black people in New Jersey had to prove they were not enslaved. This law is clear evidence that free Black people were usually considered enslaved when encountered by White people who did not know them. Altogether, these laws made a mockery of the word "free Black" by confining their lives. The thirteen colonies had won their War for Independence in 1783. However, the Revolution for equal rights for "all men" continued.

No other than a free white person shall be employed to convey the mail.
- *Centinel of Freedom,* June 22, 1801, 3.

20

Settling in Flemington 1800-1809

ABOUT 1800 OR 1801, JACOB AND MARY PURCHASED A FARM JUST OUTSIDE the north end of Flemington village. While no recorded deeds exist to substantiate the date of their farm purchase, Mary mentions the year in her widow's pension application, and Jacob's 1836 death notice suggests it. They likely purchased the farm later labeled as owned by their son Nathaniel on an 1851 map of Hunterdon County.[1] This farm was convenient to Asher Atkinson's store on the north side of the village, where members of the Francis family are known to have shopped between 1809 and 1817.[2]

Jacob turned 46 in 1800 and Mary 34. Phebe was about ten or eleven, John nine, Jacob six, Jane, Abraham, and Isaac B. a few years younger. Nathaniel, named for Mary's former enslaver, was just a year old, having been born February 1, 1799, bringing the number of Jacob's and Mary's children to seven, including Phebe.

—

Black people made up nine percent of the New Jersey population in 1800, of which 12,422 were enslaved and 4,402 free. The overall Hunterdon County population had grown by about 1,000 to 21,261. The number of free Black persons had more than doubled from 191 to 520, with Jacob and Mary's children adding to the number. Although the number of enslaved people had declined by about 80 to 1,220, seventy percent of Black persons remained enslaved in the county.[3] The 1802 and 1803 tax lists show between 55 and 60 enslaved men in Amwell Township, with most White enslavers owning just one male capable of working, while four owned two, and one, miller James Stout, owned three. This document did not include enslaved women, children, or elderly males.[4]

The largest acreage holding listed in the tax records for a White man was 400 acres. Few holdings exceeded 200, and many were less than 100 acres. Jacob appears to be the only acreage-owning Black farmer in the Flemington area. The 1802 and 1803 tax documents list Jacob as a Black man owning 115 improved acres in addition to two horses and some cattle, four in 1802 and seven in 1803. Only one additional free Black man is listed each year, but neither of them owned land. Benjamin Bake paid taxes just for a house in 1802 and William French for a house and one cow in 1803. Jacob thus stands out among the area's free Black men, and his taxable property indicates he was economically approaching the middle class.[5] More than ever, Jacob did not fit the stereotypical concept held by many Whites of the impoverished, lazy, free Black man.

—

The Gulicks, whose family name Jacob had used before 1777, left the area in 1802, moving to Northumberland County, Pennsylvania, where Minne died about 1804.[6]

—

During the first decade that the Francis family lived at their Flemington farm, New Jersey passed two laws significantly affecting Black people. In 1804, New Jersey finally legislated a gradual abolition of slavery law that took effect on the significance packed date of July 4. Politicians could now hypocritically tout July 4, 1804, as the Independence Day for enslaved people, even though not even one enslaved person gained freedom that day. Enslaved persons born before that date remained "slaves for life," while children born to enslaved women after that date would later become free at age 25 for boys and 21 for girls. To calculate their freedom dates, the law ordered enslavers to record the birth dates of children born to enslaved women with their county clerk.

In practice, this law did very little to alter conditions favorably for enslaved people in New Jersey. It did, however, stimulate more discussion, if not direct action, among White leaders concerning slavery and its eventual complete abolition. The gradual abolition act brought on new perceptions and vocabulary to mask the fact that slavery still persisted. Over the ensuing decades, definitions of enslavement and partial enslavement were debated and modified. Jacob and Mary certainly had feelings about this law and must have heard how the White people they knew felt about the persisting conditions of their enslaved acquaintances.

For Jacob to hear Black children referred to as indentured while actually enslaved must have given him pause about his indenture. Had he been treated more like an enslaved person himself? Did the owners of his "time" feel more like they owned "him?" Under the 1804 law, young "indentured" or "apprenticed" Black children could be sold away from their parents, similarly to how Jacob's "time" had been sold. While he had been removed from his family and community for many years, it was always with clear expectations concerning his treatment and eventual release date.

Due to the ambiguous and evolving aspects of the gradual abolition act, Flemington's Black community consisted of people living with varying degrees of legal freedom, including enslavement for life, enslavement for a term, freed from enslavement, or free from birth. During the last years of the eighteenth century and the first decade of the nineteenth, Jacob and Mary could establish their family much more securely than the many Black families trying to deal with the changing patterns and expectations of the gradual abolition movement.

When visiting Flemington village to shop or attend church, Francis family members met White people and the free and enslaved Black people who worked in white households and businesses. Jacob and Mary became aware of the lives of those people and the obstacles to a truly free life that they continued to encounter daily. They became aware of people who ran away seeking freedom from their enslavement and those whose owners sold them.[7] On February 15, 1806, tavern owner Samuel Taylor offered for sale "A healthy strong active Negro Girl, sixteen years of age."[8] Born before 1804, she was a slave for life.

For many White people, abolition had nothing to do with creating a community in which people of all complexions and ethnic heritage were equal. The gradual abolition law did nothing to remove the racist assumption by White people that Black people unknown to them should be considered enslaved until shown otherwise – such as with the freedom-certifying pass required by the 1798 law. Paternalistically, politicians and abolitionists could declare freedom from slavery as a gift from those who had fought for and won their freedom from Great Britain in the Revolution. However, this overlooked the fact that Black men had enormously assisted that fight for human freedoms still denied to them after the victory. White politicians who fully believed that free Black people could never be equal to Whites in intelligence, skills, and moral behavior proposed, supported, and ultimately enacted the 1804 law.[9] While the 1804 law did not directly affect Jacob and his family, they certainly knew people whose lives had hardly been changed by it, and Mary especially could identify with them.

A second law directly affected Jacob. It involved voting rights for women and free Black people. When White males wrote the July 1776 New Jersey State Constitution, they did not explicitly deny those rights to property-owning women and free Black men, thereby inadvertently establishing voting rights for them. However, amendments made to the State Constitution in 1807 revealed their original intent and denied the vote to free Black men and women and White women.[10] No voting records still exist for Amwell Township before that 1807 change to show whether Jacob ever voted in an election. However, knowing what we do about him and the lives of his children as adults, it would be fair to believe that he did vote, and with pride. Since Mary did not own any property, she would not have been eligible.[11]

—

Jacob must have bristled when he heard White people express the belief that Black people could not survive independently without the help or guidance of, and sometimes the use of force by, Whites. He repeatedly heard this belief expressed when White people sought to justify Black colonization to Africa as part of abolition. The Francis family even encountered this belief when they attended church.[12]

Jacob and Mary decided to join the Baptist Church at Flemington in 1805 and may have attended services there for several years previously.[13] Although the congregation did not formalize itself until 1798, early members had built a small, rude, wooden meetinghouse in 1764 at the village's southern end. Similar in design to a country schoolhouse, by 1805 it was "not only old, but old-fashioned, remarkably plain and bare, without carpet or cushion, and having but one room for all purposes." The wooden floor retained marks inflicted by military muskets when American troops had briefly used the building during the Revolution. Congregants sat in high, straight-back chairs, and the building lacked any means for heat and light. "Evening meetings were called at 'early candlelight,' the candles themselves were slender tallow 'dips,' mounted in plain brass sticks or tin sconces, requiring frequent snuffing, and then only making the darkness visible."

The church sexton in 1799 was named Frank, probably a Black man because no surname appears in the Church records. The church enforced strict rules and, the year Jacob and Mary joined, one male member was "excommunicated" for believing in doctrines not agreeable to the church. Rev. James McLaughlin had become the pastor in February 1804, dividing his time with the Kingwood Church, and would serve for five years. During his tenure, he welcomed 25 new members, including Jacob and Mary.[14]

Jacob and Mary joined at least three other Black members. Church records listed William Minck and "W. Thomas" as members in 1799 and "Sarah S." joined in 1802.[15] On March 2, 1805, Jacob satisfactorily gave a public account of his Christian experience as a prelude to being baptized into membership. However, White parishioner Peter Obert who owned just one-half of a Flemington village lot along with one horse and one cow in 1802 and 22 acres and two cows in 1803,[16] accused Jacob of having brought "a false account against him." The Church put Jacob's baptism on hold and appointed Levi Stout, William Merrill, and John Carr to examine the case.

They reported on April 6 that a clerk had made a mistake when copying the account so that it was off by a bushel and a half of rye. This report exonerated Jacob to everyone's satisfaction, and the Church finally baptized Jacob and Mary and accepted them into church membership on May 11. Two additional free Black people, Harry Q. and Dinah, also joined the church in 1805. Church records include the subsequent adult baptisms of several of their children, including Abraham and Jane.[17]

Jacob and Mary's seventh child, Asa, joined the family that year.

—

Flemington was small, but vibrant and growing when the Francis family took up residence just outside the village. Rather than a village of houses and businesses on small lots, it presented the visitor with many buildings situated on farmland, with some buildings near each other while others were spaced further apart. All structures faced the main street running north/south through the town center, but not all buildings sat adjacent to the road.

Visitors saw the many open areas where houses would be constructed in the future and where side streets could branch out as the town grew in population. The busy village constantly underwent changes accompanied by flurries of activity as houses were built and house lots were broken up, sold, and purchased.

The advertisements for these properties help us visualize Flemington as it was changing when Jacob and Mary first lived nearby and then in the village itself. On March 14, 1801, Amos Gregg put up for sale at public vendue:

> *a well finished two story house, with a brick front and kitchen of the same, ..., with upwards of forty acres of land, a great proportion of which is good meadow, with every necessary building to render it convenient for any kind of public business, situated in a wealthy neighborhood, four public roads forming a junction, viz. From Philadelphia, Trenton, Morris-Town and Sussex.*[18]

Evidence of Flemington's growth includes proposals for carrying mail in New Jersey. One 1801 newspaper advertisement reported that a carrier left Trenton every Tuesday at 9:00 am and passed through Pennington and Flemington to arrive at Plumstead and return to Trenton by 6:00 am the following Tuesday. Racial discrimination stood out prominently in these advertisements that blatantly stated, "No other than a free white person shall be employed to convey the mail."[19] Additional routes and more frequent contacts developed over the succeeding years. Several decades later, the local newspaper noted letters to Jacob's children available for pick up at the post office.[20]

By 1808, there were only about 16 houses between the Presbyterian and Baptist churches, located respectively at Flemington village's northern and southern ends. Several buildings operated as taverns serving the many people coming to Flemington for county court business or community gatherings, such as militia training days. The taverns competed for business in the growing town, and several went out of business or changed owners or operators over the years.[21]

Neal Hart kept a "large and commodious" tavern with extensive stables on a one and a quarter acre lot across the main street from the County Court House, the clerk's office, and the surrogate's offices; on about the site of today's Union Hotel.[22] Joseph Atkinson operated a tavern owned by Samuel

Taylor in 1805, located "within four rods of the Court House." A description promoted the house as:

> *large and well finished; it contains a cellar, has four rooms on the first floor, with fire places in each; on the second floor are four rooms, two of them contain fire-places; and on the third floor are three rooms. There is also a kitchen annexed to the house, and a well of water in the yard. There is on the lot a large stable about eighty-two feet by twenty-two and a shed seventy five feet long.*[23]

John Jemes owned another tavern opposite the courthouse and touted it as "thought by gentlemen of the bar who frequent the house four times in every year, to be superior to any county stand in this state."[24] On April 21, 1806, "the barn and stables of Mr. Alexander Bonnell, innkeeper, at Flemington, ..., took fire and with their contents were entirely consumed. The fire broke out about 9 o'clock in the evening, and strong suspicions are entertained, that it was communicated to the buildings by some wicked incendiary."[25]

Aside from tavern operators, the diverse village residents consisted of lawyers, merchants, professionals, and craftsmen serving the county government and farmers on the surrounding lands, including the Francis family. Among those involved with the law, John T. Blackwell, living just north of Neal Hart's tavern, was appointed judge of court on February 8, 1804, served as county clerk for 19 years, and surrogate for seven.[26]

Professional men occupying houses on Main Street often owned undeveloped lots that they sold as the town grew. Prominent lawyer Nathaniel Saxton living on Main Street south of the Court House, offered house lots for sale on January 20, 1809. These included "six lots of one acre each, near the Baptist Meeting House, Flemington, on the road leading to New Brunswick [today's Church Street], suitable for building lots." There was also a 25-acre lot adjoining them "whereon is a house, barn and other out buildings, and a number of fruit trees; there is a lasting spring of water near the house, and a small stream of water running thro' the lot – it is an eligible situation for a tradesman." In addition, a 45-acre lot adjoined it, "which will be sold together with it or separately. All the above lots are well calculated for grass, a considerable part now in with clover and timothy, and are about half a mile distant from the Court House."[27]

Flemington's doctors included Dr. John Gregg, a Quaker, who practiced from about 1790 to 1808 when he relocated to Pennsylvania. Dr. William Geary, a Scotsman "small of stature, quick, shrewd, a good horseman, an excellent doctor, and a popular man," succeeded him in 1808 and lived at the south end of the village, just south of the Baptist Church.[28]

Craftsmen residing in the village included carpenter Peter Haward who purchased a German indentured servant for $70 for several years to aid him in his craft. He lived at the southern end of the village, while his relatives Mary and Jane Haward owned several tenant houses near him on Main Street. Haward was busy in civic activities and became very friendly with the Francis family.[29]

Frequent real estate sales modified the town during the first decade of the nineteenth century. On July 5, 1806, Peter Obert, who had tried to block Jacob's Baptist Church membership, put up for sale a one-half-acre property in Flemington containing a "handsome" 56- by 23-foot house with two rooms on one side and one on the other side of the entry. It had "two rooms above and two more may be made, a good cellar under the house." An attached stable was large enough to house four horses, a horse-drawn riding chair, and a sleigh. Poplars and various fruit trees, including peach, apple, and cherry, grew in the front and back yards and a large kitchen garden produced "an abundance of vegetables and fruit." Obert also sold three building lots in town on Main Street. Each had a good well and contained roughly two, well-fenced hay-producing, acres planted in timothy and clover, in addition to a variety of grafted fruit trees, including peaches.[30]

On October 10, 1808, John Finley offered to sell four lots in the village. Three of them lay "on the street, 25 chains in front, containing 25 acres, and the fourth on the rear, containing 14 acres; the whole is in a high state of cultivation, there is a comfortable dwelling house, barn, store house & on the first lot opposite the court house."[31]

In 1808, the villagers began bringing in water from Coxe's Spring using hollowed wooden logs as pipes to supplement their wells and cisterns for water. Two springs on the lands of John Capner and J. C. Hopewell had provided the primary water source when wells and cisterns gave out, and village residents hauled water from them. Lack of maintenance of the log pipes led to water supplies from this source being very short in dry seasons.[32]

Flemington Academy

c1901 photo from: Kline, "The Flemington Academy."

On this thirteenth day of August AD1819 before me the subscriber one of the Judges of the Court of Common Pleas for the County of Hunterdon Personally appeared Jacob Francis aged Sixty six years resident in Flemington in the County of Hunterdon who being by me first duly sworn according to law, doth on his oath make the following declaration, in order to obtain the provision made by the late act of congress entitled "An act to provide for certain persons engaged in the land and naval Services of the United States in the revolutionary war." - Jacob Francis pension application

21

Life in Flemington 1810-1819

IN 1810, JACOB WAS 56 AND MARY 44 YEARS OLD. PHEBE WAS ABOUT 20, JOHN 19, Jacob 16, Jane, Abraham, and Isaac B. a few years younger, Nathaniel 11, and Asa about five years old in their growing family. New Jersey's Black population was up almost 2,000 from 1800 while the enslaved population had declined to 10,851, and the free Black population had risen to 7,843. These numbers work out to 4.5 slaves and 2.8 free Black persons among every 100 persons in the State. After this time, the enslaved population began a rapid decline. The ten members of the Francis family were among the 687 free Black persons living in Hunterdon County, an increase of 167, along with 1,119 enslaved people, down about 100 over the past decade.[1]

Jacob and Mary contributed to Flemington village's growing and changing population and businesses when they relocated from their farm into the town. Sometime about 1810 to 1815, Jacob and Mary left the farm under the control of their older sons and rented a house in town belonging to the Baptist Church. This house sat on the Baptist Church lot on the northeast corner of the Main and Church Street intersection, directly across Main Street from where the Flemington Academy would be established just about the same time.[2] An indebtedness note in the church files shows that Jacob owed the Church $36.76 on April 15, 1818, for house and lot rent. The memo, signed by Thomas Capner, confirmed Jacob's payment, stating, "The above said Jacob Francis confesd payment this 23 day of April and desired me to enter it as such."[3] One source describes their rented structure as "a small shanty built by 'Daddy Mink,'" who was probably William Minck, the early Black member of the Flemington Baptist Church mentioned previously.[4]

Jacob and Mary's youngest child, Abner Hunt Francis, joined the family about 1812 and like older brother Nathaniel carried a name in honor of Mary's former enslaver.

—

At least several of the Francis children received some education and could read and write as adults. A biographical sketch of their youngest son, Abner, written in 1863 states that Jacob owned a "small farm" in Flemington and provided his sons with "a good English education" in "the rudimental branches taught in the common school" at Flemington.[5] However, the educational facilities and opportunities for children in Flemington when the Francis children were young only accepted White students. So, just how Jacob and Mary arranged for their children's education is an intriguing mystery whose solution no doubt affirms Jacob and Mary's determination and skill to overcome racist obstacles.

An English maiden lady, Miss Allen conducted one of the earliest village schools in a small, 20- by 30-foot, one-story frame house built by Jacob and Mary's future neighbor, Peter Haward. It stood on the east side of Main Street, just north of the present railroad track crossing and not far from the Baptist Church.[6] Perhaps Jacob and Mary were able to work out some informal arrangements with her to teach their children.

A group of citizens founded The Flemington Academy in 1811 to serve White children. For one dollar, they purchased from Alexander Bonnell and his wife a roughly one-half acre lot located just across Main Street from the Baptist Church and the house rented by Jacob and Mary. Peter Haward served as president of the school trustees in 1813 when they voted to construct a 20- by 33-foot, two-story brick building with a shingled roof. Among the locally made red bricks, workers set the date "1811" in black bricks under the north gable. The building stood at the back of the fenced school lot that extended out to Main Street.[7]

Jacob and Mary's move into the village raises the question, did they rent that house from the church to be close to the Academy or the small school of Miss Allen? Was this part of their effort to educate their children? Asa and Abner were young enough to take advantage of the Academy, and the older children could also benefit to some degree from it.

The Baptist Church still had fewer than 80 members in 1811, and money was scarce. The congregation experienced occasional conflicts between members over religious doctrine and congregation rules, and the church declared March 21, 1811 to be a "day of humiliation and prayer for this church."[8] Some of the issues may have related to the pastor or even abolition. Presbyterian Church member Peter Haward, the Francis's neighbor, entered in his diary on August 5, 1811, that he "Heard a black man preach at the Baptist Church."[9] It would be interesting to know more about that and whether Jacob and his family heard the Black man also. Several significant changes took place in 1812. The church ordained Rev. Charles Bartolette as pastor on May 11, beginning what ultimately extended to 34 years of service, and the congregation made additional repairs to the aging church building.[10] Phebe married Thomas Hickson, noted on their marriage record as a Black man, the following year on September 19, 1813, with Rev. Bartolette officiating.[11]

While teaching at the Flemington Academy in 1817, future Presbyterian minister W. W. Blauvelt helped organize a Sunday school for Black people. This Sabbath School first met at the Academy in 1818 and continued to meet there for three years, after which the Presbyterian and Baptist churches took it up. Miss Hannah Clark served as its first teacher, and Charles Bartles taught the school in 1822.[12] Young Abner was about six years old when the Sabbath School began, while his next oldest sibling, brother Asa, was about thirteen. The other Francis children were nearing or already into their twenties and thirties, but it may have been this Sabbath School that introduced and helped develop Abner's education. Whether or not Abner began his education at the Sabbath School, somehow, he went far beyond just learning to read and write and achieved a profound and broad education. However he achieved them, as an adult he used the skills he acquired in inspirational ways.

The Flemington Academy advertised for students in March 1818, informing parents of potential scholars that it was now a school at which students could board "in respectable families at a moderate rate." The courses included Latin, Greek, English grammar, geography, mathematics, and "such other branches as are usually taught in other Academies." This notice, signed by academy President John F. Clark, pointed out that "Flemington is the seat of justice for the county of Hunterdon, in this state. It lies three miles north of what is commonly called the old York road, on which there is a regular line of stages that ply daily between New York and Philadelphia."[13]

Mary made ginger cakes and root beer which she gave to the Academy children during their daily recesses. It may be that Mary and Jacob did this to show their appreciation for some sort of informal help from the teachers in educating several of their children. During the three years that the Sunday school met at the academy, the parents employed Mary to make her root beer for both the children and their parents to enjoy, and this may have continued when the Sunday School moved to the Baptist Church building. Mary always kept her root beer cold and on tap in a cold water spring down in their cellar. Sunday worshippers at the Baptist Church also frequently stopped at Mary and Jacob's house to purchase root beer.[14]

—

Several other changes in town took place about the time Jacob and Mary settled into their rented house. Village merchant Joseph P. Chamberlin announced his new partnership in August 1815 with John Chamberlin, Jr. in Joseph P Chamberlin & Co., advertising steel, putty, and other items for sale.[15] This partnership dissolved in February 1817, and Joseph noted that he would carry on the business at his "old stand," in Flemington, "where he had for sale dry goods, groceries, hardware, stationary, a good assortment of paints, oil, window glass, cutlery, &c. Also, bar iron, and nails of all sizes." Typical of the time, he would take country produce for payment in place of cash.[16]

Twenty-two-year-old Samuel Hill built his pottery on Main Street toward the southern part of town just several lots from the Francis house about 1815 and would operate it until his death in 1858.[17]

—

Property sale advertisements help us to imagine Flemington's appearance at this time. Joseph P. Chamberlin offered his house and a one-acre lot, with many fruit trees, on February 23, 1813, describing the house as one-story with seven rooms on the first floor and a kitchen. It had a water-well near the door. He also offered four one-acre building lots as well as "a new two story frame house, with two rooms on the first floor and three on the second, well finished, on a one-acre lot."[18] In 1817, Chamberlin advertised the private sale of "a new two story frame house in the village of Flemington, with an acre of excellent land, a new frame barn, a large garden, well enclosed."[19]

John Finley offered land for sale on January 29, 1812. One package contained several contiguous lots adjoining the Baptist Church lot totaling about fourteen acres.[20] On June 29, 1816, Robert Finley and James S. Manners, administrators of the estate of John Finley, offered "about 14 acres of land, in and about Flemington, adjoining lands of James Clark, Peter Haward, and others."[21]

Dr. Geary expected to remove from Flemington early in the spring of 1816 and offered for sale his property located just south of the Baptist Church and visible from the house rented by Jacob and Mary. Geary described his property as:

> *Twenty four acres of land under the highest state of cultivation, divided into convenient lots, all in good fence. An orchard of upwards of 100 trees, chiefly grafted, and of the best selected fruit. The house is large and commodious, being two stories high, with four rooms on each floor, a good garret, and cellar under the whole, a convenient kitchen adjoining – a well of good water near the door, and a spring of soft water at some distance from the house. The garden is large and stored with a variety of fruit, and the house is surrounded with fruit and ornamental trees, interspersed with flowering shrubbery of various kinds. The outbuildings consist of a good barn and cowshed, also a small building detached from the house, suitable for an office or mechanic's shop. With the above property will be sold two shares of the Flemington Aqueduct Company, together with three acres of woodland, about two miles and a half from Flemington. Possession will be given on the 1st of April.*[22]

In January 1814, Thomas Gordon advertised for sale his lot and two-story tavern house on a lot containing seven acres of meadow, a large stable, another small house and barn, a good water-well, and some young apple trees.[23] On December 20, 1815, William Maxwell advertised his house as "large, two stories high and in excellent repair, and from its situation well calculated for a professional man, or to be kept as a boarding house or tavern." He also offered two beautiful building lots near his house.[24]

—

The Francis family knew those Black people enslaved for life under the 1804 gradual emancipation act in addition to those free Black people who lived and worked at the various village businesses. They also knew the conditions that continued to cause these friends to seek their freedom. On July 16, 1813, tavern owner Alexander Bonnell offered a ten-dollar reward for his enslaved girl Nance who ran on July 4, an especially appropriate day to seek independence. She was "about twenty years old, short and stout made, full face, had on when she went away a reddish calico frock, a purple silk bonnet, &c. pretends she is hunting a master."[25] Born before 1804, Nance was a slave for life.

The year before he planned to relocate from Flemington, Dr. Geary offered a fifteen-dollar reward for a runaway enslaved woman who ran on July 18, 1815. He described her as:

> *aged about 35 or 40, of small stature, has lost her front teeth, is remarkably fond of smoking tobacco, her dress not ascertained; she calls herself Caty, and some times Catharine Merrit, she is capable of doing all kinds of house work, it is supposed she has a forged pass, she is an excellent spinner and probably will enquire for employ in that way.*

The "forged pass" was probably the certificate required since 1798 to be carried by a free Black person to prove they were not enslaved.[26]

The Francis family also must have shared in the suffering when an enslaver sold a person. Village lawyers William and John Maxwell, Jr. offered for sale in 1812 "a smart healthy Negro wench, about 22 years of age, a slave for life."[27] John Maxwell, Jr. advertised in May 1816 a Negro wench for sale whom he described as "a smart active wench about 18 years of age, who understands all kinds of house-work." She was a slave for life, and Maxwell had also offered her for sale the previous December.[28]

Some of the Black servants Jacob and Mary knew were indentured and experienced having their time sold like Jacob had many years earlier. Tanner Philip Case offered a 30-dollar reward in 1813 for his runaway "servant for a term of years" James Baldwin about 28 years old. Baldwin was "about five feet 7 or 8 inches high, well set, of the yellow or mulatto color; is fond of liquor, and after drinking, very forward and talkative. Whilst with the subscriber, he worked principally in the tan yard, sometimes on the farm, and was expert at both."[29]

On May 12, 1813, William Maxwell offered for sale "an active, healthy Negro girl, of the age of 20 years. She has to serve about 11 years."[30] Born before the 1804 law, this woman must have been indentured, but, interestingly, he advertised her for sale, not just her time. White people often considered an indentured Black person to be virtually the same as an enslaved individual. On February 24, 1814, William Maxwell offered to sell "the time of a Negro boy who is nineteen years of age and has nine years to serve, he is sober and industrious, and has been accustomed to doing house work and waiting in a public house." He was another probable indentured person.[31]

Slave purchases also continued and Flemington resident Thomas Capner paid $180 "for a Black Woman named Rachail."[32]

After the 1804 gradual manumission law, the owners of women enslaved for life had to register the births of their children with the county to calculate their freedom date. John Maxwell held an enslaved woman named Suck, who gave birth to Elisa on May 30, 1815, and Susan, who gave birth to Jeremiah on June 3, 1821. George C. Maxwell owned enslaved woman Flora who gave birth to Lydia on November 23, 1808. Merchant Joseph P. Chamberlin's enslaved woman Phebe gave birth to Jacob on April 2, 1816, and Hetty on December 20, 1817. All the enslavers recorded these children's births with the county clerk.[33]

—

The federal Revolutionary War Pension Act of 1818 marked a significant shift in public policy toward veterans, including free Black men like Jacob. President James Monroe, like Jacob, a veteran of the Battle of Trenton, signed the act into law. By this act, officers and enlisted men who had served in the Continental Army or naval service for at least nine months and now required assistance were eligible to apply. Service in a state militia did not count. Jacob's 14 months in Colonel Sargent's regiment exceeded the minimum requirement.

This act terminated the long neglect in rewarding Continental army veterans for their meritorious service. In addition, it also engendered patriotism during the recovery from the War of 1812, often seen as a second American Revolution. Since adopting the Declaration of Independence, the young United States had struggled to develop its national identity. Rewarding veterans of the Continental army would help bring together and strengthen the federal government while celebrating its survival as a republic under the Constitution.[34]

Jacob decided to apply for a pension. On August 13, 1819, he dictated a short sworn statement at the Hunterdon County Court House in Flemington outlining his Continental service to common pleas court judge and near neighbor, Thomas Capner. Although Jacob had no official documents to prove his service, such as a discharge paper, Capner attached a statement indicating that he was satisfied that Jacob served as he stated. Afterward, four men, including Capner and lawyer William Maxwell, an enslaver who had sold an enslaved woman in 1813, certified that Jacob had always maintained a "fair character for honesty and truth" and that he was "an industrious, sober, useful man, having raised a large family, and stands in need of the assistance of his country for support."

However, Jacob did not complete his application by submitting a statement listing his economic assets and liabilities to prove his need for government assistance. Initially, such a statement had been optional. But, a May 1, 1820 pension law modification made it a requirement. Jacob may have come to feel he did not meet the financial need requirement, unlike so many other veterans. He was 66 years old with a growing healthy family. While he certainly could have benefitted from the pension, he was living comfortably without it.[35]

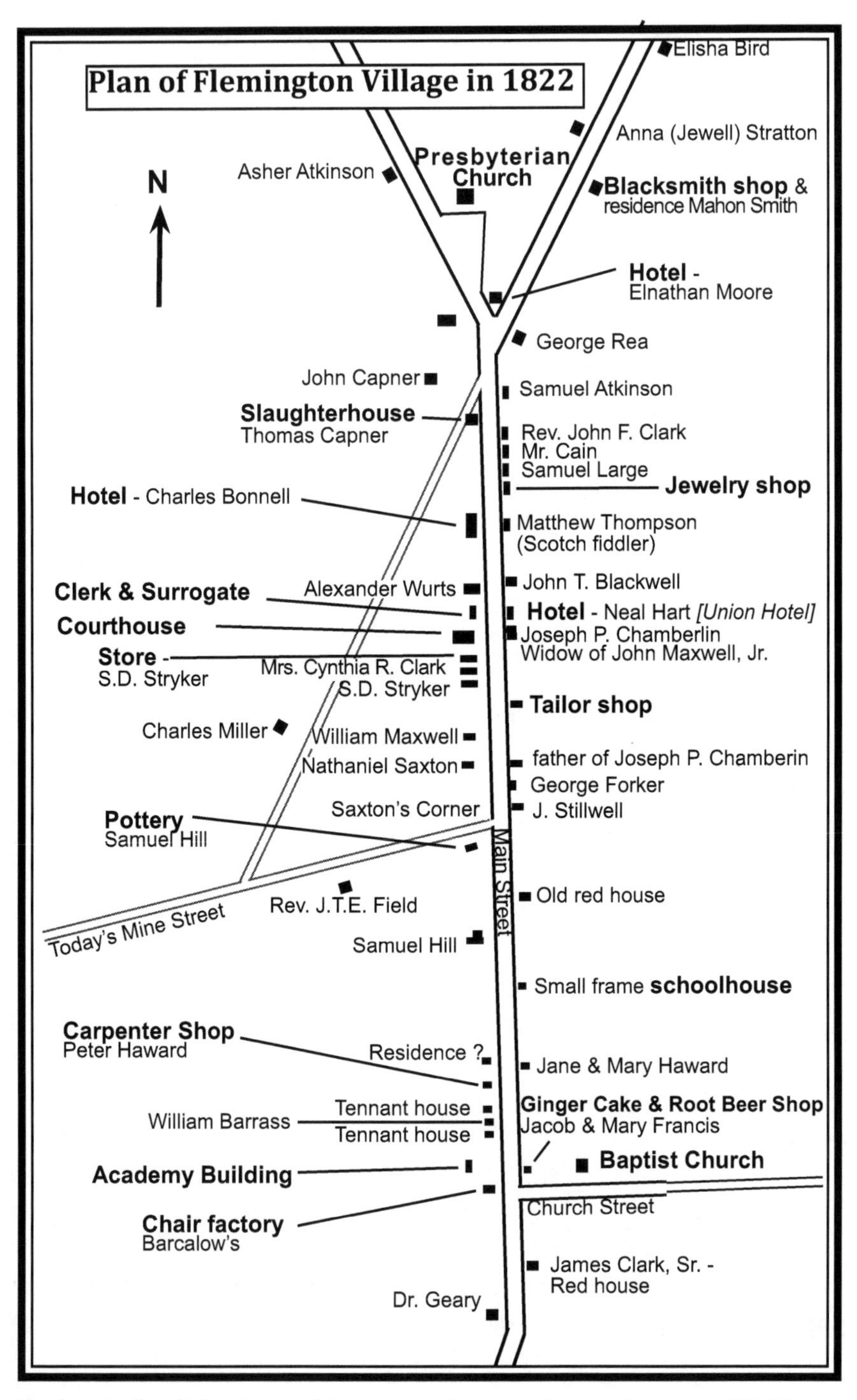

Based on: Snell and Ellis, *History of Hunterdon and Somerset Counties, New Jersey*, 328-329.

Few witnessed this scene without emotion. This corps was assembled for the first time since the revolution, and to-day they came out to attest their love of country, and to bequeath afresh the inheritance that they had so dearly purchased. Our rulers may rest assured of one thing, that however a niggardly economy on their part may withhold from the poor old soldier a bare living, the voice of the people awards to him a generous support. – Hunterdon Gazette, July 12, 1826

22

Life in Flemington 1820-1829

IN 1820 JACOB WAS NOW 66 AND MARY 54 YEARS OLD. PHEBE WAS MARRIED and about 30, John 29, Jacob 26, Jane, Abraham, and Isaac B. a few years younger in their twenties, Nathaniel 21, Asa about 15, and Abner Hunt about eight years old. The Baptist Church received Isaac and Abraham into Church membership along with adult baptism on May 14, 1820.[1] Hunterdon County still had 616 enslaved persons, down from 1,119, while free Black persons, including the Francis family, now numbered 1,443; up significantly from 687. This was the greatest one decade shift in Hunterdon's history.[2]

On a map of Flemington residences and businesses in 1822 created for the *History of Hunterdon and Somerset Counties* in 1881, Jacob and Mary Francis are the only people identified as being Black. While they are the sole Black property owners or renters shown in Flemington Village, many White residents still had Black servants and "slaves for life" living and working in their homes and businesses. The names of those servants and slaves do not appear on the map.[3]

—

People enslaved for life under the 1804 gradual abolition act and known to the Francis family continued to resist enslavement by running away to seek the freedom still being denied them. Around 1821, 40-year-old Joe left his enslaver, Tunis Quick, who advertised on November 26, 1822, a $50 reward for his return. He described Joe as "about 5 feet 6 inches high, well set – has a black spot on the white of the right eye, a scar over the same eye, and a piece of his right fore-finger gone. He is supposed to be in or near Philadelphia."[4]

This may be the same man recorded in the Baptist Church records for March 23, 1822, where it states that "Whereas Joe, a black man, a member amongst us, has eloped from his master and been charged with other immoral conduct, a committee be appointed to enquire into the business and report." The following year Joe was "excluded" from the Church "for the sins of drunkenness and excessive love of liberty." How ironic that while "excessive love of liberty" had been a positive attribute for White people at the time of the Revolutionary War, they saw the trait negatively in Black people. Twenty-five years after the gradual abolition act, on October 3, 1829, Dinah H., presumably the Dinah owned by Jonathan Hogeland, who had joined the Baptist Church in September 1815, found herself excluded from the church because she had run away from her master.[5]

Problems with alcohol were common to both races and resulted in cases of Church discipline.[6] As 1826 began, the *Hunterdon Gazette* carried a notice offering a $20 reward for a runaway 25-year-old enslaved man named Harry, known to be very fond of liquor. Harry also belonged to Tunis Quick, and the notice described him as "5 ft. 3 in. high, very black, strong and well built." He had a downcast look and avoided looking at a person in the face when addressed. Whoever apprehended Harry should deliver him to the Flemington jail.[7]

Children born after 1804 to enslaved mothers, although having a known freedom date similar to an indentured servant, continued subject to having their "time" sold. The September 1, 1825 issue of the *Hunterdon Gazette* contained an offer to sell the remaining three years and six months before freedom at age 21 of a healthy young Black woman with cooking and other housework skills. She must have been born about January 1808, several years after the July 4, 1804 gradual manumission law date, so she was not a slave for life.[8]

—

The effort to remove free Black people from the United States and establish them in African colonies gained strength during the 1820s. The

Hunterdon Gazette supported the New Jersey Colonization Society and provided it with free publicity. In an early issue on April 28, 1825, editor Charles George advertised the need to raise money to send a shipload of free Black persons to Liberia. He promoted the racist argument that free Black persons could not expect "equal privilege" in the United States and the unfounded belief "that due to lack of education and economic opportunity a very high proportion of them were in penal institutions."[9]

The New Jersey Colonization Society drew a large gathering to its Third Annual Meeting at nearby Princeton on August 15, 1827. Princeton lawyer Robert F. Stockton presented an "animated and impressive address" that included "interesting facts in relation to the slave trade." Other prominent men, including clergymen, gave orations, read Bible passages, and led prayers in support of colonization.[10] The following year, an article published in the *New York Mirror* praising the wonders of Liberia and entitled "Interesting to Free Persons of Color" also appeared in the *Hunterdon Gazette* on February 6, 1828.[11]

Throughout this growing interest in colonization among its White members, the Flemington Baptist Church continued to accept enslaved and free Black members. The church baptized into membership an enslaved girl named Hannah, owned by George Rea, on November 9, 1823, and received Jacob's and Mary's daughter, Jane, by baptism on November 24, 1824, when she was about 29 years old.[12]

Although seldom reporting on the activities of its Black community members, the *Hunterdon Gazette* did sometimes report their deaths. One death occurred in November 1826 when prominent citizen Peter V. Quick died tragically during a late evening, hastily arranged horse race when his horse stumbled and threw him off with great force. While the paper identified all the White people mentioned in the article by full name, it noted that an enslaved man, identified simply as "a black man belonging to Mr. Hogeland," was dispatched on that same horse to fetch a doctor for Mr. Quick. The horse tragically stumbled and fell again, causing the "Black man" to suffer such severe injuries that he later died.[13]

A death notice in the *Hunterdon Gazette* in October 1828 noted, "Died, in this place, on Wednesday the 1st of October inst. Lewis, a colored man, supposed to be upwards of 70 years of age, and who has been for upwards of 30 years a faithful servant of the late Alexander Bonnell, Esq."[14] The term "servant" in this case downplayed the fact that he was enslaved.

The paper seldom provided a surname for enslaved people, whereas it often did for free Black men. Women were identified less clearly. Tene, a Black woman who had lived in Flemington for many years, was found dead in her bed one Saturday morning. Was she free or enslaved? The paper noted, "She retired to bed in her usual health the night previous, and is supposed to have died in a fit." Had she been free, the editor would likely have given her surname. If she had been enslaved, the name of her enslaver would typically have been used as an identifier. In this case, omitting an enslaver's name means she was probably free.[15]

—

By 1825, Jacob and Mary still lived in the house they rented from the Baptist Church, and Flemington continued to undergo many changes. Charles George began publishing his *Hunterdon Gazette* on March 24, 1825, as the first newspaper printed in Flemington and recorded many of those changes. For example, when a tri-weekly mail route went into service in 1829, George reported it in the *Gazette*.[16]

Other Hunterdon County towns had been experiencing a "spirit of improvement" during the past several years, and Flemington residents hoped their town would develop a similar spirit. Several new houses were under construction, with additional buildings in the planning stage, and several businesses were changing. Charles Bonnell put his well-known tavern and lot up for sale in January 1824. His lot contained three acres, accommodating the tavern house and its attached "uncommonly large and convenient shed, a carriage house, a hovel, and other out buildings."[17] Blacksmith Thomas J. Stout announced that, rather than relocate, he would remain in Flemington and had taken a shop near Mr. Bonnell's Hotel. Construction of a Methodist meeting house began in 1824 on land next to this hotel purchased from Thomas Capner. Peter Smick succeeded Charles Bonnell as the tavern owner in May 1826.[18]

After Samuel D. Stryker moved to Lambertville on April 1, 1825, the store of Anderson & Stryker continued to sell a wide variety of goods. These included "cloths, cassimeres, satinets, flannels, muslins, tartan plaids, camlets, shawls, and handkerchiefs." In addition to those textiles, he sold grass and cradling scythes, cast steel, German steel, and English of superior quality. In 1826, merchant Elisha R. Johnston began competing with general merchant Joseph P. Chamberlin. Johnston advertised a variety of foods, textiles, and other items for sale.[19] Asher Atkinson put his store, where the Francis family had traded for several decades, up for lease in 1826, and the following year Knowles & Carhart opened a "country store" at the site.[20]

Milliner Hannah Blackwell set up her shop on the hill near Hoagland's by 1826.[21] That year, tailor Samuel Nailor began business at "the old established stand next door to E. R. Johnston's store," while tailor William Iliff moved his shop to the house of George Rea.[22] Watchmakers James and John Callis opened the shop lately occupied by R. Hooley. They repaired musical, repeating, horizontal, and patent lever watches and sold musical seals, snuff boxes, and other items.[23]

In October 1826, Samuel Hill's pottery factory near Jacob and Mary's house took fire. Nearby citizens assembled to fight it and put it out in a short time without significant loss. The cause remained a mystery. Hill did ask that people who owed him money would make payment in wood suitable for burning as soon as possible because the fire repairs left him short of cash to purchase firewood for his kilns. The *Hunterdon Gazette* noted the need for the town to secure a fire engine.[24]

In an assessment of the village in 1826, the *Gazette* commented that it still needed "a few additional enterprising mechanics," especially a saddle and harness maker and a coach maker. Within a few months, P. W. Dunn advertised his saddle and harness "manufactory" open for business in the village.[25]

The dirt roads trod by the Francis family in Flemington village were notorious for their poor condition. Charles Bartles, who took up residence in Flemington in 1822, says he frequently assisted in prying out wagons and teams which had become "stalled" in main street mud. The *Hunterdon Gazette* reported in February 1828 that "the public roads have not been in a worse condition in twenty years. Those whose business required them to be at court here this week experienced many difficulties in attending. Learning that the roads were in many places impassable, we did not send our carriers on the routes of Thursday and Friday."

A public meeting held at the courthouse in early 1828 considered "turnpiking the streets" and improving the sidewalks on both sides. This announcement did not specify just what "turnpiking" would involve to improve things. The citizens appointed a committee consisting of Charles Bonnell, Samuel Hill, Neal Hart, Charles George, and E. R. Johnston to solicit subscriptions, results unknown. Improvement took time. Five years later, in 1833, Charles Bartles constructed the first sidewalk in Flemington in front of his residence. That same year, he was the first to set out shade trees along the road on his lot.[26]

In defending itself in 1828 against criticism and arguments that the Hunterdon County seat should be moved to another town, the village boasted that:

> *owing to these circumstances or some other cause, for which your memorialists feel thankful, Flemington has always been distinguished as one of the most healthy situations in the county. The town is built on elevated ground, not barren or sterile, but bountifully fertile and productive; and which, like other soils of the same description, is liable no doubt to get muddy in rainy seasons, and dusty in extreme drought – an objection to the site of a county town, which we confess has the advantage of novelty at least, as we never before understood it to be essential to a county town more than any other, that should be built upon the sand.*[27]

The town contained three churches, the county offices and courthouse, a Post Office, and "between 40 and 50 dwelling houses, all occupied, several of them with two families each; besides store houses, shops, and out buildings." Business structures included four taverns, four stores, a printing office, and Samuel Hill's "Earthen Manufactory." The village proudly supported 20 mechanics or craftsmen of different occupations, 11 professional men, the county officers, and other inhabitants.[28] Mail carriers came through once a week from New York and Philadelphia in "Swift-Sure" coaches over the Old York Road.[29]

The log-pipe water system constructed in 1808 to bring water to the village from a spring on an adjoining hill still existed. However, the pipes had been neglected and finally fallen into disuse, primarily because other sources supplied the town "with pure and wholesome water, not to be exceeded in any part of the county." Several springs of pure water existed within 100 to 200 yards on each side of the main street, three of them never failing. The village also had many wells containing excellent water, and some had never failed. In addition, a consistently strong stream fed by spring water flowed at the southern end of the village about a quarter of a mile from the Court House.

—

Jacob no doubt recalled each July 4 the setting when he had heard the Declaration of Independence read in Boston, and its announcement that "We hold these truths to be self-evident, that all men are created equal, that they are endowed by their Creator with certain unalienable Rights, that among these are Life, Liberty and the pursuit of Happiness." While fully aware that the promises of the Revolution had not yet resulted in liberty and equality for Black people, Jacob remained proud of his military service in the Revolution in support of that cause.

Early in the nineteenth century, Flemington developed the custom of publicly celebrating each anniversary of the Declaration's signing. These celebrations followed a similar pattern each year. For example, at daybreak in 1807, a discharge of cannon and raising the flag in the village began the day's events. At sunrise, "seventeen guns were fired."

At ten o'clock, the Flemington Infantry Company of militia assembled at their usual place of parade with a cannon on their right. Commanded by a Revolutionary War veteran "who on this occasion appeared with all the energy of a youthful warrior," they marched to Volunteer Hill where they went through a variety of evolutions and then returned to town and lined up at the flagstaff. Prominent lawyer George C. Maxwell read the Declaration of Independence to the crowd, followed by a "feu de joie," joyful firing from militia infantry muskets and the discharge of the cannon.

At 2:00 pm, the participants had "an elegant dinner" at Flemington's Bonnell tavern, where they gave a series of toasts.[30] The 1806 celebration the previous year must have been similar, but controversy arose when a celebratory "Liberty Pole" with a flag was lashed upright to the town whipping post. Some people had issues with the conflicting symbolism.[31]

In 1809 the Flemington Infantry Company met, and after various evolutions and firings, retired to Neal Hart's tavern, where they offered toasts to the Day, the Country, President James Madison, the memory of George Washington, the Continental Congress, the Union and Independence of the United States, friendship in foreign relations, the heroes who fought in the Revolution, the governor and State of New Jersey, the militia, agriculture and manufacturing, commerce, freedom of the press, the arts and sciences, the United States army and navy, and lastly, to "the fair sex; may their virtue, industry and economy sweeten the blessings of freedom, and soften the cares of life."

Nine cheers followed, presumably in honor of the year. A newspaper reported that "Sociability and good humour, the true demonstrations of joy, were the order of the day."[32] To whatever degree Jacob and his family participated in these early annual celebrations, they probably were relegated to the crowd of onlookers.

The celebratory event evolved by 1814 to include "an appropriate oration" delivered to the military officers, uniformed volunteer militia companies, and the citizens in general.[33] Then, by 1817 the event included a parade through the village up Main Street to the Presbyterian church. The militia officer of the day led the procession followed by a band, the militia infantry, the town clergy, two men carrying the Declaration of Independence, the orator for the day, the American flag, military officers, judiciary and bar, students and teacher of Flemington Academy, young ladies in white dresses from Miss Allen's School, ladies, and the remaining citizens. After the church service and oration, the prominent men had their dinner, complete with toasts, at Hart's tavern.[34] Again, Jacob and his family were merely onlookers to the public aspects of the day.

The local militia was a big part of these annual events and always strove to appear at their best. Militia duty in 1826 played out quite differently from what Jacob had experienced forty-some years previously. The militia was now basically ceremonial and social, rather than an actual fighting force called out on active service so often that George Washington had referred to the New Jersey militiamen as "a people harassed and exhausted."[35]

For example, the Flemington Uniform Infantry held its yearly meeting at Elnathan Moore's Hotel, tavern, on Saturday, February 18 at 6:00 pm[36] At a follow-up meeting at the same location on Monday, April 17, at 10:00 am, members arrived completely equipped for service.[37] That same date and time, the Fifth Troop of the Hunterdon Squadron met at Neal Hart's tavern for company training in uniform, and each trooper was to have eleven rounds of blank cartridges to practice firing salutes.[38] These militia units were preparing to participate in the upcoming Fourth of July 50th anniversary celebration rather than actual military service.

Final arrangements for that milestone celebration occurred in June. After meetings at Mr. Smick's tavern in late June, an invitation to participate went out to all surviving local Revolutionary War veterans, telling them to report to the committee on July 4, by 9:00 am or as soon after that as possible. The organizers did not want to miss anyone but found it challenging to identify and locate all the veterans for this special jubilee celebration.[39]

The day began by ringing the village bell and then raising the flag to a 50 gun salute. Jacob dressed formally for the occasion and walked up to Peter Smick's tavern, where he joined 42 other veterans who assembled there by 11:30 am. He found only one other Black man in the group, Lewis English. However, Jacob knew some of the White veterans, including several who had served with him in the Hunterdon County militia after his Continental Army service ended. Along with the other veterans, Jacob received a broad white ribbon badge stamped with the image of the American eagle and the notation, "Survivor of 1776." The person presenting Jacob with his badge fastened it to the left button-hole of his coat to keep him uniform with the other veterans.

Seventy-two-year-old Jacob assembled in a room at the hotel with the other veterans, ranging in age from 63 to 86, decked out in their badges. They had two jobs to do before the parade began, choose their officers for the day and select men to carry banners honoring several significant battles of the Revolution. They chose Samuel Barber and Captain Tunis Case of Amwell as their officers for the day. Next, they selected Jacob Anderson of Bethlehem to carry the banner leading the veterans and proudly proclaiming *1776*.

To carry each banner honoring a battle of the Revolution, the veterans had instructions to choose an individual who had fought in that battle. Jacob was the only veteran present who had fought in the Battle of Trenton. No New Jersey Continental or militia regiments had fought in it, although about two dozen First Hunterdon regiment militiamen guided Washington's army from the ferry crossing to Trenton. It was because Jacob served in Colonel Sargent's Massachusetts regiment that he was present at the battle.

However, the veterans chose current militia "Major" or "Colonel," David Schamp of Readington to carry the significant *Trenton* banner. Schamp was serving in the militia at the time of the battle, as were all local men, but was not directly involved in it. The men bypassed Jacob in favor of a White man who had earned high rank in the post-war militia, was much more prominent in society, and would benefit socially from the notoriety gained as the flag bearer.

The veterans assigned the *Princeton* banner to John Howe of Amwell, who had not served at that battle. However, this choice did not displace a man who had served. Flemington's James Clark, Sr., carried the *Monmouth* banner and Andrew Butterfaus of Amwell the *Saratoga* banner, and they were possibly veterans of those battles. Richard Mills of Bethlehem likely fought at the siege of Yorktown and would carry that banner. Just why Jacob did not carry the *Trenton* banner is not recorded, but racist attitudes and considerations may well have played a part.[40]

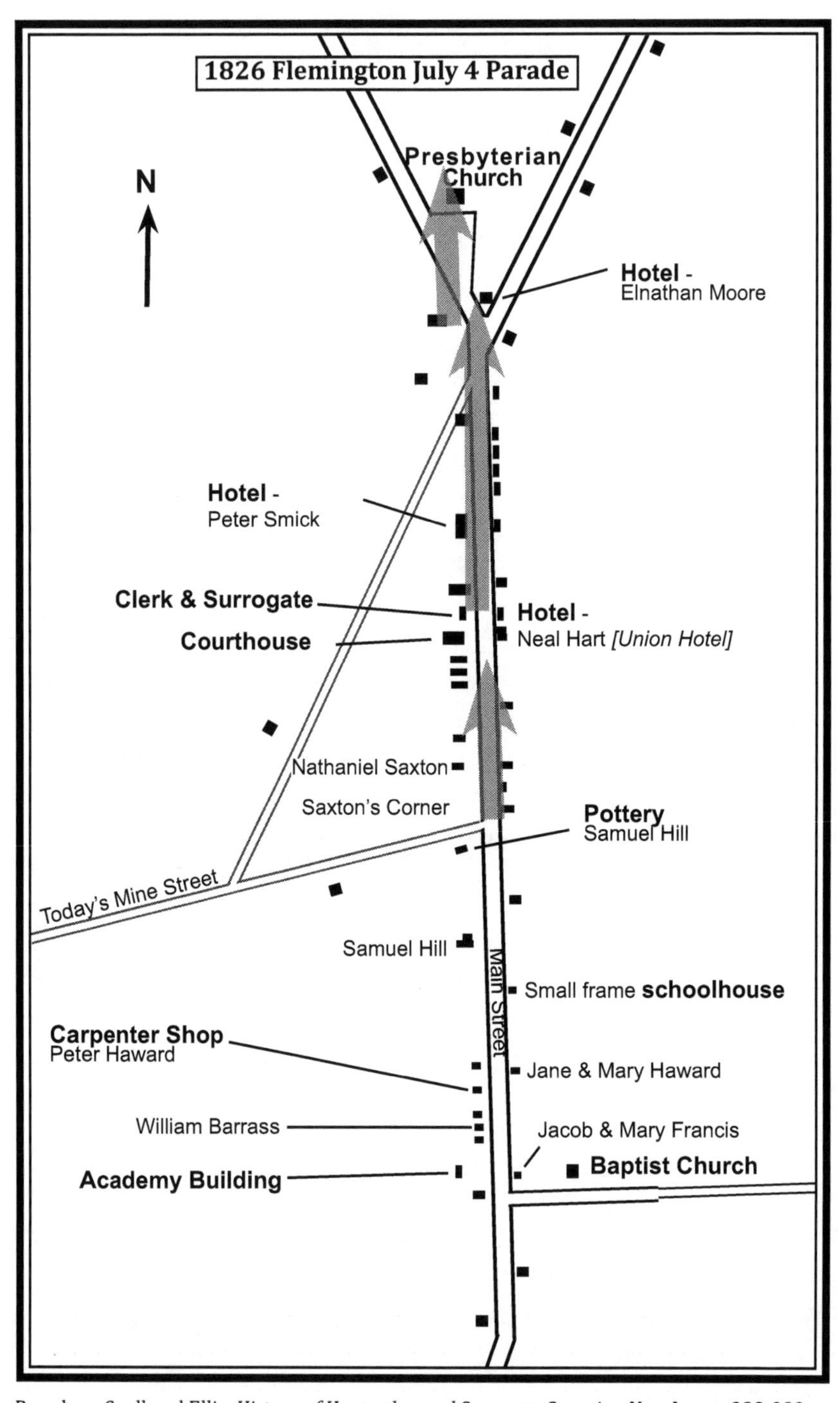

Based on: Snell,and Ellis, *History of Hunterdon and Somerset Counties, New Jersey*, 328-329.

Outside the tavern house of General Nathan Price at Saxton's Corner, the corner of today's Mine Street and Main Street intersection, the procession began marching up the dirt road led by lawyer and parade marshal John T. Blackwell and his two assistant marshals. Several companies of militiamen, both cavalry and infantry, came next, then band music, followed by the United States Flag, the clergy, the orator of the day, the reader of the Declaration of Independence, and then the Committee of Arrangement. The procession included:

> *a very interesting choir of 13 females dressed in white, each wearing a badge bearing the name of one of the original 13 states, succeeded by a younger group of females dressed in the same style, wearing badges each bearing the name of one of the eleven new states. To these succeeded a great assemblage of females from all parts of the county – the whole procession being closed by an immense concourse of citizens and strangers.*

Upon reaching the courthouse, the marchers opened up a space where Jacob and the other veterans would join in. The military marchers opened their ranks, faced inward, and presented arms to salute them. The quiet broke when the many spectators heard "three roles of the drum" announcing that the veterans were joining the procession. When they had all joined, the band "immediately struck up the tune 'Hail Columbia' in a very superior style" and joined the parade, just behind the militia units, continuing to play during the walk to and settling in at the Presbyterian Church. The newspaper reported that:

> *This scene was witnessed with the most tender emotion: many of these hoary veterans, whose trembling limbs and agitated frames seemed to call out for the repose of the tomb, electrified by the recollections of their early days, rallied suddenly their exhausted strength, stepped with the firmness of youth, their eyes speaking joy, that the old soldier, though neglected by his country, was not forgotten by his neighbors and friends.*

Upon entering the church, Jacob saw that the local women had richly decorated it and "large wreaths of laurel encircled the whole interior of the building; the pillars most delicately entwined with the richest of the Evergreen, while the Holy altar was literally embowered with all that could delight the eye or gratify the taste; the whole being studded with the richest and choicest of the flowers of the forest and garden."

Jacob and Mary found seats in the area set aside for Black people. Most likely, 14-year-old Abner attended with them and perhaps also Nathaniel and Jane. We know that Abner felt very proud of his father's service in the Revolution, fighting for freedom and independence. This event would highlight and embed a strong memory relating to those feelings.

The proceedings began with a short service of song and prayer followed by prominent lawyer Alexander Wurts reading the Declaration of Independence and then another "ode from the choir." The service concluded with an oration presented by lawyer Andrew Miller, who gave a "speech replete with good sense, lucid arrangement, and breathing through, sentiments of the purest patriotism."

In his conclusion, Miller spoke directly to the veterans, and "upon their being especially addressed by him, they spontaneously rose in their seats, and continued standing with the most fixed and solemn attention." The newspaper reported:

> *Few witnessed this scene without emotion. This corps was assembled for the first time since the revolution, and to-day they came out to attest their love of country, and to bequeath afresh the inheritance that they had so dearly purchased. Our rulers may rest assured of one thing, that however a niggardly economy on their part may withhold from the poor old soldier a bare living, the voice of the people awards to him a generous support.*

We don't know if Jacob or Lewis English read this newspaper account or had it read to them, but the editor's choice of a word that, although derived from non-racist origins, could be race-charged and would not have surprised them if it were. They must also have felt it would be more appropriate if the White people accepted them as equals every day of the year and not just this one occasion.

After singing another psalm and hearing the benediction, the procession reformed and returned south to Peter Smick's hotel while the band played *Washington's March*. While several works have borne that name, the tune played may have been the one written by Philip Phile, ironically one of the Hessian musicians Jacob helped capture at Trenton, although Jacob would not have known that. At the hotel, Jacob heard the booming 24-gun salute fired in honor of the 24 United States.

At the end of the hot day, hotel owner Smick furnished "a cold collation" to the veterans. However, according to newspaper editor George, "It seemed to be less their care to refresh a fatigued body than to gratify the deep feelings of the soul springing from the vivid recollections and strong impressions of revolutionary times. It was, 'Don't you remember when we lay at such a place,' &c." Jacob had often discussed his Continental and militia service with men he knew, so he must have joined in such conversations with the several veterans present who had served with him in the militia. He probably also related his Continental experience with Colonel Sargent. Six years later, his White militia companions would testify to the veracity of his statement of service when he applied for a government pension.[41]

—

This complex jubilee celebration did not set a pattern for future July 4 celebrations, and the 1827 event reverted to a much simpler format. A smaller procession of military and civilian contingents marched to the Presbyterian Church "in the order that shall be fixed upon that day." After reading the Declaration of Independence, Presbyterian minister Rev. John F. Clark ironically delivered a sermon "on behalf of the American Colonization Society," the organization that strove to remove to Africa the Black veterans like Jacob who had fought for American independence. After this sermon, the town took up a collection to aid the Society. If any members of the Francis family attended, they, along with other Black people present, would have been insulted and angered. Here, during a celebration of the document declaring all men equal, the clergyman and celebrants were calling to raise funds for an organization seeking to remove free Black people from America because they would never be truly equal.[42]

Many Flemington residents supported the colonization movement. Jacob's Baptist minister, Rev. Charles Bartolette, was a local leading voice calling for the colonization of free Blacks back to Africa. Also, at least one Hunterdon County man freed a slave whom he helped move to Africa, where the freed man eventually became a leading merchant in Liberia. However, Jacob's family remained active in the Baptist Church, although young Abner became involved in abolition groups that strongly opposed the colonization movement.[43]

—

By 1828 Flemington had long been subject to efforts seeking to move the Hunterdon County seat to another location, although the county Freeholders had declined to act on several relocation proposals. Carrying the designation

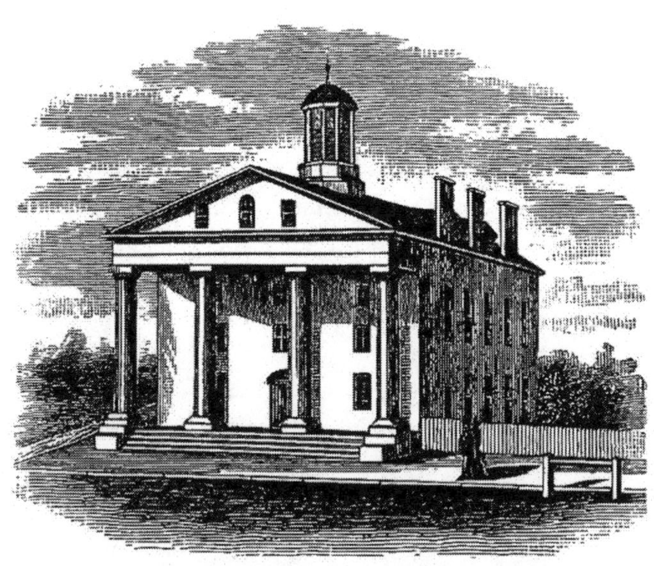

Hunterdon County Court House c1828.

From: Snell, *History of Hunterdon and Somerset counties, New Jersey*, 202.

1828 Hunterdon County Court House

Author photo November 2021.

of the county seat and the business that it brought to the town helped make Flemington a boomtown even in times of financial difficulty. Local craftsmen had built the sturdy Hunterdon County Courthouse in Flemington in 1793, and its architectural design was characteristic of the area.

Tragedy struck when a fire broke out in the courthouse late in the evening on February 13, 1828. The fire alarm aroused people too late to prevent the flames from burning through the roof near the southwest corner of the building. No fire engine was available, so people shifted their efforts to protect adjacent buildings, especially those containing public records. Although the fire destroyed the courthouse, the calm night air prevented more extensive damage to the town. Fortunately, the fire developed slowly, allowing the county clerk to remove the records in his office to a safer location. Authorities removed all the prisoners to safety at the Somerset County jail, and no lives were lost. However, Sheriff Steven Albro and his family, who lived in the building, lost all their possessions. People believed the fire to be arson.

The Freeholders met on March 10 at Smick's tavern, where they appointed a committee to survey the damage and debated whether to relocate the County Courthouse to another town or rebuild in Flemington. Finding the courthouse beyond repair but wanting to maintain Flemington as the county seat, the committee recommended building a new courthouse on the same site and use stone from the destroyed building to construct a separate jail to the rear of the new courthouse.

Lawyer Nathaniel Saxton recommended an innovative Greek Revival design for the courthouse that was accepted. The freeholders hired a Mr. Springer to be the architect and designated Thomas Capner to manage the construction. By March 23, Capner began paying laborers to remove the rubble of the destroyed building and then construct the new one. His records continue until December 1829 and list expenses for masonry, carpentry work, boards, shingles, lath, and other items. The total cost was $13,513.86. The new courthouse floor plan mirrored the previous structure, even though the Bar Association had complained about its inconvenient arrangement. A building just north of the new courthouse became the home to the Surrogate and County Clerk offices.[44]

Jacob's sons Nathaniel and Jacob, or possibly Jacob himself, received pay for working on the new building. The record shows Jacob Francis paid $43.72 on July 16, 1829, for five days of work assisting the mason, and on August 12, Nathaniel Francis received $47.80.[45]

—

About two months after the Court House fire, on April 11, 1829, Jacob and Mary purchased a two-story house with a garret (attic) and cellar from Peter and Sarah Haward. This house stood across Main Street from the dwelling they rented from the church and just north of the Flemington Academy. The modest house probably had only one or two rooms on each floor. Furnishings included four beds, complete with bedding, quilts, and blankets. A lower room was carpeted, and there was a rag carpet upstairs. The well-furnished rooms contained the usual bureaus, chests, tables, and about a dozen chairs, half of them with rush bottoms. One room had a fireplace complete with a pair of andirons, tongs, and trammel for holding pots over the fire. Several noteworthy items were some wine glasses, a pair of brass candlesticks, and several looking glasses.

The kitchen area had a stove, two iron pots, a copper pot, a tin pail, a large iron kettle, a tea kettle, an iron bake pan, a dough trough, a coffee mill, and a collection of crockery in a corner cupboard, among other items. The garret stored various pieces of lumber, and the cellar contained a barrel of soap, five barrels and two kegs, and more lumber. The seventeen one-hundredths of an acre lot, part of a large parcel Peter Haward had purchased from William and John Maxwell in April 1810, accommodated a kitchen garden where Jacob and Mary grew corn, cabbage, beets, and other vegetables and raised pigs and hogs.[46]

This house sat two lots north of the Flemington Academy and adjoined William Barrass's house lot to its south. After Jacob and Mary moved across the street, people still celebrated Mary's ginger cakes and the homemade root beer that Mary kept on tap in a spring of cold water in the cellar. Over 50 years after their deaths, the author of a short history of the Flemington Academy still recalled Mary and Jacob's friendliness. The article also noted that their fellow parishioners at the Baptist Church often stopped to purchase refreshments after services.[47]

Jacob and Mary's son, Nathaniel, married free Black woman Hannah Reading on January 24, 1829, with Rev. J. P. Pearson officiating. It seems probable that Nathaniel had taken over the family farm by this time.[48]

The entire family had long been interested in supporting the abolition movement but strongly opposed the colonization proposals associated with it. Son Abner was already corresponding with abolitionists. The local newspaper listed him as having a letter at the Flemington Post Office in June 1829, just months before he assumed an important position at an abolitionist/ anti-colonization meeting in Trenton in 1831.[49] Abner was on the verge of contributing significantly to the movement to secure emancipation, along with respect and equality, for all Black people. His efforts would continue the work begun by Jacob during the American Revolution and after. Mary and Jacob had frequent conversations with Abner and found ways to provide him with a sophisticated education that would inspire him and allow him to inspire others.

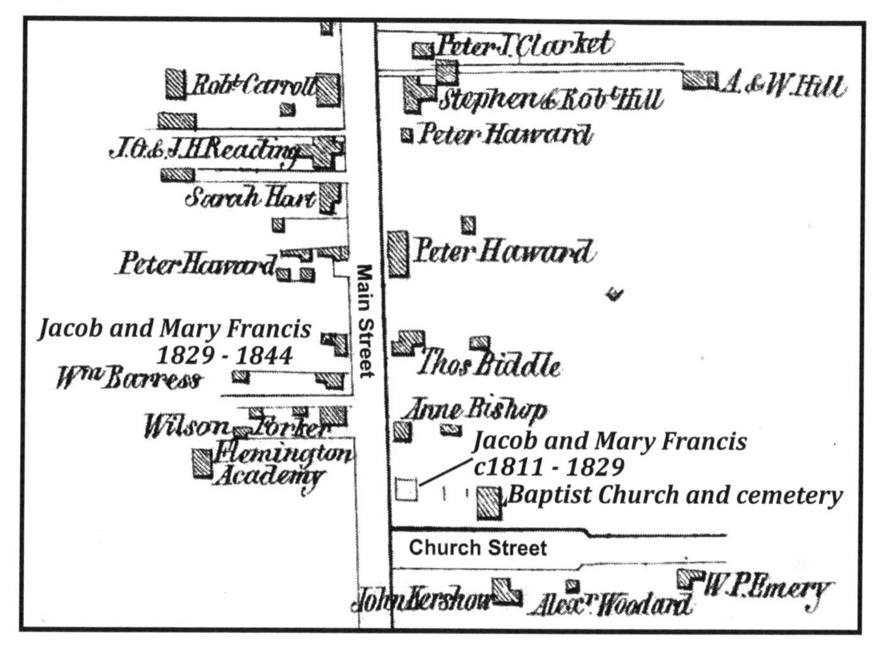

Jacob and Mary Francis Dwellings, 1811 - 1844

Cornell, Samuel C, and Lloyd Van Derveer. *Map of Hunterdon County, New Jersey: entirely from original surveys.* Philadelphia?: Lloyd Van Derveer & S.C. Cornell, 1851.

The house purchased in 1829 from Peter Haward became the residence of Mary Higgins after heirs sold the property to her after the death of Mary Francis.

Jacob and Mary are both buried in the Baptist Church cemetery.

He has resided in this place thirty-five years; has been an orderly member of the Baptist church for thirty years; he has raised a large family, in a manner creditable to his judgment and his Christian character, and lived to see them doing well; and has left the scenes of this mortal existence, deservedly respected by all who knew him. – Hunterdon Gazette, August 3, 1836

23

Life as a Pensioner 1830-1836

THE BAPTIST CHURCH WARNED BROTHERS ABNER AND ISAAC FRANCIS ON February 6, 1830, that they had not been conforming to the Church's rules and would suffer the consequences if they did not change.[1] Perhaps this had something to do with their abolitionist work opposing the African colonization movement supported by their pastor. Whatever caused their rebuke by the Church, both brothers were on the verge of leaving Flemington to pursue their economic and activist lives elsewhere.

New Jersey's abolition policies remained out of step with other northern states. Outside of the South, by 1830, only 3,568 Black people remained enslaved, but more than two-thirds of them lived in New Jersey.[2] Amwell Township's 1830 census showed a total population of 7,358, of which 434 were Black. There were 247 free Black people, 108 males and 139 females, and 187 enslaved people, 100 males and 87 females.[3] The Census accurately lists Jacob and Mary as between 55 and 100 years old; Jacob was 76 and Mary 64. Both Abner and Jane still lived at home, but the census only records one female between ten and 24-years old living in the household. This entry was likely a mistake and should have recorded either a male of that age, Abner, who was about 18 years old, or a female, likely Jane, although a little older than 24. Why both were not recorded is unknown.

Son, John, lived in Trenton, New Jersey, and was listed as a free Black male age 24 to 35, although he was 39. His wife was between 36 and 54, and they had a son under ten years of age and a daughter between 10 and 23 years old. All are listed as free Black people. Nathaniel was listed in Amwell as a free Black man aged between 24 and 35, he was 31, whose household also contained one female age 24 to 35, Hannah, and one female under age ten, Mary Jane, named for her grandmother and aunt.[4] Jacob's and Mary's other children have not been identified in the census, but Phebe was married and about 40, Jacob 36, and Asa about 25. Isaac B. and Abraham were probably in New York City, having been given a letter of dismissal from the Baptist Church in Flemington to the Abyssinian Church in New York on July 25, 1830.[5]

—

New Jersey's gradual abolition continued to keep Black people in situations they could not control. Black children born to enslaved mothers after 1804 continued to deal with having their "time" sold until they reached the age of their freedom. An 1830 notice stated, "A Black Girl, Eleven years old, smart and obedient, wants a place to serve till she shall be 21. Any person wanting such a girl, may learn further particulars, by inquiring at this office."[6] An October 30, 1830 notice offered a six-cent reward for capturing an indentured Black boy named Charles, aged about 20 years, who had run away from tanner Joseph Case. Charles was "about 5 feet 8 inches high, thick set, thick lips, flat nose, black complexion," and stuttered when talking.[7] Describing him as indentured may have referred to the fact that he was born of an enslaved woman after 1804, and the term "indentured" hid the fact that he was in reality still enslaved, but not for life.

James N. Reading offered in 1836 to sell the time of a colored boy aged 18 years. Reading noted, "He has been brought up to the farming business, with which he is well acquainted, is a good size, strong, active, healthy, sober, and honest; his services are no longer required by the present owner, which is the only cause of his being offered for sale." Notice that Reading mistakenly said the boy was for sale, not just his remaining time until age 25.[8]

—

The Baptist Church organized a Sunday school in 1830 using a corner of the gallery and the little library contained in a "small unpainted closet."[9]

—

Francis neighbor and carpenter Peter Haward recorded several jobs that he did for Jacob between 1831 and 1835. These jobs give a glimpse of Jacob and Mary's lifestyle in their later years. Haward's work included mending an unspecified type of wheel (perhaps a spinning wheel); doing a little work on the house requiring boards, nails, scantling, hinges and screws; making a pigpen; sharpening a wood saw; repairing a washboard; making a well curb; creating a new twelve and a half foot spout; and, mending a table. For Mary, he made two dozen clothes pins in 1832, and he repaired a fan handle for Jane in 1835.[10]

—

Flemington continued to experience constant changes in population and appearance. In February 1831, John H. Anderson put up some items for sale because he planned to remove from the town.[11] The firm of Johnston & Hoff, consisting of Joseph J. Johnston and Joseph C. Hoff, announced the sale of their "entire stock" of goods in March, and the firm dissolved on April 1.[12] While some businesses closed, others opened, and in March, John Durant announced "that he has commenced the manufacturer of HATS, in Flemington, where he makes *hats* of the various kinds in general use; and will be glad to supply all orders in his line. He will give the customary price for all skins brought to him. DYEING – He also takes in woolen, cotton, and silk goods, to dye black, which will be done in the best manner."[13] The new firm of Miller & Chamberlain advertised in April that "having entered into partnership in the Mercantile business," their store offered a large assortment of dry goods including a wide variety of textiles, hosiery, gloves, fancy handkerchiefs, ribbons, and laces. They also offered groceries, including molasses, sugars, teas, and coffee. Patrons could also purchase crockery and hardware, paints, and medicines. For payment, they accepted all kinds of country produce in addition to cash.[14]

Dr. Geary departed Flemington shortly after 1832 for Trenton, which had been a previous residence. Other doctors at Flemington before 1840 included John Manners, Henry B. Poole, John F. Schenck, and William Duryea.[15]

—

Growing up in Flemington with parents who cared deeply about abolition and the rights of free Black people, Abner became very active in the abolition movement while vehemently opposed to the ideas of the colonization advocates. In some of his later writings, Abner expresses his pride that his father had served the cause of liberty by taking up arms, and it is likely that Jacob and Mary supported Abner's views and actions with pride. Abner kept a significant library of his books at Mary and Jacob's Flemington house. Very mature at the young age of about 19, he attended "a respectable meeting of free people of color in Trenton, convened in the Mount Zion Church, November 30, 1831, to consider the subject of colonization on the coast of Africa."

The assembled people commenced the meeting by naming Rev. Lewis Cork chairman and appointing young Abner secretary, a strong indication that Abner was well educated and could read and write articulately. William Lloyd Garrison, who had commenced publishing *The Liberator* in January at Boston, printed a report of the Trenton meeting in December, undoubtedly written by Abner, summarizing the committee discussions and stating its resolves.

The report stressed that "free people of color, have done all that is in our power to convince the white inhabitants of these United States, that it is our wish to live peaceably with all men." The group expressed support for the establishment of a college for Black students and the work of Garrison. They proclaimed that "inasmuch as our general demeanor has been that of industry and sobriety, notwithstanding there are some among us to the contrary, as well as among the whites," the negative statements continuing to be made about the qualities of Black people as a "vagrant race" constitute "a positive libel on our general character." They argued that the goals of African colonization were not to benefit free or enslaved people of color but rather to achieve the "extermination of the free people of color from the Union."[16]

In their efforts to move the country toward a fuller achievement of the goal expressed in the Declaration of Independence that all men are created equal and have equal rights, Black activists in Newark formed an auxiliary to Garrison's American Anti-Slavery Society. Black New Jersey residents also supported, and some of them attended, the various meetings of the Colored Conventions Movement that developed in the 1830s to debate ways to improve conditions for Black people. This movement brought a broad spectrum of northern Black leaders to the forefront of political protest.[17] Abner's involvement in these activities would take him away from Flemington, first to the Trenton area and then to western New York, California, Oregon, and eventually British Columbia.

—

After several modifications, the final version of the federal law to provide pensions for Revolutionary War veterans became effective on June 7, 1832. It extended pension eligibility to all officers and enlisted men who had served a minimum of two years in Continental or State service, land or sea. The pension would provide full pay for life without requiring proof of need. The applicant need only include evidence of service in his application.

Less than two months later, on August 18, 1832, Jacob again applied for a pension, this time at the new court house two of his sons had helped build in 1828. A group of men he knew from the Amwell and Flemington area all applied between August 14 and 18. The applicants included former lieutenant Jacob Johnson on August 14, Moses Stout, Peter Snook, John Manners, and Andrew Bellis on August 15, and Samuel Corwine on August 18. Jerome Waldron testified in support of Jacob on August 18 but did not apply for a pension himself and did not corroborate other applicants' statements. The four men who applied on August 15 mutually supported each other with sworn statements. Stout, Manners (also a member of the Flemington Baptist Church), Jerome Waldron, and Samuel Corwine also made sworn statements supporting the veracity of Jacob's application. As usual, several of them noted Jacob was Black in their support statements.

However, Jacob did not supply corroborating statements for any of the White applicants who had supported him. The White pension applicants each had several White witnesses to their service to speak for them whose testimony would far outweigh Jacob's, simply because he was Black. Even though Jacob

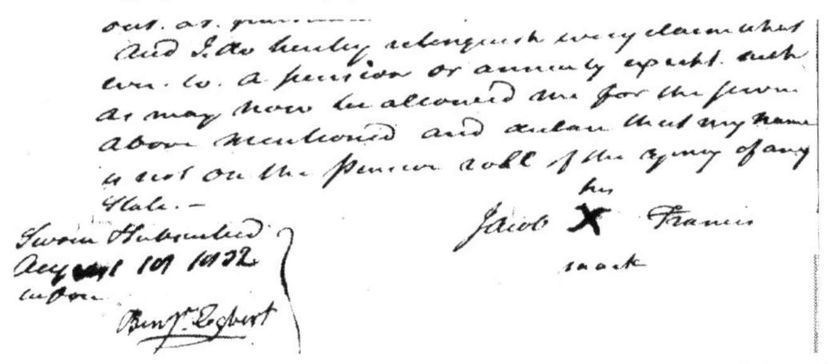
And I do hereby relinquish every claim whatever to a pension or annuity except such as may now be allowed me for the pension above mentioned and declare that my name is not on the pension roll of the agency of any State. —

Sworn & subscribed August 18 1832 before
Benjn. Egbert

Jacob his X mark Francis

Jacob signed his pension application statement with his "X".

had fought capably and honorably for freedom and equality alongside White men in the Revolution, he was still not considered the equal of White men over 50 years later.[18]

—

Abner's abolitionist activities spread beyond New Jersey. In 1832 and 1833, the first page of each issue of William Lloyd Garrison's *The Liberator* listed him as its Trenton agent, and several issues mention letters Abner sent to Garrison. An 1833 article on creating a proposed manual labor school for colored youth lists Abner as the Trenton member of the Board of Managers of the New England Anti-Slavery Society, founded by Garrison in 1832.[19] By then, 20-year-old Abner lived in Nottingham Township, Burlington County adjacent to Trenton, where he may have made himself somewhat unwelcome with his abolitionist fervor. Abner found himself accused of fathering a male child born to Susan Wiles, a single woman of Trenton on July 24, 1833. Trenton merchant Wesley P. Hunt put up surety on July 30, 1833 for Abner's court appearance.[20] This accusation seems to have gone nowhere and may have resulted from local people not approving his abolitionist activities or simply because he was a young Black man.

The Colored Conventions Movement emerged and grew in the 1830s. Abner represented Trenton at the Third Annual Convention for the Improvement of the Free People of Colour in these United States, which met in Philadelphia between June 3 and 13, 1833. He served on the committee appointed to investigate prospects for establishing a "Manual Labour School to instruct coloured youth" that reported progress in New York and Philadelphia.[21] Abner also attended the Fourth Annual Convention held at the Asbury Church in New York City between June 2 and 12, 1834. The convention president appointed Abner to the committee to nominate convention officers, and that body chose Abner to be the Assistant Secretary. He also served on a committee to investigate and resolve the differences between contending delegations from Philadelphia.[22]

—

The Flemington Baptist Church turned 30 years old in 1828, but membership was still just 90. Membership increases commenced strongly in 1829 with 57 new members, followed in 1832 with 23, 1833 with 33, 1835 with 42, and 1836 with 15.[23] The breakdown of White and Black members is not given but may be similar to that seen in the Methodist Church. Between 1834 and 1835, the membership of the Methodist Episcopal Church in Flemington increased from 127 White and five Black members to 170 White and 13 Black members.[24]

—

Abner's abolition work became his primary life's purpose, in addition to making a living. A friend from later in his life noted that Abner "started out from his native State New Jersey to conquer fortune at a time when his path was beset with almost insurmountable difficulties from the accursed institution of slavery." While never enslaved himself, Abner, like his father before him, had to deal with the systemic racism that grew from and supported slavery. Also, like his father, "he had aggressiveness enough in him to clear a way notwithstanding."

He arrived in Buffalo, New York in 1835 where he first appeared in the 1836 city directory as Abner H. Francis, a barber, living on Pearl Street, near Commercial Street. He was about the same age his father had been when he left the Continental Army and set out to establish himself in Amwell Township. Abner's 1863 biographical sketch says at some point in Buffalo, he acquired "a knowledge of Book Keeping and Mathematics" and also learned the "tailor's trade." Starting out simply, "He carried on a prosperous business there for some 15 years." While living in Buffalo, "he was always found acting in concert with those who were unremiting in their efforts to ameliorate the sufferings of slavery and to obtain the beneficent blessing of freedom for his race."[25]

During the mid-1830s, the debate in New Jersey over abolition and colonization was very heated. Jacob, entering his eighties, and his family were particularly aware of it, only partly because of Abner's involvement. On the negative side, New Jersey Senator Garret D. Wall, close to men in the Hunterdon County Democrat party, gave a speech to the Senate on February 29, 1836, beginning with, "We all, north and south, abhor abolition incendiarism." He then stated that he knew no one in New Jersey who was an abolition incendiary. Even though many may desire to see abolition, they would not want to dissolve the Union to do it.[26] The following June, the benefits of the American Colonization Society were extolled in a sermon at the Methodist Episcopal Church in Flemington and money raised for the Society.[27]

—

The growing Baptist congregation constructed a new Church in 1836 to replace the 70-year-old small wooden building where the Francis family had worshiped for about 35 years.[28] Workers laid the cornerstone on July 2, "with appropriate religious service, in the presence of a numerous assembly convened for the purpose." Rev. Bartolette, assisted by Rev. John F. Clark of the Presbyterian Church, carried out the appropriate pastoral duties.[29] We do not know 82-year-old Jacob's health situation at this time, but living so close he probably attended the ceremony if he was able.

—

Just three weeks after the cornerstone laying ceremony, Jacob departed life on July 26, 1836. While many deceased Black people were denied burial in cemeteries that included White people, Jacob was interred just behind where the new Baptist church was being constructed and among the White people of the community. His grave was even marked by a carved gravestone bearing his name and date of death. It did not indicate he was "colored."

Jacob's dictated will reveals that he had been living comfortably in his old age. He opened with the usual statement that he was of sound mind and memory and then expressed his estate wishes. He bequeathed his entire real and personal estate to his "beloved wife Mary." Their daughter Jane, probably then in her late thirties, had not yet married and probably still lived with her parents. Jacob bequeathed her "one turned bedstead, one feather bed, one straw bed, three bed quilts, three blankets, four sheets, two pillows and pillow cases, one new bureau, one candle stand, and one set of crockery ware."[30]

He did not leave any money to his oldest sons John and Jacob, instead noting that he had "paid a considerable sum of money for them already." He made bequests to the other children as follows: Isaac, $170; Nathaniel, $100; Jane, $100; Abner, $50; Abraham, $5; and Asa, $5. The difference in amounts probably reflected the degree to which he had previously helped them. Phebe was married and about 46 years old, and as noted earlier, Jacob listed her as Mary's daughter and bequeathed her $10. He ordered the residue of his estate sold after Mary's death with the proceeds to be divided equally one year after her death among his sons Isaac, Nathaniel, Abner, Abraham, and Asa and daughter Jane. He appointed Isaac and Nathaniel as his executors, and they were sworn in on August 5, 1836.[31] The bequests indicate that Jacob was close to all his children and proud of their achievements. They had belied the White racist stereotype of incapable, dishonest, drain on society, dangerous, and needy free Black people.

Jacob left no record of how he felt about Abner's work with abolition and his recent relocation to Buffalo. However, all indications are that he approved and was immensely proud. The item with the highest cash value in the inventory of Jacob's estate was Abner's library. Jacob and Mary had somehow found ways to provide Abner with an education that went well beyond the rudiments of reading and writing. They appear to have wanted Abner to carry on the fight for liberty and equality that had motivated Jacob's military service. For the rest of his life, Abner commented on his pride in his father's military service fighting for the ideals of freedom and equality for all people that motivated his actions in life.

The Jacob Francis headstone in the Flemington Baptist Church Cemetery.
The stone reads: "In Memory of Jacob Francis who died July 26, 1836."

Author photo.

Jacob's August 3 death notice in the *Hunterdon Gazette* stands out as the most extensive one published that year. The usual death notice contained just one or two sentences reporting the deceased's name, residence, date of death, age, and not much more.[32] One notice, for a 24-year-old man, did give a more personal short statement, apparently because the editor knew him. But, in contrast to Jacob's, the death notice for prominent 74-year-old Revolutionary War veteran Major Tunis Quick was only a single sentence. The announcement for a 40-year-old former member of the State Assembly mainly consisted of praise for his personal qualities but was shorter than Jacob's. The notice about 60-year-old Captain David Manners was about half the length of Jacob's and dealt with the cause of death and the community respect and liking for him in general without specifics.[33]

In some ways, editor Charles George's more extensive statements about Jacob suggest that his high-quality characteristics were not those expected in a Black man. George did not praise Jacob for his material wealth or achieving high public, military, or government office. Instead, he praised Jacob for living the quality of life expected of a respectable White man. For a White man, those qualities would not have been so noteworthy, just expected. That may be unfair, but it is curious.

After noting that Jacob was "a colored man," the notice stressed his 30-year membership in the Baptist Church and that he had "raised a large family in a manner creditable to his judgment and his Christian character, and lived to see them doing well." George described Jacob's military service, although reversing the States for which he performed his Continental and militia service. This minor error undoubtedly resulted from the many intervening years since the Revolution. More importantly, George particularly noted that "his fidelity and good conduct as a soldier were the subject of remark and received the approbation of his officers." In common with death notices for prominent White men, Jacob's expressed the high respect everyone had for him. Editor George must have personally known and respected Jacob.

Jacob had demonstrated pride in his military service in defense of liberty throughout his long life. It comes across clearly in his pension application and death notice. People in Flemington knew about his service in the Revolution and how important that service was to him as he navigated through the complex world of changing rights and conflicting attitudes toward free Black people during his long lifetime.[34]

—

At the time of Jacob's death, the idea that an unknown Black person could automatically be assumed to be enslaved was still strong enough to be used as a defense in legal cases. The year of his death, a court tried the case of an under-fifteen-year-old free Black boy sold into slavery. The purchaser of the boy put forth the defense that he should be able to assume the seller owned what he was selling, even a human being, the same as he would for "any other chattel." However, this defense did not hold up in court, and from this and other cases, the judgment stood that, under the law, one could not presume that a Black person was a slave simply because they were Black.[35] This ruling was at least a little progress, but still far short of the equality that Jacob and his family had struggled to achieve.

Part IV

Continuing the Fight for Equal Rights for All

DIED, In Flemington, Monday, Mary Francis, (colored woman) at an advanced age. – Hunterdon Gazette, February 28, 1844

24

Mary and the Children 1837-1844

A LITTLE OVER A YEAR AFTER JACOB'S DEATH, DAUGHTER JANE MARRIED Jacob Innis/Innes on September 30, 1837. Rev Bartolette officiated and recorded in his records that both were from Flemington and "couloured."[1] It appears that Jane and Jacob removed to Easton, Pennsylvania after the wedding in Flemington.[2]

While evidence of friendships between Black and White people in 1830s Flemington is rare, it does appear that Mary and Jane Francis belonged to an integrated Flemington social group connected with the Baptist Church. William and Mary Bailey had been members of the Church before they removed to Randolph, New York. On August 28, 1838, they wrote to their former pastor asking him to give their respects to William Barrass and wife, Mr. Bush and wife, Mrs. Capner, Mary Frances & Jane, and all the rest of their inquiring friends & acquaintances. All the people mentioned except Mary and Jane were White. Prominent lawyer William Barrass lived next door to Jacob and Mary and would later help inventory Mary's estate when she died in 1844.[3] The Bailey's seem unaware of Jane's recent marriage.

—

The revolution leading to independence from Great Britain that had determined much of Jacob's life was over, but the struggle for human rights that he had also fought for continued in the revolutionary world of his children, especially Abner. African colonization continued to be a frequently debated topic in Flemington. Three years after Jacob's death, Peter Haward entered in his diary in September 1839 (no specific day) that "A. D. Warren spoke in the Court House on the subject of Colonization of Free Colored people."[4]

Abner's abolitionist activities took him away from Flemington during the last years of Jacob's life. Sometime after moving to Buffalo, New York in 1835, and definitely by 1837, Abner married free Black woman Sydna Edmonia Robella Dandridge, the daughter of John and Charlotte Dandridge. The Dandridge family had moved from Virginia to Buffalo, where John worked as a waiter in 1850.[5]

By 1837, Abner partnered with Robert Banks in the firm of R. Banks & Co., selling old and new clothing at their shop on Pearl Street, near Commercial Street opposite the city hotel. The following year, the company appeared in the city directory as drapers & tailors at 9 Trowbridge block. Their business became one of the top clothing stores in Western New York, known for their extensive inventory and prompt service. Fashion was so important that working in the clothing business gave Abner access to a wide variety of people.[6]

Unfortunately, Abner encountered civil unrest in Buffalo that threatened its Black citizens.[7] In late January 1838, Abner penned a letter, signed by 46 people, identified as "An appeal to the citizens of Buffalo" that appeared in *The Colored American*. Referring to the harassment Buffalo's Black citizens had been suffering, he wrote:

> *Fellow Citizens, -- Although incompetent to do this appeal justice, still, the present crisis demands that something should be done. The opprobrious epithets continually poured out against the colored citizens, and the contemptuous manner in which we are treated by the aged and the young, is enough to debase our minds and paralyze our efforts. We would ask where can be found, under heaven, a class of men that have been thus treated, that have been more subservient to, the laws, made a more rapid progress, and less expense to the city, than we, the colored citizens of Buffalo? And we would also ask if this has not always been the case with the respectable part of the colored community; and why are we thus treated; why is it that on almost every subject brought up that leads to excitement, no matter where it originated, that the heaviest threats and greatest prejudices rest upon the colored people? Are we deserving of such treatment? Is it right that the whole colored community should be implicated for the opinions of misconduct of some of their people? Is*

it that we have proved untrue to our country? Surely not. Does not Botta's History, page 113, of your own country prove to the contrary! You will there find among the first American blood shed in defence of her rights, that of a colored man [Crispus Attucks at the Boston Massacre]; and in the last war they were efficient auxiliaries in the navy, and received the thanks of the Commander-in-chief for their services after the victory of New-Orleans. – Yes, sires, and the one who penned this appeal, my father endangered his life and boldly stood up to defend the institutions of the country, and there are others in this city whose fathers were slain in battle to achieve that glorious victory and obtain those inalienable rights which have been so cruelly wrestled from us; and as far as we can ascertain respecting the present excitement against us, it originated from the fact that a number of colored people were engaged with the Government forces in Canada. – Is it justice to implicate us on their account? Our interest are not identified with theirs; they serve under a separate government, and are amenable to the laws under which they live, and we do assure you our interests are as much at stake, our feelings as strongly attached to this government, and as fully prepared to act in its defence, if necessary, as any other citizens amongst you, and we hope and trust such feelings will no longer be harbored against us. It must be expected that there will be some thoughtless and malicious persons in the community; but the undersigned, and numbers whose names are not here, are willing to protect the city against any aggressors.[8]

The following month, a letter from Abner dated February 1, 1838, appeared in the abolitionist newspaper *The Friend of Man* published at Utica, New York. He wrote:

I noticed in the 83d number of your paper a publication copied from a hand-bill which we (the colored citizens of Buffalo) felt bound to circulate for our safety, expressive of our sentiments, and to allay the excitement against us, brought on by some true calumniator. Previous to the appeal which you published, we circulated hand-bills stating the causes of the excitement against us. As you have not seen that hand-bill, I address a few lines to you informing you why such bills were circulated, & the effect. At the time of the great excitement in this city, occasioned by the interference of some of the citizens with Canadian affairs, a rumor went the rounds that the colored

> *citizens of this city had held public meetings and passed resolutions expressive of our determination to aid and abet the government of Canada, which was strictly false, but produced quite a desperate feeling against us. Shortly after it was ascertained that among the Canadian forces were a number of colored people, and as usual (as if we had an interest at stake with them) the rabble become furious towards us and it was almost impossible for us to walk the streets without molestation. One colored man was taken up upon charge of attempting to fire the city, which upon trial proved unfounded, and if we had not circulated the said hand-bills as soon as we did, some of us, no doubt, would have shared the fate of our esteemed and much lamented friend, [Elijah] Lovejoy – murdered by the hands of an infuriated and lawless mob [at Alton, Illinois in 1837]. But thank God, the excitement ceased, and we were once more permitted to pursue our daily avocations in peace. O prejudice! Thou fell destroyer of human life and happiness. When will thy progress be stayed, and human beings no longer suffer by thy blighting influence. Alas! not until slavery is banished from our land. It produces more suffering than any evil that has existed since its first commencement – It is the foundation of all that unholy prejudice which is harbored against us and which prostrates us in the dirt. It enters the soul, and when its effects present to us scenes like that of Alton, all our sympathies should be engaged. The sufferings of the oppressed should be printed in flowing letters on our foreheads. All well-wishers of humanity should arouse from their lethargy. Abolitionists! Arouse – invigorate your efforts by a firm reliance on him whose cause you are espousing. It is the cause of God and must prevail.*[9]

Not ignoring his business activities, in 1839, Abner partnered with James Garrett at a different location, and the name of the firm changed to Francis, Garrett & Company.[10]

—

Back in Flemington, about two years after Jacob's death, Mary learned that she could apply for a pension as a Revolutionary War veteran's widow. Congress had passed a law authorizing those pensions on July 7, 1838. When Mary made her application on September 22 that year, the law required that she prove her marriage to Jacob and that he had been a pensioner who was now deceased. Her application statement contained information relating to Jacob's and her identity and her description of their marriage ceremony, including information about her situation as an enslaved woman at the time of the marriage.

Just as Jacob had no documentary proof of his military service, such as a written discharge, Mary did not have a marriage certificate or other document proving her marriage to Jacob. Therefore, she included supporting statements about their marriage ceremony from her formerly enslaved friend Phillis Duncan; even though, as a person of color, her testimony would not be sufficient. Samuel Hunt, the son of her former enslaver Nathaniel Hunt, also affirmed the wedding.

To add White testimony to her file, Mary also included a statement from her neighbor and friend Peter Haward, made the same day as Phillis Duncan's, attesting to the "excellent character" and "good repute for honor truth and veracity" of Phillis and Mary. Several additional White men, including Peter C. Rea, Samuel Hill, and Jacob J. Young, affirmed Haward's statement. The government accepted Mary's application and began paying her $60 per year, commencing from July 27, 1836, the date of Jacob's death.

—

In 1840, Hunterdon County, then somewhat reduced in size resulting from the creation of Mercer County in 1838, still had 35 enslaved persons, and 13 of them lived in Raritan Township, which included Flemington. The Hunterdon free Black population had decreased to 778.[11] Mary was 74, Phebe married and about 50, John 49, Jacob 46, Jane, Abraham, and Isaac B. a few years younger in their forties, Nathaniel 41, Asa about 35, and Abner Hunt about 28-years old. Nathaniel was probably the only child of Jacob and Mary still residing in Raritan Township and on the old family farm just north of Flemington village. The 1840 census shows Mary living in Raritan Township. Living with her were a free Black woman between 36 and 54 years old and a young free Black girl under ten years old.[12] Could these have been Jane and a daughter visiting or staying with Mary for a time? Had Jane left her husband, or had he died? No record for a suitable Jacob Innes is found in the 1840 census. Just who was living with Mary at this time remains a mystery.

—

In Buffalo, Abner continued to build his business. The firm of Francis & Garrett was located at Number 9 of the United States Block on Pearl Street and employed George Sagfield as a tailor. An advertisement for the firm appeared in June 1842 in Buffalo's *Commercial Advertiser and Journal*, showing that the firm offered clothing, boots, hats, and other items both wholesale and retail.[13]

Abner continued his involvement in civic causes and attended the August 18-20, 1840 State Convention of Colored Citizens held at Albany to consider their political condition. He was the only representative from Buffalo. When the meeting opened, delegates appointed Jacob to the Business Committee, even though he had not yet arrived. He also served on a committee working on finding a way to remove the property qualification for voting.[14]

A meeting held at the African Methodist Episcopal Church in Buffalo on July 13, 1841, protested the actions of the Maryland Colonization Convention by passing several resolves critical of the colonization movement. Abner served as secretary for this meeting and signed the letter reporting on the forum published at the end of the month in *The Colored American*. The letter emphasized how Black men had "fought, bled, and died for the liberties of their country, that we might have equal rights with other citizens. Therefore, we will never be forced from the shores of America – here we shall live, and here we will die and be buried by the side of our fathers." Then, in August, he served as one of the three secretaries for the New York State Convention of Colored Citizens held at Troy.[15]

Great Bargains!

FRANCIS & GARRETT,

MERCHANT TAILORS,

No. 9 U. States Block, Pearl street,

Have just received a handsome assortment of

BROADCLOTHS CASSIMERES, VESTINGS, &c.,

which they will make up in the most *fashionable* style, and warranted to fit, at very reduced prices.

All kinds of Ready Made Clothing and Fancy articles on hand cheap for Cash.

Persons desirous of purchasing articles in this line of business will do well to call before purchasing elsewhere.

Buffalo City Directory, 1841, 61.

As part of his efforts for equal rights, toward the end of 1842, Abner signed a letter to retiring Governor William H. Seward of New York thanking him for his efforts toward securing voting rights for Black people in New York.[16]

Abner served as one of the secretaries for the 1843 New York State Convention and also on the rules committee. In addition, he served on a committee investigating the condition of people of color in New York State. This committee reported that Buffalo had 700 colored inhabitants, including twenty mechanics and two merchants. He was one of those merchants. Buffalo had one common school serving eighty students, a society advocating the total abstinence of alcohol with upwards of two hundred members, a Methodist and a Baptist church, and one Sabbath school with sixty members.[17]

—

Abner caused a considerable stir in September 1843 by serving on jury duty in Buffalo. The *Buffalo Daily Gazette* simply reported on September 12 under the heading "A Colored Juryman" that "among the petit jurors impaneled at the present term of the Recorder's Court, is Abner H. Francis, a colored man." The editor stated that this was "the first instance of the kind, we believe, which has ever occurred in this country." While unprecedented, the editor felt, "It does not appear that justice was defeated by this innovation."[18]

However, an inhabitant of Buffalo wrote a letter on September 11 concerning this event that soon appeared in several geographically diverse papers in either full or abbreviated form. The letter began by reporting the regular news that "You have been apprised that the political Abolitionists held a convention in this place on the last three days of August, for the purpose of nominating candidates for President and Vice President of the United States, as well as candidates for county officers, at the ensuing election." Then the writer announced acidly, "To-day has shewn up a new feature in *amalgamation*," and then explained that when the Recorder's Court began its morning session and when petit jurors were called, Abner H. Francis answered to his name. Abner is listed as mulatto in the 1850 Buffalo census, so he may intentionally have been trying to "pass" for White. The letter noted that he "had the *wool* shaved off his head, and its place supplied by a wig of *straight black hair*." Abner was among the first jurors called for a case determining the rightful owner of some goods. The upset letter writer lamented that "while I write[,] he sits cheek by jowl in the jury box with eleven *white men*."

The writer continued to express his displeasure saying, "If the impudence of amalgamation can go farther than this, I know not how. Francis is a tailor here, and the owner of a small property, and as he has been regularly drawn, is perhaps not so much to blame as the *whites* who have urged him to go forward and take his seat." The writer judged Abner according to the White racist beliefs in the inferiority of Black people who had to be controlled by White people because they could not succeed independently. It is far more likely that Abner arranged and carried out his plan to serve equally with White citizens without any prompting from White abolitionists desiring to make Black men equal with White men. His actions fit in perfectly with his other self-motivated efforts to achieve equal rights. The writer then put some blame on the other jurors and explained, "The Court of course can do nothing unless the jurymen protest, and if they do not do so, I only wish the mercury in the thermometer marked 90° for their especial comfort."

In closing, the writer noted despairingly, "this is, I believe, the first instance on record, in this country where a black man has been permitted to sit in the jury box, but it will not probably be the last."[19] Other newspapers picked up the story from this letter and repeated it with modifications indicating their opinion of the event. In Louisiana and Mississippi, a short article appeared under the heading "A Negro Juryman" that intolerantly modified several sentences to make them read, "The writer hopes that if this be tolerated, the mercury in the thermometer may mark 90 for the special comfort of the associates of the sable juror. We would advise the jurymen to provide themselves with a supply of cologne."[20]

In Indiana, under the heading "A Colored Juror," the occurrence received only brief mention without comment.[21] However, a New York paper labeled the story "A Black Juror" and reported, "A 'nigger' juror sat on the trial of civil suits, in which white men were the parties, the other day at Buffalo. His fellow jurors were all white men."[22]

At least some Pennsylvanians did not view the event favorably. Under the heading "A Black Juryman," the *Jeffersonian Republican* of Stroudsburg commented, "The friends of negro emancipation in Western New York carry matters to a great length," before summarizing the event very briefly. After stating the basic fact, the editor pettily commented, "Our readers will remember that a property qualification of $250.00, in New York, enables a negro to vote, and exercise all the other rights of a freeman. Martin Van Buren was a member of the Convention that framed the present constitution of New York, and voted for the above provision, which forms a part of it. Glad we have nothing of the kind in Pennsylvania! – We should not like to have black men to be the judges of our life and property." The *Hillsborough Recorder* in North Carolina reprinted this story.[23]

In Boston, the *Emancipator and Republican* quoted part of the letter in October with the sarcastic expletive "Horrible!"[24] The *Boston Investigator* published a short summary on November 1, noting, "*Some objections* were raised against his being allowed to set as a juryman, but the objection was overruled by the judge, who decided that he was legally qualified."[25] Another short notice printed in several papers stated simply that "a black man, named A.H. Francis, has been drawn as juror in the Recorder's Court, and he sits cheek by jowl in the jury box, with the eleven white men." In closing, it simply asks, "Well, what of that?"[26]

—

Abner's wife Sydna gave birth to their daughter Theodosia in 1843, but the baby must have died very young because she does not appear in the 1850 US Census and receives no further mention. An 1863 biographical sketch mentions Abner's qualities as a son and husband, but not as a father.[27]

—

Mary Francis died on February 26, 1844. The only identifying information mentioned in her brief death notice was that she was a "colored woman" and died at an "advanced age."[28] She was 78 years old and the family buried her beside Jacob in the Flemington Baptist Church cemetery behind the church. Her gravestone matched Jacob's in style.

Author photo.

—

The New Jersey State Constitution of 1844, replacing the Constitution of 1776, referred to the ideas of the Declaration of Independence in stating that "all men are by nature free and independent and have certain natural and unalienable rights, among which are those of enjoying and defending life and liberty, acquiring, possessing, and protecting property and of pursuing and obtaining safety and happiness." However, the courts soon ruled that these words did not apply to enslaved people and did not amount to abolition.[29] The language also did not mean that free Black people would have equal rights with White people. So, the revolution to ensure equal rights for Black people continued and continues today.

We learn by letter from our esteemed friend A.H. Francis of Buffalo, that he is soon to sail for the gold regions of California. We wish him much success and the anti-slavery cause will expect to hear something from his pen while he is in that country. - Henry Bibb

Chapter 25

The Children Carry On the Revolution

THE LIVES OF ISAAC B. AND ABNER HUNT AFTER MARY'S DEATH CONTINUED the vital story of abolition and the fight for equal rights. Frederick Douglass initiated his newspaper, *The North Star*, on December 3, 1847, to express himself independently from William Lloyd Garrison. Whereas Garrison was a White man promoting abolition, Douglass' *North Star* would be edited by a formerly enslaved man and advocate for equal rights for Black people.[1] Having supported William Lloyd Garrison and then Frederick Douglass, Abner wrote to Douglass from Buffalo on December 17, 1847, telling him, "I am much pleased with the first number of your paper, and am convinced that the principles there set forth, strictly adhered to, will effect more to accomplish the end designed than any similar organ ever commenced in this country. Time forbids, in this hasty scrawl, to say more, but I intend that you shall hear from me frequently." He signed it Abner H. Francis.[2]

At a March 2, 1848 meeting of the colored citizens of Buffalo at the Vine Street Methodist Church, Abner delivered a lengthy eulogy to the life and character of John Quincy Adams, who had died on February 23. The attributes Abner extolled in praising Adams reflected beliefs his mother and father had instilled in him. Abner wrote that for Adams, "In the family circle, in the public gatherings of his native State, or in the councils of the nation, that principle of the largest liberty, was his principle." During his life, Adams, "single handed and alone, amid sarcasm and rebuke, threats and persuasions, the knife and the bullet," had been "an unflinching advocate" of "the right of the oppressed and the right of petition." With regard to improving life for Black people:

> *It was mainly through his influence that the sacred right of petition had been sustained, and the discussion on the subject of slavery in the United States reached such prominence by his labors, at a time when it required more moral stamina than was possessed by any other on that floor; and at the present time no fear need ever be entertained of expelling it from among the subjects of deliberation, until the trial is complete and the end gained.*

While analyzing the importance of Adams' work, Abner noted:

> *I should like to have the world know that the same principles of '76, which led the great mind of John Q. Adams to energetic action, to advise in behalf on his country to throw off the British yoke, actuated my father to shoulder his musket and serve through a bloody contest. And not only my father's but the blood of colored men was freely shed in that struggle for national independence.*[3]

Abner would only have known about his father's motivations if Jacob had talked about his military service on many occasions, especially when conversing with Abner about his abolition beliefs and desire to be involved in the movement. However, their conversations went far beyond just abolition. They discussed the fight for equal rights and opposition to the African Colonization movement that they heard strongly supported in Flemington, even at church.

While it was essential to throw off the bonds of slavery, Abner also profoundly believed that the White supremacy and institutionalized racism that accompanied it must also be abolished. He stated, "I base my abolition on the doctrine of universal freedom. My field of action is the world; wherever there can be found beings possessing undying, imperishable and immortal spirits, regardless of the land that gave them birth, they in like proportion share my sympathy, and shall have my support."[4]

During the 1840s, the Black citizens of Buffalo protested the lack of opportunities for their children to acquire a quality education simply because of their complexion. Somehow, Abner's parents had overcome similar obstacles in Flemington and found a way for him to become educated. Abner used his considerable influence to promote Black protests concerning this obstacle to improvement in life. Part of those protests involved enrolling Black children in public schools. However, school officials humiliated Black children sent to school by their parents in defiance of segregation policies, by denying the children seats and instruction. Officials removed some children from school by physical force. Voters continued to approve segregation, and many fearful Black parents removed their children from the district schools.[5] This problem could not be resolved during the time Abner lived in Buffalo.

Free Black people traveling outside an area where people knew them frequently experienced racist abuses. Abner was just one of many Black convention delegates who experienced such incidents that produced inconveniences and extended travel time on their journeys to and from the convention sites. To reduce the possibilities of encountering ugly situations, delegates routinely planned out in advance their routes and locations to stay or refresh themselves. There was always the possibility of encountering White travelers or conductors who would react to them aggressively with racial prejudice rather than seek to assist them and facilitate their journey.

Abner opened a men's clothing store in 1848 in Buffalo, with his older brother Isaac B., who usually signed himself "I. B." Francis. Born in 1798, Isaac was about fourteen years older than Abner. Abner traveled with Frederick Douglass in 1848 to deliver a joint address to the national anti-slavery convention. Sydna accompanied him on this trip. She had become an active force in women's reform efforts, and was president of the Ladies' Literary and Progressive Improvement Society of Buffalo and a leader in the city's Dorcas society.[6]

The Delegates to the 1848 National Convention of Colored Freemen met in the Court House in Cleveland between September 6 and 8. At its opening, the Convention named Abner the chair, and he appointed an organization committee of five that nominated Frederick Douglass to be convention president. The nomination was adopted, and Abner conducted Douglass to the president's chair. The Convention added one Vice President from each of the three states represented, Ohio, Michigan, and New York, including Abner H. Francis of New York. The meeting made many resolutions relating to education, enhancing the liberty of colored people, the curse of slavery, and the "American Colonization Society as the most deceptive and hypocritical" oppressive scheme against the colored people of the United States. They also resolved to invite females to participate in their future deliberations because they believed in the equality of the sexes.[7]

Abner and Sydna had traveled from Buffalo to Cleveland on the steamboat *Saratoga*. When Abner had asked for a cabin, clerk Alexander Bowman, a resident of Cleveland, refused the request. This action became a topic at the convention when Abner and Frederick Douglass proposed a modification to a resolution thanking the people of Cleveland for their hospitality to read "all the citizens of Cleveland *excepting one*." The convention adopted the amended resolution. Then another resolution was proposed, "That Alexander Bowman of the Steamboat Saratoga and resident of Cleveland, receive the burning reprobation of this Convention, until he repents." The Convention records note Bowman received "a unanimous shout against him" so that "he was fairly ostracized."[8]

During the convention, Abner commented that an article in the *Cleveland Plain Dealer* was "false in fact and cringing to prejudice in principle" in its reporting on an escaped enslaved man, Henry Bibb, and the Buffalo Convention. Abner also commented on a resolution respecting the dignity of all occupations, relating that "He had been in nearly all the avocations named in the Resolution; he had been waiter, etc., and he had been in a mercantile business of $20,000 or $30,000 a year, and was in mercantile business now."

Abner prominently supported a resolution that "Negroes everywhere use every just effort in getting their children into schools in common with others in the several communities."[9]

Sydna continued to be very active in efforts to include women in the cause. The *Buffalo Morning Express* for February 19, 1849, contained the announcement that "The Colored Ladies of this city will hold a PUBLIC FESTIVAL, on Tuesday Evening, Feb. 20th, at the Vine street District School House, at which time an Address will be delivered by Mr. A. H. FRANCIS. There will be Vocal and Instrumental Music on the occasion." The paper erroneously gave her signature as "Mrs. SYDNEY FRANICS, President."[10]

A large assembly of Black people at the Baptist Church in Buffalo celebrated the anniversary of West India Emancipation on August 1, 1849, with a parade, orations, music, and a dinner. Abner was one of the two principal speakers. The celebration took place at the grove of leading Buffalo citizen Judge Bennett, and the paper rather overly optimistically noted that "Acts like this show that prejudice is rapidly abating."[11]

In July 1850, Abner escorted Frederick Douglass to board the "new and beautiful steamer 'Alabama' at Buffalo to take him to Cincinnati. Douglass noted that "my esteemed friend ... did what he could to secure me a comfortable passage."[12]

Abner was no doubt interested in the Underground Railroad and the Fugitive Slave Act of 1850 and, about that time, decided to relocate to California. The previously mentioned formerly enslaved man Henry Bibb had escaped from Kentucky to Canada in 1850, and in 1851 he published a newspaper dedicated to abolition and equal rights for Black people. In his June 18, 1851 edition, he noted, "We learn by letter from our esteemed friend A.H. Francis of Buffalo, that he is soon to sail for the gold regions of California. We wish him much success and the anti-slavery cause will expect to hear something from his pen while he is in that country."[13]

—

Lured by the gold excitement, in 1851, brothers Abner and Isaac immigrated that summer to California by steamship on a two-month journey by way of New York, Chagres, through New Grenada, Mexico, and finally California. While establishing themselves there, they soon decided to establish a business in Portland, Oregon, where they arrived on August 10. They launched their mercantile store in the Columbian Hotel located at Front and Washington Streets. Drawing supplies from San Francisco, Abner would conduct "an extensive and thrifty business" there for about the next ten years.[14]

However, after only a few weeks, while Abner was away on business, authorities arrested Isaac under Oregon's 1849 law excluding Black people. While Oregon Territory had early prohibited slavery, Black exclusion laws had existed since December 1844. Oregon had passed that law to discourage Black seamen from jumping ship, as well as other Black men who might settle with Indians and arouse hostility toward the White Oregonians. A reported sailor from the West Indies, Jacob Vanderpool, had been arrested and expelled from the territory in 1850.

In September 1851, Associate Justice Orville C. Pratt of the Oregon Supreme Court presided over an extensive defense arguing the law's unconstitutionality as a violation of the right of citizens of one state to have the same rights "as the same class of citizens enjoy in the state which they visit" and that the law did not provide for a jury trial. However, Justice Pratt upheld the law and ordered both Francis brothers to be expelled from Oregon within four months.

The brothers began to make preparations to depart. However, a petition on their behalf, signed by more than 200 White citizens of Portland, helped them avoid expulsion. The petition urged revising the law to exempt the popular Francis brothers. Although the legislature did not change the law, Abner and Isaac did not leave and were not forced out. In a series of letters to Frederick Douglass, Abner denounced the law as "unjust and devilish in all its features." Douglass gave Abner's letters a national audience in his abolitionist newspaper. Oregon rescinded the law in 1854.[15]

Isaac managed the brothers' store and, late in 1855, announced its relocation to a new two-story brick building at Front and Stark.[16] The newspaper frequently advertised their wares, and they regularly traveled and shipped goods on craft sailing to and from San Francisco. They became prominent merchants with solid financial worth that grew through the 1850s.

Sydna and Abner purchased residential property in San Francisco in 1853. Abner continued his work seeking to bring equal rights to Black citizens. He circulated petitions to the California legislature seeking to remove laws barring court testimony from Blacks and chaired public meetings supporting Black causes. Abner also worked to expand knowledge of Frederick Douglass's newspaper among West Coast residents. In his continuing correspondence with Douglass, he described the institutionalized prejudice he and Isaac encountered on the Pacific Coast. Douglass welcomed these letters from "our old friend" and wrote in 1854: "Distance does not damp his zeal in the cause of his people's freedom and elevation."

Isaac died in California in April 1856 when he was about 58 years old, and in 1857 Abner enlisted his former business partner from Buffalo, James W. Garrett, to join him in Portland at A. H. Francis & Co. He placed a notice to that effect in the newspaper in August 1857.[17]

The Oregon Territory had been created in 1848 and a decade later moved toward statehood. The issue of slavery delayed statehood while Congress debated whether Oregon should be admitted as a free or slave state. It became the thirty-third state, a free state, on February 14, 1859. The citizens voted for a state constitution that prohibited slavery but still included a "whites only" clause that, although never enforced, was a factor reducing Black movement into the State. The 1860 census recorded just 128 Black citizens out of a population of 52,465. Struggling against the Oregon racism, Abner continued to advertise in the city's newspapers without regard to their political bent,

Copartnership Notice.

A. H. FRANCIS has this day associated with him in business JAMES GARRETT. The business hereafter will be known under the name of

A. H. FRANCIS & CO.

We purpose entering more largely in the Jobbing Business; one partner remaining a greater part of the time in San Francisco. Francis & Co. will be able, by this new arrangement, to hold out as fine inducements to Country Merchants as have ever before been offered in this Territory. The reputation of this House has been six years before the inhabitants of this portion of the Pacific; we leave it to them to judge whether the public have derived any benefit therefrom; one thing certain, greater inducements for the future

Recollect, at the old stand, corner of Stark & Front streets, opposite the Ferry Landing

A. H. FRANCIS & CO.

Portland, Aug. 10, 1857.

NOTICE.

All persons indebted to A. H. Francis or I. B. Francis, deceased, are hereby requested to call and settle their accounts on or before the 10th of September next, or the accounts will be placed in the hands of others for collection. A. H. FRANCIS.

Aug. 7, 1857. 38:3m

Weekly Oregonian, September 12, 1857, Portland, OR, 3.

with subtly worded copy encouraging customers to visit his store regardless of the day's controversies.

—

In late 1858, Abner purchased the lot containing his store at Front and Stark and expanded his trade to Victoria, British Columbia. In the 1860 census for Portland, Oregon his real estate was valued at $16,000 and personal estate at $20,000. He also appears in San Francisco the same year showing real estate at $12,000 and personal estate at $1,200. He would soon branch out even further than these two locations. The provincial governor of British Columbia had issued an invitation for Blacks to emigrate and become citizens, and in August 1861, Abner and Sydna left Oregon and moved to Victoria. Abner continued advocating for civil and political rights for the flourishing black community and engaged in real estate most of his time there.

The citizens of Victoria elected Abner as their first Black City Councilor in 1865. Announcing Abner's election, a local paper described him as "formerly a merchant in Portland, and is a fine, intelligent mulatto, for whom our misguided southern brethren would have paid about $2,500, five years ago."[18] Another paper stated that "a better representative could not be found. He is a gentleman of liberal education, refined manners, and progressive principles. He will be a valuable addition to the City Council of Victoria."[19] However, because he was not listed on the 1863 Assessment Role, a requirement for holding public office, he resigned the day after being sworn in. His resignation led citizens to question the use of the Assessment Role as a requirement for election.[20]

A short biographical sketch of Abner, written in San Francisco, appeared in the *Pacific Appeal* in July 1863 as the third in a series on the *Colored Men of California*. For this series, the term "California" referred to the entire Pacific coast area. No matter where on the Pacific coast each man currently lived, each had first lived in California. The writer does not give a source for his information on Abner, but it must have been from people who knew him well, and perhaps Sydna. The sketch notes that he first came to California and "subsequently removed to Portland, Oregon, in which place he conducted a large mercantile business." He left Oregon primarily because of the oppressive and anti-Black laws "and the unfair opposition waged against him" and settled in Victoria. The author commented "we hope he will soon be engaged in business, for which his talents and habits are well suited."[21]

This biographical sketch presented his overall character, stating:

> *Mr. Francis is not a public man; he is best known as a merchant, in which capacity he has done much to elevate the character of colored men. Although he makes no pretentions to literary excellence, he is a graceful, easy writer, as his letters in Frederick Douglass' paper, to which he was an occasional correspondent, evinced. He is no orator, but when forced to speak in public, his remarks show sound sense, practical judgment, and are enlivened by a vein of humor.*
>
> *He is of brown complexion, a man of aldermanic proportions; of easy manners, and gentlemanly deportment; he shines most in conversation, in which only his extensive reading, his keen wit, and practical knowledge of men and things can be elicited. His constitution is sanguine and bilious, his habits plethoric; fond of good living, of refined and cultivated taste; a dutiful son, a fond, obedient husband, to one of the most loving and least exacting of wives, a good social companion, but withal, a strict business man.*[22]

In Victoria, Abner often expressed to friends how much he would like once more to see "the great centres of *light* and *life* on the other side of the continent," but he was denied that wish. Abner took ill "with a malignant attack of inflammation" during the evening on March 25, 1872. After a short, painful illness, he died on March 27, aged 59 years. Sydna and a few of his devoted friends ministered to him in his final hours, and his departing words to Sydna were, "Meet me in Heaven." The funeral took place at his home on Quadrastreet in Victoria at 2:00 pm on March 29.

The editor of the *British Colonist and Victoria Chronicle* commented that he was "a leading and influential colored resident" whose "father was a revolutionary soldier, and fought under General Washington in the war of independence, and his mother received a pension from the United States Government up to the time of her death."[23] A memorial written by Abner's friend and Victoria photographer J. Augustus Craigg in Frederick Douglass's *The New National Era* described him as a man with "much natural ability," "much intelligence," "a pleasing address," and "considerable commercial activity." Craigg also mentioned the attribute that Abner seems to have been incredibly proud of, that "He was the son of a Revolutionary soldier who sealed his devotion to his country with his blood on the battle-field."[24]

—

Ironically, the month after Abner's death, a call went out in New Jersey for a New Voter's State Convention to be held on April 9. The call noted that the Fifteenth Amendment to the United States Constitution created "new citizen voters of the State of New Jersey." The rights and privileges of those voters depended "on some well digested plan of operation, some determined settled course of action." However, because "we have never as yet given an expression to matters of public policy on State or National affairs, we, the undersigned, in behalf of the aforesaid voters of the State of New Jersey, do call a convention to be represented by delegates elected by the new citizen voters of each of the cities, towns, townships, and villages in each of the counties of the State." The importance of such a convention could "only be estimated by the fact that the people of the State of New Jersey have never yet realized to the fullest extent that we are now American citizens, entitled to all the immunities, rights, and privileges conferred upon any other class of citizens." Notice the word "colored" was not used to designate the new voters. A note at the end of the article stated, "The word colored is intentionally omitted; as the word white is stricken from the constitution of the State, we should also drop the word colored." In addition, to develop unity of purpose and plan, the convention can also "disabuse the public mind of the impression that we are satisfied with what they choose to accord us. We shall, therefore, set forth respectfully our views on public schools, juries, and all other subjects of honor, trust, and profit, pertaining to our interest and welfare. We shall also set forth our line of policy and basis of operation." Among the people signing the call for the convention was Nathaniel Francis of Hunterdon County, who signed along with White farmer James Williamson of Hunterdon.[25] Abner would have been proud of his brother, and Jacob and Mary of their son.

—

It is also ironic that just two months before his death, the *Weekly Louisianian* for January 4, 1872, noted Abner's service in Buffalo "many years ago" in an article entitled "Jurymen, Without Regard to Color."[26] While progress toward equal rights was being made in fits and starts, Jacob and Mary's legacy continued through the lives of their children. Their story has been told here in the hopes that it will assist the struggle for equal rights to continue moving forward.

Epilogue

Following the lives of Jacob and Mary's children after Mary's death in 1844 has proven difficult. All the children struggled against the obstacles created by racism and not all of them left children to carry on the struggle.

—

Phebe still lived when Jacob made his will in 1836, but she and her husband, Thomas Hickson, disappear from the records beyond that.

—

John was living in Trenton in 1830 with his young wife and son, but after that, he cannot be positively identified in the US Census.

—

Son Jacob cannot be positively identified in US Census records. He may be the Jacob Francis who died on May 3, 1854, age 60, born about 1794. This Jacob was buried at the Alms House Burial Ground in Philadelphia.[1]

—

Jane married Jacob Innis/Innes on September 30, 1837, and it appears that they removed to Easton, Pennsylvania, where they disappear from the records.

—

Abraham married a Margaret or Mary, and they settled in Alexandria Township in Hunterdon County, where Abraham was a day laborer. He appears in the 1850 through 1870 US Census records and the 1855 New Jersey State Census.

—

Asa may be the Asa Francis enumerated in the United States and New York Census records between 1840 and 1870, living in the Fifth Ward and then the Sixteenth Ward in New York City where he worked as a waiter, then a porter, and finally as a bartender. If so, he moved to New York when he was 19, about 1824. Asa may have had three successive wives, Ann, Matilda, and Sarah. The fact that this Asa Francis had sons named Asa and Abner provides strong evidence that he was the son of Jacob and Mary.

—

Nathaniel and his family continued to live on their Flemington farm, and in the 1850 census, Nathaniel was one of only two Black farmers owning property in Raritan Township. The 1850 census for Raritan Township shows

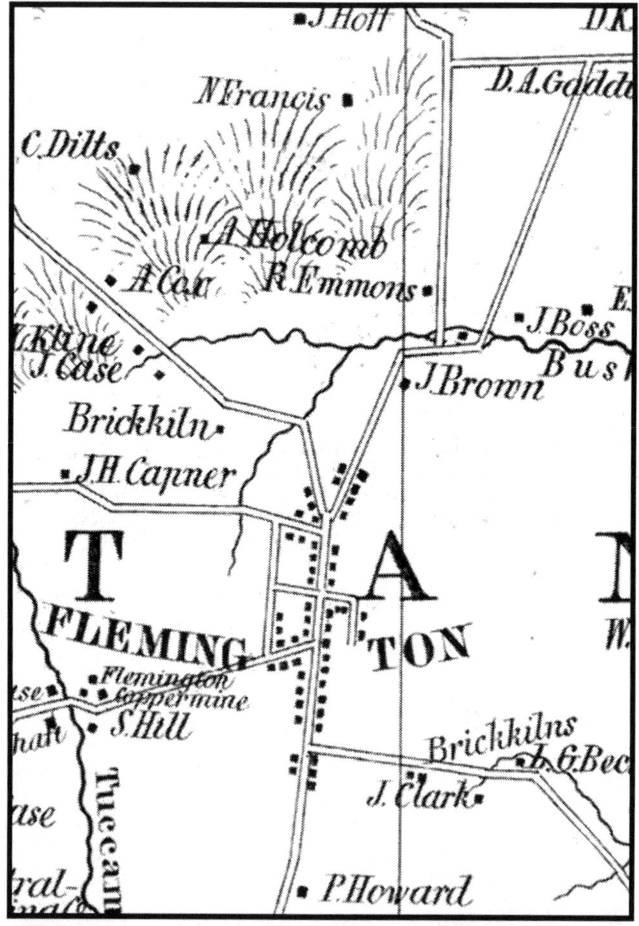

Portion of 1851 Map of Hunterdon County showing farm of Nathaniel Francis

Cornell, Samuel C, and Lloyd Van Derveer. *Map of Hunterdon County, New Jersey: entirely from original surveys.* Philadelphia?: Lloyd Van Derveer & S.C. Cornell, 1851.

him owning real estate valued at $2000. The only other Black man listed as a farmer and owning real estate is 55-year-old Moses Hunt, with real estate valued at $1600. Samuel and Caroline McIntire are listed as Mulattos in their twenties who own real estate valued at $500, but no occupation is given. Thirty-three-year-old Henry Wycoff had no real estate or occupation listed, but his mother-in-law, who lived with Henry and his wife, was listed as having real estate worth $300, perhaps the land her daughter and son-in-law lived on with her. Twelve other households headed by Black men of various ages are listed with no real estate values and either working as a laborer or listing no occupation.[2] Nathaniel also appears in the 1855 New Jersey State Census.

In 1870 US Census shows Nathaniel's farm valued at $5,000 and his personal estate at $1,000. Twenty-eight-year-old David and 26-year-old Anna live on the farm with their parents. Thirty-two-year-old son Nathaniel with his wife and six-year-old daughter live separately on the next assessed, probably adjoining, property.

Nathaniel lived until November 2, 1881, when he died at age 82. He was buried at the Flemington Baptist Church cemetery some distance from his parent's graves in a family cluster which ultimately included his wife and several children. No members of the family are listed in the 1880 US Census for Raritan Township.

Nathaniel Francis family cluster in cemetery of the Flemington Baptist Church.

Author photo

The inventory of Nathaniel's estate made on November 25, 1881, showed that he owned a house containing a well-equipped parlor, a hall, four bedrooms, a kitchen, and a cellar. The property also contained an old house and a barn. As the essential social room that it was, the parlor contained the most furniture and the library. The farm animals include two horses, a steer, three cows, two hogs, three pigs, a lot of poultry, and a lot of turkeys. The farm equipment is the usual mix of horse and human-powered items. Crops mentioned include rye, corn, hay, wheat, and oats. Nathaniel's son, David, administered the estate and took the inventory appraised by two disinterested men. The total value of the estate came to $6,952.25.[3] Heirs sold the farm out of the family in 1885.

In the 1900 US Census, David lived in East Raritan Township as a day laborer. He reported that he was single, 54 years old (born in 1845), was literate, rented a house, and had been unemployed for six months that year. He also appears in the 1910 US Census as single and age 65 living on Clover Hill Road in East Raritan Township.

—

The people in Flemington remembered Jacob and Mary long after their deaths. An article published in 1901 recounting the history of the Flemington Academy devotes a substantial paragraph to them, and their ginger cakes and root beer. Most of the article is about the evolution of the school and the trustees and faculty. The story of Jacob and Mary is a significant digression since they had no direct role at the school. To be remembered that long and given so much space in the article is very meaningful. The focus on Mary is also interesting. The fact that they are included on the 1822 map of Flemington in the 1881 *History of Hunterdon and Somerset Counties* and noted for the "cakes and beer" is another indication of community memory. In both cases, they are identified as "colored."

While Jacob, Mary, or any of their children never achieved greatness, they do represent the thousands of free Black people who struggled for equality daily during the last years of legal enslavement in New Jersey and the systemic racism that accompanied it, and that has continued beyond it. Jacob and his family did not just survive the racism that infused their world; despite it they became well-liked and highly respected by those they encountered. Their lives helped the White people they lived among to see the errors in the arguments of racists for not extending equal rights to Black people.

They also helped prove that when given a chance, people of color could win the respect and friendship of White people on their own and not just under the guidance or force of White people. They could achieve a lifestyle similar to that of Whites living in a system of White privilege while they fought the obstacles of racism. And, they never lost sight of their goal to help achieve equality for all people. The struggle to end the racism they lived with in Flemington demonstrated the wide diversity in attitudes of White people toward Black people with which we continue to live. Hopefully, knowledge of their lives will help the movement toward racial equality continue to improve so that "all" humans can live in equality.

Appendix A

New Jersey Black Population 1745-1860

Year	Total Population	Black Total	Black %	Black Free	Enslaved
1745		4,600			4,600
1790	184,139	14,185	7.7	2,762	11,432
1800	211,149	16,824	9.0	4,402	12,422
1810	245,562	18,694	7.6	7,843	10,851
1820	277,575	20,017	7.2	12,460	7,557
1830	320,823	20,557	6.9	18,303	2,254
1840	373,306	21,718	5.8	21,044	674
1850	489,555	24,046	4.9	23,810	236
1860	672,035	25,336	3.8	25,318	18

Chart based on Calligaro, Lee, "The Negro's Legal Status in Pre-Civil War New Jersey," *New Jersey History*, Fall and Winter, 1967, 176. Citing: Interracial Committee of N.J. Conference of Social Work, *Negro in New Jersey 77* (1932), and U.S. Bureau of the Census, Population Statistics, 1737-1860.
Wright, Giles, R., Afro-Americans in New Jersey: A Short History, Appendix 2.

Hunterdon County Black Population 1790-1840

Year	Total Population	Black Total	Black %	Black Free	Enslaved
1790	20,253	1,492	7.4	191	1,301
1800	21,261	1,740	8.2	520	1,220
1810	24,556	1,806	7.4	687	1,119
1820	28,604	2,059	7.2	1,443	616
1830	31,060	1,942	6.3	1,770	172
1840*	24,789	813	3.3	778	35

Wright, Giles, R., Afro-Americans in New Jersey: A Short History, Appendix 3.

*Hunterdon County reduced in size with creation of Mercer County in 1838/1839

Amwell Township Black Population 1830

Year	Total Population	Black Total	Black	Black Free	Enslaved
1830	7,358	434	%	247 108 male 139 female	187 100 male 87 female

Appendix B

16th Continental Regiment
January 1, 1776 – December 31, 1776

Colonel Paul Dudley Sargent (wounded October 28, 1776 at White Plains – returned ca December 3, 1776)
Lieutenant Colonel Michael Jackson (wounded September 23, 1776 at Montressor's Island – returned ??)
Major Jonathan Williams Austin (dishonorably discharged by court martial November 13, 1776)
Adjutant - Second Lieutenant Peter Dolliver of Captain Perry's company (collateral duty)
Quartermaster - Ensign Osgood Carleton of Captain Keith's company (collateral duty)
Surgeon - John Slomans, Parker Cleaveland,
Chaplain - Eleazer Swetland

Companies

1. Captain Frederick Pope

First Lieutenant Isaac Fuller
Second Lieutenant Zacheus Thayer (Jan 1776)
Ensign Zacheus Thayer then Isaiah Fuller
Sergeants: __ Hooper
Privates: Samuel Bisbee, Solomon Bryant, Christopher Capen, Samuel Capen, Luther Cary, Benjamin Croswell, Noah Drake, Benjamin Hanks, William Hanks, Moses Hayden, Daniel Porter, William Snow, Joshua Stearns

2. Captain William Scott

First Lieutenant Lemuel Holmes (went into Ranger service - second in command to Knowlton - captured at Fort Washington, November 16.)
Second Lieutenant Isaiah Monroe or Morrow
Ensign Josiah Cleveland
Privates: Luke Fletcher (switched to Barnes company), Daniel McGuire

3. Captain Asa Barnes

First Lieutenant Ephraim Cleveland (went into Ranger service)
Second Lieutenant Aaron Stratten (taken prisoner at Tappan Dec 7, 1776)
Ensign Matthew Macumber (dishonorably discharged September 21, 1776)
Privates: Robert Bradford, Obadiah Brown ^ (in ranger service wounded by shot in elbow at Harlem Heights, September 16, 1776), Oliver Cory, John Curtis, Luke Fletcher, Thomas Powell, Tony Sherman, Frederick Temple, Thomas Williams, Titus Wood

4. Captain John Vinton

First Lieutenant Silas Hollis
Second Lieutenant Ichabod Holbrook
Ensign Thomas Hartshorn
Musicians: John Faxon, Francis Faxon - fifer
Privates: John Dobel, Ichabod Dyer, Samuel Ellenwood, Lemuel Field, Daniel Hayden, Jacob Hayden, Nathaniel Holbrook, Silas Howard, Joseph Mann, Jedidiah Russell, David Sloan, John Vinton (son of captain), Nathaniel Wales

5. Captain James Perry

First Lieutenant Jonathan Brown
Second Lieutenant Peter Dolliver
Ensign Benjamin Snow - promoted to Lieutenant
Corporals: __ Hathaway (killed at Horn's Hook)
Privates: Josiah A. Crossman, Oliver Jones, Adam Nichols, Daniel Woodward

6. Captain James Keith

First Lieutenant David Chandler (died of smallpox February 21, 1776), David Thomas
Second Lieutenant David Thomas (June 28, 1776), Osgood Carlton
Ensign David Thomas, Osgood Carleton, Joshua Eddy
Fifer: Hezekiah Packard
Privates: James Churchill, John Cooper, William Dolliver, Isaac Fowls, Zaccheus Goldsmith, David How^ (promoted to Corporal), Isaac Huse, James Ide, Joseph Jackson, David Keith, James Keith, Caleb Leach, Edward Masters, John Melcoy, Samuel Paris, William Parker, Ebenezer Smith, Robert Stewart, Andrew Thomas, Robert Thomas, Eleazer Wood

7. Captain Thomas Farrington

First Lieutenant Nathaniel Doubleday
Second Lieutenant Woody Dustin
Ensign Richard Welch
Privates: Michael Barry (colored), Abel Blood, Simeon Blood, March/Mark Farrington (waiter for father), Thomas Farrington, Jr., Isaac Green, Isaac Lee, James McCormick

8. Captain John Wiley

First Lieutenant William Scott (went into Ranger service)
Second Lieutenant Timothy Whiting, Aldridge Wiley
Ensign Aldridge Wiley, Ebenezer Fish (enlisted as a sergeant - promoted)
Orderly Sergeant: Timothy Whiting
Corporals: Jacob Wilder
Privates: __ Barnes, Jacob Gulick/Francis (colored), Thomas Herbert, William McIlvaine

Enlisted men given are those mentioned in the text. or known to be in the regiment.
Individuals with an "*" are known to have pension application files. Those with an "^" have a journal of their experiences.

Appendix C

16th Continental Regiment - Colonel Paul Dudley Sargent

(Established April 23, 1775)

Assignments – June 14, 1775 – December 31, 1776

Main Army

General George Washington

Cambridge, Massachusetts - June 14, 1775 – April 4, 1776

Siege of Boston

Division

Major General Israel Putnam's

Brigade

"Vacant" – commanded by Gen Israel Putnam - until January 24, 1776

General William Heath's – after January 24, 1776

Eastern Department/Division

Major General Artemas Ward

Boston, Massachusetts - April 4, 1776 - July 11, 1776

Main Army

General George Washington

New York City - July 11, 1776 – Trenton - December 31, 1776

Division

General Joseph Spencer's on Manhattan at Horn's Hook - July 11 - July 29, 1776

Brigade

General Thomas Mifflin's – August 12, 1776

Colonel Paul D. Sargent's – created August 31, 1776

Division

General William Heath's – July 29, 1776 - September 18, 1776

General Charles Lee's – Late October 1776 to December 13, 1776

General John Sullivan's - after capture of General Lee, December 13, 1776

Brigade

Colonel Paul D. Sargent's - October 15, 1776

Colonel John Chester's – Temporarily beginning November 10, 1776 due to Sargent's wound

Colonel Paul D. Sargent's – upon return of Sargent in December 1776

Divisions: Normally commanded by a Major General
Brigades: Normally commanded by a Brigadier General, but sometimes by a senior Colonel

Appendix D

16th Continental Regiment - Colonel Paul Dudley Sargent

Muster Returns during the 1776 New York campaign and retreat across New Jersey

	May 4	Sept 12	Sept 21	Sept 27	Oct 4	Oct 25	Nov 2	Nov 9	Nov 24	Dec 22
Officers Present										
Captains (8)	6	8	7	7	6	5	3	3	5	6
First Lieutenants (8)	5	6	5	4	4	5	3	3	1	3
Second Lieutenants (8)	6	7	2	1	3	3	2	2	1	-
Ensigns (8)	7	2	7	6	6	5	5	3	2	4
Rank & File										
Present and fit for duty	331	295	298	292	250	270	242	225	169	122
Present sick	26	63	42	65	65	71	50	60	41	6
Absent sick	14	71	79	86	91	67	106	107	139	235
On Command*	126	98	90	84	97	89	100	104	100	72
Total	516	527	508	508	503	497	498	496	449	435
Needing to complete	124	113	-	132	137	143	143	144	191	-

Captain John Wiley's Company

Officers Present					
Captain	1	1	1	-	-
First Lieutenant	On command with rangers				
Second Lieutenant	-	1	1	-	-
Ensign	1	-	-	1	1
Rank & File					
Present and fit for duty	52	51	46	46	34
Present sick	8	7	18	9	17
Absent sick	1	6	2	6	8
On Command*	8	6	5	11	11
Total	69	70	71	72	70
Needing to complete	11	10	9	9	10
Sergeants (3)	1	3	2	2	4
Fife & drum (2)	2	2	1	0	2

*These were men temporarily absent from normal company service performing duties such as tending the sick, serving as an officer's waiter, serving as a camp colorman (sanitary cleaning force), serving as a teamster with the baggage train, guarding the cattle or baggage, serving as barber, running balls/making cartridges, serving with the rangers, and other special duties.

These returns show the accelerating drop in strength suffered by the regiment in company in which Jacob Francis served in the months leading up to the Battle of Trenton on December 26, 1776 as his one-year enlistment came to a conclusion.

Source Notes

Chapter 1

1 Gigantino, *Ragged Road to Abolition*, 15. Jacob Francis PF W459. Unless otherwise noted, all quotes attributed to Jacob Francis come from this source.
2 Price, *Freedom Not Far Distant*, 4; Wright, *Afro-Americans in New Jersey*, 14; Wright, "New Jersey Laws and the Negro," 156-167.
3 Gigantino, *Ragged Road to Abolition*, 14; Pingeon, *Blacks in the Revolutionary Era*, 9-15.
4 Schmidt, *Rural Hunterdon*, 243; Schmidt, *Slavery and Attitudes on Slavery*, 3. Probate records up to 1780 for Hunterdon County show thirty estates with slaves. Sixteen showed just one slave, four should two, two cases showed three, two cases, four, three cases, five, and in one case, six.
5 Gigantino, *Ragged Road to Abolition*, 1.
6 Price, *Freedom Not Far Distant*, 32.
7 Price, 21.
8 Schmidt, *Rural Hunterdon*, 244-245; Gigantino, *Ragged Road to Abolition*, 15.
9 Price, *Freedom Not Far Distant*, 22.
10 Price, 29. Woolman, John. *Considerations on the Keeping of Negroes*, 4.
11 Schmidt, *Rural Hunterdon*, 248.

Chapter 2

1 Amwell Township, Township Meeting Records, Hunterdon County Historical Society, However, the records do occasionally indicate a child's indenture. For example, the entry for March 20, 1770, well after Jacob's indenture began, reads, "John Huff to keep Mary Bones Black boy to age of 21."
2 Gigantino, *Ragged Road to Abolition*, 74.
3 Stryker-Rhoda, "1780 Amwell Township Tax Retables," 80.
4 Schmidt, *Rural Hunterdon*, 238
5 Schmidt, 248, 241.
6 David E. Gulick, *Gulicks of the U.S.A.*, 1961 no copy write, page 251. His name is also variously spelled Minner/Minnie/Minnah. Minne and Elizabeth did not have the first of their eleven children until 1769, several years after selling Jacob's remaining indenture time.
7 Stryker-Rhoda, "New Jersey Retables, 1778-1789," 41 shows Gulick owning one enslaved man in May 1778, but not in January 1780. It may be that after Gulick sold Jacob's remaining time, he replaced Jacob with an enslaved man or it may be that Jacob worked alongside one while at Gulick's.
8 Schmidt, *Rural Hunterdon*, 244-245.
9 From Jacob Francis PF W459 – "I always understood I was bound by my mother a colored woman when I was young to one Henry Wambough, (or Wambock) in Amwell he parted with me to one Michael Hatt [Hart?], he sold my time to one Minner Gulick (called Hulick) a farmer in Amwell he sold my time when I was a little over 13 years of age to one Joseph Saxton, he went in the spring of the year 1768 and took me with him as his servant to New York from thence to Long Island where we took shipping in May 1768

and went to the Island of St. John. We visited different parts of that Island and spent the summer there towards fall we came to the town of St Peters when we took shipping and returned to Salem Massachusetts where we arrived about the month of November 1768." Interestingly, Jacob phrases it that they "returned" to Salem. Salem merchants engaged in much trade in the islands, and it is probable that the ship they took regularly transited between the islands and Salem. It is also possible that Saxton had taken him from New York to St. John by way of Salem.

10 Wright, *Continental Army*, 8-9.

Chapter 3

1 Phillips, *Salem in the Eighteenth Century*, 274-275; Hoffer, *Prelude to Revolution*, 12.
2 National Park Service, *Salem: Maritime Salem in the Age of Sail*, 10-11, 27-28.
3 Drake, *Old Landmarks and Historic Personages of Boston*, 177.
4 Streeter, "Salem before the Revolution," 48.
5 Felt, *Annals of Salem*, II: 264-265; Streeter, "Salem before the Revolution," 61.
6 Streeter, "Salem before the Revolution," 49, 53-54, 61-62, 65, 70; *Essex Gazette*, July 24, 1770, 104; August 18, 1772, 11; May 26, 1772, 175; March 17, 1772, 135. These vendue announcements are just a sampling.
7 *Essex Gazette*, December 27, 1768, 89.
8 Felt, *Annals of Salem*, II: 108-109, 117. This was the "September Hurricane of 1769" also known as "The Great Chesapeake Bay Hurricane of 1769." See: Ludlum, *Early American Hurricanes*, 24-25.
9 Felt, II: 101, 117. This was also likely a hurricane. See: Ludlum, *Early American Hurricanes*, 25-26.
10 *Essex Gazette*, June 1, 1773, 175; *Essex Gazette*, July 6, 1773, 195; *Essex Gazette*, July 13, 1773, 201.
11 "John Jenks of Salem to Cotton Tufts of Weymouth."(dated Salem, August 26, 1774) *Historical Collections of the Essex Institute*, XLVII, 230-232.
12 Felt, *Annals of Salem*, II: 410; Phillips, *Salem in the Eighteenth Century*, 272; Hoffer, *Prelude to Revolution*, 11-13; Streeter, "Salem before the Revolution," 50.
13 Felt, *Annals of Salem*, II: 154; Streeter, "Salem before the Revolution," 47-48, 50.
14 Phillips, *Salem in the Eighteenth Century*, 270-271.
15 National Park Service, *Maritime Salem*, 25.
16 Felt, *Annals of Salem*, II: 426-427, 450.
17 *Essex Gazette*, August 24, 1773, 15; Felt, *Annals of Salem*, II: 432.
18 *Essex Gazette*, October 19, 1773, 47.
19 Felt, *Annals of Salem*, II: 432.
20 *Essex Gazette*, March 29, 1774, 139.
21 Felt, *Annals of Salem*, II: 450; Streeter, "Salem before the Revolution," 50.
22 Felt, *Annals of Salem*, II: 453. In October 1772, the *Essex Gazette* carried a tract signed Temperanteriae Amator, stating that "among the causes, that are conspiring to bring on the ruin of this country, there is one that, in my apprehension, is none of the least fatal and destructive; I mean the unnecessary multiplying of taverns and public houses, and the scandalous abuse that is made of them, by turning them into places of rendezvous for drunkards and drones; by which means a set of men is upheld and encouraged, that will be as vermin on the body politic, and prey like vipers upon the very vitals of the state." *Essex Gazette*, October 20, 1772, 45. The county Court of General Sessions (1692-1827), consisted of justices of the peace and heard all criminal cases and also had authority over county affairs, including licenses for liquor, levying taxes, highways, jails, and administration of poor laws.

23 *Salem Tabernacle Church Records* images 97, 99; Leete, *The Deland family*, 82-85, 94. Jacob never indicates there were two men with the same name and the sparse town records do not need to avoid confusion by specifying which Benjamin is involved, even in election of town officials or when a Benjamin Deland was involved in a non-importation violation and reprimanded publicly. Without looking at the Deland genealogy, one would not think there was more than one Benjamin Deland in Salem and one in Danvers. Jacob clearly states that he was in Salem.
24 *Essex Register*, Dec 19, 1810, 3.
25 *Essex Gazette*, March 26, 1771, 140; March 23, 1773, 135.
26 "Papers Relating to the North church in Salem,"*Essex Institute Historical Collections*, VI*:* 68-69. Document of February 1772 lists Benjamin Daland as yeoman. Rantoul, "A Historic Ball Room," 77.
27 "List of Houses Built in Salem from 1750-1773," *Historical Collections of the Essex Institute*, LVIII, 292-296. Salem Land Deeds, Sarah Campbell to Benjamin Daland, book 108, page 276.
28 *Essex Gazette*, Salem, MA, December 17, 1771.
29 Rantoul, "A Historic Ball Room," 82; *Salem Land Records*, Book 132, page 165.
30 *Essex Gazette*, December 6, 1774.
31 Streeter, "Salem before the Revolution," 51.
32 Visitation by Dr. Whitaker of church members in January-February 1771, *Tabernacle Church Records*, image 137-140.
33 Streeter, "Salem before the Revolution," 72.
34 *Essex Gazette*, Salem, MA, February 22, 1774.
35 *Salem Land Records*, Book 133, page 242.
36 *Salem South Church Records*, on line, image 4.
37 Rantoul, "A Historic Ball Room, 80-81.
38 *Salem South Church Records*, on line, image 6.
39 Streeter, "Some Historic Streets and Colonial Houses of Salem," 193-194; Streeter, "Salem before the Revolution," 59, 65; National Park Service, *Maritime Salem*, 26.
40 Phillips, *Salem in the Eighteenth Century*, 174; Streeter, "Some Historic Streets and Colonial Houses of Salem," 193-194; Streeter, "Salem before the Revolution," 59.
41 Streeter, "Salem before the Revolution," 49-51, 54; Hoffer, *Prelude to Revolution*, 11. Salem had about 450 to 500 houses at this time.
42 "John Jenks of Salem to Cotton Tufts of Weymouth."(dated Salem, August 26, 1774) *Historical Collections of the Essex Institute*, XLVII, 230-232.
43 "Extracts from the Interleaved Almanacs of William Wetmore of Salem, 1774-1778." *Historical Collections of the Essex Institute*, XLIII, 116; Perley, "The Court Houses in Salem," 115.
44 Visitation by Dr. Whitaker of church members in January-February 1771, *Tabernacle Church Records*, image 137-140.
45 *Essex Gazette*, Salem, Massachusetts, December 18, 1770.
46 Phillips, *Salem in the Eighteenth Century*, 272.
47 *Essex Gazette*, May 25, 1773, 171.
48 Felt, *Annals of Salem*, 416-417.
49 Visitation by Dr. Whitaker of church members in January-February 1771, *Tabernacle Church Records*, image 137-140.
50 *Essex Gazette*, October 19, 1773, 48; Felt, *Annals of Salem*, II: 417.
51 Felt, *Annals of Salem*, II: 416-417; Phillips, *Salem in the Eighteenth Century*, 272.
52 Phillips, *Salem in the Eighteenth Century*, 272; "Black Kings and Governors of New England," *The New England Historical Society* https://www.newenglandhistoricalsociety.com/black-kings-governors-new-england/ accessed September 27, 2020.
53 Streeter, "Salem before the Revolution," 66-67.

54 *Essex Gazette*, March 1, 1774, 123.
55 Felt, *Annals of Salem*, II: 461-462; *Essex Gazette*, March 31, 1772, 144.

Chapter 4

1 Phillips, *Salem in the Eighteenth Century*, 298; Streeter, "Salem before the Revolution," 70-71.
2 Streeter, "Salem before the Revolution," 73, 75.
3 Streeter, "76.
4 Felt, *Annals of Salem*, II: 11, 15-16, 24; National Park Service, *Maritime Salem*, 36; Phillips, *Salem in the Eighteenth Century*, 295; Streeter, "Salem before the Revolution," 76.
5 Felt, *Annals of Salem*, II: 17.
6 Felt, II: 192.
7 Hoffer, *Prelude to Revolution*, 16-18.
8 Phillips, *Salem in the Eighteenth Century*, 381.
9 *Felt, Annals of Salem*, II, 549.
10 *Essex Gazette*, August 22, 1769, 15; October 10, 1769, 43; November 21, 1769, 67; December 19, 1769, 73.
11 Felt, *Annals of Salem*, II: 196.
12 *Essex Gazette*, January 22, 1771, 103; Annals, II: 196. Labaree, *Colonial Massachusetts*, 238.
13 *Essex Gazette*, March 20, 1770, 135.
14 *Essex Gazette*, October 2, October 9, November 13, 1770; *Boston Gazette*, October 8, 1770; *Massachusetts Spy*, October 6, 1770.
15 *Essex Gazette*, Salem, MA, October, 2, 1770.
16 Felt, *Annals of Salem*, II: 550; *Boston Evening-Post*, Mar 18, 1771, 3.
17 A listing of officers in the First Regiment of Essex County on August 20, 1771 gave William Browne, Esq. as Colonel, disgraced merchant Peter Frye, Esq. as First Lieutenant Colonel, Benjamin Pickman, Jr., Esq. as Second Lieutenant Colonel, and Abner Cheever, Jr. Esq., as Major - *Essex Gazette*, August 20, 1771, 15. These were men from the group being overtaken by a new leadership group favoring the Whigs.
18 Wright, *The Continental Army*, 10.
19 *Felt, Annals of Salem*, II: 196; *Essex Gazette*, December 21, 1773, 83; December 28, 1773, 85-88.
20 The term Coercive Acts was used by the British for the series of acts passed to punish Boston but the term Intolerable Acts was not used at the time by the colonists. It developed in the nineteenth century. For a complete discussion of this see: Bell, J.L., "Intolerable Acts," *Journal of the American Revolution*, June 25, 2013 or Bell's blog for April 27, 2008 at https://boston1775.blogspot.com/2008/04/no-tolerance-for-intolerable-acts.htm.
21 Wright, *Continental Army*, 10; Labaree, *Colonial Massachusetts*, 279.
22 Phillips, *Salem in the Eighteenth Century*, 318; *Essex Gazette*, March 22, 1774, 135.
23 Curwen, *Journal and letters*, 487.
24 Force, *American Archives*, Series 4, I: 246-247.
25 *Essex Gazette*, May 3, 1774, 3; Felt, *Annals of Salem*, II: 499.
26 *Essex Gazette*, May 17, 1774, 165.
27 Phillips, *Salem in the Eighteenth Century*, 322; *Essex Gazette*, June 7, 1774, 176.
28 *Essex Gazette*, June 7, 1774, 176.
29 Streeter, "Salem before the Revolution," 79; *Essex Gazette*, June 7, 1774, 176.
30 Perley, "The Court Houses in Salem," 112.
31 Felt, *Annals of Salem*, II: 107-110; Perley, "The Court Houses in Salem," 101- ; Streeter, "Salem before the Revolution," 59, 62, 77.
32 National Park Service, *Maritime Salem*, 26.

33 Streeter, "Salem before the Revolution," 79-80.
34 Stark, *The Loyalists of Massachusetts*, 131.
35 Streeter, "Salem before the Revolution," 79-80.
36 Address of Salem merchants and freeholders to Gage, June 18, 1774 and his response – Force, *American Archives*, Series 4, I: 424-425
37 *Essex Gazette*, June 28, 1774;
38 *Essex Gazette*, July 26, 1774, 3.
39 *Essex Gazette*, August 9, 1774, 3; Streeter, "Salem before the Revolution," 79-80.
40 Raphael, *First American Revolution*, 90-93; Felt, *Annals of Salem*, II, 514; Salem Town meeting August 20, 1774 – Force, *American Archives*, Series 4, I:730; "John Jenks of Salem to Cotton Tufts of Weymouth."(dated Salem, August 26, 1774) *Historical Collections of the Essex Institute*, XLVII, 230-232.
41 Perley, "The Court Houses in Salem," 116.
42 *Norwich Packet*, September 15, 1774, Norwich, CT, 3; Force, *American Archives*, Series 4, I: 787-788.
43 Wright, *Continental Army*, 11.
44 *Essex Gazette*, November 1, 1774, 2; Wright, *Continental Army*, 11; Labaree, *Colonial Massachusetts*, 278-279.

Chapter 5

1 Greene, *The Negro in Colonial New England*, 332.
2 Greene, 333.
3 Rantoul, "A Historic Ball Room," 85; Salem South Church records, on line, image 45.

Chapter 6

1 Hoffer, *Prelude to Revolution*, 60.
2 "Copy of a Circular Letter in the Handwriting of Col. Pickering," *Essex Institute Historical Collections*, II, 155; October 26, 1775, *The Journals of each Provincial Congress of Massachusetts*, 31- 34.
3 *Essex Gazette*, February 21, 1775.
4 Felt, *Annals of Salem*, II: 514.
5 Smith, "Biographical Sketch of Col. David Mason," 204-205; Hoffer, *Prelude to Revolution*, 62.
6 Hoffer, *Prelude to Revolution*, 59.
7 Phillips, "Why Colonel Leslie Came to Salem," 314.
8 Hoffer, *Prelude to Revolution*, 63-64. The author explores the various estimates of the force size and concludes about 250 men. Derek W. Beck, in his *Igniting the American Revolution: 1773-1775* gives a lower estimate of about 120 men and explains his reasoning in his Appendix 4: Tallies of British Troops in Boston in 1774-1775.
9 Phillips, "Why Colonel Leslie Came to Salem," 118, 131.
10 Hoffer, *Prelude to Revolution*, 75-76.
11 ___, "The Affair at the North Bridge," 321.
12 Hoffer, *Prelude to Revolution*, 57-86; Felt, *Annals of Salem*, II: 514 -519.

Chapter 7

1 Greene, *The Negro in Colonial New England*, 127; Shurtleff, *Records of the Governor and Company of the Massachusetts Bay in New England*, May 27, 1652, III: 268; May 14, 1656, III: 397, IV, Part 1: 257
2 Greene, *The Negro in Colonial New England*, 303; Greene, "The Negro in the Armed Forces," 123.
3 Greene, "The Negro in the Armed Forces," 123-124.
4 *Essex Gazette*, March 7, 1775, 3.
5 Greene, *The Negro in Colonial New England*, 188.
6 *Essex Gazette*, March 28, 1775, 2; Felt, *Annals of Salem*, II: 519.
7 Wright, *Continental Army*, 12.
8 Greene, *The Negro in Colonial New England*, 190.
9 Wright, *Continental Army*, 12; Felt, *Annals of Salem*, II, 519-520; *Journals of Each Provincial Congress of Massachusetts*, 679.
10 Streeter, "Salem before the Revolution," 65.
11 Wright, *Continental Army*, 13-15.
12 Wright, 21.
13 Wright, 23.
14 Wright, 23-27.
15 July 10, 1775, letter to John Hancock – Chase, ed., *The Papers of George Washington, Revolutionary War Series*, I: 90.
16 *New York Gazette and Weekly Mercury*, July 24, 1775, 3; Force, *American Archives*, 4th Series, II: 1630; *Journals of Each Provincial Congress of Massachusetts*, July 8, 1775, Committee of Safety, 592.
17 *New York Gazette and Weekly Mercury*, July 24, 1775, 1
18 Chadwick, *First American Army*, 282.
19 Graydon, *Memoirs*, 130-131.
20 Felt, *Annals of Salem*, II: 520; Force, *American Archives*, Series 4, III: 1058; Lefkowitz, *Benedict Arnold's Army*, 56-57.
21 Smith, "Diary," 292; also in Smith, *Letters of Delegates to Congress*, II: September 1775 - December 1775, September 26, 1775, 67.
22 Smith, *Letters of delegates to Congress*, II: 122-123.
23 Felt, *Annals of Salem*, II: 267.
24 *Thomas's Massachusetts Spy Or, American Oracle of Liberty*, October 27, 1775, 3.
25 George Washington to Robert Carter Nicholas, camp at Cambridge, October 5, 1775, Fitzpatrick, ed., *Writings of George Washington*, IV: 14.
26 Frothingham, *Siege of Boston*, 266-267; Questions for the Committee of Conference at Cambridge, c18 October 1775 – Chase, ed., *Papers of George Washington, Revolutionary War Series*, II: 188.
27 Council of war October 8, Cambridge, Chase, ed., *Papers of George Washington, Revolutionary War Series*, II: 125; Force, *American Archives*, Series 4, III: 1039-1040, 1161.
28 Questions for the Committee of Conference at Cambridge, c18 October 1775 – Chase, ed., *Papers of George Washington, Revolutionary War Series*, II: 188. See: item 7 for October 23 in the *Proceedings of the Committee of Conference, 18-24 Oct. 1775*, Document II, Minutes of the Conference, 190-205.
29 Mayer, *Congress's Own*, 8.
30 General Orders, October 22, 1775, Fitzpatrick, ed., *Writings of George Washington*, IV: 37.
31 William Heath, camp at Cambridge, October 23, 1775 to John Adams, in Taylor, ed., *Papers of John Adams*, III: 230-231.

32 John Thomas to John Adams, October 24, 1775, in Taylor, ed., *Papers of John Adams*, III: 239–241.
33 Frothingham, *Siege of Boston*, 256-257, 258+.
34 Journal of Dr. Jeremy Belknap for October 19, 1775. Marcou, *Life of Jeremy Belknap*, 92.
35 Frothingham, *Siege of Boston*, 263-264.
36 Mayer, *Congress's Own*, 35.
37 Gough, "Black Men and the Early New Jersey Militia," 227.
38 Mayer, *Congress's Own*, 110.
39 Abner H. Francis, Eulogy to John Q. Adams, *The North Star*, March 24, 1848, 1 - Library of Congress Digital Collections Frederick Douglass Newspapers, 1847 to 1874.
40 Gigantino, *Ragged Road to Abolition*, 96.

Chapter 8

1 Fitzpatrick, *Writings of George Washington*, IV: 21.
2 Price, *Diary*, 212.
3 How, *Diary*, 3. Some sources give his birth as Salem although his father was from Gloucester.
4 Mayer, *Congress's Own*, 4, 19-20.
5 The men were from Essex, Bristol, Middlesex, Plymouth, Worcester, Suffolk, and Hampshire Counties in Massachusetts and Hillsborough and Cheshire Counties in New Hampshire.
6 NARA M881 Compiled Service Records of Soldiers Who Served in the American Army During the Revolutionary War
7 Wiencek, *An Imperfect God*, 201-202.
8 For the oath see: June 14, 1775, *Journals of the Continental Congress*, II: 90; Oct 12, 1775, *Journals of the Continentl Congress*, III: 289; *Pennsylvania Packet*, 30 October, 1775. For the Articles of War see: June 30, 1775, JCC, II: 112.
9 General Orders, Cambridge, October 31, 1775, Fitzpatrick, *Writings of George Washington*, IV: 56-58; General Orders, Cambridge, November 12, 1775, Fitzpatrick, *Writings of George Washington*, IV, 86. The General Orders do not indicate what the two dollars meant. It was probably Spanish dollars.
10 Commager and Morris, *Spirit of 'Seventy-Six*, 154. Just how accurate Thompson's specific observations were is open to debate, but they do not vary from the horrible conditions mentioned by other observers.
11 Frothingham, *Siege of Boston*, 263.
12 General Orders, August 1, 1775, Fitzpatrick, *Writings of George Washington*, III: 382; Chadwick, *First American Army*, 46.
13 Also, Jacob does not mention serious illness in his pension application statement and if he missed any significant time from duty ill, he would probably have mentioned it as other veterans often did.
14 Thacher, *Military Journal*, 40-41.
15 How, *Diary*, 4-6 and various; Brown, *Diary*, 3, 10 and various.

Chapter 9

1 Frothingham, *Siege of Boston*, 263-264.
2 Fitzpatrick, *Writings of George Washington*, IV: 84-86. General Orders, Cambridge, November 12, 1775 Chase, ed., *The Papers of George Washington, Revolutionary War Series*, II: 354. See: Don Hagist, *British Soldiers American War*, Yardley: Westholme, 2014.
3 George Washington, Cambridge, to Joseph Reed, November 8, 1775, Fitzpatrick, *Writings of George Washington*, IV: 77.

4 Price, *Diary*, 216.
5 Fitzpatrick, *Writings of George Washington*, IV: 124-125.
6 Price, *Diary*, 217.
7 Gen. Sullivan to New Hampshire Committee of Safety, December 3, 1775, Hammond, *John Sullivan Letters and Papers*, I: 135. See letter of Washington to Hancock, December 4, 1775 for more of the same. Fitzpatrick, *Writings of George Washington*, IV: 141+. Frothingham, *Siege of Boston*, 273.
8 Quintal, *Patriots of Color*, 174-180.
9 Price, *Diary*, 218; Frothingham, *Siege of Boston*, 266.
10 Thacher, *Military Journal*, 42.
11 See: "Journal of Simeon Lyman of Sharon," *Collections of the Connecticut Historical Soc*iety, VII (1899): 128-131.
12 Tomlinson, Abraham, ed., *The military journals of two private soldiers, 1758-1775*, ... 84.
13 Thacher, *Military Journal*, 42; Frothingham, *Siege of Boston*, 273-274.

Chapter 10

1 General Orders, October 31, 1776, Fitzpatrick, *Writings of George Washington*, VI: 233-235.
2 Mayer, *Congress's Own*, 125-127.
3 General Orders, July 23, 1775 - Chase, ed., *Papers of George Washington, Revolutionary War Series*, I: 158; Rapp, *Accomplishing the Impossible*, 105.
4 Fitzpatrick, *Writings of George Washington*, October 28, 1775 General Orders, IV: 49-50; Chase, ed., *Papers of George Washington, Revolutionary War Series*, II: 277 – Nov 1, 1775.
5 *Journals of the Continental Congress*, III: 323.
6 George Washington to President of Congress, Cambridge, February 9, 1776, Fitzpatrick, *Writings of George Washington*, IV: 317.
7 Joseph Barrell, Westown, to Joseph Green, November 3, 1775, Webb, *Correspondence and Journals*, I: 112, 114.
8 Moses Brown, Providence, to William Wilson, January 2, 1776, "An Unwritten Chapter in the History of the Siege of Boston," *The Pennsylvania Magazine of History and Biography*, I (1877), 168-174, 171.
9 Frothingham, *Siege of Boston*, 276.
10 General Orders, December 24, 1775, Fitzpatrick, *Writings of George Washington*, IV: 180.

Chapter 11

1 Rapp, *Accomplishing the Impossible*, 75.
2 For more on Inman and his house see: "Old Cambridge and New," *New England Historical and Genealogical Register*, vol 25, 1871, 231.
3 Wright, *Continental Army*, 209-210.
4 Rapp, *Accomplishing the Impossible*, 109.
5 Frothingham, *Siege of Boston*, 259.
6 Greene, "Orderly Book," 12-13.
7 Chadwick, *First Army*, 19; Shaw, *Journals*, 8 – letter of February 14, 1776.
8 Heath, *Memoirs*, 39.
9 General Orders for November 5, 1775. Fitzpatrick, *Writings of George Washington*, IV: 65.
10 Price, *"Diary,"* 213-214, 216.
11 Atkinson, *British are Coming*, 234-237.

12 Webb, *Correspondence and Journals*, 131.
13 B. P., Maryland, to The Earl of Dartmouth, December 20, 1775, Force, *American Archives*, Series 4, IV: 359-360.
14 Chadwick, *First Army*, 15.
15 "Journal of Simeon Lyman of Sharon," *Collections of the Connecticut Historical Society*, VII (1899), 124-125; Heath, *Memoirs*, 38-39.
16 Philbrick, *Bunker Hill*, 255.
17 Frothingham, *Siege of Boston*, 249, 251, 255.
18 Atkinson, *British are Coming*, 227, 232. Invoice of stores onboard the Nancy, Force, *American Archives*, Series 4, III: 1721-1722; newspaper article copied in file.
19 Reed, *Life and Correspondence of Joseph Reed*, I: 133. See also: "Journal of Simeon Lyman of Sharon," *Collections of the Connecticut Historical Society*, VII (1899): 129-130 who saw the "christening."
20 Price, *Diary*, 220; *Boston Gazette*, December 11, 1775, 2.
21 Greenwood, *Revolutionary Services*, 21.
22 Heath, *Memoirs*, 39-41; Baldwin, *Revolutionary Journal*, 18. Baldwin says finished Cobble Hill fortifications on December 11. Frothingham, *Siege of Boston*, 270-271.
23 Jacob Francis PF W459.
24 Heath, *Memoirs*, 41-42.
25 Heath, *Memoirs*, 43; Baldwin, *Revolutionary Journal*, 19.
26 Frothingham, *Siege of Boston*, 270-1; Baldwin, *Revolutionary Journal*, 19-29.
27 Baldwin, *Revolutionary Journal*, 20.
28 Stephen Moylan, Washington's Aide, to Joseph Reed, January 2, 1776, Reed, *Life and Correspondence*, 1:137.
29 How, *Diary*, 1; Frothingham, *Siege of Boston*, 272.
30 Holton, *Liberty is Sweet*, 210.
31 From George Washington to Richard Henry Lee, 26 December 1775," *Founders Online,* National Archives, https://founders.archives.gov/documents/Washington/03-02-02-0568. [Original source: *The Papers of George Washington*, Revolutionary War Series, vol. 2, *16 September 1775–31 December 1775*, ed. Philander D. Chase. Charlottesville: University Press of Virginia, 1987, pp. 610–613.] See also: Charles Patrick Neimeyer, *America Goes to War: A Social History of the Continental Army*, New York: New York University Press, 1996, 72. Washington's letters and general orders are in: Philander D. Chase, ed., *The Papers of George Washington, Revolutionary War Series*, Charlottesville: University Press of Virginia, 1985+, I: 90; II: 125, 188, 269, 354, 620.
32 See page 94 for information on this petition.
33 Holton, *Liberty is Sweet*, 210-211.
34 General Orders, December 30, 1775, Cambridge, Chase, ed., *The Papers of George Washington, Revolutionary War Series*, II:620
35 General Orders, December 30, 1775; GW to John Hancock, December 31, 1775 – Fitzpatrick, *Writings of George Washington*, IV: 194, 195)
36 See: Wiencek, *An Imperfect God*, 204-205 and his thoughts about Washington's changing attitude toward Black people that developed during the war.
37 Heath, *Memoirs*, 43-44; Frothingham, *Siege of Boston*, 285.
38 Rapp, *Accomplishing the Impossible*, 111.
39 William Gordon letter, April 6-May 6, 1776. Collection of Harold Murdock, printed in *Massachusetts Historical Society Proceedings*, 60: 360.
40 Felt, *Annals of Salem*, II: 417.
41 See: Emily Blanck, "Seventeen Eighty-Three: The Turning Point in the Law of Slavery and Freedom in Massachusetts," *The New England Quarterly*, Vol. 75, No. 1 (Mar., 2002), 24-51.

Chapter 12

1 Heath, *Memoirs*, 39.
2 Philbrick, *Bunker Hill*, 264-265.
3 Frothingham, *Siege of Boston*, 284.
4 Fitzpatrick, *Writings of George Washington*, IV: 202-204.
5 Wright, *Continental Army*, 209.
6 Daniel Woodward PF S30,227 of Perry's company.
7 George Washington to John Hancock, Cambridge, January 4, 1776, *Founders Online*, National Archives, https://founders.archives.gov/documents/Washington/03-03-02-0013. [Original source: *The Papers of George Washington*, Revolutionary War Series, vol. 3, *1 January 1776–31 March 1776*, ed. Philander D. Chase. Charlottesville: University Press of Virginia, 1988, pp. 18–21.]
8 Atkinson, *British Are Coming*, 232-233.
9 Heath, *Memoirs*, January 8, 1776, 44; Atkinson, *British Are Coming*, 221; Greenwood, *Revolutionary Services*, 23-24.
10 See; Frothingham, *Siege of Boston*, 287, 288; Washington to Reed, January 14, Fitzpatrick, *Writings of George Washington*, IV: 240-245; Diary of Colonel Samuel Pierce of Dorchester.
11 General Orders, Cambridge, January 1, 1776, Fitzpatrick, *Writings of George Washington*, IV: 202-204; Frothingham, *Siege of Boston*, 285.
12 Fitzpatrick, *Writings of George Washington*, IV: 227-229; Philbrick, *Bunker Hill*, 267.
13 *Journals of the Continental Congress*, 4: 60.
14 Caleb Leach PFS13,738; How, *Diary*, 4.
15 Isaac Huse – PF S10,900; David How PF S29,912.
16 How, *Diary*, 4-6.
17 Brown, "Diary," 3. Brown said he heard the fine was one shilling but it was actually four pence in the orders of February 17.
18 Baldwin, *Journal*, 20-27.
19 Wright, *Continental Army*, 209.
20 Frothingham, *Siege of Boston*, 291. See Washington's general orders for this day – Fitzpatrick, *Writings of George Washington*, IV: 276.
21 Brown, "Diary," 2-3. See also: Obadiah Brown PF S14,994. He noted that a man died very suddenly on February 11 in Cambridge. He went again to the hospital on February 22, when it rained.
22 Chadwick, *First American Army*, 23-25.
23 Greene, "Orderly Book," 24.
24 How, *Diary*, 4-6; Brown, "Diary,"2.
25 Chadwick, *First American Army*, 23-25, 46.
26 How, *Diary*, 4-6; Heath, *Memoirs*, 46.
27 Frothingham, *Siege of Boston*, 290; Washington's two letters to Congress of February 9 in Fitzpatrick, *Writings of George Washington*, IV: 312-317.
28 George Washington to President of Congress, Cambridge, February 9, 1776, Fitzpatrick, *Writings of George Washington*, IV: 316.
29 Frothingham, *Siege of Boston*, 290.
30 Greene, "Orderly Book," 4.
31 Fitzpatrick, *Writings of George Washington*, IV: 344. Brown, "Diary," 2.
32 How, *Diary*, 4-6; Brown, "Diary," 3; Heath, *Memoirs*, 46.
33 Bell, *George Washington's Headquarters and Home, Cambridge, Massachusetts*, 350-351.
34 Greene, "Orderly Book," 6.

35 Greene, 6.
36 Brown, "Diary," 3.
37 Greene, "Orderly Book," 9, 24 -February 28.
38 Greene, 12-13.
39 Greene, 13-14, 18-20.
40 Heath, *Memoirs*, 48.
41 Baldwin, *Revolutionary Journal*, 27.
42 Greene, "Orderly Book," 21-22; Resolve for paying Parker Cleaveland £8 16s passed October 19, 1776, Force, *American Archives*, Series 5, III: 400-401.
43 Heath, *Memoirs*, 48.
44 Greene, "Orderly Book," 25-29.
45 How, *Diary*, 7; Brown, "Diary," 2- 4.
46 Frothingham, *Siege of Boston*, 296.
47 Brown, "Diary," 2-4; Greene, "Orderly Book," 31-36.
48 "From George Washington to Burwell Bassett, 28 February 1776," *Founders Online*, National Archives, https://founders.archives.gov/documents/Washington/03-03-02-0280. [Original source: *The Papers of George Washington*, Revolutionary War Series, vol. 3, *1 January 1776–31 March 1776*, ed. Philander D. Chase. Charlottesville: University Press of Virginia, 1988, pp. 386–387.]
49 Force, *American Archives*, 4th series, V, 112; Greene, "Orderly Book," 38.
50 How, *Diary*, 8. In March, David How became a corporal in the company. David How PF S29912.
51 Frothingham, *Siege of Boston*, 297; Washington to Massachusetts Legislature, February 26, 1776, Fitzpatrick, *Writings of George Washington*, IV: 351.
52 How, *Diary*, 8, Brown, "Diary," 4; Heath, *Memoirs*, 48.
53 Greene, "Orderly Book," 39.
54 Greene, 44-45.
55 Webb, *Correspondence and Journals*, 134; Frothingham, *Siege of Boston*, 298. Citing report of Henry Knox.
56 Heath, *Memoirs*, 49; Brown, "Diary," 4.
57 Commager and Morris, *Spirit of 'Seventy-Six*, 174.
58 Greene, "Orderly Book," 46; How, *Diary*, 9.
59 Rapp, *Accomplishing the Impossible*, 129.
60 Goodwin, M.C., "The Castle – A Sketch of Fort Independence," *The Bostonian*, II: 644-654 – 651; Heath, *Memoirs*, 49-50.
61 How, *Diary*, 9; Brown, "Diary," 4-5. It is unclear just who Captain Spalding was. Perhaps Captain Edward Spaulding of the Rhode Island artillery. Identifying the man as his Negro would indicate the man was enslaved to him.
62 Greene, "Orderly Book," 49.
63 How, *Diary*, 10; Brown, "Diary," 5; Heath, *Memoirs*, 51.
64 Greene, Orderly Book," 52-53.
65 Frothingham, *Siege of Boston*, 305.
66 Brown, "Diary," 5; Heath, *Memoirs*, 51.
67 How, *Diary*, 10; Heath, *Memoirs*, 51.
68 Brown, "Diary," 5.
69 Greene, "Orderly Book," 55-57.
70 Greene, "Orderly Book," 58-63; Heath, *Memoirs*, 51.
71 Brown, "Diary," 5.
72 Greene, "Orderly Book,", 63-64.
73 Brown, "Diary," 5-6.
74 How, *Diary*, 7, 10.
75 Brown, "Diary," 6; Heath, *Memoirs*, 52. See "From George Washington to Captain John Manley, 28 January 1776," *Founders Online*, National Archives, https://founders.archives.

gov/documents/Washington/03-03-02-0149. [Original source: *The Papers of George Washington*, Revolutionary War Series, vol. 3, *1 January 1776–31 March 1776*, ed. Philander D. Chase. Charlottesville: University Press of Virginia, 1988, 206–207.]

76 Greene, "Orderly Book," 69.
77 Brown, "Diary," 6.
78 Frothingham, *Siege of Boston*, 309.

Chapter 13

1 How, *Diary*, 11; Brown, "Diary," 6. "Brother Jonathan" was a British slang expression for Americans.
2 Greene, "Orderly Book," 71; Adam Nichols – support statement for Josiah A. Crossman PF S29,105 and Nichols' PF S35,538.
3 Brown, "Diary," 6.
4 Robertson, *Diaries and Sketches*, 80-81; Brown, "Diary," 6.
5 Warren, *Life of John Warren*, 72.
6 Atkinson, *British Are Coming*, 267.
7 Greene, "Orderly Book," 76; Brown, "Diary," 6.
8 Heath, *Memoirs*, 53.
9 How, *Diary*, 11; Brown, "Diary," 6.
10 Philbrick, *Bunker Hill*, 264; Thacher, *Military Journal*, 51; Bangs, *Journal of Lieutenant Isaac Bangs*, 13.
11 Based on comments in Price, "Diary," 24-25. Price was from Boston but had fled the city and was apparently living in Stoughton, about 17 miles south of Boston. He frequently visited areas closer to Boston, such as Roxbury and Cambridge.
12 Warren, *Life of John Warren, M.D.*, 69-74. Contains entries from his journal.
13 Frothingham, *Siege of Boston*, 329-330; Warren, *Life of John Warren, M.D*, 69-71.
14 Thacher, *Military Journal*, 50-51.
15 Philbrick, *Bunker Hill*, 256. Basically all theater was considered immoral in puritanical New England.
16 Rev. Andrew Eliot, Boston, to Isaac Smith, London, April 9, 1776, Foote, *Annals of King's Chapel*, II: 293. It is interesting that Eliot talks of coal rather than firewood.
17 "From George Washington to Lieutenant Colonel Joseph Reed, 1 April 1776," *Founders Online*, National Archives, https://founders.archives.gov/documents/Washington/03-04-02-0009. [Original source: *The Papers of George Washington*, Revolutionary War Series, vol. 4, *1 April 1776–15 June 1776*, ed. Philander D. Chase. Charlottesville: University Press of Virginia, 1991, pp. 9–13.].
18 How, *Diary*, 11; David How Pension File S29,912; Brown, "Diary," 6.
19 Josiah A. Crossman PF S29,105.
20 Greene, "Orderly Book," 75-76.
21 Brown, "Diary," 7.
22 "Hutchinson's Orderly Book", 339-340; Brown, "Diary," 7, How, *Diary*, 12.
23 Samuel Capen PF S29,064.
24 "Hutchinson's Orderly Book", 339-340; Brown, "Diary," 7; Frothingham, *Siege of Boston*, 312. Same arrangement given on April 16.
25 Wright, *Continental Army*, 209; George Washington, Cambridge, to Artemas Ward, April 4, 1776, Fitzpatrick, *Writings of George Washington*, IV: 467.
26 Brown, "Diary," 8.
27 "Hutchinson's Orderly Book, 341.
28 Brown, "Diary," 8.

29 Brown, 7-11.
30 "Hutchinson's Orderly Book," 343.
31 Col Hutchinson's orderly book, 340-341; How, *Diary*, 12-13.
32 Jacob Francis PF W459.
33 Warren, *Life of Dr. John Warren*, 73-74.
34 "Hutchinson's Orderly Book," 340-341; How, *Diary*, 12-13.
35 "Hutchinson's Orderly Book," 342.
36 How, *Diary*, 15; David How PF S29912.
37 "Hutchinson's Orderly Book," 347.
38 Artemas Ward to George Washington, May 4, 1776, Library of Congress, *George Washington Papers*.
39 "Hutchinson's Orderly Book," 343; George Washington, Cambridge, to Artemas Ward, April 4, 1776, Fitzpatrick, *Writings of George Washington*, IV: 469-470.
40 Brown, "Diary," 8.
41 "Hutchinson's Orderly Book," 341-342; George Washington, Cambridge, to Artemas Ward, April 4, 1776, Fitzpatrick, *Writings of George Washington*, IV: 470.
42 "Hutchinson's Orderly Book," 343-344.
43 "Hutchinson's Orderly Book," 346; Brown, 10. The six men were William Willey, John Kely, Francis Bennett, Jacob Smallwood, James Jeffers, John Andrews.
44 "Hutchinson's Orderly Book," 347.
45 Brown, "Diary," 11; How, *Diary*, 16-17.
46 "Hutchinson's Orderly Book," 353.
47 "Hutchinson's Orderly Book," 348; Artemas Ward to George Washington, May 4, 1776, Library of Congress, *George Washington Papers*.
48 How, PF S29912; How, *Diary*, 16-17; Brown, "Diary," 11.
49 Return of the Division of the Continental Army commanded by Major General Ward, stationed at Boston, Charlestown, Dorchester, & Beverly, May 4, 1776, George Washington Papers, Series 4, General Correspondence: Artemas Ward to George Washington, May 4, 1776, with Report of Troop Strength, Library of Congress, *George Washington Papers*; Frothingham, *Siege of Boston*, 313.
50 To George Washington from Major General Artemas Ward, 9 May 1776," Founders Online, National Archives, https://founders.archives.gov/documents/Washington/03-04-02-0201. [Original source: The Papers of George Washington, Revolutionary War Series, vol. 4, 1 April 1776–15 June 1776, ed. Philander D. Chase. Charlottesville: University Press of Virginia, 1991, pp. 248–250; Brown, "Diary," 12.
51 "Hutchinson's Orderly Book," 350; David How's PF S29,912: How, *Diary*, 17.
52 Jacob Francis PF W459. Jacob's description was not completely accurate but reflects his impression and memory.
53 "Hutchinson's Orderly Book," 353.
54 "Hutchinson's Orderly Book," 350; March 16, 1776, *Journals of the Continental Congress*, IV: 208-209.
55 How, *Diary*, 18; Brown, "Diary," 12.
56 Brown, "Diary," 12-13; Major General Artemas Ward, Boston, to George Washington, May 17, 1776, *Founders Online,* National Archives, https://founders.archives.gov/documents/Washington/03-04-02-0267. [Original source: *The Papers of George Washington*, Revolutionary War Series, vol. 4, *1 April 1776–15 June 1776*, ed. Philander D. Chase. Charlottesville: University Press of Virginia, 1991, 329–330.]
57 Brown, "Diary," 13-14.
58 Brown, "Diary," 11; How, *Diary*, 16-17.
59 How ,*Diary*, 18; Col Hutchinson's orderly book, 349-350.
60 How, *Diary*, 19; Brown, "Diary," 14; "Hutchinson's Orderly Book," 353.
61 "Hutchinson's Orderly Book," 353.

62 "Hutchinson's Orderly Book," 355.
63 Brown, "Diary," 19; "Hutchinson's Orderly Book," 359.
64 "Hutchinson's Orderly Book," 360.
65 "Hutchinson's Orderly Book," 355, 360; How, *Diary*, 20
66 "Hutchinson's Orderly Book," 360-362.
67 "Hutchinson's Orderly Book," 356, 361.
68 How, *Diary*, 20-22.
69 "Hutchinson's Orderly Book," 358-359. Noted again on June 18.
70 "Hutchinson's Orderly Book," 361-362.
71 *New England Chronicle*, June 20, 1776, 3; Adam Nichols – support statement for Josiah A. Crossman PF S29,105 and his PF S35,538; Brown, "Diary," 16-17. See also: Ensign Josiah Cleveland PF S44,782. Cleveland was from Connecticut and was serving in Captain Scott's company.
72 "Hutchinson's Orderly Book," 362.
73 Brown, "Diary," 20.
74 "Hutchinson's Orderly Book," 363; Thacher, *Military Journal*, 54.
75 "Hutchinson's Orderly Book," 363-364; Brown, "Diary," 21-22.
76 Brown, "Diary," 21.
77 How, *Diary*, 23; Brown, "Diary," 22.
78 Wright, *Continental Army*, 209-210.
79 Brown, "Diary," 22; Thacher, *Military Journal*, 62.
80 How, *Diary*, 23; Brown, "Diary," 22-23.
81 Thacher, *Military Journal*, 55-58; http://boston1775.blogspot.com/2007/07/sheriff-greenleaf-and-col-crafts-read.html; *New England Chronicle*, July 25, 1776, 3.
82 Mayer, *Congress's Own*, 3-4, 8, 17, 70, 77.
83 How, *Diary*, 23; Jacob Hayden – PF S33,281; Support statement of Ichabod Holbrook – 2nd Lt in company; Caleb Leach PF S13,738; Brown, "Diary," 23.

Chapter 14

1 Samuel Capen PF S29,064.
2 Gannett, *The Origin of Certain Place Names in the United States.*
3 Brown, "Diary," 23-25. The fort site is now a part of Carl Schurz Park, near intersection of 89th Street and East End Avenue and the site of Gracie Mansion, the traditional home of the New York City Mayor. Walton's Belview mansion occupied the site of today's Gracie Mansion. See also: Jeffrey B. Evans, *A Short History of Carl Schurz Park*, https://www.carlschurzparknyc.org/the-history-of-the-park.
4 Paul Dudley Sargent PF W24.
5 George Washington to President of Congress, July 29, Fitzpatrick, *Writings of George Washington*, V: 346; To Artemas Ward, July 29, V: 352. General Heath also notes Sargent's regiment arrival at horn's Hook on July 29 along with Colonel Hutchinson's regiment. Heath, *Memoirs*, 60.
6 Heath, *Memoirs*, 60.
7 General Orders, August 4, 1776, Fitzpatrick, *Writings of George Washington*, V: 368.
8 Brown, "Diary," 26.
9 General Orders, August 6, 1776, Fitzpatrick, *Writings of George Washington,* V: 376,
10 General Orders, August 7, 1776, Fitzpatrick, *Writings of George Washington,* V: 378.
11 Brown, "Diary," 26-27.
12 Heath, *Memoirs*, 61.
13 General Orders, August 9, 1776, Fitzpatrick, *Writings of George Washington*, V: 407.

14 Heath, *Memoirs*, 62.
15 General Orders, August 9, 1776, Fitzpatrick, *Writings of George Washington*, V: 407.
16 General Orders, August 12, 1776, Fitzpatrick, *Writings of George Washington*, V: 422; David How PF S29,912; Wright, *Continental Army*, 210; Brown, 28; Heath, *Memoirs*, 62.
17 General Orders, August 13, 1776, Fitzpatrick, *Writings of George Washington*, V: 424 -245.
18 General Orders, August 14, 1776, Fitzpatrick, *Writings of George Washington*, V: 436-437.
19 Heath, *Memoirs*, 62. The settlement was originally spelled King's Bridge after the bridge crossing from Manhattan Island to Westchester County. Today it is generally spelled Kingsbridge.
20 Brown, "Diary," 29.
21 Brown, 28-31.
22 Caleb Leach PFS13,738.
23 Confirmation of their location at Horn's Hook at this time is found in: General Washington to the President of Congress, September 16, 1776, in Force, *American Archives*, 5th Series, II: 351. How, *Diary*, 26.
24 A return of the officers and men killed, captured, or missing in Sargent's Brigade since January 1, 1776 was made sometime after November 5. Force, *American Archives*, series 5, III: 723-724.
25 Jacob Francis PF W459; Brown, "Diary," 32-33. Brown also recorded that a number of men from Sargent's regiment went onto Long Island but returned after seeing the defeat and the advancing regulars.
26 Brown, "Diary," 34.
27 "General Orders, 30 August 1776," *Founders Online*, National Archives, https://founders.archives.gov/documents/Washington/03-06-02-0136. [Original source: *The Papers of George Washington*, Revolutionary War Series, vol. 6, *13 August 1776–20 October 1776*, ed. Philander D. Chase and Frank E. Grizzard, Jr. Charlottesville: University Press of Virginia, 1994, pp. 162–164.].
28 Wright, *Continental Army*, 210.

Chapter 15

1 Robertson, *Diaries and Sketches*, 95.
2 Johnston, *Campaign of 1776*, 225.
3 Johnston, 228.
4 George Washington to William Heath, August 26, 1776, George Washington, New York, to William Heath, September 1, 1776, Fitzpatrick, *Writings of George Washington*, V: 493, VI: 2-4; How, *Diary*, 27-28.
5 How, *Diary*, 27-28; Brown, "Diary," 34.
6 General Orders, September 2, 1776, Fitzpatrick, *Writings of George Washington*, VI: 7-8.
7 Brown, "Diary," 35.
8 General Orders, September 3, 1776, Fitzpatrick, *Writings of George Washington*, VI: 8.
9 Robertson, *Diaries and Sketches*, 96; Heath, *Memoirs*, 68.
10 "Jedidia Swan's Orderly Book," *Proceedings of the New Jersey Historical Society*, III: 30.
11 How, *Diary*, 27-28; Brown, "Diary," 36.
12 Samuel Capen PF S29,064; Robertson, *Diaries and Sketches*, 96; David How PF S29,912; How, *Diary*, 27-28; Brown, "Diary," 28, 36. George Clinton to Abraham Yates, Jr., this date, in Hastings, *Clinton Papers*, 1:338–42; Robertson, *Diaries and Sketches*, 96; Heath, *Memoirs*, 69. Jeffrey B. Evans, *A Short History of Carl Schurz Park*, https://www.carlschurzparknyc.org/the-history-of-the-park.
13 Sunday, September 8, Nine O'clock AM – Captain Eliphalet Howell to Colonel Henry Knox, *Papers of the Continental Congress*, M247, Ltrs from Gen George Washington, June 3 - September 18, 1776, Vol 2: Jun 3-Sept 18, 1776, Page: 542, Roll Number: 166. Also in Force, *American Archives*, Series 5, II: 240.

14 "From George Washington to John Hancock, 8 September 1776," *Founders Online,* National Archives, https://founders.archives.gov/documents/Washington/03-06-02-0203. [Original source: *The Papers of George Washington*, Revolutionary War Series, vol. 6, *13 August 1776–20 October 1776*, ed. Philander D. Chase and Frank E. Grizzard, Jr. Charlottesville: University Press of Virginia, 1994, pp. 248–254.].
15 Heath, *Memoirs*, 69; How, *Diary*, 27-28.
16 Colonel Reed to General Mifflin, Head -Quarters, 8 o'clock PM, September 9, 1776, Force, *American Archives*, Series 5, II: 259; Brown, "Diary," 37.
17 General Washington to the President of Congress, September 16, 1776, Force, *American Archives*, Series 5, II: 351.
18 George Washington, HQ, to Governor Jonathan Trumbull, September 9, 1776, Fitzpatrick, *Writings of George Washington*, VI: 40.
19 Robertson, *Diaries and Sketches*, 96.
20 Brown, "Diary," 37.
21 Solomon Bryant PF S29,657 includes statements from two other members of his company, Ebenezer White and Joseph Wright.
22 Brown, "Diary," 38.
23 Johnston, *Campaign of 1776*, 230.
24 How, *Diary*, 27-28; Brown, "Diary," 38; A return of the officers and men killed, captured, or missing in Sargent's Brigade since January 1, 1776 was made sometime after November 5. Force, *American Archives*, Series 5, III: 723-724; Robertson, *Diaries and Sketches*, 96.
25 Isaac Huse PF S10,900 - David How gives support statement. Huse continues, "when we were marched to the White Plains where I was in charge of the stores at Weeks Liberty Pole during the battle we then went to North Castle and remained there a short time in company with Capt. Corey who then superintended the stores. We then were ordered to remove with all the Laboratory stores to Fishkill and remained there in guard of the stores till the 1st January 1777 and were there dismissed by said Capt. Correy and returned home about 200 miles on my own expence."
26 Force, *American Archives*, 5th series, II: 329-330, ca September 12, 1776.
27 General Orders, September 12, 1776, September 14, 1776, Fitzpatrick, *Writings of George Washington*, VI: 50, 54-55.
28 Johnston, *Battle of Harlem Heights*, 33; Mackenzie, "Diary," September 9, 1776, in Commager and Morris, *Spirit of 'Seventy-Six*, 461-462.
29 Schecter, *Battle for New York*, 180.
30 A return of the officers and men killed, captured, or missing in Sargent's Brigade since January 1, 1776 was made sometime after November 5. Force, *American Archives*, Series 5, III: 723-724.
31 Brown, "Diary," 38.
32 Serle, *Journal*, 104.
33 Johnston, *Battle of Harlem Heights*, 170; Heath, *Memoirs*, 70.
34 Force, *American Archives*, Series 5, II: 551.
35 Joseph Williams, camp one mile from Kingsbridge, to William Coit, September 30, 1776, United States. Naval History Division, Michael J Crawford, William James Morgan, and William Bell Clark. *Naval Documents of the American Revolution*, Volume 6, Washington: Naval History Division, Dept. of the Navy, 1972, 1062-1063; How, *Diary*, 28-29; David How PF S29,912; A return of the officers and men killed, captured, or missing in Sargent's Brigade since January 1, 1776 was made sometime after November 5. Force, *American Archives*, Series 5, III: 723-724; Brown, "Diary," 39; General Orders, September 26, 1776, Fitzpatrick, *Writings of George Washington*, VI: 120; Colonel Smallwood to the Convention of Maryland, October 12, 1776, transcribed in Johnston, *Battle of Harlem Heights*, 158; Johnston, *Campaign of 1776*, Part II: 90.
36 Robertson, *Diaries and Sketches*, 99.

37 Brown, "Diary," 39. It also meant that he was not captured at the fall of Fort Washington when the rangers were captured there.
38 Adjutant General Joseph Reed, Heights near Kingsbridge, to his wife, September 17, 1776, Commager and Morris, *Spirit of 'Seventy-Six*, I: 468.
39 Johnston, *Battle of Harlem Heights*, 82.
40 "An Extract from the Journal of Lieut. David Dimock," *American Monthly Mgazine*, I (October 1892), 353-354.
41 Johnston, *Battle of Harlem Heights*, 82-86.
42 Johnston, 92.
43 A return of the officers and men killed, captured, or missing in Sargent's Brigade since January 1, 1776 was made sometime after November 5. Force, American Archives, Series 5, III: 723-724; How, *Diary*, 28-29; David How PF S29912; Caleb Leach PFS13,738; George Washington, Head Quarters Colonel Morris's House, to Governor Nicholas Cooke, September 17, 1776, Fitzpatrick, *Writings of George Washington*, VI: 60-64; Johnston, *Battle of Harlem Heights*, 193.
44 Johnston, *Battle of Harlem Heights*, 90-91; Atkinson, *British are Coming*, 397. Aktinson's source notes give a number of references to this change in feeling.
45 Court-martial report of September 19, 1776 at Harlem Heights, Force, *American Archives*, Series 5, II: 499-500.
46 General Orders, September 18, 1776, Fitzptrick, *Writings of George Washington*, VI: 70-71.
47 Force, *American Archives*, Series 5, II: 382-383; Heath, *Memoirs*, 71.
48 How, *Diary*, 28-29; Caleb Leach PFS13,738. There were two Valentine's Hills at the time, one in the Bronx and the other in Yonkers. The one they encamped on was Isaac Valentine's Hill in the Bronx not far from where they crossed at King's Bridge. Time Abbott, *A Bronx (and Yonkers) Tale of Two Valentines* online at: http://notfellows.blogspot.com/2018/11/a-bronx-and-yonkers-tale-of-two.html
49 Force, *American Archives*, Seris 5, II: 499-500. Brigade Major Daniel Box had been a British sergeant who deserted at Boston and had been entrusted by Nathanael Greene to become his drillmaster and then brigade major. Box had no solid status within New England society. American officers knew that he was a deserter, and not a gentleman in England, so they might have held him in some contempt. See: J. L. Bell, *Daniel Box, from Deserter to Brigade-Major*, http://boston1775.blogspot.com/2011/09/daniel-box-from-deserter-to-brigade.html.
50 Force, *American Archives*, Series 5, II, 500-501; "Jedidiah Swan's Orderly Book," *Proceedings of the New Jersey Historical Society*, III: 43.
51 General Orders, Headquarters, Harlem Heights, September 25, 1776, Force, *American Archives*, Series 5, II: 566.
52 Reed, *Life and Correspondence of Joseph Reed*, I: 240.
53 Heath, *Memoirs*, 73.
54 General Return of the Army in the service of the United States of America, at King's Bridge and its Dependencies commanded by His Excellency George Washington, Esq., General and Commander-in-Chief. Sept. 21, 1776. Force, *American Archives*, Series 5, II: 449-450.
55 Force, *American Archives*, Series 5, III: 1038-1039.
56 General Orders, September 21, 1776, Fitzpatrick, *Writings of George Washington*, VI: 87-89.
57 How, *Diary*, 30.
58 Force, *American Archives*, Series 5, II: 452-453; How, *Diary*, 29.
59 General Orders, September 13, 1776, Fitzpatrick, *Writings of George Washington*, VI: 52.
60 Extract of a Letter from Mount Washington, dated September 26, 1776, Force, *American Archives*, Series 5, II: 552; Jacob Francis PF W459; Heath, *Memoirs*, 75-76; General Orders, September 29, 1776, Fitzpatrick, *Writings of George Washington*, VI: 131-132; Court Martial proceedings, September 30-31, 1776, Force, *American Archives*, Series 5, II: 610-613. Nathan Cary PF R1,681 Capt John Weisner's company – says British

were trying to surround the Americans - therefore the attack on Blackman's island - Montressor's Island - no comment about Weisner except that he was cashiered for cowardice.

61 Major General Henry Knox, Heights of Harlem, to his brother, September 23, 1776, Commager and Morris, *Sprit of 'Seventy-Six*, I: 479-480.

62 Heitman, *Historical Register*, 592.

63 George Washington, Heights of Harlem, to President of Congress, September 24, 1776, Fitzpatrick, *Writings of George Washington*, VI: 107-108. This letter is very long and goes into great detail on Washington's advice for improving the army and the critical need to do so.

64 Force, *American Archives*, Series 5, II: 550. For his story see: Kidder, Larry, *A People Harassed and Exhausted*, 2013, 136-140.

65 Force, *American Archives*, Series 5, II: 550.

66 How, *Diary*, 30.

67 Force, *American Archives*, Series 5, II: 569.

68 NARA M246. Muster rolls, payrolls, strength returns, and other miscellaneous personnel, pay, and supply records of American Army units, 1775-83. Weekly Return of the 16th Regiment Commanded by Colonel Paul Dudley Sargent, September 27, 1776.

Chapter 16

1 General Orders, October 1, 1776, Fitzpatrick, *Writings of George Washington*, VI: 144; Force, *American Archives*, Series 5, II: 551. The charge of firing on his own party could not be sufficiently supported.

2 How, *Diary*, 30.

3 Return of Field Officers of Sargent's Brigade at King's Bridge, October 5, 1776, Force, *American Archives*, Series 5, II: 874-875.

4 NARA M246 Revolutionary War Rolls, Regimental Return for Sargent's Regiment, October 4, 1776.

5 Force, *American Archives*, Series 5, II: 883.

6 George Washington, Harlem, to the President of Congress, October 4, 1776, Fitzpatrick, *Writings of George Washington*, VI: 152-156.

7 General Orders, Harlem Heights, October 4, 1776, Fitzpatrick, *Writings of George Washington*, VI: 157.

8 How, *Diary*, 31-32.

9 *Journals of the Continental Congress*, II: 119.

10 October 9, 1776, General Orders, September 28 General Orders, Fitzpatrick, *Writings of George Washington*, VI: 190-191, 127.

11 Heath, *Memoirs*, 79. The *Turtle* was later recovered but not further employed.

12 October 9 orders from General Heath to Colonel Sargent from King's Bridge, Force, *American Archives*, Series 5, II: 962.

13 Force, Series 5, II: 976; How, *Diary*, 32-33.

14 How, *Diary*, 32-33.

15 General Orders, Harlem Heights, Fitzpatrick, *Writings of George Washington*, VI: 207-208; Force, *American Archives*, Series 5, II: 1036.

16 Force, Series 5, II: 1119.

17 Johnston, *New York Campaign*, 271.

18 Jacob Francis PF W 459; How, *Diary*, 33-34; David How PF S29912.

19 Heath, *Memoirs*, 85-86.

20 NARA M246. Muster rolls, payrolls, strength returns, and other miscellaneous personnel, pay, and supply records of American Army units, 1775-83. Weekly Return of the 16th Regiment Commanded by Colonel Paul Dudley Sargent, October 24, 1776.

21 General Orders, White Plains, October 24, 1776, Fitzpatrick, *Writings of George Washington*, VI: 226-227.
22 A return of the officers and men killed, captured, or missing in Sargent's Brigade since January 1, 1776 was made sometime after November 5. Force, *American Archives*, Series 5, III: 723-724.
23 NARA M881. Compiled service records of soldiers who served in the American Army during the Revolutionary War, 1775-1783. Roll:0054.
24 Heath, *Memoirs*, 87.
25 David How PF S29,912.
26 Johnston, *New York Campaign*, 273, 275.
27 Samuel Capen PF 529.
28 Paul Dudley Sargent PF W24.
29 "Extract of a Letter from a Gentleman in the army, dated camp near the mills, about three miles north of White-Plains, November 1, 1776, Force, *American Archives*, Series 5, III: 474.
30 Schecter, *Battle for New York*, 241. Schecter cites Joseph Plumb Martin as an example.
31 Johnston, *New York Campaign*, 275; Steadman, *History of the Origin, Progress, and Termination of the American War*, I: 215.
32 "Extract of a Letter from a Gentleman in the army, dated camp near the mills, about three miles north of White-Plains, November 1, 1776, Force, *American Archives*, Series 5, III: 474; Heath, *Memoirs*, 90.

Chapter 17

1 General Orders, White Plains, November 3, 1776, Fitzpatrick, *Writings of George Washington*, VI: 238.
2 Force, *American Archives*, Series 5, III: 500.
3 How, *Diary*, 36.
4 Samuel Capen PF 529.
5 David How PF S29,912.
6 Muster roll and a return of the officers and men killed, captured, or missing in Sargent's Brigade since January 1, 1776 was made sometime after November 5. Force, *American Archives*, Series 5, III: 723-724.
7 General Orders, White Plains, November 2, 1776, Fitzpatrick, *Writings of George Washington*, VI: 238.
8 General Orders, White Plains, November 6, 1776, Fitzpatrick, *Writings of George Washington*, VI: 252; General Orders, White Plains, November 8, 1776, Fitzpatrick, *Writings of George Washington*, VI: 259.
9 For more on Austin see: Waters, Wilson, and Henry Spaulding, *History of Chelmsford, Massachusetts,* Lowell, MA: 1917, 195, 198-200,206-207, 303, 620, 760, 791, 806, 828. Mentions the plundering incident on page 828 but claims, without any evidence, it was a different Major Austin.
10 Lee to Washington, Phillipsburg, November 12, 1776, Force, *American Archives*, Series 5, III: 653.
11 George Washington, Peekskill, to Major General Charles Lee, November 12, 1776, Fitzpatrick, *Writings of George Washington*, VI: 275.
12 Force, *American Archives*, Series 5, III: 654-655. See: *Journals of the Continental Congress*, V: 804 for the applicable Rule of War.
13 Alden, *General Charles Lee*, 145 – citing the Lee Orderly Book, entry for Nov. 11, 1776, Library of Congress.
14 Force, *American Archives*, Series 5, III: 709-710.
15 Luther Cary PF S18,755.

16 William Grayson, Hackensack, to General Charles Lee, November 20, 1776, Lee, "The Lee Papers, volume II 1776-1778," 289-290.
17 Force, *American Archives*, Series 5, vol 3, 831-832.
18 General Charles Lee, Campt, to Joseph Reed, November 24, 1776, Commager and Morris, *Spirit of 'Seventy-Six*, I: 499.
19 David How PF S29,912; Alden, *General Charles Lee*, 151-152
20 Alden, *General Charles Lee*, 152; How, *Diary*, 40.
21 Thomas Powell PF 44,257 – Captain Asa Barnes company - support statement of Titus Wood.
22 David Keith PF S32,943.
23 Caleb Leach PFS13,738.
24 Samuel Capen PF S29,064.
25 Force, *American Archives*, Series 5, III: 939; Zaccheus Goldsmith PF S32,746. From Sargent's regiment the men were Zac. Goldsmith, James Linsey, Jo. Trobes, Edward Master, Joshua Hubbard, James Churchill, Benj. Leonard, Simeon Blood, Abel Blood, John Edmund, Samuel Fletcher. Zaccheus Goldsmith was a blacksmith of Andover, Massachusetts in Captain Keith's company and was discharged at White Plains. Edward Masters was in Keith's company. James Churchill was Keith's company. Simeon Blood was in Farrington's company – not discharged – reenlisted for a year in same company for 1777. Abel Blood also in Farrington's company and served in 1777 as well as Saratoga and Monmouth.
26 Jacob Francis PF W459.
27 Paul Dudley Sargent PF W24,894.
28 Force, *American Archives*, Series 5, III: 1167.
29 Alden, *General Charles Lee*, 153-158.
30 David How' PF S29,912.
31 How, *Diary*, 40.
32 Coryell's Ferry was at today's Lambertville and Howell's Ferry at Stockton, both in Hunterdon County, New Jersey.
33 Hooper to Hewes Nov 5, 1776, Smith, *Letters of Delegates to Congress*, V: 439
34 Force, *American Archives*, Series 5, III: 1401-1402.
35 How, *Diary*, 40.
36 Stryker, *Battles of Trenton and Princeton*, 133 – See Thomas Rodney description at Bristol in his diary.
37 Stryker, *Battles of Trenton and Princeton*, 138.
38 H.E. Scudder, ed. *Recollections of Samuel Breck with Passages from his Note-Books (1771-1862)*, Philadelphia: Porter & Coates, 1877. 208-210. Breck was not present at the crossing as he was only a child then. His description of Knox developed during the 1790s when he knew him as Secretary of War. In his book of recollections he draws portraits of a number of men from the Revolution whom he met in Boston and Philadelphia.
39 Greenwood, *Wartime Services*, 80-81; Avery, "Battle of Trenton, 154-155.
40 Washington's General Orders, December 25, 1776, Chase, *The Papers of George Washington, Revolutionary War Series*, VII:434; Smith, *Battle of Trenton*, 20; Fischer, *Washington's Crossing*, 222-223.
41 Greenwood, *Wartime Services*, 39; Wilkinson, *Memoirs*, I: 128.
42 Powell, *Bostwick's Memoirs*, 102.
43 The road followed today's modern road Route 546, Washington Crossing/Pennington Road. It passes on the border of Washington Crossing State Park and roughly parallel to a previously labeled "Continental Lane" inside the park that was long thought to have been the original road used by the troops, but this has been disproven. – See: Peter Osborne, *Where Washington Once Led: A History of New Jersey's Washington Crossing State Park*, Yardley, PA: Yardley Press, 2012, 44.

44 Wheaton J. Lane, *From Indian Trail to Iron Horse: Travel and Transportation in New Jersey, 1620-1860*, Princeton: Princeton University Press, 1939, 38-41. See also: New Jersey Historic Roadway Study, Prepared for New Jersey Department of Transportation and Federal Highway Administration, New Jersey Historic preservation Office, prepared by KSK Architects Planners Historians, Inc. With Armand Corporation, Inc., and Michael Baker, Jr. Inc., January 2011, HPO Log #03-1895-6, Chapter 6.
45 Fischer, *Washington's Crossing*, 226-227; Powell, "Bostwick's Memmoirs," 102.
46 Greenwood, *Wartime Services*, 81.
47 Greenwood, 82.
48 Powell, "Bostwick's Memmoirs," 102.
49 Paul Dudley Sargent PF W24,894. He made this comment in the statement for his pension application stating that process with its repetitions and delays "has given me more pain, anxiety, and fatigue, than my march to Trenton Decm 26, 1776, thro one of the most Boisterous Nights ever experienced by Man."
50 Today's Upper Ferry Road. The crossroads settlement of Birmingham is today's West Trenton.
51 Conrad Beam PF W25,323.
52 Fischer, *Washington's Crossing*, 222.
53 Fischer, 239 – citing several Hessian accounts. Stryker, *Trenton and Princeton*, 150-151; Dwyer, *Day is Ours*, 251; Smith, *Battle of Trenton*, 22.
54 White, *Eagle Tavern*, 2-2.
55 Stryker, *Trenton and Princeton*, 151-152, 189; Dwyer, *Day is Ours*, 251. Quotes Wilkinson who says the early fugitives going over the bridge were joined by some of the musicians, the surgeons, and some of the women. The Trenton Prisoner List includes the musicians, medical officers, and some wives. It does not list any Jägers.
56 Stryker, *Trenton and Princeton*, 176-182; Smith, *Battle of Trenton*, 25.
57 Benjamin Titus PF W6287.
58 Smith, *Battle of Trenton*, 25.
59 Stryker, *Trenton and Princeton*, 176-182
60 Smith, *Battle of Trenton*, 25.
61 Smith, 25.
62 Jacob Francis PF W459.
63 Stryker, *Trenton and Princeton*, 182-184. On December 27 Washington ordered that the swords and knapsacks that had been taken from officers and sergeants were to be returned.
64 Dwyer, *Day is Ours*, citing Major Apollos Morris.
65 On his way home after discharge he sold it to a young officer for $8. White, "Good Soldier," 77.
66 This cap is now at the Smithsonian. See: Kenneth S. Jones, *Captain Oliver Pond's Hessian Fusiliercap*: A Monograph. Worcester, MA: Kenneth S. Jones, 1986.
67 Jacob Francis PF W459. No other source discusses this effort with the prisoners. His account is interesting because it reflects Washington's original plan but not what other accounts describe. In other accounts all the Hessian prisoners and their families were marched back to Johnson's Ferry. It might be that Jacob was detailed as one of the guards for the prisoners on their way back to Johnson's and he just did not remember it that way. For the purposes of this work, I decided to describe Jacob's "world" as he recalled it whenever possible. Although, in this case his memory does not seem to fit with evidence from other sources other than the one given next.
68 John Cadwalader, Bristol, December 26, 1776, to PA Council of Safety, Force, *American Archives*, Series 5, III: 1441. Two letters both of same date.
69 Howe, *Diary*, 41.
70 For more on after battle conditions in Trenton and these wounded Hessians see: Kidder, *Crossroads of the Revolution*, 162-164.
71 Root, "The Battle of Princeton," 515-516.

72 Josiah A. Crossman PF S29,105.
73 Adam Nichols – support statement for Crossman and his PF S35,538
74 Jacob Hayden – PF S33,281.
75 Lemuel Field - PF S5,393.
76 John Vinton (his son) PF S41,284.
77 Samuel Bisbee PF S34,031 and Joshua Stearns PF S33,712.
78 Hezekiah Packard PF S20,501.
79 Jedidiah Russell PF S45,127.

Chapter 18

1 David How PF S29,912.
2 Private Noah Drake PF 45,334 – statement of Lot Drake.
3 Fischer, *Washington's Crossing*, 401.
4 How, *Diary*, 41-42.
5 Gulick, *Gulicks of the U.S.A.*, 251.
6 See for example: Geni.com/surnames/francis and https://www.ancestry.com/name-origin?surname=francis
7 Gough, "Black Men in the Early New Jersey Militia," 228.
8 Jacob Francis PF W459.
9 For a complete discussion of the New Jersey militia laws, how the system worked in actual practice, and how duty affected men's lives, see: Larry Kidder, *A People Harassed and Exhausted: The story of a New Jersey Militia Regiment in the American Revolution*, CreateSpace: 2013. Captain Snook's Company was part of the Third Hunterdon County Militia Regiment. See also, Edmund Dalrymple PF S988 for a very good description of how the class system worked.
10 Jerome Waldron statement of support in Jacob Francis PF W459.
11 See supporting statements in Jacob Francis PF W459.
12 Peter Snook PF S 835.
13 Jacob Francis PF W459, Jacob Johnson PF W796, Moses Stout PF R10,245, and Peter Snook PF S 835.
14 The tours of duty with Captain Snook are corroborated partly in other pension files, such as Matthias Abel S2,028 and Jacob Johnson W796, and in New Jersey State Archives, Auditor's Book B, pages 181, 185, 465. The wounding of Captain Snook by a bullet through the thigh is confirmed in New Jersey State Archives, New Jersey Adjutant General's Office, Revolutionary War Manuscripts, New Jersey, Mss 6005 – a Certificate made out by Colonel Joseph Phillips accounting for expenditures during his three month recovery. More on the wounding of Captain Snook is found in the support affidavit of Jerome Waldron in Jacob Francis' PF W459.
15 Waldron statement in Jacob Francis PF W459.
16 See: Calligaro, "The Negro's Legal Status in Pre-Civil War New Jersey."
17 Gigantino, *Ragged Road to Abolition*, 27.
18 Tax Rateables for Amwell Township during the 1770s and 80s list numbers of enslaved men capable of working owned by residents and subject to taxation. Only enslaved men were taxed so women and children do not appear.
19 NJSA, Amwell Township Tax Ratables, Books 865 and 866. See also: Ken Stryker-Rhoda, "New Jersey Rateables: Amwell Township, January-February 1780 and June 1780," *Genealogical Magazine of New Jersey*, Volume 47, Number 2, May 1972, 66-84. Omer Jupiter is listed as Omer Jupe in June.
20 *New Jersey Gazette*, April 30, 1783, 3.
21 *New Jersey Gazette*, April 1, 1778, 4.

22 *New Jersey Gazette*, July 19, 1780, 4.
23 *New Jersey Gazette*, February 26, 1783, 4.
24 *New Jersey Gazette*, August 29, 1785, 3. Otherwise, description is the same. Advertised only by John Lequear on August 23, 1785.
25 *New Jersey Gazette*, May 3, 1780, 4.
26 *New Jersey Gazette*, June 14, 1780, 3.

Chapter 19

1 Amwell Township Tax Rateables Book 867.
2 Amwell Township Tax Rateables July/August 1786, Book 868.
3 Gedney, *Town Records of Hopewell*, 38-39.
4 *New Jersey Gazette*, May 2, 1785, 4.
5 Schmidt, *Slavery in Hunterdon County*, 13. – citing letter in Capner collection.
6 Schmidt, *Slavery*, 6-7; Gigantino, *Ragged Road to Abolition*, 73.
7 Gigantino, *Ragged Road to Abolition*, 28-30.
8 New Jersey State Archives, County Tax Rateables, Hunterdon County, Amwell Township, Book 867 1784 (he is a householder but no land), Book 868 1786 (he is not listed), Book 869 1789 (living with John Reid).
9 Although Samuel Hunt states in Jacob's pension file that he thought Mary was the property of Ralph W. Hunt, "his brother in law" who also lived with Nathaniel Hunt, both Mary and Phillis state they were owned by Nathaniel.
10 Mary Francis statement in Jacob Francis PF W459. A search of the incomplete Hunterdon County records relating to marriages and manumissions does not provide evidence of the sequence of events or their details. However, had he not freed her, their children born before 1804 would have been born as slaves rather than as free Blacks.
11 Calligaro, "The Negro's Legal Status," 168.
12 Wright, *Afro-Americans in New Jersey*, 21-23.
13 Schmidt, *Slavery in Hunterdon County*, 4.
14 *The New York Packet*, January 11, 1792, 3; *The New-York Journal, & Patriotic Register*, June 15, 1791, 185.
15 James S. Norton, *New Jersey in 1793: An Abstract and Index to the 1793 Militia Census of the State of New Jersey*, Salt Lake City: 1973, xvi; Gough, "Black Men and the Early New Jersey Militia," 232-235. In 1799, when he reached age forty-five he was no longer in the militia age range.
16 Gough, "Black Men and the Early New Jersey Militia," 237.
17 Alexis De Tocqueville, *Democracy in America*, 336-360.
18 Snell, *History of Hunterdon and Somerset*, 338.
19 Wright, *Afro-Americans in New Jersey*, 25.
20 Gigantino, *Ragged Road to Abolition*, 65-68, 70, 78, 81.
21 Gigantino, 80.
22 Schmidt, *Slavery in Hunterdon County*, 5-7.
23 March 14, 1798, Acts 22nd General Assembly. 2nd sitting, ch. DCCXXVII, p. 364-373.

Chapter 20

1 Cornell, Samuel C, and Lloyd Van Derveer. *Map of Hunterdon County, New Jersey: entirely from original surveys*. Philadelphia?: Lloyd Van Derveer & S.C. Cornell, 1851.
2 Hunterdon County Historical Society, Bound Mss 434, *Ledger 1796-1807, Atkinson, Asher, General Store, Flemington, NJ*. The ledger actually continues beyond 1807. Atkinson Store

Records October 23, 1809 – 12.10 paid by John Francis – insert between pages 105, March 10, 1810 – payments by John Francis, December 30, 1815 – list of debts Jacob Francis – insert page 94, May 9, 1816 – debts insert page 93, February 4, 1817 – Phebe Francis, John Francis –insert page 93, 1817, April 22 – John Francis insert p.92, May 5 – Phebe Francis, September 2 – Jacob Francis

3 Schmidt, *Slavery in Hunterdon County*, 4

4 New Jersey State Archives, County Tax Rateables, Hunterdon County, Amwell Township, Book 870 1802. County Tax Rateables – Hunterdon County – Amwell Township, Reel 11, 12; New Jersey State Archives, County Tax Rateables, Hunterdon County, Amwell Township, Book 871 1809.

5 New Jersey State Archives, County Tax Rateables, Hunterdon County, Amwell Township, Book 870 1802. County Tax Rateables – Hunterdon County – Amwell Township, Reel 11, 12; New Jersey State Archives, County Tax Rateables, Hunterdon County, Amwell Township, Book 871 1809.

6 Gulick, *Gulicks of the U.S.A.*, 251.

7 Gigantino, *Ragged Road to Abolition*, 110-111.

8 *True American*, March 10, 1806, 1. The newspaper add gives the date as 1805 but this is probably a misprint.

9 Gigantino, *Ragged Road to Abolition*, 92-93.

10 Van Buskirk, *Standing in Their Own Light*, 183. Wright, "New Jersey Laws and the Negro."

11 Thank you to Matthew Skic of the Museum of the American Revolution for information on the search made by museum researchers for voting records in New Jersey previous to 1807.

12 Gigantino, *Ragged Road to Abolition*, 98.

13 Its name would be formally changed to the Baptist Church of Flemington in 1853.

14 *One Hundredth Anniversary Exercises*, 12, 15, 16, 143-144. Hunterdon County Historical Society, Bound Mss 655, *Records of the Flemington Baptist Church,*, 7, 34.

16 NJSA, Amwell Township Tax Ratables 1802, Book 870; 1803, Book 871.

17 Hunterdon County Historical Society, Bound Mss 655, *Records of the Flemington Baptist Church,* 44, 10. The records show it was extremely rare for a potential member to be challenged as Jacob was.

18 *Centinel of Freedom*, Newark, New Jersey, March 10, 1801, 4.

19 *Centinel of Freedom*, Newark, June 22, 1801, 3.

20 See *Hunterdon Gazette,* July 1, 1829 for example.

21 Snell, *History of Hunterdon and Somerset*, 328, 334.

22 Snell, *History of Hunterdon and Somerset*, 328, 334. Hart died September 4, 1837, age 59.

23 *Trenton Federalist,* November 25, 1805, 3.

24 *Trenton Federalist,* November 20, 1809, 4.

25 *Trenton Federalist,* April 28, 1806, 3.

26 Snell, *History of Hunterdon and Somerset*, 327. His father, James H. Blackwell, served as postmaster for ten years from 1820-1830.

27 *Trenton Federalist,* February 27, 1809, 4.

28 Snell, *History of Hunterdon and Somerset*, 327, 332.

29 Snell, *History of Hunterdon and Somerset*, 327.

30 *Trenton Federalist,* July 21, 1806, 1.

31 *Trenton Federalist,* October 17, 1808, 4.

32 Snell, *History of Hunterdon and Somerset*, 328, 334.

Chapter 21

1 Schmidt, *Slavery in Hunterdon County*, 4. Wright, *Afro-Americans in New Jersey,* Appendix 2 and 3.

2 Shown on a sketch of structures and their owners in 1822 published in Snell, *History of Hunterdon and Somerset Counties.*

3 Capnerhurst Papers, Box 16, Folder 963, Hunterdon County Historical Society.
4 Snell, *History of Hunterdon and Somerset Counties*, 328-329.
5 *The Pacific Appeal*, 4 July 1863, 2.
6 Snell, *History of Hunterdon and Somerset*, 333.
7 Kline, "The Flemington Academy," 18-19.
8 Flemington Baptist Church, *One Hundredth Anniversary Exercises*, 16.
9 Schmidt, *Slavery in Hunterdon County*, 15.
10 Flemington Baptist Church, *One Hundredth Anniversary Exercises*, 16-17.
11 Abner's birth year is estimated from his age given in various documents, such as his death notice that says he was 59 years old upon death in 1872, and the 1850 and 1860 Census records. For Phebe's marriage see: "New Jersey, County Marriages, 1682-1956," database with images, FamilySearch (https://familysearch.org/ark:/61903/3:1:939Z-18HJ-Z?cc=1803976&wc=9XR9-929%3A146363301: 20 May 2019), 004541217 > image 458 of 816; New Jersey State Archives, Trenton.
12 Kline, "The Flemington Academy," 18-19. Hunterdon County Historical Society, Capner Papers, Box 16, Folder 963, Rental payment note of Jacob Francis signed by Thomas Capner, April 15, 1818.
13 *Trenton Federalist*, April 6, 1818, 1; *True American*, April 6, 1818, 3. The Old York Road got its name when it was one of several main colonial roads across New Jersey connecting to New York.
14 Kline, "The Flemington Academy." 17-19; Snell, *History of Hunterdon and Somerset*, 333. The oldest deed of school property is dated Jan 1, 1812. Early teachers included Leigh, Mendham, Kissam, and Brown. Brown was last teacher in the old building that stood in rear of the Baptist Church. First trustees were Peter Haward, Thomas Capner, James Clark, Jonathan Hill, and John Maxwell.
15 *Trenton Federalist*, September 25, 1815, 1.
16 *Trenton Federalist*, March 3, 1817, 2.
17 Snell, *History of Hunterdon and Somerset*, 328.
18 *Trenton Federalist*, March 15, 1813, 4.
19 *Trenton Federalist*, March 3, 1817, 2.
20 *Trenton Federalist*, February 3, 1812, 3.
21 *True American*, July 15, 1816, 4.
22 *Trenton Federalist*, April 15, 1816, 4.
23 *Trenton Federalist*, February 7, 1814, 1.
24 *Trenton Federalist*, December 25. 1815, 3.
25 *Trenton Federalist*, July 26, 1813, 5.
26 *Trenton Federalist*, January 8, 1816, 4.
27 *Trenton Federalist*, July 13, 1812, 1.
28 *Trenton Federalist*, May 6, 1816, 1.
29 *Pennsylvania Correspondent, and Farmers' Advertiser*, Doylestown, PA, August 9, 1813, 4.
30 *Trenton Federalist*, May 17, 1813, 3.
31 *Trenton Federalist*, May 2, 1814, 4.
32 Schmidt, *Slavery in Hunterdon County*, 15.
33 Hunterdon County Birth Certificates of Children of Slaves, 1804-1835.
34 Ann Becker, "The Revolutionary War Pension Act of 1818," *Historical Journal of Massachusetts*, Summer 2019, 98-137, 102-103.
35 Jacob Francis PF W459. The Francis family was well known to Maxwell and in a promissory note dated October 2, 1819, John Francis promised to pay to John Maxwell, Jr. on order the sum of eight dollars and sixty one cents. Capnerhurst Papers, Box 11 Folder 567.

Chapter 22

1 Flemington Baptist Church Records, 90.
2 Schmidt, *Slavery in Hunterdon County*, 4. Wright, *Afro-Americans in New Jersey*, Appendix 2 and 3.
3 Snell, *History of Hunterdon and Somerset Counties*, New Jersey, 1881, 328-329.
4 *Emporium and True American*, December 7, 1822, 2.
5 Flemington Baptist Church records, 117.
6 Flemington Baptist Church. *One Hundredth Anniversary Exercises*, 19.
7 *Hunterdon Gazette*, January 19, 1826.
8 *Hunterdon Gazette*. Sept. 1, 1825.
9 Schmidt, *Slavery in Hunterdon County*, 24, referring to *Hunterdon Gazette*, April 28, 1825.
10 *Princeton Pat.* August 22, 1827.
11 Schmidt, *Slavery in Hunterdon County*, 24.
12 Flemington Baptist Church Records, 100, 104.
13 *Hunterdon Gazette*, Nov 8, 1826.
14 *Hunterdon Gazette*, October 8, 1828.
15 *Hunterdon Gazette*, October 6, 1830.
16 Snell, *History of Hunterdon and Somerset*, 333.
17 *Trenton Federalist*, February 9, 1824, 4.
18 Snell, *History of Hunterdon and Somerset*, 330; *Hunterdon Gazette*, May 31, 1826.
19 *Hunterdon Gazette*, March 24, 1825; February 23, 1826; May 31, 1826; September 20, 182; September 27, 1826.
20 *Hunterdon Gazette*, December 27, 1826.
21 *Hunterdon Gazette*, April 26, 1826.
22 *Hunterdon Gazette*, April 12, 1826; April 26, 1826.
23 *Hunterdon Gazette*, May 3, 1826.
24 *Hunterdon Gazette*, October 27, 1825; December 1, 1825.
25 *Hunterdon Gazette* editorial, April 19, 1826; July 26, 1826.
26 Snell, *History of Hunterdon and Somerset*, 331; *Hunterdon Gazette*, January 17, 1828; February 13, 1828.
27 *Hunterdon Gazette*, February 20, 1828.
28 *Hunterdon Gazette*, February 20, 1828.
29 Snell, *History of Hunterdon and Somerset*, 330.
30 *The True American*, July 20, 1807, 2.
31 John Hall (Capner) to Mary Hall, July 20, 1806, Capner Papers, Folder 286.
32 *The True American*, July 17, 1809, 4.
33 *Trenton Federalist*, June 27, 1814, 3.
34 *Trenton Federalist*, July 14, 1817, 3; August 2, 1824, 2.
35 George Washington to William Livingston, September 1, 1777, Library of Congress, *George Washington Papers*. See: Kidder, *A People Harassed and Exhausted* for the story of the First Hunterdon County regiment in the War for Independence.
36 *Hunterdon Gazette*, February 16, 1826.
37 *Hunterdon Gazette*, April 12, 1826.
38 *Hunterdon Gazette*, April 5, 1826.
39 *Hunterdon Gazette*, June 14, 1826, June 21, 1826; June 28, 1826.
40 "Celebration of the Jubilee, at Flemington," *Hunterdon Gazette and Farmer's Advertiser*, July 12, 1826, 26-28. The other veterans who attended were: Jacob Anderson, Samuel Barber, William Bennett, John Besson, sen., William Bilby, William Bowne, Robert Butler, Andrew Butterfaus, Capt. Tunis Case, John Chamberlin, James Clark, sen., Albert Conover, Paul Cool, sen., Adam Conrad, Samuel Corwine, Nicholas Danbury, William Danbury, William C. Dilts, Lewis English (a Colored man), Daniel Ent, Joseph Fish, William Fulper,

Peter Geary, Capt. Jon. Higgins, John Howe, Adam Hummer, Martin Johnson, Christopher Kuhl, John Maxwell, sen., James Metlar, Richard Mills, George Pownell, Tunis T. Quick, David Schamp, George N. Schamp, John Servis, Michael Shurts, Moses Stout, William Taylor, Elijah Thatcher, John Trimmer, and Jerome Waldron.

41 *Hunterdon Gazette*, Wednesday, July 12, 1826.
42 *Hunterdon Gazette*, June 27, 1827.
43 Schmidt, *Rural Hunterdon*, 255.
44 Schreiner, Kathleen J., "Our Courthouse," *Hunterdon Historical Newsletter*, vol 14, No 2, Spring 1978, Hunterdon County Historical Society, 3-4; Snell, *History of Hunterdon and Somerset*, 330-331; *Hunterdon Gazette*, February 20, 1828.
45 County of Hunterdon Cash Book, 1828-1829 – MS 392. Hunterdon County Court House MS 393 also lists the same amounts, but gives date of August 1 for Jacob and August 11 for Nathaniel and both men are listed as "labourer."
46 Hunterdon Deeds, 499-500; New Jersey State Archives, Hunterdon County Probate Records, Jacob Francis file 4303J.
47 Kline, "The Flemington Academy," 18-19.
48 "New Jersey, County Marriages, 1682-1956," database with images, FamilySearch (https://familysearch.org/ark:/61903/3:1:939Z-18WM-Z?cc=1803976&wc=9XRM-T38%3A146362901 : 20 May 2019), 004541226 > image 529 of 889; New Jersey State Archives, Trenton.
49 *Hunterdon Gazette*, June 30, 1829.

Chapter 23

1 Flemington Baptist Church Records, 119-121.
2 Litwack, *North of Slavery*, 14.
3 *Hunterdon Gazette*, October 6, 1830.
4 US Census 1830.
5 Records of the Flemington Baptist Church, 16, 23, MSS 655.
6 *Hunterdon Gazette*, Sept. 29. 1830.
7 *Hunterdon Gazette*, January 5, 1831.
8 *Hunterdon Gazette*, June 15, 1836.
9 Flemington Baptist Church, *One Hundredth Anniversary Exercises*, 138-144.
10 Peter Haward Letters, 1800-1854, Folder 37, Day Book 1830, Hunterdon County Historical Society. January 27, 1831 – Jacob Francis to mend Wheel? - $1.31 ½; March 18, 1831 – Jacob Francis to boards, nails, scantily, hinges & screws, and work on little house $3.00; April 11, 1831 – Jacob Francis for making pig pen $1.25; Nov 18, 1831 – Jacob Francis for sharping wood saw - $ .12 ½; Oct 1832 – Mary Francis for 2 doz close pegs $1.37 ½; August 27, 1834 – Jacob Francis for repairing washing board $1.19, making well curb $1.75, ½ pound? Nails $1.04; September 1, 1834 – Jacob Francis for new spout 12 ½ feet long $1.53; September 2, 1835 – Jacob Francis for mending table; June 1, 1836 – Jane Francis for handle to fan; September 29, 1837 – Isaac Francis for sharpening saw $2.12 ½; January 29, 1839 – Isaac Francis for frale? [flail?]
11 *Hunterdon Gazette*, Flemington, Feb. 23, 1831. 3.
12 *Hunterdon Gazette*, Flemington, Feb. 23, 1831. 4; *Hunterdon Gazette*, Flemington, April 6, 1831,1.
13 *Hunterdon Gazette*, Flemington, March 9, 1831, 3.
14 *Hunterdon Gazette* Flemington, April 4, 1831.
15 Snell, *History of Hunterdon and Somerset*, 327, 332.
16 "A Voice from Trenton," The *Liberator*, December 17, 1831, 2.
17 Wright, *Afro-Americans in New Jersey*, 32.

18 An example of a White applicant for a pension who had no White men to testify for him was John Ferrell of North Carolina, PF S6836. Ferrell testified "he has no documentary evidence that he can prove his service by and that he knows no man now living, who was with him but old Arthur Toney a Coloured man; and whose evidence (being a Coloured man) would not be good Testimony."
19 "Important Mission," *The Liberator*, March 9, 1833, 3.
20 D'Autrechy, *More Records of Old Hunterdon*, II: 185. Citing: Recognizance Bond 2246 at the Office of the Hunterdon County Clerk.
21 *Minutes and Proceedings of the Third Annual Convention, for the improvement of the Free People of Colour in these United States*, New York: 1833, 3, 14.
22 *Minutes of the Fourth Annual Convention, for the improvement of the Free People of Colour, in the United States*, New York: 1834, 8-10, 17.
23 Flemington Baptist Church, *One Hundredth Anniversary Exercises*, 17-18.
24 Schultz, *History of the Methodist Episcopal Church of Flemington*, 5. A note in the church history says that "in those days the colored members were reported separately."
25 *New National Era*, Washington, DC, May 16, 1872, 1. – Frederick Douglass, editor; *The Pacific Appeal*, 4 July 1863, 2.
26 Schmidt, *Slavery in Hunterdon County*, 32.
27 *Hunterdon Gazette*, June 29, 1836.
28 Flemington Baptist Church, *One Hundredth Anniversary Exercises*, 18.
29 *Hunterdon Gazette*, July 6, 1836.
30 New Jersey State Archives, Hunterdon County Probate Records, Jacob Francis file 4303J, will and inventory 1836. The will is fairly long and provides something for each child. It also states how the estate should be divided after the death of Mary. He owned a house and lot and the inventory of the house contents indicates a modest middle class lifestyle.
31 Ancestry.com. *New Jersey, U.S., Wills and Probate Records, 1739-1991* [database on-line]. Provo, UT, USA: Ancestry.com Operations, Inc., 2015. 523-425
32 *Hunterdon Gazette*, Wednesday, August 3, 1836. The obituary also appeared in other papers, including the Cleveland, Ohio, *The Cleveland Whig*, August 16, 1836, 1.
33 *Hunterdon Gazette*, April 27, 1836; May 11, 1836; November 30, 1836; December 7, 1836.
34 *Hunterdon Gazette*, Wednesday, February 28, 1844. Died In this village, on Tuesday the 26th of July, Jacob Francis, a colored man, in the 83d year of his age. He has resided in this place thirty-five years; has been an orderly member of the Baptist church for thirty years; he has raised a large family, in a manner creditable to his judgment and his Christian character, and lived to see them doing well; and has left the scenes of this mortal existence, deservedly respected by all who knew him. – Jacob Francis was a soldier of the Revolution – he served a long tour of duty in the Massachusetts militia, and was some time in the regular army in New Jersey; and we have learned from those who knew him in those days of privation and peril, that his fidelity and good conduct as a soldier were the subject of frequent remark, and received the approbation of his officers. – For the last few years he received a pension from government; an acknowledgement of his services to his country which, though made at a late day, came most opportunely to minister to his comfort in the decline of life, and under the infirmities of old age. August 3, 1836.
35 Calligaro, "The Negro's Legal Status," 173. State v Heddon, 1 N.J.L. 377 1795.

Chapter 24

1 "New Jersey, County Marriages, 1682-1956," database with images, Family Search (https://familysearch.org/ark:/61903/3:1:939Z-18CD-G?cc=1803976&wc=9XR9-929%3A146363301 : 20 May 2019), 004541217 > image 420 of 816; New Jersey State Archives, Trenton.

2 The 1840 census recorded them in a too young age range column, but as free colored persons.
3 Hunterdon County Historical Society Collection Part II: Records of the First Baptist Church of Flemington (1803-1927), Folder 38. Mr. Bush may be tailor John Bush. The Capner family was quite prominent and there were several Mrs. Capners.
4 Schmidt, *Slavery in Hunterdon County*, 24.
5 1850 US Census for Buffalo, New York.
6 *The Pacific Appeal*, 4 July 1863, 2.
7 Buffalo, New York directories for 1837 and 1838.
8 *The Colored American*, New York, January 27, 1838, 1. The story of Crispus Attucks appears on page 113 of volume I, Book III in Carlo Botta, *History of the War of Independence of the United States of America*, New Haven, 1837.
9 *The Friend of Man*, February 28, 1838, 2; *The Emancipator*, March 15, 1838.
10 Buffalo, New York directory 1839.
11 Schmidt, *Slavery in Hunterdon County*, 4-5.
12 US Census 1840.
13 *Commercial Advertiser and Journa*l, Buffalo, New York, June 6, 1842, 1; October 8, 1842, 1.
14 Minutes of the State Convention of Colored Citizens, Held at Albany, on the 18th, 19th, and 20th of August, 1840, for the purpose of considering their political condition. Piercy & Reed, New York, NY, 1840, 8, 13, 19.
15 *The Colored American*, New York, July 31, 1841, 1; *The Colored American*, New York, September 11, 1841, 1.
16 *Buffalo Commercial Advertiser and Journal*, December 30, 1842, 2. Seward would serve as Secretary of State under President Abraham Lincoln.
17 Minutes of the National Convention of Colored Citizens: Held at Buffalo on the 15th, 16th, 17th, 18th, and 19th of August, 1843 for the purpose of considering their moral and political condition as American Citizens, New York: 1843, 7, 8-9, 37-39.
18 *Buffalo Daily Gazette*, September 12, 1843, 2.
19 *Alexandria Gazette and Virginia Advertiser*, September 16, 1843, 1; *Daily Madisonian*, Washington, DC, Saturday, Sep 16, 1843, 2; *Tarborough Press*, Tarborough, Edgecombe County, N.C., September 30, 1843, 1.
20 *Baton Rouge Tri-Weekly Gazette & Comet*, September 30, 1843, 3; *The Natchez Weekly Courier*, Natchez, Mississippi, September 27, 1843, 3.
21 *Richmond Indiana Palladium*, September 30, 1843, 3.
22 *New York Herald*, Saturday, September 16, 1843, 3.
23 *Jeffersonian Republican*, Stroudsburg, Pennsylvania, September 21, 1843, 3.; reprinted in *Hillsborough Recorder*, Hillsborough, North Carolina, October 5, 1843, 3.
24 *Emancipator and Republican*, Boston, October 26, 1843, 102.
25 *Boston Investigator*, November 1, 1843, 3; see also *Vermont Religious Observer*, Middlebury, VT, November 28, 1843, 1.
26 *Massachusetts Spy*, Worcester, MA, September 20, 1843, 3; *The Liberator*, Boston, MA, October 06, 1843, 160.
27 US Census for 1850 – Buffalo, New York; *The Pacific Appeal*, July 4, 1863, 2.
28 *Hunterdon Gazette*, February 28, 1844.
29 Schmidt, *Slavery in Hunterdon County*, 8.

Chapter 25

1 For more on Douglass at this point in his life see: Blight, David W., *Frederick Douglass: Prophet of Freedom*, New York: Simon & Schuster, 2018, 191 and chapter 11.
2 *Frederick Douglass's Paper*, January 7, 1848, 2.

3 *The Liberator*, Boston, March 24, 1848, 1; *North Star,* March 24, 1848.
4 *North Star*, March 24, 1848, Eulogy for John Quincy Adams, 1.
5 Arthur O. White , "The Black Movement against Jim Crow Education in Buffalo, New York, 1800-1900," *Phylon*, Vol. 30, No. 4 (4th Qtr., 1969), pp. 375-393, 380.
6 *North Star*, August 17, 1849, 1.
7 *The Liberator*, October 20, 1848, 1; *Frederick Douglass' Paper*, Rochester, NY, September 15, 1848, 2.
8 Report of the Proceedings of the Colored National Convention, Held at Cleveland, Ohio, on Wednesday, September 6, 1848, Rochester: *The North Star*, 1848, 8-10; *The Colored Conventions Movement: Black Organizing in the Nineteenth Century*, edited by P. Gabrielle Foreman, Jim Casey, and Sarah Lynn Patterson, University of North Carolina Press, 2021. Pages 37-38.
9 Report of the Proceedings of the Colored National Convention, Held at Cleveland, Ohio on Wednesday, September 6, 1848, Rochester: 1848, 3, 4.
10 *Buffalo Morning Express*, Feb 19, 1849, 2.
11 *Buffalo Weekly Republic*, August 14, 1849, 2; *Anti-Slavery Bugle*, New Lisbon, OH, August 18, 1849, 3.
12 Letter of Frederick Douglass, *Frederick Douglass' Paper*, July 18, 1850.
13 *Voice of the Fugitive*, Sandwich, Canada West, June 18, 1851, 3.
14 *New National Era*, Washington, DC, May 16, 1872, 1. – Frederick Douglass, editor. This dual location helps explain their appearance in both places in the 1860 US Census.
15 *Frederick Douglass' Paper* (Rochester, N.Y.), November 13, 1851, 2.
16 *Weekly Oregonian*, Portland, Oregon , February 02, 1856, 4.
17 *Weekly Oregonian*, Portland, Oregon, September 12, 1857, 3.
18 *The Daily Mountaineer*, Dalles, Oregon, November 21, 1865; *New National Era*, Washington, DC, May 16, 1872, 1. – Frederick Douglass, editor.
19 *Elevator*, December 1, 1865.
20 British Columbia Black History Society, https://bcblackhistory.ca/firsts/.
21 *The Pacific Appeal*, 4 July 1863, 2.
22 *The Pacific Appeal*, 4 July 1863, 2.
23 *The British Colonist and Victoria Chronicle*, Victoria, British Columbia, March 28, 1872, 3.
24 *The New National Era*, Washington, DC, May 16, 1872, 1. – Frederick Douglass, editor. This is the only reference to Jacob being wounded in action. Jacob does not mention such an incident in his pension application. The writer might more accurately have commented about Jacob's willingness to shed his blood for the cause. Abner also hinted in general that Jacob had been wounded in battle in his eulogy for J. Q. Adams. Since no specifics are ever given and Jacob makes no mention of it, it must be hyperbole. It may also be that Jacob may have commented about bleeding from injuries associated with fatigue duty and combat in general rather than directly from enemy fire in a specific battle.
25 *New National Era*, Washington, DC, March 28, 1872, 1. – Frederick Douglass, editor.
26 "Jurymen, Without Regard to Color," *Weekly Louisianian*, January 4, 1872.

Epilog

1 Ancestry.com. Philadelphia, Pennsylvania, Death Certificates Index, 1803-1915 [database on-line]. Provo, UT, USA: Ancestry.com Operations, Inc., 2011. Original data: "Pennsylvania, Philadelphia City Death Certificates, 1803–1915." Index. FamilySearch, Salt Lake City, Utah, 2008, 2010. From originals housed By the 1850 census, Nathaniel was one of only two Black farmers owning property in Raritan Township. He owned real estate valued at $2000 while the other farmer owned land worth $1600.
2 1850 US Census, Raritan Township, Hunterdon County, New Jersey.
3 NJSA, New Jersey Probate Records, file 8146J, Volume 18, page 684, Estate of Nathaniel Francis.

Bibliography

Manuscripts Collections

Hunterdon County Historical Society, Deats Library
Amwell Township, Township Meeting Records, Hunterdon County Historical Society
Hunterdon County Historical Society, Bound Mss 655, *Records of the Flemington Baptist Church Organized June 19, 1798, as the Baptist Church of Amwell, from Jun 19, 1798 to November 11, 1867*, Copy for Hiram Deats, Flemington, NJ

Library of Congress,
George Washington Papers, online at: https://www.loc.gov/collections/george-washington-papers/about-this-collection (GWPLOC)

Massachusetts Historical Society Collections
Brown, Obadiah, "Obadiah Brown Diary, 1776-1777." *Online*, https://www.masshist.org/database/1908.

NARA M246. Muster rolls, payrolls, strength returns, and other miscellaneous personnel, pay, and supply records of American Army units, 1775-83

NARA M804 Revolutionary War pension files

NARA M881. Compiled service records of soldiers who served in the American Army during the Revolutionary War, 1775-1783

New Jersey State Archives
Amwell Township Tax Rateables Book 867, 868, 869
Hunterdon County Birth Certificates of Children of Slaves, 1804-1835
Hunterdon County Probate Records
Hunterdon County Land Deeds

Salem Land Deeds -
Commonwealth of Massachusetts, Southern Essex District Registry of Deeds
https://salemdeeds.com/salemdeeds/Defaultsearch2.aspx

Salem Tabernacle Church records

Salem South Church records

US Census 1830, 1840, 1850, 1860, 1870

Yale University Library
Greene, "Orderly book: from General Nathanael Greene's headquarters, 1776 Feb 13-May 19," online at https://collections.library.yale.edu/catalog/10602506

Newspapers

Source note citations reference over fifty newspapers, including the papers published by Abolitionists such as Frederick Douglass. The papers used most extensively are those associated with locations where Jacob Francis lived. These include Salem and Boston, Massachusetts, and Trenton and Flemington, New Jersey. See source notes for specific references.

Published Document Collections

Buffalo, New York directories for 1837, 1838, 1839, online at: https://newyorkgenealogy.org/erie/buffalo-new-york-city-directories-1828-1893.htm.

Chase, Philander D., ed., *The Papers of George Washington, Revolutionary War Series*, Charlottesville: University Press of Virginia, 1985+.

Commager, Henry Steel, and Richard B. Morris, eds., The *Spirit of 'Seventy-Six: The Story of the American Revolution as Told by Participants*, New York: Bobbs-Merrill, 1958.

D'Autrechy, Phyllis B., *More Records of Old Hunterdon County, Volume 2*, Flemington: Hunterdon County Historical Society, 2000.

Fitzpatrick, John C., ed., *The Writings of George Washington from the Original Manuscript Sources, 1745-1799*, Washington: U.S. Government Printing Office, 1931-44.

Force, Peter, *American Archives*, Washington: Prepared and published under authority of an act of Congress, 1837-53.

Gedney, Lida Cokefair, comp., *The Town Records of Hopewell, New Jersey*, New Jersey Society of the Colonial Dames of America, 1931.

Hammond, Otis G., *Letters and Papers of Major-General John Sullivan, Continental Army*, Concord, NH: New Hampshire Historical Society, 1930-39.

Hutchinson, Israel, "Colonel Hutchinson's Orderly Book," *Proceedings of the Massachusetts Historical Society*. XVI (1878), 335-364.

____, *Journals of the Continental Congress*, Washington: U.S. Government Printing Office, 1904-37.

____, *Journals of Each Provincial Congress of Massachusetts in 1774 and 1775, and of the Committee of Safety*, Boston: Dutton and Wentworth, 1838.

Lee, Charles, "The Lee Papers, Volume II 1776-1778," *Collections of the New York Historical Society for the year 1872*, New York: 1873.

Minutes and Proceedings of the Third Annual Convention, for the improvement of the Free People of Colour in these United States, New York: 1833,

Minutes of the Fourth Annual Convention, for the improvement of the Free People of Colour, in the United States, New York: 1834.

Minutes of the National Convention of Colored Citizens: Held at Buffalo on the 15th, 16th, 17th, 18th, and 19th of August, 1843 for the purpose of considering their moral and political condition as American Citizens, New York: 1843.

"New Jersey, County Marriages, 1682-1956," database with images, FamilySearch (https://familysearch.org/ark:/61903/3:1:939Z-18WM-Z?cc=1803976&wc=9XRM-T38%3A146362901 : 20 May 2019), 004541226 > image 529 of 889

Norton, James S. *New Jersey in 1793: An Abstract and Index to the 1793 Militia Census of the State of New Jersey*, Salt Lake City: 1973

Prince, Carl E. ed. *The Papers of William Livingston*, Trenton, New Jersey Historical Commission, 1980.

Reed, William B. *Life and Correspondence of Joseph Reed*, Philadelphia: Lindsay and Blakiston, 1847.

Report of the Proceedings of the Colored National Convention, Held at Cleveland, Ohio on Wednesday, September 6, 1848, Rochester: 1848.

Shurtleff, Nathaniel B.,ed., *Records of the Governor and Company of the Massachusetts Bay in New England*. Boston: 1853-54.

Stryker-Rhoda, Ken, "1780 Amwell Township Tax Retables," *Genealogy Magazine of New Jersey*, vol 47, no 1, 80.

____, "New Jersey Ratables: Amwell Township, January-February 1780 and June 1780," *Genealogical Magazine of New Jersey*, Volume 47, Number 2, May 1972, 66-84.

____, "New Jersey Retables, 1778-1789," *Genealogy Magazine of New Jersey*, vol 48, no1, January 1973, 41

Robert J. Taylor, ed., *Papers of John Adams*, Cambridge: Belknap Press of Harvard University Press, 1979.

Smith, Paul H., ed., Gerard W. Gawalt, Rosemary Fry Plakas, Eugene R. Sheridan, assistant eds. *Letters of Delegates to Congress, 1774-1789*, Washington: Library of Congress, 1976-.

Published Diaries and Memoirs

Avery, Rev. David, "Battle of Trenton – From the Diary of the Rev. David Avery," *The American Monthly Magazine*, XIX (July-December 1901) Washington, DC: National Society, D.A.R., 1901, 151-156.

Baldwin, *The Revolutionary Journal of Col. Jeduthan Baldwin 1775-1778*, edited with memoir and notes by Thomas Williams Baldwin, Bangor: Printed for The DeBurians, 1906.

Bangs, Edward, ed., *Journal of Lieutenant Isaac Bangs, April 1 to July 29, 1776*, Cambridge: John Wilson and son, 1890.

Belknap, Jeremy, *Life of Jeremy Belknap, D.D.: The Historian of New Hampshire*, New York: Harper & Brothers, 1847.

Curwen, Samuel. *Journal and letters of the late Samuel Curwen judge of admiralty, etc., a loyalist-refugee in England, during the American Revolution. To which are added, illustrative documents and other eminent men*. By George Atkinson Ward ... New York: Leavitt, Trow & co., 1845.

De Tocqueville, Alexis, *Democracy in America*, Henry Reeve, trans., New York: George Adlard, 1838.

Graydon, Alexander, *Memoirs of a Life, Chiefly Passed in Pennsylvania, within the last Sixty Years*, Edinburgh: 1822.

Greenwood, John, *The Wartime Services of John Greenwood, A Patriot in the American Revolution 1775-1783*, Westvaco, 1981.

Heath, Major-General William, *Heath's Memoirs of the American War*, Reprinted from the Original Edition of 1798, introduction and notes by Rufus Rockwell Wilson, New York: A. Wessels, 1904.

How, David, *Diary of David How: A Private in Colonel Pau Dudley Sargent's Regiment of the Massachusetts Line, in the Amy of the American Revolution*, Morrisania, NY: 1865.

Price, Ezekiel – "Diary of Ezekiel Price, 1775-6," *Proceedings of the Massachusetts Historical Society*, VII: 1863-1864, 185-262.

Powell, William S., "A Connecticut Soldier Under Washington: Elisha Bostwick's Memoirs of the First Years of the Revolution," *The William and Mary Quarterly*, Third Series, VI (1949), 94-107.

Robertson, Archibald. *Archibald Robertson: His diaries and sketches in America, 1762-1780*. Reprint edition. New York: New York Public Library and Arno Press, 1971.

[Root, Nathaniel] Sergeant R---, "The Battle of Princeton," from *The Phenix* of March 24, 1832, published at Wellsborough Pennsylvania, *Pennsylvania Magazine of History and Biography* XX (1896), 515-516.

Serle, Ambrose. *The American Journal of Ambrose Serle, 1776-1778*. Edward H. Tatum, ed. and intro. New York: New York Times, 1969. (Reprint of 1940 edition)

Shaw, Samuel, *The Journals of Major Samuel Shaw, the first American consul at Canton. With a life of the author, by Josiah Quincy*, Boston: W. Crosby and H. P. Nichols, 1847.

Smith, Richard, "Diary of Richard Smith in the Continental Congress, 1775-1776, "*The American Historical Review*, Vol. 1, No. 2 (Jan., 1896), 288-310.

Thacher, James. *Military Journal during the American Revolutionary War*, 1775-1783, Boston: Richardson and Lord, 1823.

Tomlinson, Abraham, ed., *The Military Journals of Two Private Soldiers, 1758-1775*, Poughkeepsie: Abraham Tomlinson, 1855.

Webb, Samuel Blachley, *Correspondence and Journals of Samuel Blachley Webb*. Collected and edited by Worthington Chauncey Ford, vol 1, New York: 1893.

White, Joseph, "The Good Soldier White: A Revolutionary Veteran Speaks," *American Heritage* VII (1956): 74-79.

Wilkinson, General James, *Memoirs of My Own Times*, Philadelphia: Abraham Small, 1816.

Woolman, John. *Considerations on the Keeping of Negroes*. Philadelphia: 1754.

Dr. John Warren Diary, 19 April 1775–May 1776 MS N 1731, John Collins Warrren Papers, vol. 1A, Massachusetts Historical Society, Boston,

Secondary sources

___, "List of Houses Built in Salem from 1750-1773," *Historical Collections of the Essex Institute*, LVIII, 1922, 292-296

___, "The Affair at the North Bridge, Salem, February 26, 1775," *Historical Collections of the Essex Institute*, 38, October 1902, 321-352.

Alden, John Richard, *General Charles Lee: Traitor or Patriot?*, Baton Rouge: Louisiana State University Press, 1951.

Atkinson, Rick, The *British are Coming: The War for America, Lexington to Princeton, 1775-1777*, New York: Henry Holt, 2019.

Becker, Ann, "The Revolutionary War Pension Act of 1818," *Historical Journal of Massachusetts*, Summer 2019, 98-137.

Bell, J. L., *George Washington's Headquarters and Home, Cambridge, Massachusetts, Longfellow House – Washington's Headquarters National Historic Site*, Historic Resource Study, National Park Service, U.S. Department of the Interior, February 2012.

Calligaro, Lee. "The Negro's Legal Status in Pre-Civil War New Jersey," *New Jersey History*, LXXXV, Fall and Winter, 1967, 167-179.

Chadwick, Bruce, *The First American Army: The Untold Story of George Washington and the Men behind America's First Fight for Freedom*, Napierville, IL: Sourcebooks, Inc., 2007.

Drake, Samuel Adams. *Old Landmarks and Historic Personages of Boston*, Boston: J.R. Osgood and Company, 1873.

Dwyer, William M. *The Day is Ours! November 1776-January 1777: An Inside View of the Battles of Trenton and Princeton*. New York: Viking Press, 1983.

Felt, Joseph Barlow, *Annals of Salem*, Salem: W. & S.B. Ives, 1849.

Fischer, David Hackett, *Washington's Crossing*, Oxford: Oxford University Press, 2004.

Flemington Baptist Church. *One Hundredth Anniversary Exercises of the Baptist Church, Flemington, N.J. June 17th, 18th and 19th*, 1898. Flemington, NJ: Published by the church, 1898.

Foote, Henry Wilder, *Annals of King's Chapel from the Puritan age of New England to the present day*, Boston: Little, Brown, 1882-1940, c1881-c1940.

Foreman, P. Gabrielle, Jim Casey, and Sarah Lynn Patterson, eds., *The Colored Conventions Movement: Black Organizing in the Nineteenth Century*, University of North Carolina Press, 2021.

French, Allen, *The Siege of Boston*, New York: Macmillan, 1911.

Frothingham, Richard, *History of the Siege of Boston*, Boston: Little and Brown, 1851.

Gannett, Henry, *The Origin of Certain Place Names in the United States*, Washington, D.C.: Second Edition, Government Printing Office, 1905.

Gigantino, James J., *The Ragged Road to Abolition: Slavery and Freedom in New Jersey, 1775-1865,* Philadelphia: University of Pennsylvania Press, 2015.
Goodwin, M.C., "The Castle – A Sketch of Fort Independence," *The Bostonian*, II: 644-654
Gough, Robert J. "Black Men and the Early New Jersey Militia." *New Jersey History*, 88 (1970), 227-338.
Greene, Lorenzo Johnston. *The Negro in Colonial New England, 1620-1776*, New York: Columbia University Press, 1942.
____, "The Negro in the Armed Forces of the United States, 1619-1783," *Negro History Bulletin*, XIV, no. 6 (March 1951, 123-127, 138.
Gulick, David E., *Gulicks of the U.S.A.*, 1961.
Heitman, Francis Bernard, *Historical Register of Officers of the Continental Army During the War of the Revolution, April 1775, to December, 1783*, Washington, DC: 1914.
Hoffer, Peter Charles, *Prelude to Revolution: The Salem Gunpowder Raid of 1775,* Baltimore: Johns Hopkins University Press, 2013.
Holton, Woody, *Liberty Is Sweet: The Hidden History of the American Revolution*, New York: Simon & Schuster, 2021.
Horton, James Oliver. *Free People of Color: Inside the African American Community*. Washington: Smithsonian Institution Press, 1993.
Hufeland, Otto, *Westchester County during the American Revolution: 1775-1783*. White Plains, N.Y.: Published for Westchester County by the Westchester County Historical Society, 1926.
Johnston, Henry P., *Battle of Harlem Heights, September 16, 1776; with a Review of the Events of the Campaign*, New York, Columbia University Press, 1897.
____, *The Campaign of 1776 around New York and Brooklyn*, Brooklyn: Long Island Historical Society, 1878.
Kaplan, Sidney and Emma Nogrady Kaplan, *The Black Presence in the Era of the American Revolution*, Amherst: University of Massachusetts Press, 1989.
Kline, James A., "The Flemington Academy," *The Jerseyman*, VII, 1719, August 1901, 18-19.
Labaree, Benjamin W., *Colonial Massachusetts: A History*. Millwood, NY: Kto Press, 1979.
Lane, Wheaton J., *From Indian Trail to Iron Horse: Travel and Transportation in New Jersey, 1620-1860*, Princeton: Princeton University Press, 1939.
Leete, Frederick Deland, *The Deland family in America, a Biographical Genealogy*. Deland, FL: 1943.
Lefkowitz, Arthur S. *Benedict Arnold's Army: The 1775 American Invasion of Canada during Revolutionary War*, El Dorado Hills, CA: Savas Beatie, 2008, 2014.
Litwack, Leon F. *North of Slavery: The Negro in the Free States, 1790 - 1860*, Chicago: Chicago University Press, 1961.
Ludlum, David M., *Early American Hurricanes, 1492-1870*, Boston: American Meteorological Society, 1963.
Marcou, Jane Belknap, *Life of Jeremy Belknap, D. D.: The Historian of New Hampshire*, New York: Harper & Brothers, 1847.
Mayer, Holly A., *Congress's Own: A Canadian Regiment, the Continental Army, and American Union*, Norman: University of Oklahoma Press, 2021.
Perley, Sidney. "The Court Houses in Salem." *Historical Collections of the Essex Institute*, XLVII April 1911, 101-
Philbrick, Nathaniel, *Bunker Hill: A City, A Siege, A Revolution*, New York: Viking, 2013.
Phillips, James Duncan, *Salem in the Eighteenth Century*, Salem: Essex Institute, 1969.
____, "Why Colonel Leslie Came to Salem, *Historical Collections of the Essex Institute*, 1954, XC, 313-316.
Pingeon, Frances D., *Blacks in the Revolutionary Era*, Trenton: New Jersey Historical Commission, 1975.
Price, Clement Alexander, ed. *Freedom Not Far Distant: A Documentary History of Afro-Americans in New Jersey*. Newark: New Jersey Historical Society, 1980.
Quarles, Benjamin, *The Negro in the American Revolution*, Chapel Hill: The University of North Carolina Press, 1961.

Quintal, George, Jr., *Patriots of Color "A Peculiar Beauty and Merit,"* Boston: Boston National Historical Park, 2004.

Rantoul, Robert S. "A Historic Ball Room." *Historical Collections of the Essex Institute*, XXXI (1894), 69-87.

Raphael, *The First American Revolution*, New York: The New Press, 2003.

Rapp, William E., *Accomplishing the Impossible: Leadership That Launched Revolutionary Change*, New York: Knox Press an imprint of Permuted Press, 2021.

Rees, John U., *'They Were Good Soldiers': African-Americans Serving in the Continental Army, 1775-1783*, Warwick, England: Helion & Company, 2019.

Scudder, H.E., ed. *Recollections of Samuel Breck with Passages from his Note-Books (1771-1862)*, Philadelphia: Porter & Coates, 1877

Schecter, Barnet, *The Battle for New York,* New York: Walker Books, 2002.

Schmidt, Hubert G., *Rural Hunterdon: An Agricultural History*, Westport, CT: Greenwood Press, 1945.

____, *Slavery and Attitudes on Slavery in Hunterdon County New Jersey*, Flemington: Hunterdon County Historical Society, 1941.

Schreiner, Kathleen J., "Our Courthouse," *Hunterdon Historical Newsletter*, vol 14, No 2, Spring 1978, Hunterdon County Historical Society, 3-4

Schultz, Rev. John H. E., *History of the Methodist Episcopal Church of Flemington, N.J. 1822-1914*, 1914

Smith, Samuel Steele, *The Battle of Trenton* (Reprint of 1965 edition): Yardley, PA: Westholme, 2009.Trenton

Smith, Susan. "Biographical Sketch of Col. David Mason of Salem," *Historical Collections of the Essex Institute*, 1912, XLVIII, 197-216.

Snell, James P., *History of Hunterdon and Somerset Counties*, New Jersey, Philadelphia: Everts & Peck, 1881.

Stark, James H., *The Loyalists of Massachusetts and the other side of the American Revolution*. Boston: W.B. Clarke Co., 1907.

Steadman, Charles, *The History of the Origin, Progress, and Termination of the American War*, London: 1794

Streeter, Gilbert L., "Salem before the Revolution." *Historical Collections of the Essex Institute*, XXXII, 1859, 47-98.

____, "Some Historic Streets and Colonial Houses of Salem," *Historical Collections of the Essex Institute*, XXXVI, July 1900, 185-213.

Stryker, William S., *The Battles of Trenton and Princeton*, Boston: Houghton, Mifflin and Company, 1898.

United States. National Park Service. Division of Publications. *Salem: Maritime Salem in the Age of Sail.* Washington, D.C.: U.S. Dept. of the Interior, 1987.

Van Buskirk, Judith, *Standing in Their Own Light: African American Patriots in the American Revolution*, Norman: University of Oklahoma Press, 2017.

Warren, Dr. Edward. *The Life of John Warren, M.D.*, Cambridge: Houghton and Co., 1873.

White, Rebecca, Nadine Sergejeff, William Liebeknecht and Richard Hunter. *A Historical Account and Archaeological Analysis of the Eagle Tavern, City of Trenton, Mercer County, New Jersey*. Trenton: Hunter Research, 2005.

Wiencek, Henry, *An Imperfect God: George Washington, His Slaves, and the Creation of America*, New York: Farrar, Straus and Giroux, 2003.

White, Arthur O., "The Black Movement against Jim Crow Education in Buffalo, New York, 1800-1900," *Phylon*, Vol. 30, No. 4 (4th Qtr., 1969), pp. 375-393

Woodson, Carter G. *The Education of the Negro Prior to 1861*, Washington, D.C.: The Associated Publishers, 1919.

Wright, Giles R., *Afro-Americans in New Jersey: a short history*. Trenton, NJ, New Jersey Historical Commission, 1989.

Wright, Marion M. T., *The Education of Negroes in New Jersey*. New York: Teachers College, Columbia University, 1941.

____, "New Jersey Laws and the Negro," *The Journal of Negro History*, XXVIII, No. 2, April, 1943, 156-199.

Wright, Robert K., Jr., *The Continental Army*, Washington, DC: Center of Military History, U.S. Army, 1983.

Index

A

B

Q

R

S

Acknowledgements

The author acknowledges the many people who have helped keep him focused and determined to complete this book.

Roger Williams, my friend, and publisher of several of my books, was a driving force with his enthusiasm for this book and helped in so many ways.

Beverly Mills and Elaine Buck, authors of *If These Stones Could Talk* provided both encouragement and feedback that was very helpful.

John Allen Watts and Jason Huza, creators of the musical *The Crossing and the Ten Crucial Days* not only accepted the suggestion to include Jacob Francis as a role, but were just always so supportive of getting the story of Jacob Francis to a wide audience.

David Harding and John Allen of the Hunterdon County Historical Society both strongly encouraged this project as well as read drafts and offered important feedback. David also helped make available the resources of the Society for research.

Jim Labbe and Ken Hawkins shared their research on Abner Francis and encouraged and supported my work in various ways.

J. L. Bell of the Boston1775.net website is a font of information and guidance who helped with several significant searches and has been very supportive of telling the story of Jacob Francis.

Historian John U. Rees who has also written about African-American soldiers in the American Revolution was very supportive and read portions of an early draft offering important feedback.

Matthew Skic of the Museum of the American Revolution has always supported my work and greatly helped with this one.

Wanda McNeill read early draft portions and provided important feedback.

David Brush, my former college roommate, fellow history teacher, and historian read and provided valuable feedback on an early draft and his been an important supporter of the project.

Kimberly McCarty, Museum Curator at the Washington Crossing Historic Park in Washington Crossing, Pennsylvania has been a consistent and enthusiastic supporter of this project.

The interest and encouragement of George Leader of the College of New Jersey Anthropology and Sociology Department, and his students, has been most helpful.

David Price, a fellow writer of history and friend consistently and publicly promoted the importance of this project.

Friends who discussed various aspects of the project with me include: Algernon Ward, Chuck Monroe, David and Kathy Ludwig, Stuart and Meg Rich, Melchior Baltazar.

Friends in the Hopewell Valley Historical Society, Princeton Battlefield Society, Historical Society of Princeton, Washington Crossing State Park in New Jersey, Washington Crossing Historic Park in Pennsylvania, The Old Barracks Museum in Trenton, The William Trent House Museum, and many other historical organizations I work with have consistently asked about the progress of the story and expressed their desire to see and read the finished product.

I cannot forget the contribution of my cat Izzy who vocally told me each day to get to work and kept me company while I worked at the computer. I must also add retired Belgian draft horse, Chester, with whom I took many walks during the writing process. His calmness and friendship gave me opportunities to think through my understandings and how I expressed them, allowing me to later get back to work with a fresh mind.

I am sure my acknowledgements are incomplete because there have been so many helpful conversations but I extend my sincere thanks to everyone who has encouraged and contributed to the success of this project. Any mistakes a reader discovers are my responsibility.

Note on the Author

William L. Kidder, universally known as Larry, was born in California and raised in California, Indiana, New York, and New Jersey. He received his bachelor's and master's degrees from Allegheny College in Meadville, Pennsylvania.

He retired after forty-years teaching high school history in both public and private schools. During his 32 years at The Hun School of Princeton he enjoyed designing courses that gave his students the opportunity to develop the thinking, research, and writing skills that result from "doing history" and not just learning facts for a test.

Larry served four years of active duty in the US Navy. He was assigned to the US Navy Research and Development Unit, Vietnam and then the destroyer USS Brownson (DD868) homeported in Newport, Rhode Island. In the 1980s he was the lead researcher and writer for the creation of the Admiral Arleigh Burke National Destroyer Museum aboard the destroyer museum ship USS Joseph P. Kennedy, Jr. (DD850) at Battleship Cove in Fall River, Massachusetts.

For over thirty-three years, Larry has been a volunteer at the Howell Living History Farm, part of the Mercer County Park System, in Hopewell, New Jersey. For varying lengths of time he has served as an historian, interpreter, webmaster, and draft horse teamster. He is a member of the Association for Living History, Farm, and Agricultural Museums (ALHFAM).

Larry continues his teaching through his writing and giving a number of talks on local history to a variety of groups in New Jersey, Pennsylvania, New York, and Virginia. He is also a volunteer for the Crossroads of the American Revolution National Heritage Area, assisting with several projects. A member of the Princeton Battlefield Society and past board member, he develops tours of the Princeton Battlefield for both adults and children and contributes to a number of projects. He is a member of the board of TenCrucialDays.org, a non-profit organization dedicated to promoting the historic sites associated with the Ten Crucial Days and educating the public about them.

His website is at: wlkidderhistorian.com.

He can be contacted by email at larrykidder@gmail.com.

Made in the USA
Middletown, DE
31 March 2023